LOVE, MONEY, CONTROL

REINVENTING ESTATE PLANNING

THE ESPERTI PETERSON INSTITUTE CONTRIBUTORY SERIES

Eileen Sacco, Publisher

Generations: Planning Your Legacy
Giving: Philanthropy for Everyone
Legacy: Plan, Protect, and Preserve Your Estate
Love, Money, Control: Reinventing Estate Planning
Strictly Business: Planning Strategies for Privately Owned Businesses
21st Century Wealth: Essential Financial Planning Principles
Ways and Means: Maximize the Value of Your Retirement Savings
Wealth Enhancement and Preservation, 2d ed.

LOVE, MONEY, CONTROL

REINVENTING ESTATE PLANNING

---

*Practical Answers
from America's Foremost
Estate Planning Advisors*

Robert A. Esperti

Renno L. Peterson

The editors and contributors are not engaged in rendering legal, tax, accounting, estate, and financial planning, or similar professional services. While legal, tax, accounting, estate, and financial planning issues covered in this book have been checked with sources believed to be reliable, some material may be affected by changes in the laws or in the interpretations of such laws since the manuscript for this book was completed. For that reason the accuracy and completeness of such information and the opinions based thereon are not guaranteed. In addition, state or local tax laws or procedural rules may have a material impact on the general recommendations made by the contributing authors, and the strategies outlined in this book may not be suitable for every individual.

CFP™ and Certified Financial Planner™ are certification marks owned by the Certified Financial Planner Board of Standards, Inc.

ISBN 0-9674714-6-X
Library of Congress Control Number: 2003096862

Publisher and managing editor: Eileen Sacco
Senior technical editor: Richard Gumm, J.D., LL.M.
Project editor: Connie Brands
Project manager: Christy Allbee
Marketing services: Lydia Monchak
Jacket design: Rick Frye
Composition, design, and editing services: Glacier Publishing Services
Printed and bound in the United States by Johnson Printing

An Esperti Peterson Institute Contributory Series Book
by Quantum Press LLC
Quantum Alliance³ Companies
621 17th Street, Suite 2250
Denver, CO 80293
303.893.2663
quantumpress.net

Contents

Preface

Estate planning is a term that has changed dramatically over the years. At one time, estate planning meant having a will that would go through probate and, if a person was married, titling property jointly with a spouse. It conjured up visions of death and of wealthy families gathered in attorneys' wood-paneled offices listening to wills being read. It suggested that only the wealthy should plan so that they could avoid estate taxes. Changes in the laws and changing views of finance, lifestyle, privacy, nontraditional families, and longevity of life have made estate planning far more interesting and, frankly, more compelling for a larger group of people than ever before.

During the 1980s and early 1990s, estate planning attorneys debated wills and probate versus living trust planning. That argument has been settled. Most Americans now recognize that living trust–centered estate planning is more suited for the modern, mobile society in which we now live.

For these and many other reasons, *estate planning* is no longer will planning or tax planning only for the wealthy. It is what we have espoused for our combined 60+ years of practice experience: *Estate planning* is financial, retirement, business succession, charitable, medical, disability, legacy, and gift planning. Its scope is not daunting, as it might seem from this list; it is exciting and rich in opportunities.

In *Love, Money, Control* our contributors explain the reinvention of estate planning and what it can do for individuals and families. Here are some examples:

Planning to maintain control: "Control of what?" you might ask. Whether we consciously think about it or not, we all want to control our financial and personal affairs while we are mentally and physically capable of doing so. Most of us have had the experience of watching parents or grandparents mentally decline while determined not to relinquish decision-making control over their financial and personal affairs. Many of us have seen the results of individuals and families thrown into the position of having to make crucial decisions for their loved ones without the proper authorization or understanding of what their loved ones want done. With proper planning, you can control your financial and personal affairs while you are well and competent and can leave instructions for how your affairs should be managed—in essence, still maintaining control—if you become physically or mentally disabled.

Planning for loved ones: The options available for "how and when" to give what you own to your friends, family, loved ones, and charity are limited only by your goals and your imagination. That statement may not sound logical, but we believe it to be factual based on our experience. You have tremendous opportunities to ensure that your heirs receive your property in a manner that best fits their needs and your goals. You have the ability to plan for your spouse, to create a legacy for future generations of your family and for your community, to remember friends, and to make a difference.

Retirement planning: According to the Department of Health and Human Services, the average life expectancy in the United States is a little more than 77 years. As medical science improves, that figure will increase. According to a survey by Employee Benefit Research Institute, the average retirement account balance (net of loans) for participant-directed plans at the end of 2001 was a scant $43,215. For most of us, that's not nearly enough retirement savings, and none of us wants to outlive our money. There is no more important reason to plan for retirement than that profound concept. It is critical that you design and implement a retirement plan as soon as possible so that you have sufficient time to accumulate the resources you need to retire comfortably.

Planning for seniors: Governmental studies further indicate that if we live to age 65, we are likely to live to age 83, and that people today aged 65 or older face a 40 percent lifetime risk of entering a nursing home. The projections are that these figures will get worse: We will live longer, and as we do, our risk of entering a nursing home will go up. It is critical for all of us who want to retain our privacy, dignity, and control to understand the issues of medical care and long-term-care costs and our options to plan for them.

Business planning: Some studies indicate that only about 50 percent of all family-owned businesses last more than one generation and that very few last more than two generations. Estate tax plays a role in these losses, but failing to plan for the succession of the business plays an equally important role. In our experience, saving estate taxes is usually the aftereffect of planning for other goals, those being primarily a happy and comfortable retirement and a successful transition of the business to co-owners, family, or key employees in order to support the retirement.

Love, Money, Control is the product of a national research project that involved the planning knowledge, ideas, and expertise of some of the most talented estate planning attorneys and financial advisors from across the United States. It is not an annotated reference book intended to cover everything about estate planning in the tiniest detail. *Love, Money, Control* is organized in three parts and covers what our contributors' clients consider the most important aspects of estate planning today. In Part One, Love, our contributors emphasize that people should be motivated to plan out of love of family, friends, and personal causes. In Part Two, Money, our contributors explain the challenges and opportunities that the new gift and estate tax laws create and strategies to overcome the challenges and to take advantage of the opportunities. Part Three, Control, covers all of the aspects of estate planning that satisfy our needs to protect our wealth and to preserve our dignity and independence as well as possible until our deaths.

All of our contributing authors were challenged with a single goal: to provide readers with the best possible answers to the questions they are most frequently asked by their clients. Because of the book's question-and-answer format, even the newest reader to the topic will be able to make sense out of the many aspects of estate planning.

Love, Money, Control offers insights into the issues that are important for planning. For many, just knowing which questions to ask a competent advisor will be of help and will encourage participation in the planning process. Armed with the information in this book, you will be able to enter into the estate planning process with more confidence.

The consistency of the questions provided by the contributors reinforced our belief that most clients have similar concerns, regardless of differences in their cultures, economics, geographic locations, and size of their estates. This consistency has been the highlight of every Esperti Peterson Institute Contributory Book Series project.

The responses of our contributing authors reflected their differing professional views and feelings with regard to virtually every estate planning issue. As editors, we have attempted to blend these differences into an overall perspective that provides readers with the best overview and understanding possible. At times, we included differing opinions in the responses in order to present a variety of good approaches and to allow readers to choose the one with which they are most comfortable.

Readers may find a subtle repetitiveness in the text. Rather than always referring readers back and forth among chapters of the book, we have attempted, whenever possible, to include some of the same information in various sections. Our goal is to ensure that readers turning to virtually any section of the book will find complete information there. Experience tells us that few readers will read this book cover to cover. As you skip around, reading specific sections, you will encounter much of the background information necessary to understand each topic. We encourage you to read the introductions at the beginning of the three parts of the book to gain a broad view of the topics under discussion and a better understanding of the focus of each chapter in that part. At the end of each chapter we've included a set of action steps to help you implement the concepts contained in the chapter.

In addition to the thirteen chapters in *Love, Money, Control*, we have included five appendixes. Appendix A provides a broad range of useful resources for more information about many of the topics covered in this book. Recognizing that it is difficult to know what professional designations and accreditations mean, we included in appendix B definitions of the major designations; the agencies that regulate attorneys, accountants, and financial planning professionals; and the major professional organizations. Appendix B also includes the names of organizations that provide referrals of professionals.

The professionals who contributed to *Love, Money, Control* were chosen to participate in this project through a stringent application process that is fully described in appendix C. Alphabetical and geographical lists of all the contributors are presented in appendixes D and E. We have also included a glossary of the most commonly recognized terms that we use in the text.

Love, Money, Control contains the most current information available on estate planning. However, a few statistics relevant to estate planning are indexed for inflation and are not yet available for 2004 and beyond. For this reason, our contributing authors used 2003 figures in a few explanations. In all cases, the theories and strategies behind the figures are completely up to date and incorporate the latest legislation.

As with all general reference works, readers should be careful not to treat the information in *Love, Money, Control* as a recommendation for any particular course of action in individual circumstances. No other concept came through to us more clearly than the diversity of successful strategies available to individuals and families, as well as the damage that can result from using the wrong strategy. This is even more critical now in light of the 2001 tax act. The act may affect retirement plans, buy-sell agreements, lifetime gifts to children, marital trusts, and other crucial planning strategies. *Love, Money, Control* addresses these impacts, but we specifically recommend that, in planning for your well-being and that of your family, you seek advice from competent professionals in each relevant discipline.

Love, Money, Control is a collaborative effort of a number of planning professionals. We are proud of the efforts that our contributing authors made to bring you such practical information and strategies to implement a "reinvented" estate plan. We hope that the information in this book helps you to attain a better understanding of estate planning as it stands today so that you can confidently and successfully participate in your own planning process.

Robert A. Esperti
Renno L. Peterson
October 2003

Introduction

Love, Money, Control: Reinventing Estate Planning is the ninth in a continuing series of collaborative books published by Quantum Press for the Esperti Peterson Institute. These books are designed to provide valuable information that you can understand and implement to enhance and to protect your financial well-being. The 69 contributors to this book are some of the country's top estate, tax, and financial planning attorneys and financial advisors. They have worked hard to share with you vital information that you need to make informed decisions when planning for your estate. The professionals who contributed to *Love, Money, Control* were selected for participation in this project through a stringent application process. Each contributor has significant credentials and a rare quality of expertise in his or her discipline and practice. The contributors to *Love, Money, Control* are dedicated professionals who provide superior estate, tax, and financial planning services that are tailored to the specific needs of their clients.

This book is sponsored by the Esperti Peterson Institute (EPI) and published by Quantum Press. EPI is a cutting-edge educational institution whose mission is to enhance the quality of estate and wealth planning in the United States. EPI offers professionals advanced education in planning for high-net-worth clients and their families. Graduates of EPI's 3-year Masters Program concentrate on planning for families with more than $25 million in assets, and its graduates are among the best estate and wealth strategies planners in the United States. EPI also offers an Advanced Studies Program in which estate and wealth planning professionals learn the techniques that are most effective for clients and their families having a net worth of $10 million to $25 million. Graduates of this program have helped thousands of clients to plan for their wealth.

The foundation of the Esperti Peterson Institute is its commitment to collaborations of professionals who work together to offer the best and most effective planning possible for the benefit of their mutual clients. EPI believes that when professionals combine their respective talents and skills, rather than compete with one another, clients and professionals alike are the winners.

Acknowledgments

One of the most difficult parts in writing any book is the acknowledgments. How does one give credit to the many—perhaps thousands of—people who have had an impact on one's thinking and writing? We have written or collaborated on almost 30 books, some of which have been for the public and some of which have been for professionals. In our careers we have been fortunate to meet thousands of dedicated planners who are doing an extreme amount of good in helping their clients. Each and every one of them, in some way, has enhanced our lives. While we cannot thank them individually, we offer our appreciation for their being a part of our lives.

There are a number of people who have gone to extra lengths to make this book possible. First and foremost, we want to thank Eileen Sacco, president of Quantum Press and a person we have known for more than 25 years. Her dedication in creating, designing, marketing, producing, and distributing contributory books is simply awesome. Not only does she make our jobs much easier, but she also inspires us to be even better than we expect. Her relationship with our contributors makes their lives easier and helps them to fully express their great expertise.

Richard Gumm, J.D., LL.M., senior legal editor at Quantum Press, put in a yeoman's effort in helping to compile the raw research material, a very challenging job. Richard also does a terrific job of reviewing our final writing for technical accuracy.

We also want to thank Christy Allbee. She works tirelessly to make sure that all of the details of putting such a complex book together have been taken care of. She is always ready to help in any way that she can with a cheerful attitude.

We wish to thank our colleague and partner, David K. Cahoone, J.D., LL.M. David's professional expertise, winsome and gentle spirit, and untiring efforts as our partner and colleague in our national law and consulting firms have been enormously helpful to us for many years and are greatly appreciated. He is also a contributor to this book and gave us moral and technical support, for which we are always appreciative.

Finally, we dedicate this book to Liz and Karen.

PART ONE

Love

DEATH AND TAXES. HISTORICALLY, ESTATE PLANNING HAS BEEN about little more than planning for death and taxes. Given the unpopularity of these two subjects, it is not surprising that people are unmotivated to plan their estates. The message of this book, and in particular Part One, is that estate planning is no longer just planning for death and taxes. Our contributors emphasize in Part One that you should be motivated to plan out of love of family, friends, and personal causes.

To be honest, no one is obligated to plan. As you will discover in this book, state governments have, for decades, assumed that people will not plan their estates, and have created, by statute, a bare-bones estate plan for everyone. So, for people who are not particularly concerned about who (including the government) gets what and when after they die, rest assured that your state legislature has a plan in place for you. And, if you feel confident that nothing will ever go wrong for your family, you do not need to plan. If you are sure that your spouse will live comfortably after your death, that your children will never be sued or divorced, that your grandchildren will get a college education without your help, then no planning is necessary.

If you do want to protect your loved ones and to provide for their future as best you can, then you must plan. You can plan for how and when they will receive their inheritances. You can plan to provide for your life partner after your death, in spite of what your family may want. You can plan to support your community and important causes through charitable donations. You can plan to pass along your values and beliefs to future generations. In this way, planning becomes a life-affirming symbol of your love. Death and taxes take a back seat to what you really want to accomplish.

Ultimately, planning requires a great deal of self-knowledge along with professional advice. The purpose of this book is two-fold: to help you to discover your individual planning needs and to offer the information you need to make informed decisions.

Part One, Love, is the first leg of your journey to design and to implement a successful estate plan. It contains three chapters that focus on planning for the people and things we love. As Stephen R. Covey says in his book *The Seven Habits of Highly Effective People,* "start with the end in mind." It is much easier to reach your destination when you know, from the outset, where you want to go. We and our contributors believe that you must have some idea of what it is that you want to accomplish before you can truly begin the estate planning process. So, in chapter 1, our contributors address some of the more common goals of estate planning: to provide a legacy for loved ones and charity, to maintain control of your personal and financial affairs, to minimize taxes, and to avoid probate. Your goals will be unique to you, and with your advisors' help, you will be able to determine your precise goals and priorities for your estate plan. To understand the many planning techniques that abound in estate planning, one must understand the fundamentals. These include the concepts of an estate plan, how it is planned, and the importance of ownership in estate planning, all of which are discussed in chapter 1.

Chapter 2 is one of the most important chapters in the book. While providing for your loved ones is a priority, *what* you leave them and *how* you leave it to them are what you will decide as part of the estate planning process. Many people want to leave more than cash or property to loved ones; they also want to pass on to future generations their values, experiences, family heritage, and beliefs. Our contributors offer techniques that you can use to preserve your memories and values and pass them on to your heirs along with their financial inheritance.

Chapter 2 discusses the various ways to leave property to your surviving spouse and the criteria you should use in deciding which method is best for your situation. Our contributors offer detailed descriptions of the various marital trusts that are available, because in most situations one of these trusts is preferable to an outright bequest to a surviving spouse.

Your choices for how to leave property to your children at your death are as diverse as the children themselves. Our contributors provide in-depth information about structuring an inheritance for adult and minor children, grandchildren, and children with special needs. Readers who are looking for ways to encourage or discourage certain behavior in their children, to shield their assets from creditors, or to provide for children with disabilities should read this chapter thoroughly.

Chapter 3 is a masterful overview of charitable planning. Philanthropy is an important part of our culture—in 2001 Americans gave $212 billion to charitable causes. Charitable giving is the way we express our love and support for our communities and our causes—it is an extension of our love of family. This commitment to charity was reflected in the submissions from our contributors. The questions and answers in this chapter cover a broad range of charitable topics, from the basic (albeit complex) tax-deduction rules to sophisticated giving techniques. Whether you currently make small donations to charity or would like to become a major supporter of charities, this chapter will offer you wise counsel.

The most important aspect of chapter 3 is its explanation of how charitable giving can simultaneously enhance other important goals such as estate planning, saving for retirement, and financial planning. In particular, the chapter emphasizes charitable remainder trusts as a powerful tool for people who want to make substantial gifts to charity while also benefiting themselves and their loved ones financially. For readers who want more control over their donations, our contributors provide helpful information on private foundations, supporting organizations, and donor-advised funds. Our contributors' submissions also reflect the complexity of this area of estate planning and the importance of your working with an advisor who is proficient in charitable planning before making a major gift to charity.

Even if you do not consider yourself charitably inclined, we encourage you to read this chapter to discover the full potential of well-planned charitable giving.

chapter 1

Introduction to Estate Planning

WHAT'S AN ESTATE?

ଔ *What's in an estate?*

Your estate is, simply, everything that you own. An estate consists of your investments such as stocks, bonds, mutual funds, annuities, bank accounts, and certificates of deposit; your retirement accounts such as individual retirement accounts and 401(k) plans; real estate; and life insurance policies. It also consists of your "stuff"—furniture, appliances, jewelry, collectibles, and all the other items of personal property. The value of your estate is the value of all of these assets, less mortgages and any other debt.

WHAT IS ESTATE PLANNING?

ଔ *What is estate planning?*

In its most basic form, *estate planning* is the process of planning for

5

the management and disposition of your assets and resources when you are deceased or no longer able to manage your own affairs. While most people think estate planning is just worrying about assets or minimizing income and estate taxes, it is really much more. Estate planning is really about accomplishing your goals during your life and beyond.

Although many people share similar goals, the process of estate planning involves identifying your own specific goals. Once you identify them, you can, along with your advisors, determine the best strategies to achieve them. Since people are different, this estate planning process will be very different from person to person.

  Isn't estate planning just for rich people?

It's not how much wealth you have accumulated that's important; it's about what and who are important to you. Take as an example a widow with two grown children who has only a house and $200,000 from a life insurance policy on her late husband. Does she need estate planning to protect herself and her two children? To some people, $200,000 isn't a lot of money. Even so, the widow wants to be assured that she can live in comfort in her own home. What if her son has an alcohol problem? Wouldn't she worry that he will just drink up whatever amount she leaves him at her death? Wouldn't she feel better leaving money to him in such a way that it could be used for his rehabilitation? It's not whether you have an estate that requires planning, it's whether planning will provide you with a sense of comfort and well-being about your and your family's future.

WHAT ARE SOME ESTATE
PLANNING GOALS?

  How do we determine what our goals are?

Your attorney doesn't need to meet with you to know that you want to reduce your estate taxes and pass on your money to your children—he or she already knows that. Attorneys and financial advisors who focus on estate planning counseling will spend time asking questions and listening to you. They will take you through "what if" scenarios and ask you other questions to help you define your estate and financial planning goals. The types of questions counselors will ask you are similar to those we present in the action steps at the end of this chapter.

We find that many people are unaware of the estate planning opportunities available to them. And sometimes the opportunities themselves can suggest goals and objectives. Experienced estate planning advisors know how to elicit the goals you have already and how to help you craft some new goals based on their knowledge of estate planning law. Our experience indicates that estate planning is more about what's in your heart and head than what's in your pocketbook. Effective estate planning begins with finding out what is *really* going on inside.

∝ *How do I begin the estate planning process?*

It requires thinking about what things will be like after you're gone. No one likes to think about his or her own mortality. Here are some points from which to start:

1. Organize your affairs to develop an accurate picture of your estate. Don't overlook life insurance policies.
2. Analyze your current estate plan. Do you have a will or trust? How are your assets titled?
3. Look into the future. Your assets will most likely grow in value and may be subject to death taxes.
4. Ask yourself the questions listed in the action steps at the end of this chapter and spend some time thinking about how you would answer them—perhaps even writing down your answers.
5. Talk to your family. Have an open dialogue regarding your wishes.
6. Plan a meeting with your trusted advisors to help you to establish your goals and to be sure your planning reflects your wishes.

∝ *Who can help me develop my estate plan?*

Your planning team should consist of an attorney, an accountant, a securities broker, a life insurance agent, and a financial advisor, if possible. We discuss how to find and work with the advisors on your team in Chapter 13, Finding and Working with Professional Advisors.

Goal #1: Plan for Loved Ones

℘ Do people plan primarily to take care of their assets?

Not really. People plan their estates because they care about their loved ones. They want to provide their families and advisors with clear instructions about what is important to them and how to take care of things in the event that they become disabled or when they die. Many of our clients' children tell us that the time we take to detail and communicate our clients' wishes through their estate planning documents provides them with a great deal of comfort and confidence especially when they are called upon to act on behalf of a disabled or deceased family member. They tell us that since the plan already makes the tough decisions for them, it takes the burden off the family to make numerous choices during this difficult time.

Estate planning also lets people have one last "conversation" with the ones they love. As with disability, the depth and clarity of the instructions on death ease the grief experienced by the family since the hopes, dreams, and aspirations of the deceased person have been expressed through their estate plan. Many children express gratitude that their mothers or fathers cared enough about them to put on paper the things that were most important and to provide guidance.

℘ My spouse and I are newlyweds. We have no children. Our estate is modest. We have all our assets in joint tenancy, and we have named each other as the beneficiaries of our life insurance and retirement plans. Why should we do any estate planning?

If one of you becomes incapacitated and you have done no planning, a guardian may need to be named for you. If you have an asset, such as a retirement plan or a life insurance policy, in your name when you become incapacitated, your spouse does not have the automatic right to control that asset. He or she may need to petition the probate court to be named guardian of your estate. If you are in an accident together and one of you dies immediately but the other lingers on for a period of time, the entire estate will pass to the family of the second of you to die, and the family of the first to die will get nothing.

Goal #2: Plan to Pass On Your Legacy

଼ *Can I promote my values in my estate plan?*

Perhaps one of the most important reasons to create your estate plan is to pass on your values and beliefs. These values can include your beliefs on religion, education, marriage, work ethic, and the use of drugs or alcohol. For example, you can encourage family members to get a college education by providing to pay for tuition in your estate plan and even offer them a "bonus" if they complete their college education in 4 years. You can discourage alcohol and drug abuse by cutting off funds from heirs who have substance abuse problems. You can promote your religious beliefs through a gift to your church or synagogue. For many people, passing on their values is more important than passing on their wealth.

଼ *The world is changing so rapidly; I'm worried that my grand-children may never learn about our family history. What can I do about this?*

Like you, many of our clients want to pass on their values, history, traditions, and culture to their children, grandchildren, and future generations. Estate planning offers an excellent opportunity to do so. There are many different ways that you can pass on your legacy as part of your estate plan, ranging from simple letters to more elaborate documents, videotapes, and family mission statements. Some people also include a charitable component to their estate plan in which present and future generations can be involved.

Leaving a personal family history to your children and grand-children is certainly a part of a meaningful estate plan because you can include important lessons that you learned during your lifetime. Also, a family mission statement is something that your whole family can create together now, and it can serve as a vehicle for family involvement and collaboration for generations.

Goal #3: Plan to Avoid Probate and Intestacy

଼ *I don't have minor children or a taxable estate so why should I plan?*

If you do not plan your estate, the state in which you live has drafted a plan for you through what are known as the intestacy laws. If you become disabled, these laws will determine who takes care of you and how. At your death, these laws will determine who receives your estate; when they are going to receive it; and if they are minors, who is going to manage it for them until they reach the age of majority. For these reasons, everyone who has assets and loved ones or favorite charities needs to plan for what should happen if they become incapacitated and at their death.

CR Are there considerations as to why a small estate should have a living trust?

A properly drafted and fully funded living trust will save your family substantial costs at your death. While probate costs generally are related somewhat to the size of the estate, the process involves certain minimum costs and fees which will accrue regardless of the size of the estate (such as opening and closing the probate, advertising, etc.). Those costs and fees tend to be a larger percentage of a small estate than they are for a large estate. On this basis alone, a living trust can potentially be more valuable to the small estate than to a larger estate.

Goal #4: Plan to Minimize Taxes

CR My friend tells me that estate planning is not as important now because the estate tax has been repealed. Is that true?

As we will explain in detail in Chapter 4, Tax Basics, the federal estate tax has not actually been repealed. But more importantly, estate planning is about far more than estate taxes. Estate planning is about achieving your personal goals for yourself and your family. Accomplishing those goals requires careful planning and professional assistance, with or without tax concerns. Yes, reducing estate taxes is a common planning goal, but it is only one of many.

Goal #5: Plan for Disability

CR I don't have many assets. Why do I need an estate plan?

Estate planning is much more than deciding who gets what at the time of your death. If you have an opinion as to whether you would prefer to receive long-term care at home rather than in a nursing home in the event that you become disabled, then you are a candidate for estate planning. If you want to choose the people who should have the power to decide if you are disabled, as opposed to leaving it up to the court system or to doctors whom you may never have met, then you are a candidate for estate planning.

WHAT IS PROBATE?

Wills

CR *What is a will?*

A *last will and testament* is a legal document designed to tell the probate court what to do with your assets at your death. To be valid, a will must comply with the laws of the state where you live. For example, all states require that a will be in writing. All states require that there be a certain number of people who witness the signing of your will. The requirements vary from state to state. If you fail to meet your state's requirements, your will will be invalid.

A will only governs the distribution of property that is left in the deceased person's name at death. If property passes to a new owner at death, for example by a beneficiary designation or by joint tenancy with right of survivorship, then that property is not in the deceased person's name at his or her death. It is therefore not part of the probate estate and is not governed by the provisions of the will.

CR *If I have a will, does there need to be a probate?*

A will guarantees probate. A will generally has no validity until after your death and after it has been submitted to, and accepted by, the probate court. A judge will decide whether the will conforms to state law, and if the judge decides the will is valid, then the judge will order that it be admitted into probate.

CR *Is a preprinted, fill-in-the-blank form a valid will?*

Every jurisdiction varies. Some states do permit preprinted fill-in-the-blank forms when all the "material" portions of the will are in the decedent's own handwriting. And not only does the form have to comply with state law, but there are limitations on what types of property can pass under the will and the formalities of signing the will. But, even if accepted in your state, think carefully before using these do-it-yourself wills. Your family is unique, and they have unique issues, which can't be addressed through a generic form. No matter what the value of your estate, it's taken you a lifetime to create and build it—you and your family deserve the care an attorney will give you in crafting a plan that is best for you.

ᐯ *Do I have to list in my will every personal possession I own and who I want to leave it to when I die?*

No. If you have heirlooms or special property that you want to leave to a particular person, you may want to identify that property individually. On the other hand, if you simply want to leave "everything" you have to your spouse, or daughter, or friend, you can simply do that.

In some states, you can write a *memorandum* along with your will naming the beneficiaries of your personal property. The advantage of a memorandum is that you can change it at any time without all the formalities of signing a new will.

ᐯ *I wrote my will several years ago but I need to add a gift to my niece. Do I have to rewrite the whole thing?*

You can rewrite the will and update the whole thing (most attorneys recommend that a will be reviewed and updated *at least* every 2 to 4 years) or you can execute a *codicil* (a legal word for an amendment to the will). A codicil only amends your original will by adding, deleting, or changing a specific provision and generally has language in it that specifically states the rest of the original will remains in effect.

ᐯ *My sister isn't in very good health, but I don't want to leave her out of my will. What will happen if I leave her something and she dies before I do?*

Most states have an *anti-lapse* statute. These statutes try to ensure that your bequests are honored to the extent possible. So, for example, your sister's children would get her bequest if she predeceased you. You can also override the anti-lapse statute in your will and specify who receives the property if she predeceases you.

᚛ *My kids can't get along now, and I don't expect things to improve once I'm gone. Can I do anything to prevent one of them from contesting my will in the hopes that they can get more money?*

Sure. Clients often include a "no contest" clause in their wills or trusts. The clause says, essentially, that if beneficiaries contest a will in court and lose, then they will receive nothing; not even what was originally left them. A no contest clause won't guarantee that a child won't attack your will, but it should make the child think long and hard before doing it. However, each state's laws are different, so the advice of an attorney is critical in this regard.

᚛ *What happens if my family can't find my will when I die?*

In most states, when the decedent's will cannot be located, it is presumed that the person destroyed the will with the intent to revoke it. Therefore, it is very important to keep your will in a safe place. Tell your family members where you have stored your original will; and keep a copy of it in a place where your family is likely to find it, with a note telling them where the original is located.

᚛ *What happens if I die without a will?*

In a sense, no person can die without a will. Even if you have not created one for yourself, the laws of your state specify how your property is distributed on your death. The state essentially writes a will for you. These laws are referred to as the *intestate succession statutes*, and a person who dies without a written will is said to have died *intestate*. These laws distribute your property to your family members based on their relationship to you. The process of distributing your property is supervised by the probate court, much the same as with a will. It is a very poor practice to rely on these statutes for your estate planning needs. With a will, even though it will go through probate, you control to whom, when, and in what portions your estate is distributed.

ᘓ *What is probate?*

There are actually two types of probate:

1. Living probate
2. Death probate

Living Probate

ᘓ *What does living probate mean?*

Living probate, more commonly known as a *guardianship*, is a legal proceeding to appoint a guardian or a conservator for a person who cannot manage his or her own affairs. When a person becomes incapacitated and can no longer make financial or health care decisions, then the court appoints someone (usually a family member, but not always) to make decisions for that person. Living probate can be very involved and expensive. You can avoid it with proper planning—a combination of a revocable living trust, health care powers of attorney, and living wills. We will discuss disability planning techniques that avoid living probate in Chapter 8, Planning for Disability.

Death Probate

ᘓ *What is death probate?*

Death probate is the legal proceeding to verify and administer a decedent's will. The probate court oversees this process of transferring title of assets as well as making sure all taxes are paid and creditors are satisfied. The court will transfer ownership of the decedent's assets from the name of the deceased person into the name of a living person according to the deceased person's will. If there is no will, then the court will distribute the assets according to state law.

ᘓ *What's so bad about death probate?*

Some professionals and nonprofessionals will tell you that probate is not so bad and that there is no need to be concerned about it. Some who have been though the probate process will say that they never want to experience it again. The usual disadvantages associated with death probate include:

- *Delay.* The probate process usually lasts from 9 months to 2 years. During this time, the decedent's assets are usually frozen so that the personal representative can make an accurate inventory of the assets. In many cases, while the assets are frozen, nothing can be distributed or sold without court approval. If your family needs money to live on, they must request a living allowance from the court.

- *Cost.* Probate and its related expenses aren't cheap. The *Wall Street Journal* and the AARP have done studies that show probate costs range from 5 to 7½ percent of the value of the decedent's estate. Small estates pay even more than that as a percentage of the entire estate.

- *Publicity.* Every probate proceeding is a matter of public record. Anyone can go to the probate court and look at your probate file. Anyone can see an inventory of your assets, whom you're leaving things to, whom you've left out, and other private matters.

- *Control.* Omitted or disgruntled heirs can contest your will and hold up distribution for everyone else, effectively blackmailing the other heirs.

- *Multiple probates.* If you own real estate in other states, your estate could face multiple probates, each one according to the laws in that state.

WHAT ARE THE PROBATE ALTERNATIVES?

CR *What are the alternatives to probate?*

There are several ways to avoid living and/or death probate. They include:

- Giving away assets
- Using joint and contractual forms of property ownership
- Using a revocable living trust

Give Away Assets to Avoid Probate

ℂℛ *Why can't I just give my property to my children while I'm alive? Isn't that an alternative to probate?*

Yes, it will avoid living and death probate. However, there are several reasons why this is not a recommended alternative to probate:

1. First, by giving your property away, you give up control of your property. Regardless of your good intentions and the good intentions of your children or others to whom you give the property, you have no guarantee that they will use the property as you wish or that they will use the property to take care of you.

2. If you give the property to your children, it becomes subject to the claims of the children's creditors, including their spouses. Also, if a child predeceases you, the property will pass in accordance with that child's estate planning. If no planning is in place, the property will pass to the child's spouse or children. If those grandchildren are minors, their share cannot be used for any purpose other than for their care. If the child divorces, your son- or daughter-in-law will have a claim against the property.

3. Also, if the property you give away is valued at more than the gift tax annual exclusion (which we explain in chapter 4), you must file a federal gift tax return and pay the appropriate gift taxes, if any.

Use Certains Forms of Property Ownership to Avoid Probate

Role of Ownership Form to Estate Planning

ℂℛ *Does the way that I own property play any role in my estate plan?*

Think of your estate plan as written instructions about the management of your property and the care of yourself and your family. For your estate plan to be effective, your property must be subject to those instructions. But with certain types of ownership, such as joint tenancy and contractual ownership, those instructions do not control the property at your death. That property will not be a part of your estate plan, and an estate plan is only as good as the amount of your property that it controls. So, if you create a will or revocable living trust that you intend to control your assets but have property titled in joint tenancy, the joint tenancy ownership will control disposition of the property at your death, not your will or trust. For these reasons, you may need to change the ownership of some of your assets as part of implementing your estate plan.

Joint Tenancy with Right of Survivorship

ᚸ *What is joint tenancy with right of survivorship?*

Joint tenancy with right of survivorship (WROS) is a form of ownership where two (or more) people each own an equal, undivided interest in an asset. Although a great many individuals may use this form of ownership, married couples most commonly use it. In terms of value, each joint tenant owns an undivided interest in the whole asset. In terms of control, all joint tenants must consent to sell, give away, or dispose of the asset.

ᚸ *What is tenancy by the entirety and how is it different from joint tenancy with right of survivorship?*

Tenancy by the entirety is a term used in some states for joint tenancy WROS when the joint owners are husband and wife. Like joint tenancy WROS, on the death of one spouse, the surviving spouse is vested with sole ownership through operation of law. Depending on the state where you live, there may be added creditor protection for married couples owning assets in this form.

ᚸ *How does joint tenancy with right of survivorship ownership avoid death probate?*

Joint tenancy WROS avoids probate because of the survivorship aspect of this form of ownership. When one joint tenant dies, his or her interest passes to the surviving joint tenant, or tenants, automatically by operation of law without the need for a probate proceeding for that property. This is what the "with right of survivorship" means. Looked at from another point of view, however, joint tenancy WROS means that the first tenant to die loses all control over to whom or

how his or her interest in the asset will ultimately be distributed—
the survivor takes all.

CR *Besides avoiding a death probate, does joint tenancy achieve any
other estate planning goals?*

Let's examine joint tenancy in relation to the common goals we
mentioned earlier in this chapter:

- *Avoid probate.* Joint tenancy will avoid the probate process when
  the *first* joint tenant passes away. However, when the second
  joint tenant dies, the property will likely go through probate; so,
  you really haven't avoided probate, just delayed it.

- *Plan for disability.* With some assets, especially real estate, all
  joint tenants must sign the necessary documents to sell or lease
  the property. If one of the joint tenants becomes disabled, the
  other tenant cannot sell the asset for the disabled tenant's benefit
  without court intervention. For instance, if you need to sell your
  home after your husband becomes incapacitated, joint tenancy
  will not help you avoid a probate guardianship proceeding for
  him. For other assets, such as bank accounts, it may be easier
  for the healthy tenant to access the account to assist the disabled tenant, but if there is a guardianship proceeding for the
  disabled tenant, the asset may become subject to the probate
  court's jurisdiction.

- *Control property during life.* Depending on the type of asset you
  own in joint tenancy, you may no longer be free to do as you wish
  with the property. For many assets, all joint tenants must act
  together in managing the property. For real estate, if the joint
  tenants disagree, they may have to go to court for a partition of
  the property—a judicial separation of the joint tenancy that frequently results in a court-ordered sale of the property.

- *Control property at death.* When one tenant dies and the property passes to the surviving tenant, the property will be in his or
  her name only. The surviving tenant now controls the property
  totally, and the wishes of the deceased owner (expressed through
  a will or living trust) for its future use may be totally disregarded. By placing property in joint tenancy, you potentially lose
  your ability to control the property. For many, this loss of control at death is a significant drawback. Many people mistakenly

think that their will or trust will dictate distribution of the property and instead ends up unintentionally disinheriting their loved ones.

℞ *I'm a widow with two children. Each of my children has two children. Can't I put my checking and savings accounts in joint tenancy ownership with my children and avoid probate?*

Joint ownership is a good intention headed for trouble. The accounts will avoid probate when you die. However, there are even more dangers associated with this form of ownership:

- Either of your children can access the accounts at any time without your permission and without telling you first. This may be all right, so long as neither of your children abuses the power they have over your accounts.

- If one of your children predeceases you, the accounts will then be held jointly in your name and the name of the surviving child. If you die before correcting this situation, the account will pass to your surviving child, thus disinheriting the children of your deceased child.

- If your surviving child becomes incompetent, he or she would not be able to give half of the account to the children of your deceased child. Or he or she may die before "doing the right thing," and the accounts may pass to his or her spouse, who may not carry out your or your deceased child's wishes.

- If either of your children has a creditor (such as the Internal Revenue Service), the creditor can seize the account to satisfy the child's debts.

- By placing your children's names on the accounts, you are making a gift to them as soon as you create the joint ownership. This is usually an unintended result and catches many people by surprise. You may need to file a gift tax return when you add their names to the accounts, and possibly pay state and/or federal gift tax.

We generally find that joint tenancy WROS is a shortcut to trouble. There are many other ways to avoid probate that have far fewer risks and smoother operations. Generally, joint tenancy WROS should be avoided.

❦ My husband is dead. My children don't help me, and they don't need my money. All I really have is my house. The ladies in my church group say that I should just put my granddaughter, Sarah, on the deed with me so she gets the house after I'm gone. That way I won't have to leave the house to her in a will that my other children can contest. Is this a good idea?

In addition to all of the dangers outlined in the previous questions and answers:

- If you give half the house to Sarah now, you are giving her a present gift of half the value of the house. You'll have to prepare and file a gift tax return.
- If you need Medicaid assistance within the next 3 years, you may have made yourself ineligible by virtue of making this gift.
- If you need to take out a home equity line of credit or need to sell the home, you will need Sarah's consent and signature. If you do sell the house, Sarah will be entitled to half of the sale proceeds.

You can certainly give your home to Sarah at your death, but please don't give up control of it while you are living. There are much better ways to accomplish this gift to her, such as through a living trust.

❦ If I have a will that leaves everything equally to my four children and I have a bank account in joint tenancy with one child, what controls the distribution of the bank account on my death—my will or the joint tenancy?

The joint tenancy designation on the account controls distribution. This asset will pass, by law, to the child who is the joint tenant. The only assets controlled by your will are the assets titled in your name only.

Contractual Ownership

❦ What is contractual ownership?

Contractual ownership generally refers to a person's right to direct the disposition of an asset at death as part of the agreement that created the asset. For example, a life insurance policy is a contractual agreement between the policy owner and the insurance company, and as part of that agreement the owner has the right to designate who receives the insurance proceeds at the insured's death.

Ꮽ *How does contractual ownership avoid probate?*

Contractual ownership allows for the automatic transfer of the asset at the owner's death (or at the insured's death in the case of a life insurance policy) according to the contract. The asset controlled by the contract passes to the person or entity specified in the contract, so the asset does not go through probate.

Ꮽ *What's wrong with just leaving my life insurance to my children by beneficiary designation?*

There is just so much space in that little box on the beneficiary designation form to write in the name of the beneficiary. There is no space for, nor would the insurance company allow you to write in, any special instructions about managing the proceeds. By naming your children as beneficiaries of your life insurance, you forfeit the opportunity to pass along your values and to protect the proceeds from your children's creditors and from estate taxes. Naming a trust as the beneficiary of your life insurance provides much more opportunity and protection for your children's futures.

Ꮽ *I have four children. I have established four brokerage accounts, and each child is a payable-on-death (POD) beneficiary of a separate account. Haven't I avoided probate and divided my estate equally to my four children?*

Not necessarily. First, you may have avoided death probate, but this plan does nothing to address living probate. Like a beneficiary designation, a *payable-on-death designation* only gives ownership to the beneficiary at your death, not if you become incapacitated while you are still alive. Second, your POD accounts will probably not grow at the same rate. You will need to regularly move investments among the accounts to keep them equal. If you become incapacitated, you will not be able to watch over the accounts to be sure they are kept equal. This could result in a child receiving a reduced share or no share at all.

Community Property Ownership

ᛒ *What is community property?*

Each state determines whether its system of property ownership for married couples will be community property ownership or the more common alternative, which is common law or separate property ownership. Community property is a collection of laws governing shared ownership of property between married individuals. The ten community property states are Alaska, Arizona, California, Idaho, Louisiana, Nevada, New Mexico, Texas, Washington, and Wisconsin. Each community property state has a slightly different set of rules about how and when couples acquire the community property.

Generally speaking, *community property* is the property, including real property and personal property, wherever it is located, that has been acquired by a married couple during the marriage while domiciled in a community property state. Both spouses, the members of the marriage community, have equal rights to use or dispose of their one-half interest in community property.

Ordinarily, each spouse owns a one-half interest in the property owned as community property and the presumption is that all property possessed by either spouse during marriage or upon dissolution of the marriage (death or divorce) is community property. The presumption can be rebutted by showing that the property is really the separate property of one spouse. Property titled in the name of one spouse only is frequently community property. Even if property brought to a marriage starts out as separate property, the income from the property and any appreciation in value after the marriage may acquire community property status, depending upon the circumstances and the law of that particular state.

ᛒ *What is considered separate property?*

Separate property in a community property state is generally:

1. property properly designated as separate property;
2. property owned by a spouse before marriage;
3. property acquired during marriage by gift, devise (by will), or inheritance (by intestacy); or
4. a spouse's recovery for personal injury sustained during marriage. A separate property recovery for personal injuries typically

includes damages for pain and suffering, mental anguish, disfigurement, and so forth. A recovery for loss of earning capacity and medical expenses is generally community property.

❧ *What is the significance of property being classified as community property versus separate property?*

Whether property is classified as community property or separate property is critical. From an estate planning standpoint, the classification is important because a spouse can give away only his or her separate property plus his or her one-half of the community property. The other one-half of the community property belongs to the surviving spouse. There are also special tax benefits to community property that are discussed later in this book, and for that reason it is important to distinguish between community and separate property.

❧ *Will the community property laws apply to my partner and me?*

Community property only applies to couples legally married under state law. Domestic partners cannot hold property as community property.

❧ *We've heard that there is a new form of title called community property with right of survivorship. What is that and how does it differ from regular community property?*

Community property with right of survivorship (WROS) is a relatively new form of ownership that exists by statute in California, Arizona, and a few other community property states. These laws permit married couples to take title to community property in a new form. Community property WROS combines the beneficial aspects of community property with the concept of joint-tenancy property. Property held as community property WROS, like property held as joint tenancy, passes to the surviving spouse without administration in probate. This newer form of ownership generally does not apply to all types of property, and in some states it is limited to real estate.

As we discussed earlier with regard to joint tenancy, community property WROS is also a poor substitute for proper estate planning. It does not truly avoid probate; it only defers it until the death of the surviving spouse.

Tenancy in Common

ભ *I own some property as tenants in common with my brother. Is that the same as joint tenancy?*

Tenancy in common is similar to joint tenancy in that it is a form of ownership between two or more individuals who each own an undivided interest in the property. Their interests may or may not be equal.

However, tenancy-in-common ownership differs from joint tenancy in that the deceased tenant's interest does not automatically pass to the surviving tenant, as it would with joint tenancy. Each tenant in common has the ability while living to sell, give away, or in any other way dispose of his or her interest *without* the consent of the other tenant in common. Each tenant in common also controls who receives his or her interest at death through instructions in a will or a trust. For example, with the property you and your brother own as tenants in common, at your death your undivided interest in the property will be distributed pursuant to the terms of your will or trust. The ability to direct the property at death is the major distinction between this form of ownership and joint tenancy.

ભ *Are there any estate planning benefits of owning assets as tenants in common?*

From an estate planning perspective, owning an asset as a tenant in common is much like owning an asset by yourself. You can direct the disposition of your interest in the asset at death in a will or trust. If you become disabled, your guardian or other person you have appointed controls your interest, and the other tenant remains in control of his or her respective interest. In other words, tenancy in common does not avoid probate, but it does not prevent you from doing proper estate planning either.

Use a Revocable Living Trust to Avoid Probate

ભ *What is a revocable living trust?*

First, *trust ownership* is a form of ownership where the legal title to assets is held by the trustee of the trust for the beneficial enjoyment or use by the beneficiary or beneficiaries of the trust. As the name suggests, a *revocable living trust* is a trust created during the trust-maker's life, and the trustmaker retains the right to amend or revoke the trust while alive. While the trustmaker is alive and competent, he or she can serve as the trustee and is the primary beneficiary of the trust.

Like a will, a living trust contains the maker's instructions for what is to happen to the trust property when he or she dies. But, unlike a will, a living trust also contains instructions for what is to happen if the maker becomes disabled or incapacitated and can avoid both living and death probate.

❧ *How does a living trust work?*

A revocable living trust has three distinct stages:

1. when the trustmaker is alive and well;
2. when the trustmaker is disabled; and
3. after the trustmaker dies.

As the trustmaker, when you are alive and well, you will notice little difference in how you conduct your finances. You still write checks and file tax returns as you did before the trust. If you become disabled, the disability trustee that you named in the trust document will make decisions for you based on the instructions you included in the document. This generally avoids living probate. After you die, the trust assets will be distributed to your beneficiaries or held in the trust according to the terms you included in the trust.

❧ *Can a living trust allow me to avoid probate at my death?*

Yes. A revocable living trust avoids probate after your death *as long as it is fully funded. Funding* is the act of transferring (or retitling) your assets from your name individually to you as the trustee of your living trust. If your trust is not fully funded, then the assets titled in your name and not in the trust will have to go through probate.

❧ *Can I transfer all of my assets to my living trust?*

Though most assets can be transferred to your trust, there are some assets that must not be transferred to your trust during your lifetime.

These are your tax-deferred assets, including your individual retirement accounts, 401(k) plans, 403(b) plans, and tax-deferred annuities. Transferring the ownership during your lifetime, even if it is to the trustee of your trust, can cause these assets to become immediately subject to income tax. Always consult a knowledgeable estate planning attorney before transferring assets to your trust.

CR *What are the benefits of a revocable living trust?*

In relation to the common goals we mentioned earlier in this chapter, a revocable living trust can provide the following benefits:

- *Avoid probate.* As long as all of the trustmaker's assets are funded to the trust, a revocable living trust avoids a death probate, which, among other benefits, results in privacy and lower administration costs.
- *Plan for disability.* If the trustmaker becomes disabled, the successor trustee takes care of the trustmaker's affairs according to the instructions in the trust. There is no need for guardianship proceedings.
- *Control property during life.* Because the trustmaker is both the trustee and the beneficiary of the trust, the trustmaker retains the same control over the property as he or she had before transferring the property to the trust. The trustmaker is free to do as he or she wishes with the property, and there are no worries about a co-owner's creditors or whether the property will end up in the hands of the wrong heirs.
- *Control property at death.* The trust controls the property at the death of the trustmaker, and the trust contains the trustmaker's instructions for what is to happen to that property—whom it goes to, how much, and when. It can also provide creditor protection for beneficiaries.

CR *What are the basic differences between a will and a revocable living trust?*

Both documents are sets of instructions for the management and distribution of your assets after your death. A will takes effect at your death and triggers the probate of your estate. A will does not prevent guardianship if you become disabled. A revocable living trust provides instructions for the management of your assets during your life, disability, and after your death. In this way it eliminates the need for court-controlled guardianship proceedings during life and probate at your death. Table 1-1 compares joint tenancy WROS, wills, and revocable living trusts as estate planning tools.

TABLE 1-1 Comparison of Traditional Estate Planning Tools

Goal	Joint tenancy ownership	Contractual ownership (beneficiary designation)	Will	Revocable living trust
To take care of you in case of disability or incapacity and to avoid a living probate				✓
To maintain control over your property during life	✓	✓		✓
An option to measure trustees' abilities while you are alive				✓
To provide for loved ones and charitable causes at your death according to your instructions			✓	✓
To avoid death probate and intestacy	✓	✓		✓
To minimize federal estate taxes			✓	✓
To provide asset protection to heirs			✓	✓
To maintain privacy at death	✓	✓		✓
To use a planning tool that will work in every state without having to go through probate in other states	✓	✓		✓
To minimize the post-death administrative burdens on your family	✓	✓		✓

Action Steps

We respectfully present the following action steps to summarize the concepts that we discussed in chapter 1 and to suggest steps that you can take to prepare for meetings with your estate planning team of professionals.

❑ *Locate existing estate planning documents.* These might include, but not be limited to, your will, living trust, powers of attorney, living will, and retirement plan and life insurance ownership and beneficiary forms.

❑ *Make an inventory of your major assets and liabilities.* Whether or not you have an existing estate plan, prepare a list of your major assets with estimates of their values. Don't forget assets such as retirement plans and life insurance policies. Note on the list how each asset is titled, that is, how you own it—sole ownership, trust ownership, joint tenancy, community property, and so forth. Also, add up your major debts and other liabilities.

❑ *Consider your values and experiences.* Think about the experiences that have shaped your life and your values. Consider how you want to preserve those values and to pass them along to future generations.

❑ *Outline your major planning goals.* List your goals in the broadest possible terms and, if possible, prioritize them. Working from that initial list, rewrite your goals in more specific terms. For example, your goals might include paying the cost of your grandchildren's college education or making a large donation to your alma mater.

❑ *Read your existing estate planning documents.* Ask yourself the following questions:

   ■ Do you understand the terms of the documents?

- Compare your list of assets and liabilities to the documents. Does your plan account for all of your assets and their total value? Does the plan make provisions for your debts and other liabilities?

- Will your assets pass to whom you want, the way you want, and when you want?

- Does your existing plan address your goals as you defined them?

- Does your plan address your personal, family, and financial situation as it is today, taking into account changes that have occurred in your life since you signed the documents?

❑ *Make an appointment with an estate planning professional.* Never create or revise an estate plan without working with an attorney. Contact your current estate planning attorney to set up an appointment to review your estate plan. If you do not have an estate planning attorney or would prefer to work with someone else, read Chapter 13, Finding and Working with Professional Advisors, to help you in selecting an attorney.

chapter 2

Planning for Loved Ones

LEGACY PLANNING

*CR I read an article in the paper last week about ethical wills. Is
that a special kind of will?*

Ethical wills are not legal documents but are a custom with roots
going back to biblical times. They are similar to personal legacy
statements or family mission statements. In Jewish tradition, the
individuals who wrote these documents wished not only to leave certain assets to certain heirs, but also to sum up the meaning they had
found in their own lives. Often these documents were used to pass
on, in written form, the decedent's life story and core values; the
hopes, dreams, and aspirations that they had for themselves and for
their families and heirs; and messages of love and gratitude to family
and friends. Oftentimes they would contain instructions, guidance,
and even prohibitions intended to influence or control what heirs
did with their inheritances.

Most of us who have lost close family members would treasure
letters from them talking about their lives, their hopes, and their

31

dreams. Regardless of your religious beliefs, estate planning provides you an excellent opportunity to leave behind these kinds of thoughtful communications.

℞ *How does a personal legacy statement relate to the rest of my estate planning?*

The process of writing the statement can help you to identify your priorities. For example, it may make it easier to choose a trustee or guardian for your children, or it may clarify your goals for distributions to your beneficiaries. Most of all, when you describe your personal beliefs and values in writing, there is a greater likelihood that your plan will be respected and understood. Providing beneficiaries with an understanding of your motivations may make them more comfortable with your decisions.

℞ *Can you give me some ideas about how to write a personal legacy statement?*

There are as many different ways as there are individuals. One way to start is to write down a description of your childhood—your parents, who they were, the values you learned from them, lessons you learned in life—and describe the people who most influenced you during your childhood.

℞ *Are there resources available to help me write a legacy statement as part of my estate plan?*

Some estate planning attorneys are trained to work with individuals who want to prepare personal legacy statements as part of their estate plans. There are books that present questions to parents and grandparents so that they can write something of an autobiography and talk about their hopes and dreams. There are also resources on the Internet that can give you ideas on how to proceed. We include some suggestions in Appendix A, Estate Planning Resources.

℞ *If our family mission statement includes giving to the community as an important goal, how can we implement this goal?*

Some families hold regular meetings to discuss how they will collectively contribute time and money to charitable causes. Some families set up charitable private foundations or contribute to donor-advised funds as a way of establishing charitable legacies for their families to maintain. The point is that there are a number of ways to implement your family's charitable goals, and those goals should be integrated with your estate plan to ensure they are accomplished.

PLANNING FOR A SPOUSE

Planning for a U.S. Citizen Spouse

Q What common issues do you see when planning for couples?

Planning for spouses involves a number of personal as well as tax issues. Here are some of the more common personal concerns that we address:

- A spouse is concerned about taking care of his or her spouse first, above all others.

- A spouse wants to ensure that whatever assets remain at the second death will pass to the children, whether they are children from a prior marriage or their joint children.

- Many people are concerned that their spouses are not experienced in handling financial matters.

- Sometimes clients have partners and worry about how to provide for them after death so that disapproving family members cannot interfere.

Q I want to take care of my wife after I die. What can I do to make her life more comfortable after I'm gone?

You can provide your wife with a lot of comfort if your estate plan goes beyond just the assets themselves. One of the planning goals you may want to consider is shielding the assets from your wife's creditors. You may want to plan for your wife's current or future disability and take advantage of the public assistance that may be available to her. If you want to provide your wife with these benefits, you would give her the use of your property without giving her so much control that a creditor could seize the property or that the property might disqualify her from receiving public assistance.

ᴄᴙ *Am I required by the laws of my state to leave a portion of my assets to my husband?*

The inheritance and succession statutes of every state contain provisions designed to prevent spouses from being disinherited. Such statutory provisions, often called *elective-share statutes*, entitle a surviving spouse to a minimum distribution from the estate of a deceased spouse and can be used to override the terms of a will or will substitute. If you do not take this into consideration when designing your estate plan, the enforcement by your husband of his elective share can significantly disrupt the settlement of your estate.

ᴄᴙ *Is there a preferred way to leave assets to my husband?*

The best way to leave assets to a spouse is through a revocable living trust or a will that creates a marital trust for your husband after your death. Following are some of the advantages of using marital trust planning:

- By using a marital trust, you are able to eliminate federal estate tax on the first spouse's death.

- You can name a cotrustee for the marital trust to serve with your husband after your death to provide him with asset and financial management assistance.

- Depending on the laws of your state, leaving assets to your husband in a marital trust can provide him with creditor protection if he is sued.

- The assets you leave in trust can be protected if your husband were to be involved in a later, unsuccessful second marriage. Additionally, your husband may be able to more comfortably refuse to give away assets or to loan money to other family members or friends by stating that the assets were left in trust and he cannot use them for those purposes.

If you use a revocable living trust as your basic planning document, you have the added advantages of avoiding probate on your death and avoiding a living probate if your husband is disabled after you die and is unable to manage his financial affairs.

❧ *What options do I have for leaving my estate to my wife when I die?*

There are basically two ways to leave assets to a spouse. The first and simplest way is to leave the assets "outright" to your wife with no strings attached, but this method does not provide any of the protections of a marital trust, which is the second way of leaving your estate to your wife. There are three marital trusts that couples commonly create in their revocable living trusts or wills:

1. Total control trust
2. Qualified terminable interest property (QTIP) trust
3. Total return trust

❧ *What is a total control marital trust and how would it benefit my wife?*

By *total control trust,* we mean a marital trust that you establish at your death for the benefit of your wife, over which she has total control. The purpose of this trust is to avoid probate at your wife's later death and in the event of her incapacity. With this trust, your wife:

- has the right to receive all income earned on the investments of the trust;
- has the right to withdraw all or any amount of the trust property for any reason and without any restrictions; and
- has complete authority to decide who receives the rest of the trust property at her death.

Because the spouse has total control of this trust, it generally does *not* provide any asset protection. If someone sues your wife and gets a judgment against her, the judgment creditor can usually attach the assets held by the trust.

❧ *What is a QTIP marital trust and how would it work for my wife?*

The *qualified terminable interest property (QTIP)* trust provides the following:

- Your wife must receive all income earned on the trust property at least annually.

- Your wife does not have unrestricted rights to the principal of the trust, but you would probably want to add a provision in the trust instructing the trustee to distribute principal, if necessary, for her health and support and to maintain her lifestyle. These provisions can be very broad and even include distributions for vacations, maintaining a second home, and so forth.

- You can give your wife some authority to choose who receives the marital trust property at her death; or when you create the trust you can decide who will receive it after your wife's death.

Because of her limited rights in the trust property, the QTIP marital trust protects the property from your wife's creditors. It will also protect the trust's principal for your children in the event she remarries after your death.

✃ What is the total return marital trust and how would it work for my wife?

The *total return trust* is a fairly new concept for a marital trust. The total return trust pays your wife the greater of the trust's income or a fixed percentage of the trust's value, determined annually. For example, if you decide your spouse should receive at least 5 percent of the trust's value each year, in a year that the trust is worth $500,000, your spouse would receive at least $25,000 (more if the trust's income for the year is greater than that). Some people prefer this type of trust because it allows the trustee to provide adequately for the spouse without investing heavily in bonds or other income-producing investments. Otherwise, this trust offers all the benefits of a QTIP trust, and you can include in the trust the added provisions described above.

✃ There seem to be a lot of rules and restrictions if I want to leave property to my husband in a marital trust. Why is that?

Actually, it's not as bad as it may appear. You have a lot of options in structuring the marital trust. Most of the rules concerning marital trusts are required by the Internal Revenue Code for the estate tax marital deduction. This deduction is very important in estate planning because by taking the deduction, you can eliminate estate taxes at the death of the first spouse. There are really only three rules that marital trusts have to follow to ensure that they qualify for the marital deduction.

1. The spouse *must* have the right to all of the trust's income, paid at least annually, for life.

2. The spouse *must* be the only lifetime beneficiary of the marital trust; none of the income or principal can be paid to anyone else while the spouse is living.

3. The spouse *must* be able to direct the trustee to convert non-income-producing assets to income-producing assets.

℞ *I have always handled the finances; how can I protect my wife if I should die first?*

If at all possible, you should explain your financial situation to your wife and help her to have a working knowledge of your finances before your death. To spare your wife from the drudgery and stress of making financial decisions, you should leave your assets in a trust for her benefit with others acting as trustees. These qualified trustees can hold the assets, manage their investment, and make distributions under your instructions given in the marital trust. You should select trustees who are experienced in investments and other financial matters and in whom you and your wife repose trust and confidence.

℞ *I have heard about probate and death taxes; however, when my husband passed away several years ago, there was no probate and no taxes were due. Am I missing anything?*

We assume that everything you and your husband owned was in joint ownership and everything passed to you at his death. In 1982, the federal government passed a law that exempted most transfers between spouses from estate and gift taxes. This exemption is called the *unlimited marital deduction*. We explain the marital deduction in this chapter and in Chapter 4, Tax Basics, so you can understand its benefits and limitations in planning. Even though your husband's estate avoided probate and taxes, if you do not plan, at your death there will be a probate and possibly estate taxes due, depending on the value of your estate and whether you own property jointly with others.

Planning for a Noncitizen Spouse

CR My husband and I have lived in the United States for the past 10 years, but I am not a U.S. citizen. My financial advisor has just told me that the rules about estate planning are different for us than what I have been reading. Can you explain?

The U.S. federal estate and gift tax laws allow married couples to transfer any amount of property to each other, free from federal estate or gift taxes, as long as the spouse receiving the property is a U.S. citizen. The U.S. government is concerned that a noncitizen spouse might leave the country after the citizen spouse's death, which could keep the U.S. government from collecting the full amount of estate taxes owed on the property. To prevent this from occurring, the Internal Revenue Code contains special rules for transfers to a spouse who is not a citizen. The most important rule is the requirement that any marital trust for a noncitizen spouse must be a qualified domestic trust.

CR What is a qualified domestic trust?

A *qualified domestic trust (QDOT)* functions like a marital trust for U.S. citizens, but there are also some important differences:

- The trustee of a QDOT *must* be either a U.S. citizen or a U.S. corporation.
- Depending on the value of the property or the amount of foreign real estate held in the QDOT, one trustee must be a U.S. bank.
- The trust document *must* provide that no distribution (other than one of income) may be made from the trust unless the trustee has the right to withhold estate taxes on the distribution of trust assets.

CR What happens if my spouse becomes a citizen after the date of my QDOT?

If your noncitizen surviving spouse becomes a citizen before the estate tax return is due, none of the QDOT rules will apply.

Disinheriting a Spouse

CR *Is it possible to disinherit my husband?*

It is very difficult and almost legally impossible in the United States to completely disinherit a spouse, especially a wife. A number of states still provide a wife with a "dower interest" in her husband's assets, even if his trust, will, or other documents left nothing to her. In many states, a husband or a wife is entitled to an *elective share,* which is a percentage of the estate. Election of a wife's dower interest or a spouse's elective share can be devastating to estate plans as far as estate and gift taxes are concerned. Therefore, you should plan carefully when attempting to disinherit a spouse.

CR *Can I disinherit my husband in a prenuptial agreement?*

A properly executed *prenuptial agreement,* or *premarital agreement,* can and commonly does delineate each spouse's rights to the other spouse's property on death. A prenuptial agreement can include waivers of inheritance—dower, elective share, homestead—and other property rights that your husband would have absent a premarital agreement. If you are considering a prenuptial agreement, it is important that independent counsel represent each party in the process. Full disclosure of assets is also an important factor in creating a durable premarital agreement. With independent counsel and full disclosure, the effectiveness of a successful attack on the agreement is remote.

CR *Can I disinherit my wife in a postnuptial agreement?*

A *postnuptial agreement* is a marital agreement made by spouses after they are married. In most states, but not all, these agreements are just as valid as premarital agreements, although a court may scrutinize them more closely if undue influence is suspected. Thus you can use a validly executed postnuptial agreement to disinherit your wife if both of you are willing and if both of you make full disclosure of all the assets you own. Just as for a prenuptial agreement, it is essential that each of you has separate legal counsel.

CR *Can I disinherit my wife if we own property jointly?*

You cannot disinherit your wife in regard to any property titled jointly with her. Such joint property will be automatically distributed to the surviving joint tenant. The survivor of the two of you will receive outright ownership of those joint assets along with responsibility for any liens or encumbrances on them.

Changing jointly titled assets to your sole ownership will require your wife's consent and signature.

CR *What inheritance rights does a spouse have in a community property state?*

In community property states, assets brought to the marriage and assets inherited during the marriage that are not commingled with the community property estate remain the separate property of the deceased spouse. These assets do not become part of the community property that is divided equally between the spouses when one spouse dies.

PLANNING FOR LIFE PARTNERS

CR *Why do my partner and I need to estate plan?*

The law is slowly evolving in the domestic partners arena, especially in estate planning. Generally, if a person does not have an estate plan, the state in which that person resides has a plan for him or her. It is contained in the intestacy statutes. *Intestacy* is a statutory inheritance framework that favors spouses and family bloodlines. In most states, the law does not recognize same-sex marriages or unmarried partners, so when one partner dies, there is no statutory mechanism for the surviving partner to inherit the deceased partner's property. Instead, under the intestacy law of most states, the deceased partner's biological family will inherit everything. To provide for the other domestic partner, each partner must complete an estate plan.

Anyone in a nontraditional relationship must seriously consider seeking the assistance of an estate planning attorney to create a plan to protect both partners in the event of death or disability. The good news is that, with proper planning, unmarried couples can receive many of the same nontax benefits as married couples.

⚬ *My partner and I own everything jointly. Why do we need to estate plan?*

Although joint tenancy is one method for unmarried partners to pass assets at death, it is not the most effective way to do so. There are several reasons to consider an alternative method:

- *What happens if one of you becomes disabled?* Joint tenancy does not resolve the challenges of making medical decisions for each other when one partner is unable to do so. Joint tenancy may not allow one partner to sell an asset while the other partner is disabled and unable to execute a transfer document. Joint tenancy does not allow you to leave instructions for your care and assistance in the event that you become disabled.

- *What happens if the relationship fails?* The law does not provide a mechanism similar to a divorce proceeding to untangle jointly held assets.

- *What happens if one of you gets into financial or legal trouble?* It will likely impact the other partner's half of the joint property.

⚬ *I have a large life insurance policy. Is it possible to name my partner as a beneficiary?*

Unmarried couples often name each other as life insurance beneficiaries to effectuate their planning desires. Some states require that the beneficiary have an *insurable interest* on the life of the insured. An insurable interest arises from the relationship between the person buying insurance and the insured person; if there is a reasonable expectation of benefit on the continuation of the insured's life. The benefit may be economic (as between business partners, debtor and lender, or employer and key employee) or love and affection (as between legally married spouses or parent and minor child); and a person can of course always insure his or her own life. Insurable interest serves a social purpose because it prevents speculation, as in the case of murderers insuring their victims. Some states, such as California, allow you to name anyone as your beneficiary.

⚬ *What can I do if I cannot name my partner as a beneficiary on my life insurance policy?*

You can name your estate as the beneficiary of the insurance policy and your will can name your partner as the heir. This is risky because the will may be challenged. A safer solution is to name your living trust as the beneficiary and your partner as the beneficiary of the living trust.

CR *If my partner predeceases me, I am worried that his family will challenge my inheriting his estate. What can I do?*

Unfortunately, these types of challenges by the deceased partner's family are common. Even if everyone accepts the relationship while both partners are alive, many times at death that acceptance gives way to hostility. Often, the family of the deceased partner demands that the surviving partner provide an accounting of who owns which assets, including property that was jointly purchased. Most of us do not keep these types of records. These demands place more stress on the surviving partner, who is trying to cope with the loss.

A revocable living trust will help prevent some of these problems. Generally, a trust communicates what someone intends to accomplish in his or her estate plan. Transferring assets to the trust and maintaining it while you are alive establishes your intentions, and the trust document, in fact, states your true wishes. The family's burden in challenging the decedent's estate plan in this situation is often insurmountable.

The key to this process is to work with a counseling-oriented attorney who will spend time with you to understand your goals and wishes and then to put into place the mechanisms to accomplish them. Your planning should then be backed up by regular reviews with the attorney to consider what, if any, changes to the plan are needed to reflect your revised goals.

CR *How can I provide for my significant other if I become disabled?*

Let us answer your question with a real-life client situation. We represented Dennis, a dentist who had done very well financially in his practice and through real estate investments. Dennis wanted to provide for Alice, the woman with whom he had been sharing his life for many years. Alice had a modest estate at best, and Dennis paid for almost everything.

We drafted some very specific disability instructions in Dennis's revocable living trust, so that during any period of disability, the trustee would provide for Alice. Dennis instructed his disability trustee that Alice could reside in his house and the trust would pay for maintaining the home. Alice would also be permitted to drive any car that he owned. The trust will also pay Alice's normal living expenses up to $3,000 a month. Without these instructions in his trust, the trustee would not have been permitted to care for Alice.

When planning for a significant other, you must think carefully about his or her needs, how you provide for that person now, and whether you would want to provide for him or her if someone else were handling your financial affairs during your disability.

 My partner and I are not married. Is our estate planning different than a married couple's?

One of the biggest differences is the unlimited marital deduction. A married couple can pass property to each other estate and gift tax–free through the marital deduction. So, with proper planning, usually there is no estate tax at the death of the first spouse. Unmarried couples are not eligible for the marital deduction, so there may be estate tax due when the first partner dies; leaving less property to maintain the surviving partner. The challenge in these situations is how to plan in lieu of the marital deduction.

 Before I met my partner, I had children from a prior marriage. How do I provide for my partner without excluding my children as part of my estate plan?

There are numerous ways to accomplish your goals, including creating a trust for your partner and your children—everything goes to your partner in trust until his or her death, at which time the remaining trust property passes to your children. This is by no means your only option. Rest assured that an estate planning attorney can tailor a plan to meet your specific goals. The point is that you do not have to choose between your partner and your children—most often you can accomplish both objectives.

PLANNING FOR CHILDREN

In General

 How much information should I share with my children about my estate planning?

How much information you share is a very personal question and the answer will differ from family to family. Some parents will take the position that it is they who created the wealth and they don't wish to disclose, for whatever reasons, the nature of their estate nor their plans for its disposition. This is certainly their right.

In other families, one could reasonably make the case that there is more responsibility to preserve and to grow this wealth for the benefit of the family from a multigenerational perspective.

There is no question but that the younger generation's planning could benefit from the knowledge of their parents' and grandparents' estate plans. But, there is also a real concern that knowledge of the estate plan can, in some cases, cause negative consequences.

For example, if an adult child knows that he or she will inherit substantial wealth, it may rob the child of the drive and initiative to succeed. For other adult children, such knowledge may have no effect whatsoever on their motivation and drive. In other cases, such knowledge may allow the adult child to pursue work that might otherwise be implausible. For example, with knowledge of a future inheritance, one might decide to pursue a job in the arts or teaching or even charitable work with low pay, where, without such knowledge, a different occupation with higher pay would be necessary.

Perhaps the bottom line here is that you must consider your children and the effects that knowledge of the estate plan would have on them. Often, it can be very beneficial to have a meeting with the children to explain the estate plan or aspects of it. If you are naming children as trustees or executors, it is even more important for them to know certain details. Remember, when you are gone, you are no longer available to answer their questions on the when's, where's, why's, and wherefore's. Often, family advisors can assist in planning these meetings with children and participate in making presentations according to the parents' wishes.

ଔ *Do I have to give all of my assets to my children?*

No, but unless you prepare an estate plan that reflects otherwise, the law in most states will distribute your estate to your children in equal shares. You are free to leave your property to whomever you choose, but you must affirmatively exercise that right by executing a will or trust naming others as heirs of your estate and the amount or percentage each is to receive.

ଓ *Do I have to be "fair" to all my kids and leave them equal shares?*

Our clients usually express a desire to be "fair" to their children. There can be a great difference, however, between treating your children "fairly" and treating them "equally." Fairness is ultimately a subjective term, and it refers to giving someone what he or she needs or deserves. In your estate plan, you have the freedom to do what you believe is right. If you have been significantly subsidizing one of your children during life, you may want to make up the difference to another child at your death. One child may have a financially successful career, while another has a job that pays less but is important to society, such as a firefighter or a teacher. Is it fair to divide your wealth between them equally? The key is to consider your relationships with your heirs, their relationship to each other, and the respective needs of each of your children.

ଓ *Can we leave our property equally to our children but distribute it to them differently?*

This is a common and effective planning strategy. You can create a separate trust for each child in which you provide detailed instructions that specifically meet your hopes, concerns, dreams, values, and aspirations for that child and that specifically address your assessment of that child's strengths and weaknesses.

ଓ *In planning my estate, how do I take into account the 20-year age difference between my two children?*

Start by asking yourself how you would treat your children if you were still alive when they are to receive their inheritances. If your older child has already been provided with a college education, a wedding, or a down payment on a house, would you want to make sure your younger child has those same benefits? If your estate is measured in millions, there may be enough money available for everyone. However, if you have a more modest estate, you should consider the use of a common trust.

A *common trust*, which can be incorporated into a will or a living trust, states that on the deaths of both you and your spouse, all of your assets will continue to be held in one trust for the benefit of both children until some triggering event occurs—which you designate in the document—such as your younger child reaching a certain age. At that point, the common trust can be divided into a separate share for each child. You would also designate in the trust document what happens to each share and when. Either or both can be distributed at that time or continue to be held in trust and distributed later under other criteria that you design.

This technique allows you to make sure that your younger child receives the same benefits that your older child received, just as you would have done if you were still alive.

◌ར When should the common trust terminate?

There are many alternatives as to when the common trust terminates. Two of the most traditional approaches are to have the common trust end:

1. when the youngest child reaches a certain age, such as 23; or
2. when the youngest child reaches a certain age or completes college, whichever occurs first.

At that time, any remaining trust property is divided equally (or otherwise, as you designate) into a separate share for each child. You can instruct the trustee to distribute the property in a lump sum or in some other way, depending on the provisions in your trust.

◌ར When will my children be old enough to properly manage their inheritances?

The legal age of adulthood, or majority, and—unless otherwise planned and provided for by the parents—the time at which a child is entitled to receive his or her inheritance is generally the age of 18, although this age may vary on the basis of circumstance and state law. Since it is often difficult to know how well an 18-year-old will manage money, parents are sometimes concerned about a lump-sum distribution to children. In some cases, this is true even though the children are already adults at the time the estate plan is established.

In a revocable living trust or will, you can provide a trustee with specific directions for how and when distributions should be made to your children. It is not uncommon in the situations we just mentioned for parents to stretch out an inheritance over a period of years and stagger the amounts of the distributions.

Parents who have such concerns need to know that they can achieve their goal of providing support to their children without worrying that the children will accidentally or purposefully undermine that goal.

◌⒭ What issues should I consider regarding the distribution of assets?

Once you've decided on the terms for dividing the inheritance into each child's own share or trust, you have the following additional considerations:

- Whether or not you want the trustee to make periodic distributions of the trust income and, if so, when
- When you want the trustee to distribute the trust principal (trust assets)
- The degree of discretionary distributions that you want to permit the trustee to make

◌⒭ What do you mean by discretionary distributions?

Frequently, trustmakers give their trustees the authority to make distributions for the "health, education, maintenance, and support" of the child. These are known as the *ascertainable standards* in the Internal Revenue Code. Collectively, they provide for a beneficiary's all-encompassing needs. Thus, the trustee, in his or her discretion, could pay for a child's medical needs. Similarly, the trust could provide the trustee with a standard for discretionary distributions. For example, some parents prefer a conservative standard that requires the existence of a genuine need, whereas others prefer a more liberal standard that allows financial assistance for such matters as the purchase of a residence, a business, or any other extraordinary opportunity.

◌⒭ My husband and I have two children. What are the options for distributing their inheritance to them?

There are four major methods for distributing an inheritance to a child:

1. Outright distribution

2. Convenience trust

3. Staggered distributions

4. Lifetime trust

ℭ *What is an outright distribution?*

As the term implies, the beneficiary receives the inheritance immediately and in a lump sum, so he or she has total control of the property you leave. Among the major disadvantages of this method is that it offers no creditor protection for the beneficiary.

ℭ *Should I give my adult children their inheritance all at once or over a period of time?*

Although your natural inclination may be to give your adult children their inheritances outright, that may not be the best or wisest course of action for them. A well-thought-out series of subtrusts in your living trust can provide for the specific needs of each child. Leaving property to your children in trust can often protect them from their own inexperience with money, from their inability to make wise decisions, from their creditors, or from a divorcing spouse. Adult children who do not have experience with large sums of money are often overwhelmed when they receive an inheritance. They may make poor choices and come to realize, too late, that their inheritances have gone to poor investments and frivolous spending.

Perhaps an adult child is easily influenced by friends and family and can't say "no" when asked for a handout. Perhaps he or she has a drug or alcohol problem, and a large "windfall" will only increase his or her ability to satisfy the dependency. Or, perhaps, at the time of your death, one of your children may have the misfortune of being in the middle of a nasty divorce or a lawsuit.

By using a separate subtrust for each child, you can plan for all these situations very specifically if they currently exist, or you can plan in anticipation of the possibility of those problems and provide some protection for your children if it is later needed.

ℭ *What is a convenience trust?*

A *convenience trust,* as some attorneys call it, is a trust that permits the beneficiary to withdraw the assets of the trust at any time and for any reason, without restriction. Like an outright distribution, the convenience trust gives the child total control of the inheritance but offers the advantage of not being subject to a living or a death probate, provided that he or she leaves the assets in the trust. This method may not protect the inheritance from the child's creditors and will not protect it from future estate taxes.

❧ *What are staggered distributions?*

Parents often stagger distributions from their trusts for younger children because the children are too young to have demonstrated how they will handle money as adults. Parents will stretch out the inheritance over a period of years and stagger the distributions at ages 30, 35, and 40, for example. In this way, if a child mishandles the first distribution, he or she has two more chances to learn to manage property responsibly. Until the child reaches the distribution ages, the trust directs the trustee to make discretionary distributions for the health, education, maintenance, and support of the child.

While the inheritance is in the trust, it is protected from the child's creditors, but the protection is lost as the child receives the distributions.

❧ *What is a lifetime trust?*

A *lifetime trust* keeps the inheritance in trust for the lifetime of the beneficiary. Most lifetime trusts distribute income and principal as needed for the beneficiary's health, education, maintenance, and support. This trust avoids probate and protects the inheritance from the beneficiary's creditors. The beneficiary may even be his or her own trustee.

❧ *We want to leave our money for our kids in an intelligent way. We're concerned that if they receive their inheritance too quickly, it will be harmful to them; but we also don't want to control them "from the grave." What should we do?*

Most parents are unsure about the wisdom of leaving large amounts of cash and assets to their children. The notion of an outright distribution of several hundred thousand, or even millions of dollars, to a child, at any age, fuels this concern. This is especially true when planning for younger children who have not yet developed financial responsibility. As a result, many parents seek alternative ways to distribute inheritances to their children.

Many parents utilize trusts for their children with differing standards and criteria for distributions, and there are as many strategies as there are inventive parents and grandparents. Here are some common examples:

- The trust funds can be distributed at regular intervals (for example, every 5 years).

- The funds can be held in trust until the child reaches a certain age and then be distributed in a lump sum.

- If a child has not reached middle-age maturity or does not have a track record to demonstrate financial responsibility, it might be appropriate to use a minimum two-stage distribution, 5 years apart, with quarterly payments of net income throughout the period of the trust. In this way, the child can learn from mistakes that he or she makes from the first distribution and, hopefully, become more responsible with subsequent distributions of principal.

- For the same reason, staggered distributions are also appropriate if the trust assets are significant. Distributions typically begin when the child reaches a certain age (usually at age 30 or 35) or on the death of the surviving parent and continue at specified intervals over a predetermined period of years. For example, a trust document could state:

  > Distribute 25 percent of our daughter's share to her on the death of the survivor of us, distribute 30 percent 3 years from that date, and distribute the balance in two equal distributions at 5-year intervals from that date.

- Some people create lifetime trusts for their children that never allow them to directly control the money, though they may benefit from the trust for life. These trusts can provide substantial benefits for your children and avoid turning over substantial sums to them in a lump sum.

CR *Can we provide for our children's retirement years through trust planning?*

Parents can sometimes reasonably predict that their children will frivolously waste their distributions. A strategy you can use in this situation is to provide net income to your children and to give authority to the trustee to make discretionary distributions of principal with the final distribution at age 55 or later. In other words, the assets are used to ensure the children's retirement.

○ℛ *How can I prevent my children from fighting among themselves over their inheritance?*

By doing good planning! Family squabbles are more likely to occur when people do not leave instructions that make their intentions clear. If your instructions are complete and give a clear indication of your intentions, there will be less likelihood that your children will argue over different interpretations of the instructions.

There is nothing wrong with adding language to your estate plan that describes your intentions. The problem with many "cookie-cutter" documents is that no specialized language is added. A good estate planning professional will be able to help you identify your hopes, concerns, and desires and to properly incorporate them into your legacy planning documents.

○ℛ *I don't want my son to lose his inheritance in a lawsuit or divorce. Can I do anything to prevent this?*

If you leave your property to your son outright, his inheritance will be subject to the claims of his creditors and the claims of your daughter-in-law's creditors if she and your son were to get a divorce. Leaving your property in trust to your son will shield the property from the claims of his creditors and a divorcing spouse. You can set up the trust to allow your son to make major decisions about the trust property during his lifetime but also include special instructions that prevent others from gaining access to his inheritance.

This protection is not available if the beneficiary of the trust has the right to withdraw assets from the trust at any time for any reason. Therefore, the terms of the trust must provide that the assets can only be used for specified purposes, such as a beneficiary's proper maintenance and support. Also, the creditor protection is significantly weakened if the beneficiary is the only trustee of the trust. For this reason, your son either should not be the trustee or should serve as a cotrustee with another person. With a cotrustee, your son cannot use assets of the trust without the cotrustee's agreement, and this will substantially enhance the creditor protection.

℃ *What are the special instructions that I have to include in the trust to prevent creditors from gaining access to my son's inheritance?*

If the trust has what are known as *spendthrift* provisions in it, the trust may be able to protect your son's inheritance from his creditors. These provisions allow the trustee to make distributions of income and principal *solely* in the trustee's discretion, rather than requiring the trustee to make mandatory distributions.

The purpose of a spendthrift trust is to protect the inheritance of beneficiaries who are poor at handling money. The beneficiary cannot force the trustee to make distributions on demand, which is why it is inadvisable to name the beneficiary as the sole trustee of his or her own trust. Similarly, the beneficiary's creditors cannot attach the assets held in the spendthrift trust for the beneficiary or force their early distribution to pay the beneficiary's debts. Creditors can, however, get to the assets once they have been distributed to a beneficiary, even if the assets were distributed from a spendthrift trust.

℃ *How can my children control their inheritance if the money is in a trust?*

There are many different ways you can design such a plan. One increasingly common method is to have each child serve as a cotrustee of his or her trust with someone else, often a financial advisor, accountant, or trust company. You can authorize your children to select their own cotrustees (as long as the cotrustees are not related to the child) and even remove and replace cotrustees.

℃ *I want to provide for my wife after my death, but if she remarries after I die, I want to be sure that everything we accumulated ultimately goes to our children, not to a new husband and his children. How can I accomplish this?*

Generally, if you leave property to your wife outright, she will have the unrestricted right to use those assets any way she wants, including for the benefit of a new husband. Moreover, the laws of most states entitle her new husband to a significant share of her estate upon her death, even if her will or revocable living trust leaves everything to your children. You can prevent this from happening by structuring your estate plan so that at your death your assets are divided between a marital trust for her benefit and a family trust for your children.

The marital and family trusts will provide for your wife while she is living, and at her death the remaining assets will pass to your children. Her new husband will not be entitled to any of the marital trust property while your wife is alive or after she dies.

To achieve this goal, your attorney adds provisions to both trusts, which, in the event of her remarriage, shuts off access to the income or principal, or both, of the family trust and to the principal of the marital trust. (Remember, your wife must be able to receive all the income from the marital trust for her life in order to qualify that trust for the marital deduction.) You can also provide that if your wife's marriage ends for any reason, she can once again benefit from the provisions that were terminated at the time of the remarriage.

When you use these remarriage provisions, it is important that the trustee of the marital and family trusts be someone other than your wife or that there be a cotrustee serving with her. If your wife were the sole trustee, she could deplete the marital and family trusts before the children knew about the remarriage provisions. The children would then be at the point of having to sue your wife or possibly lose the funds.

Planning with Incentives

ᴄᴿ *I have three children. Two children work in the business and are good workers. One is not interested in working and prefers to live off of the money we give him. What can we do in our estate plan to encourage him to get a job?*

Your situation is not uncommon. Parents often come to us concerned that one of their children has developed an unacceptable behavior or lifestyle. Others are worried that their children, while productive and responsible now, may "slack off" once they receive their inheritances. These clients are searching for ways to motivate their children to be productive members of society, to teach their heirs financial responsibility, or to push a family member to get help for a dependency problem. We often help clients build incentives into trusts to reward children for achieving certain goals or to discourage children from unacceptable behavior.

In an *incentive trust*, the trust offers the beneficiary certain "carrots and sticks" to reward or discourage behavior. By linking trust distributions to behavior, the trust will encourage your child to do certain things that you believe are worthwhile or discourage your child from engaging in inappropriate conduct.

CR *I want my children to lead productive, hardworking lives, which contribute to our society. How can I build incentives into the distributions without being overly controlling or just giving them too much money?*

There are a number of approaches you might consider:

■ *Opportunity funding:* You may instruct your trustee to create or buy an "opportunity" for a child. The benefits to the child will occur primarily if the child successfully develops the opportunity.

■ *Testamentary charitable foundation:* You may want to create a trust or foundation in your living trust that springs to life after your death and directs that, under certain guidelines, your children assist in the philanthropic endeavor of giving away the income of the trust. This strategy not only encourages children to look beyond themselves but also enhances their personal and social status in their communities.

■ *Staggered distributions:* You may simply want to stagger distributions to the children at certain more mature ages or after certain periods of time. A second- or third-chance formula allows your children to have resources left if they fail to handle their first distributions wisely.

■ *Trustee discretion with criteria:* Your trustee can hold a child's share for life with the discretion to make certain distributions. You can set any number of specific criteria for the exercise of that discretion, such as liberal or conservative standards for distributions; and you can suggest or direct under what circumstances the trustee should distribute that child's trust principal.

■ *Milestone incentives:* You may set conditions for distributions from your trust on your children's reaching certain milestones, which can either be clearly defined or be left to the discretion of your trustee.

The opportunities for creating incentives for your children are almost endless; however, you must also be sensitive to the risks of overcontrolling. With the assistance of an experienced, knowledgeable estate planning team, you can create the structures that encourage the desired outcome without the negative responses.

Incentives for Financial Achievements

> ℛ *I don't want my kids to become "trust-fund babies" who just live off their inheritance. How can I discourage that?*

This is a common concern for wealthy parents. To address this issue, consider adding one or more of the following provisions to your trust or will:

- The trustee makes distributions that match the child's income shown on a W-2 form. If they don't work, they do not receive a distribution from the trust.
- The child must earn a specified amount before the trustee makes distributions to him or her.
- Incentive trusts can also motivate children (and grandchildren) to choose socially important careers that do not necessarily pay well, such as teaching, the foreign service, missionary work, social services work, and so forth. For example, the trust could offer to pay a child an amount equal to the income from one of these professions.

Incentives for Educational Achievements

> ℛ *My top priority is seeing that my descendants get a good education. How can the trust encourage my family to go to college and do well?*

To encourage children and grandchildren to get an education, the trust can pay a child's educational expenses and even offer a bonus for reaching certain educational targets, such as a 3.5 grade-point average or a master's degree. In most cases, the trust requires the child to finish college within a reasonable time so the child doesn't become a lifetime student.

Incentives for Behavioral Issues

☞ *I'm concerned that my heirs will use their inheritance to support their bad habits. How can I prevent that from happening?*

For parents of children with drug, alcohol, or other addictions, their greatest concern is that their wealth will eventually go to support a self-destructive lifestyle. They fear that the money they leave behind for loved ones will end up buying their loved ones an early death. This result must be avoided at all costs. With proper drafting, a trust can actually help an addicted child recover.

This time, the trust includes "disincentive" provisions to withhold distributions to a child while he or she exhibits the specified bad habits or addictions, such as drug or alcohol addictions, compulsive gambling, and criminal behavior. With the "sticks," the trustee is empowered to require the child to enroll in school, to attend counseling programs, to submit to drug screening, or to provide objective proof that he or she is not engaging in the prohibited activities in order to qualify for the "carrot"—the trust distributions. Another carrot could be an offer to pay for counseling and treatment to help the child overcome the destructive behavior.

Minor Children

☞ *What happens if I do not plan for my minor children?*

If you do not plan for the needs of your minor children, a court will take charge of your assets in a guardianship. Even if you nominate the guardian, it is the court, rather than the guardian, who has the final say. Not only is the guardianship process expensive, but there is no way to ensure that the court will carry out your values and desires for your children. Also, court jurisdiction and the guardianship ends when your minor children reach the age of majority. At this time, the children are given unconditional control of their property.

In addition, in a guardianship, the funds for each child are maintained in separate accounts. The court does not allocate more money to one child even if that child has greater needs. Thus, if one of your children has health problems or special needs and all of his or her share is used, the court cannot divert part of the funds of another child whose share is more than adequate for his or her needs. All children are treated equally, even if they have unequal needs.

ᘔ *What should my wife and I think about when planning for our minor children?*

Begin by thinking about who should care for them and how that person will provide for them. After that, consider what is important to you. Is education, religion, or involvement in extracurricular activities (sports, music, arts, etc.) important to you? How would you like the resources you leave to be used for your children? The same thoughts you have with regard to how you would like to have your children raised also applies to the values you wish to instill in them. Are the guardians you select appropriate for your children in accomplishing these goals? Once you are clear in your own mind as to what you would like to happen, be sure to communicate clearly those hopes and dreams to your children's potential guardians in your estate plan instructions.

ᘔ *Education is important to my wife and me. How do we incorporate this priority into our estate planning should we meet an untimely death while our children are still minors?*

This goal is readily achievable. Your advisors' job is to delineate your objectives for your children and clearly state in the estate planning documents your specific instructions to your trustee and guardian. The more thorough your advisors all are in developing a clear understanding of your goals, the greater the likelihood that your goals will be met.

Your estate planning documents can be viewed as an elaborate set of baby-sitter instructions to guide trustees and guardians in making choices consistent with your educational goals for your children.

If your goal is private schooling for your children, you must also consider how the guardian will pay for private education in your absence. Your estate plan will need both directions for your guardian and a funding mechanism (typically life insurance) to pay for your children's education.

ᘔ *I am a single parent with young children and a small estate. How will a living trust benefit me?*

A single parent with minor children arguably needs a living trust more than anyone else. If you die before your children grow up, their guardian will hold all of your assets for their benefit until they reach the age of majority—18 or 21 years. Unless you have directed in a living trust that your assets are to be held in trust beyond that age, then their inheritances will be turned over to them, no strings attached, on either their 18th or their 21st birthdays. Because children, even mature children, lack the experience and judgment necessary to anticipate their future needs, they very often spend some or all of this inheritance unwisely. This frustrates the educational and other goals you have for your children. A trust also provides excellent opportunities for parents to leave detailed instructions for the person or persons who will be looking after the children and their inheritance, and to provide for financial assistance to the guardian of the children for the extra expenses required for their loving care.

All of this could be accomplished in a properly drafted will with a testamentary trust, but with one major drawback. A will has no effect until after your death, leaving you and your children unprotected if you become incapacitated. The major advantage of a living trust over a will is that the living trust can provide for you and your children during your incapacity. You will still need a will to appoint a guardian for your minor children at your death, but otherwise a trust will better provide for you and your children.

❧ How can I make gifts to a minor?

Children under 18 are generally prohibited from owning property in their own names. Parents and others have historically used trusts or *Uniform Transfers to Minors Act (UTMA)* accounts to transfer gifts to minors. With an UTMA account, or in some states, an *UGMA (Uniform Gifts to Minors Act)* account, a custodian manages the gifts and makes distributions to the child as the custodian deems necessary. A similar vehicle for these gifts is a minor's trust, which essentially works the same way as an UTMA account.

There are some potential disadvantages to using UTMA or UGMA accounts or a minor's trust:

1. The trust or account will terminate when the minor reaches the age of majority (18 or 21, depending on your state) and will distribute its assets to the child, at which point he or she will have full control of the assets.

2. The assets in the account or trust may be subjected to estate taxation when the custodian or donor dies.

3. Income from the UTMA account will be taxed at the parents' tax bracket if the minor is under age 14 and has unearned income (interest and dividends) in excess of the annual threshold amount.

4. The child's chances for financial aid for higher education may be adversely affected because assets in an UTMA account are considered the child's.

Other types of trusts, discussed later in this book, do not have these shortfalls and can be used to effectively transfer wealth to minors.

ଉ *If we have more children after we execute our estate plan, do we have to redo our trust?*

Not necessarily, but it's a good idea. The law in many states gives children the right to a share of their parents' estates even though they were not mentioned in the will or trust; but the omitted child must show that he or she was unintentionally omitted in order to receive a share of a deceased parent's estate. Also, most wills and trusts include a provision for afterborn children so that an omitted child is included in the estate plan. Still, it's a good idea to revise your estate planning documents to include the new child. By doing so, you can include the specific terms for your new child's inheritance and avoid potentially hurting the child's feelings when he or she is not included by name in your estate plan.

If you get married or have a child after you have signed your will or trust, you should have it reviewed. To avoid any confusion, you should either write a new will or trust, or re-execute the old will or trust. Your lawyer will guide you through this process.

Children with Disabilities

ଉ *How important is estate planning for children with disabilities?*

It is absolutely critical. The most important thing about planning for a child with physical, emotional, or mental disabilities is to do everything that you can to care for his or her needs after you pass away. You should never assume that your surviving family members or friends would care for your special child the way you do.

❧ *What specifically are special needs?*

Supplemental needs, or *special needs* as they are sometimes referred to, are any items that are essential for maintaining the comfort and happiness of a person with a disability and that are not being provided by any public or private agency. Special needs include medical and dental expenses not covered by Medicaid, annual independent checkups, equipment, training, education, treatment, rehabilitation, eyeglasses, transportation (including vehicle purchase and maintenance), insurance (including payment of premiums on life insurance for the beneficiary), and essential dietary needs. Special needs may also include electronic equipment such as radios, CD and DVD players, television sets, and computer equipment; camping, vacations, athletic contests, movies, and travel; money to purchase appropriate gifts for relatives and friends; payments for a companion or attendant; and other items to enhance self-esteem.

❧ *I have a son with special needs and have been told that I shouldn't leave him anything because he may not qualify for governmental benefits if I do. I want to make sure his needs are taken care of. Are there any other alternatives?*

Absolutely. There is a common misperception that a child with special needs should be completely disinherited so that the child doesn't lose governmental benefits. But disinheriting your son may be the worst thing you can do, leaving him to rely solely on public assistance. If you plan properly, you can leave assets from your estate for the benefit of your son in a way that can supplement the governmental benefits he is receiving. This planning requires the use of a supplemental-needs trust.

❧ *How should the needs of a child with a disability be met?*

A family with a special child faces many challenges, but perhaps none is more wrenching than trying to deal with an uncertain future and making an estate plan for that child. Parents want to ensure the financial well-being of their child, and the needs of such a child may continue long after the parents are gone.

For many persons with disabilities, losing eligibility for benefits is not an option. Persons with physical or mental disabilities often rely on public benefits to pay or supplement the cost of attendant care, medical care, wheelchairs, and rehabilitation. Public benefits may also provide for other basics such as food, clothing, and shelter. Historically, families resorted to the very unsatisfactory arrangement of either disinheriting the person with a disability or leaving his or her share to siblings to avoid losing benefits. A much better solution is the supplemental-needs trust.

The future of many essential governmental benefits for persons with disabilities is uncertain. There is a growing trend for the federal and state governments to provide fewer resources for persons with disabilities. Many people feel that providing for care will increasingly fall upon families, churches, and nonprofit organizations in the future.

A *supplemental-needs trust* can enable a child with a disability to inherit property without jeopardizing eligibility for governmental benefits, can coordinate the parents' estate plan so that the child will be provided for if the parents become disabled or die, and can protect the assets from the child's creditors.

To ensure that their special child will be cared for most effectively, parents must have a carefully thought-out plan, and the plan must be flexible enough to work despite an uncertain future. A proper estate plan will focus on achieving as much independence as possible for the beneficiary.

ℭ℞ *Our only son is receiving Social Security disability income and Medicare benefits. Can we leave him our estate?*

You could, but you should not. Leaving as little as $5,000 to someone receiving SSDI and Medicare benefits may result in their disqualification from receiving these benefits. While the SSDI alone may not be a significant sum of money, the Medicare benefit could prove to be priceless. What you can do in this case is to design your estate plan to include a supplemental-needs trust for your son. The trust will prohibit the trustee from using trust assets to pay for your son's food, shelter, and clothing, because basic needs are provided by the governmental benefits. Permitting the trust to provide for those needs would disqualify your son from receiving those benefits. The trust can be used, however, to supplement his basic care, to provide for his needs over and above what SSDI and Medicare provides. For example, your son may need a dental procedure that is not covered by the governmental benefits, or he may enjoy taking a trip to see family members. To qualify for this special treatment, the trust must contain special language that limits your son's rights in the trust. If this language is missing, he may lose the Social Security benefits.

❧ *May I disinherit my daughter who has a disability and instead leave her share to my son so he can provide for her?*

Leaving the share of a child with a disability to another child has many drawbacks and concerns. If your son predeceases your daughter, the property will pass according to his estate plan and may not be available for your daughter. If your son becomes disabled, he will be unable to care for your daughter. If he divorces his wife, she may claim part of the property in the divorce proceedings. Placing the money in a special trust for your daughter is a much more secure technique.

❧ *Does every person with a disability need a supplemental-needs trust?*

Absolutely not. This sort of planning is appropriate only if (1) the beneficiary lacks the capacity to manage his or her financial affairs or (2) maintaining eligibility for public benefits is important to the person's standard of living. There are many people with disabilities who do not receive benefits and have no impediment preventing them from managing their financial affairs.

❧ *How does a supplemental-needs trust protect my daughter's eligibility for public benefits and still take care of his day-to-day needs?*

A supplemental-needs trust protects eligibility for public benefits by *supplementing,* rather than replacing, essential governmental benefits that your daughter may be receiving or might later be eligible for from various governmental assistance programs.

The purpose of the supplemental-needs trust is to cover items that governmental benefits do *not* pay for—trips to visit family members, reading materials, educational tools, and over-the-counter medicines are just a few of the many purchases that can be made on behalf of the beneficiary. Assets in a supplemental-needs trust can also be used to pay for programs of training, education, treatment, and rehabilitation not covered by public benefits. The trust may also provide for certain recreation, entertainment, and consumer-goods expenses that enhance the beneficiary's self-esteem. A well-planned and well-managed supplemental-needs trust can serve as a safety net to provide for your daughter throughout her life.

෬ *Are there any limits as to how much we can put into a supplemental-needs trust?*

Since these trusts are a function of state law, each state has its own requirements concerning them. Some states do specify a maximum amount of assets that can be used to establish a supplemental-needs trust. You should check with a competent advisor in your state regarding its specific requirements.

෬ *What are some of the other planning issues that I should consider for my son who has a disability?*

Additional planning considerations for your son include:

- recording information about your son's condition and needs;
- determining his requirements for future care;
- determining your son's final arrangements;
- choosing a person to be an advocate for your son;
- choosing the guardian for your son, as well as identifying one or two additional successor guardians;
- preparing a supplemental-needs trust that will qualify him for governmental benefits;
- funding the supplemental-needs trust; and
- updating the plan regularly.

෬ *When preparing a record of our child's medical history, what types of information should we include?*

The medical summary should include a chronology of the child's medical history; a list of physicians (with addresses and phone numbers); the names, addresses, and phone numbers of any nurses or other caregivers for your child; and the types and dosages of all medication required by the child.

෬ *When determining the future needs for our child, what should we consider?*

You need to consider the following issues with regard to your child's future needs and care:

- *Residence:* Will your child live with relatives, live with friends, or be placed in a group home? You need to plan for change, as the residential needs of your child and the caregiver will change over time. You also need to consider how to pay for the child's living arrangements.

- *Environment:* You need to determine the availability of social activities for your child. Consider what activities are significant to the child, who will make sure the child participates in those activities, and how to pay the expenses of those activities.

- *Employment:* You should probably consider what employment opportunities exist for your child, and what work, if any, the child likes or dislikes, and whether the child can be trained.

ᴄᴿ *Each of our five children stands to inherit about $75,000 after my wife and I are both deceased. This includes our son, James, who has a birth defect and is permanently disabled. I doubt that we have the resources to set up a trust for James. Is there anything else we can do in our circumstances?*

Perhaps. Some states have *pooled trust funds* or a *master trust* that permit families with modest resources to provide supplemental services or special needs for their children with disabilities. There is usually an application fee to establish your child's trust account and a minimum deposit amount, such as $15,000. Once the trust account is set up, the funds are managed by one investment firm for the benefit of all accounts. The monies are pooled together providing "strength in numbers" and allowing for professional fund management when it would not be financially feasible to do so on an individual basis. Distributions from the trust are supervised by the corporate trustee, which has a legal duty to make sure that the distributions are for qualifying supplemental services or supplemental needs only. You should consult with a competent professional advisor in your state to see if this option is available to you.

Guardian Selection for Minor Children and Children with Disabilities

ᴄᴿ *Who takes care of my children if I am deceased?*

If a child under the age of majority has lost both parents, the probate court must appoint a guardian for the child. The guardian is responsible for the child's well-being, including determining all medical, educational, housing, and clothing needs.

You can nominate in your will one or more persons to serve as guardians for your children; but if you fail to name a guardian in your will or if the person named declines the post, then a judge will select a guardian for your children. When possible, the court will generally appoint a family member.

○ *What should I look for in a guardian for my children?*

Look for someone like yourself with a similar philosophy about life and raising children. Consider how that person raises his or her own children. Also, consider the strain that being a guardian would put on that person. Is it fair to ask grandparents who may no longer have the stamina for young children? If you have more than one child, you need to consider if it makes sense to break up the family among several guardians to ease the burden and what that split might do to the siblings. Selecting a guardian is a much more daunting task than many realize, and parents must take great care before asking someone to serve.

○ *Does the guardian manage my children's inheritance?*

Some states authorize the guardian to take charge of your child and his or her inheritance. Other states divide the responsibilities between a guardian and a custodian who is responsible for managing the child's property until he or she reaches the age of majority. The same person may be appointed to both positions, but you can nominate different persons for the two posts if that is your desire.

The guardian or custodian will only manage assets that you leave outright to your child. If you establish a trust for your minor child in your will or living trust, the trustee, not the guardian or custodian, will control your child's inheritance.

○ *Do my guardians have to know I named them?*

Most parents discuss the matter with the proposed guardians to make sure they are willing to serve. Other parents think that making their choice public negatively affects their relationships with siblings or close friends and, therefore, do not tell anyone.

ॐ *Should I leave a letter of instructions for the guardian of my child?*

You are the greatest and best source of information about your child. A letter of instructions for your child's guardian is invaluable. The instructions should include a summary of your child's medical history, including the current health care providers and medications and daily care needs. It is also helpful to detail your child's likes, dislikes, things that motivate the child, habits, and routines. Finally, express your hopes and dreams for your child's future so that the guardian can strive to make those dreams come true. You may be gone, but with proper planning, your goals for your child can still be achieved in your absence.

ॐ *Once my disabled daughter turns 18, do I continue to be her guardian?*

At age 18, in most states, a child reaches the age of majority and is legally considered an adult. To have the authority to continue making health care decisions for her and managing her finances, you will have to petition the probate court to appoint you as her guardian.

Planning for Children from a Previous Marriage

ॐ *I have a blended family. I have not legally adopted my wife's children although they lived with us and my children. Will they automatically share in my inheritance?*

As a general rule, your stepchildren are not your heirs. The best approach is to make clear in your estate plan your wishes for your wife's children.

ॐ *I am remarried and have children from a previous marriage. How do I take care of my present husband but also guarantee that my children are properly taken care of?*

Your goal is very common among remarried individuals and is fairly simple to accomplish. By using a qualified terminable interest property (QTIP) marital trust (described earlier in this chapter), you can provide for your husband if you die first and be certain that at his death the remaining trust property will pass to your children. The

QTIP trust is widely used in these instances because it is the only form of marital deduction transfer that gives the trustmaker control over the disposition of the trust property after the death of the surviving spouse. In addition, the balance remaining in a QTIP trust on the death of the surviving spouse is not subject to probate administration or to the claims of the surviving spouse's creditors or ex-spouses.

ᘉ *The QTIP trust sounds perfect. Are there any disadvantages?*

One potential problem is that your children will have to wait until your husband dies before they can receive a large share of their inheritance. However, this problem can be resolved through other planning techniques suggested in this book.

ᘉ *My wife has children from a previous marriage and I want to make sure they are taken care of, but how do I make sure that their father will not get control of the funds?*

You can leave assets in trust for the children and specify who will serve as trustee as well as a list of persons to serve as trustee if something happens to the initial trustee. The trustee that you name, rather than the children's father, will always control the assets and manage them in the manner in which you have directed.

Disinheriting a Child

ᘉ *My children are adults, established in their careers and financially secure. Is there anything wrong with leaving everything I own to my new wife and stepchildren who need it much more than my children?*

There is nothing inherently wrong with this choice. However, in making this choice, consider carefully the emotional and psychological consequences of disinheriting your children. Even if your children do not need your money, money has tremendous symbolic significance, especially after the death of a parent. If this is your choice, we recommend that you explain to them why you have made this particular choice. An alternative way to address this situation would be to write letters to them, to be delivered after your death.

○R What are the potential consequences of disinheriting a child?

Disinheriting a child requires very deliberate and careful thought. The emotional and financial consequences of that decision can be enormous, for both the parent and the child. When a parent wishes to disinherit a child, there is often great sadness and pain around the decision. It is a symptom of a poor relationship, and the parent is at a loss for anything else to do. The decision to disinherit a child should not be an impulsive reaction to a situation. A thorough understanding of the circumstances surrounding the decision is critical, and slowing down the planning process is often the most appropriate course to ensure that parents make the best decision. Alternatives that might heal the wounds and lessen the pain should always be explored.

○R My husband and I have a child who, as an adult, has adopted values that are contrary to just about everything we tried to instill in him as a child. He no longer has any contact with our family. We think it would be terribly unfair for this child to have any share in what we have accumulated after we die. Can we disinherit him?

Your son has no legal right to inherit from you. The laws of most states provide that a child will inherit property from his or her parents if the parents die intestate (without a will or trust). Even if you just leave the child out of your will or trust, the child may challenge your estate plan in court. He can claim that you didn't really mean to disinherit him, you simply forgot to include him in your estate plan. To avoid this result, you should affirmatively disinherit your son in your estate planning documents by identifying him as your son and making clear your desire that he is not to inherit any of your property.

○R Can our son contest our estate plan?

He can contest your plan, but only on certain grounds. Specifically, he must prove that you were not of sound mind when you signed the documents or you were acting under duress or the undue influence of someone else in making the decision to disinherit him. Absent proof of these circumstances, the court will most likely uphold your decision to disinherit him.

Are there any measures we can take to protect against our disinherited son contesting our wills?

Yes, there are. First, instead of using a will as your primary estate planning document, use a revocable living trust. In this way, your assets can pass upon your death according to the terms of your revocable living trust rather than under your will. When assets pass under your will, they must go through probate. This means that the contents of your will become a public record for your disinherited child to see. Moreover, a living trust is effective as soon as signed and funded, unlike a will that only becomes effective at your death. By creating and maintaining a living trust for the rest of your life, your child's argument that you were coerced into disinheriting him or that you simply forgot to include him is far less persuasive.

I love my child, but she has emotional problems and addictions. I feel that I must disinherit her or I will only magnify her problems and create problems for my other children. What else can I do?

Although there are ways to disinherit a child, it sounds as though you really want to give your daughter a share of your estate. Rather than disinherit your daughter, you can provide a framework for managing her inheritance without giving her any funds outright and without wreaking havoc on your other children. This requires that you decide how much of the assets your daughter will receive and design an appropriate structure to hold her share.

One planning option would be to designate that any share you give to your daughter is to be held in a lifetime trust under terms and guidelines for distribution, which you provide in your trust agreement. These distribution instructions could be liberal or conservative. They could include incentive provisions to urge your daughter to seek treatment for her problems.

There are several planning strategies available that will, with a little forethought and planning, allow you to accomplish your goals without having to take the extreme step of disinheriting your daughter.

PLANNING FOR GRANDCHILDREN

Both of our children are professionals and have more money than we do. Can we skip over them and leave our estate to our grandchildren?

Yes, in fact your children may well encourage this plan of action. But there are limitations, most notably the generation-skipping transfer (GST) tax. We explain this tax in more detail in Chapter 4, Tax Basics, but suffice it to say that the government levies an extremely high tax on transfers to grandchildren.

Currently, the law provides that you and your husband can each leave as much as $1.12 million (2003 figure; indexed for inflation) to your grandchildren without being subject to the GST tax. Even with this limitation, you can bypass your children and leave substantial wealth to your grandchildren at your death.

ᘒ *We would like to leave our assets to our children to provide for the education of our grandchildren at least through graduate school. But we are a little afraid that our children will not use the inheritance for that purpose. Is there a way to ensure that our wishes are carried out?*

Yes. You can leave your assets in trust, with the income and principal to be used as needed for the education of your grandchildren. You can also provide that after the last grandchild has been educated, the remaining principal is to be given to your children.

ᘒ *One of my two daughters is not married, and she'll probably never get married. Can I prepare my estate plan so that anything I leave her will go to my grandchildren after her death?*

Absolutely. The ability to accomplish this goal is one of the great benefits of leaving property to your children in trust. By leaving property to your unmarried daughter *in trust,* rather than through an outright distribution, you can specify that she has use of the property during her lifetime and that, when she dies, it passes according to your instructions to your grandchildren.

ᘒ *I'd like to leave some money to my grandchildren when I die, but I certainly don't want to leave out grandchildren who may be born in the future. What do I do?*

The easiest way to solve this problem is to leave what is commonly referred to as a *class gift*. A class gift leaves property to a *class* of people, rather than named individuals. For example, you could include a provision in your will or trust that says, "I leave $100,000 to all of my grandchildren who are living at the time of my death, divided equally among them." In this example, the class of persons sharing the gift is determined on the day you die, not the day that you sign your will or trust.

CƦ *I want to give particular accounts or particular life insurance policies to specific grandchildren at my death. Can I just put those items in their names now?*

Too often, loving grandparents make this basic mistake. This tactic is fraught with so many disadvantages. Unfortunately, when you die, neither the bank, the insurance company, nor the probate court will turn that money over to beneficiaries while they are minors. Instead, the probate court will appoint a guardian to manage the money for your minor children or grandchildren. A far better solution is to establish a trust to manage the assets for these minors and name the trustee as the beneficiary of the policy or account.

Even if those beneficiaries are over 18, you should think twice about naming them as beneficiaries of large lump-sum distributions. Will your 18-year-old grandson put that money toward a college education? Or will he spend it on sports cars, clothes, and exotic vacations? It takes experience and maturity to manage large sums of money, and those attributes take time to develop. Again, a trust is the best approach to see that the money is invested and spent wisely.

PLANNING FOR PARENTS

CƦ *Can I be in the meeting with the lawyer and my parents to complete my parents' estate planning documents?*

An attorney's assistance is often sought after the parents or grandparents are disabled or seriously or terminally ill. In most situations, the family member who initiates contact with an attorney has the best interests of the parent or grandparent in mind. However, there are often situations in which the family member wishes to gain control over the senior citizen's assets.

An attorney has clear-cut ethical standards to follow. He or she must ask, "Who is my client? Do I represent the senior citizen or one or more of the other family members?" So, though an initial consultation with you outside the presence of your parents is generally acceptable, the attorney should meet directly with your parents in a one-on-one setting whenever appropriate.

PLANNING FOR PETS

℞ *I've always had a dog, and I probably always will, even as I grow old. After I'm dead, I'd like to see her humanely cared for. Can I leave money to my dog to pay for her care?*

In all but a few states, the answer is "no." Technically your pet is an item of personal property that you own, and you can't leave property *to* property.

℞ *Well, can I set up a separate trust just for my pets then?*

That depends on where you live. Historically, estate plans written to benefit animals have been declared by courts to be invalid. But law evolves with changes in society, and now 17 states have enacted laws to allow trusts to benefit pets. In those states, provisions vary as far as how long the trusts can last (for example, some are limited to 21 years) and under what circumstances a court must enforce them.

℞ *But I don't live in one of those states. Is there nothing I can do?*

First, all states have historically recognized conditional gifts and bequests, in this instance, a bequest conditioned on the recipient agreeing to care for your pet. Such arrangements are referred to as *honorary trusts.* You leave a sum of money to someone, with the condition that he or she agrees to take your pet in and properly care for the animal. It's best to consult with this person before you die to make sure he or she is willing to take on the task of caring for your pet.

℞ *I'm beginning to have doubts about using will or trust provisions to provide for my pet then! Short of having her buried with me, are there any other options?*

Organizations such as veterinary colleges and local societies for the prevention of cruelty to animals have created *perpetual pet-care* programs. These programs vary widely, but a common theme is that you make arrangements with an organization for the care of your surviving pets. The arrangements can range from finding an adoptive family to housing the animals in "life-care cottages." All plans typically include veterinary care. The cost of the program, which sometimes includes a charitable donation, is paid through your estate plan.

ଓ *Is there anything else I should do for my pet's well being?*

Just as you should carry your family and medical information in your wallet in case of accident or sudden illness, you should have a plan for who will care for your pet during an emergency. Carry a card in your purse or wallet explaining that you have a pet, where it is located, who your vet is, and explaining the arrangements you have made for its care during your illness. This card can ensure that your pet is not without food or water for several days during your emergency.

ACTION STEPS

We respectfully present the following action steps to summarize the concepts that we discussed in chapter 2 and to suggest steps that you can take to prepare for meetings with your estate planning team of professionals.

❑ *Talk openly and frankly with your husband or wife.* In our experience, it is best if married couples plan their estates jointly. You need not have the exact same goals and desires, but you should discuss those goals with each other prior to meeting with your attorney. We have, regrettably, seen more than one couple start arguing in our offices because they failed to openly discuss their goals, desires, and ideas before our meeting.

❑ *Consider how you want to leave assets to your husband or wife.* Your options are an outright bequest with no strings attached or a marital trust over which your spouse has some or no control. In making your choice among the options, you must:

- ■ weigh the advantages and disadvantages of giving your surviving spouse control over the assets with your desire for providing protection of the assets from creditors;

- ■ consider whether you want to control who will receive the balance of the assets at your spouse's subsequent death or whether you will give your spouse that control;

- ■ consider whether you want to give your spouse the ability to change the disposition of your property after your death to accommodate changes in circumstances and laws.

If your spouse is not a U.S. citizen, be sure to contact an estate planning attorney who understands the limitations on planning for noncitizen spouses.

❑ *Plan your children's inheritance.* The first decision you have to make is whether you will divide your property equally or unequally among your children. Remember, "fair" and "equal" are not always the same thing. As you plan each child's inheritance, think about the following:

- Each of your children is a unique individual; there is no one best way to leave property to all children.

- How well does each child handle money?

- Do you want to encourage or discourage certain behavior?

- How and when do you want each child to receive his or her inheritance?

- Do you want to shield your children's inheritances from creditors and divorce?

- What happens if a child predeceases you?

- Do you want to provide incentives for certain achievements through your estate plan?

- Is there a particular asset you want to leave each child?

- Do you have children from a prior marriage for whom you want to plan?

Also, if one of your goals from Chapter 1, Introduction to Estate Planning, was to write a legacy statement for your children, you should start jotting down your ideas for this statement.

❏ *Plan for multiple generations.* Your estate plan can last a very long time, and in some states indefinitely, benefiting your grandchildren and future generations of your family. If one of your goals is to create a legacy, through multigenerational planning, you can minimize federal estate taxes over several generations and ensure that your wealth stays in your family.

❏ *Take care of your minor child or child with a disability.* If you have a child with physical or mental disabilities or who is a minor, decide who will care for your child after you die.

If you have a child with a disability, make plans for the child's housing, education, and other special needs. Consult with an attorney who understands how you can leave property to your disabled child while preserving his or her eligibility for public assistance.

❑ *Plan for your family's education.* Paying for your children's and your grandchildren's college education is perhaps the best gift you can give them. Before you can develop a plan to pay for their education, you first need to know how much their schooling will cost. The cost of a state university or local vocational school is less than Harvard. A financial advisor is your best resource for saving and investing for education. Consult with a financial advisor who will help you determine what the costs are and will explain the various methods of saving and investing for the costs. The sooner you begin saving, the better. Depending on the age of your children or grandchildren and the number of years you have to save, you and your advisor can have either the luxury of developing a long-term plan or be pressed to come up with a shorter-term strategy.

❑ *Consider others in your life.* Proper planning is not just for people with spouse-and-children lifestyles. Planning for your partner requires careful and thorough planning. The laws that protect surviving spouses do not apply to unmarried partners, and without an estate plan you will likely leave nothing to your partner. In addition, you may have a niece, grandchild, or even a neighbor you want to remember in your estate plan. Maybe your pets are the "family" in your life. You can provide for them, just as you would a child, through your estate plan. The key points are that an estate plan should reflect your goals, appreciation of others, and your unique lifestyle.

chapter 3

Planning for Loved Ones and Charity

CHARITABLE LEGACY PLANNING

ᑳ *We give to charity regularly but have never thought about including charitable giving as one of our estate planning goals. Should we?*

Many parents and grandparents use charitable giving to teach their families the importance of helping their community and responding to unmet social needs. While they see the tax benefits of their charitable gifts, for them it's more about shaping the legacy they leave behind and not just how many dollars they will leave to their families.

Most of our clients made their wealth from their own efforts, inheriting little or nothing from their parents. But many of their children have never known scarcity and have yet to earn their own way.

When children and grandchildren are involved in charitable activities, they learn the fragility of success and are reminded of their many blessings. Involving your children or grandchildren in charitable projects creates opportunities for you to share practical lessons about money management, goal setting, working with others, planning, and many other skills that you otherwise may not have the opportunity to share with your heirs.

Simply having the opportunity to show active caring can be an important lesson. Giving is an act of strength; caring requires self-confidence and self-awareness. When parents or grandparents offer these lessons, the lessons can be especially powerful.

CR *My wife and I started with nothing. We are proud of the wealth we have built up through our hard work and thrift. We are worried that we will deprive our children of an important growing experience if we leave them too much. We do not want to pay any more taxes than required to the government. How do we reconcile these concerns?*

There is a third alternative which many of our "self-made" clients find very attractive. These clients prefer to leave to charity the dollars that would otherwise go to the government in taxes, and many of them will give more than that, giving a large portion of their wealth to charity and a smaller amount to their children. These clients often place their wealth in certain charitable vehicles that they manage and that their children control and manage after the parents die. With this technique, future generations of your family can determine how the assets are invested and which charitable organizations should receive the assets.

The power of this planning technique should not be overlooked. It gives you the opportunity to pass on to future generations the values that you hold important and gives your family an opportunity to make a difference in their community. Moreover, you can still give your children enough of an inheritance to lay the groundwork for their future success without stunting their personal development with an excessive inheritance.

CR *How does giving to charity help my children learn about business and investing?*

Even a fund of $1,000 needs some management. A child who is responsible for this fund will have to learn about different types of investments, principles of investing, how to write checks and reconcile accounts, and how to interact with others—possibly an investment advisor, accountant, attorney, or planned-giving counselor from the local community foundation or a particular charity.

Q What can we do to help our children understand the tremendous social responsibility they have with respect to handling family wealth?

The best way to show them what is important to you is by example. For many donors, the key to giving is public involvement. If you have a need to express love and appreciation, to show support to certain organizations and the people working in them, to successfully influence others to engage in activities deemed valuable to society, or to give back to others some of what has been given to you, then your involvement in charitable giving will demonstrate to your children the importance that you place on the values upheld by the charities. Discussions about social responsibility and why charities are important are easier if your children see the results of what you do.

In our experience, parents and grandparents have used all of the charitable giving techniques that we discuss in this chapter to demonstrate their commitment to teaching children social responsibility.

Parents who want the highest level of participation by their children use private foundations. When children are on the boards of directors, they see and assess the various needs that are presented and participate in the decisions for distributions, and they decide how to invest the foundation's funds; all of which allows the children to feel like they are really making a meaningful contribution to society. This is truly a great opportunity to pass along family values and financial responsibility to your children and grandchildren while supporting the causes that are important to you.

For families who do not have the desire or wherewithal to create a foundation, donor-advised funds and supporting organizations provide middle-ground options for teaching children many of these same lessons.

Charitable remainder trusts and charitable lead trusts are the most popular tools for parents and grandparents to incorporate charitable giving into their estate planning and to pass legacies to their heirs without a great deal of expense and governmental regulations.

Q Why can't I just pay my taxes and give what's left to my family?

You can. Certainly, this is what most people have done over the years. However, we find that when people are informed about all of their choices, they often gain new knowledge, which leads to new decisions. For example, when people reflect on the role that charities have played in their lives—from the arts to religion to hospitals to parks—they often feel a sense of gratitude or responsibility to give something back. Most people want to leave the world a little better place than they found it and only need to learn that the strategies they create for charities also end up giving more to both themselves and their families.

⌘ Does the government encourage charitable giving?

Yes. There are many forms of charitable giving authorized under the Internal Revenue Code (IRC) that will allow you to exempt a certain portion of your giving for authorized social purposes. Social services are an important foundation of what has made the United States great. In fact, many of our tax laws are designed to support private giving to charities and nonprofit institutions, which can do a better job and can accomplish more from these dollars than the government in serving the general welfare of society. Government encourages taxpayers to give to qualified charitable entities and thus reduce or even eliminate their individual tax liability.

⌘ Should I give while I am alive, or should I wait until I die?

There are many ways that you can make charitable gifts, and you can give them during your life or arrange for them to be made at your death. Since every family situation is different, it is important that you structure your family giving in a way that is comfortable for you. That is why we always suggest that you do an integrated and coordinated wealth design that will allow you to make the right decisions about all of your wealth.

The timing of making charitable gifts is based on both personal and financial objectives. Different gift values made at different times produce different income and/or estate tax deductions.

The personal component to giving suggests that giving in life is preferable to testamentary (after-death) gifts, simply because you are available to experience the joy of giving and to receive the accolades for your gifts. Being acknowledged for giving can be very important to some donors. This does not mean that they are egotistical or selfish. To the contrary, just as the gift made to charity produces a financial return in the form of a tax deduction, gratitude is the personal return for the gift.

○ぴ *Are there benefits to making a charitable gift during life versus making it at death?*

It is typically more beneficial to make a charitable gift during your life rather than at death, because lifetime gifts provide you with the opportunities to see the results of your gifts and to receive income tax deductions.

○ぴ *How can charitable gifts be more meaningful to my family and me?*

A client came into my office to review his estate plan after his wife had died from cancer the previous year. During our meeting, he told me that he did not have any children and that he wanted to make a generous gift to the hospital because of the way they had cared for his wife during her illness. Although he was a very accomplished man, he was also humble. I told him that he should receive some type of acknowledgment for his gift and asked his permission to contact the planned-giving officer at the hospital. I determined that if my client were to make his gift irrevocable, the hospital would acknowledge the gift now in the form of naming a building after him and his wife. After analyzing the effect of an irrevocable gift on his estate plan, he decided that he could do it. Selecting the signage and the artwork for the building was very exciting for him. Seeing his name with his wife's on the hospital building in perpetuity was a very meaningful experience for a humble and generous man.

○ぴ *How can my wife and I even think of giving to charity while we are alive when we don't know if we have enough for the rest of our lives?*

You should never give to the point that it threatens your financial well-being or that of your family. There are ways to give to charity so that you can enjoy the process without worrying about adverse consequences. You cannot give money away comfortably unless you know you are financially secure. Before you begin to give large sums to charity, you should invest in the services of a financial planner to quantify your current situation and the capital required for the rest of your lives. Your planner will help you take a comprehensive look at your income sources such as pensions, Social Security, and investment distributions, as well as expenses and risks such as income needs, taxes, inflation, and expected investment performance. Once your resources are quantified, you will confidently know how much remains for your charitable giving.

There are many different charitable giving strategies that allow you, the donor, to retain an income interest in the gift during your lifetime. One or several of these strategies, integrated into a comprehensive plan that takes into account your future needs, various projected rates of return, inflation, and the disposition of all of your assets, should have the best chance of allowing you to make the gifts you want without the fear of running out of money.

CHARITABLE TAX DEDUCTIONS

CR What are the tax deductions for making gifts to charity?

When you give money or property to a qualified charity, you are entitled to one or more of the following deductions:

- *Income tax deduction:* You can deduct a certain amount of your charitable gifts from your income taxes. Your charitable deduction is limited in any single year to 20, 30, or 50 percent of your *contribution base* (adjusted gross income not including any net operating loss carry-back deduction). Which one of these three percentage limits that will apply depends on whether the donation is made "to" or "for the use of" a charity, the type of charity you donate to, and the type of asset you give. Except for large contributions, these rules rarely prevent you from being able to deduct 100 percent of a donation in the year in which you make it. To the extent that this limitation prevents you from taking the full deduction in the year you make the gift, you carry over the unused deduction for up to 5 additional years.

- *Gift tax deduction:* You are entitled to a gift tax deduction for lifetime transfers to charity in the same amount as your income tax deduction, but you always use 100 percent of the gift tax deduction in the year that you make the gift. There is no percentage limitation as there is for the income tax deduction. You file a gift tax return for the taxable year that you make the gift and take the full deduction on that return.

■ *Estate tax deduction:* For gifts of property to charity that take place at your death (by will, living trust, or beneficiary designation), your estate receives a charitable estate tax deduction equal to the value of the property transferred. The IRC allows a deduction from your gross estate for gifts to qualifying charities for public, charitable, and religious uses.

There are a number of rules and restrictions on the types of transfers that are eligible for these deductions. It is important to consult with a tax advisor before making a substantial gift to charity.

CR My income this year is $50,000. I want to make a cash gift of $100,000 to my church for a new building. Will I lose some of the income tax deduction?

You won't be able to fully use the income tax deduction this year, but you can carry the unused deduction forward up to 5 years. You can probably deduct $25,000 this year, and assuming your income doesn't change in the future, you can deduct that same amount in each of the next 3 years to fully utilize the deduction.

QUALIFIED CHARITIES

CR What are qualified charities?

The IRC defines a *qualified charity* in a series of complex regulations, and taxpayers only receive deductions for gifts to qualified charities. There are three basic types of qualified charities: public charities, supporting organizations, and private foundations.

Public charities are the best-known and most common type of qualified charity. Churches, educational institutions, hospitals and medical research institutions, university endowment funds, governmental units, museums, and ballet companies are public charities. To qualify as a public charity, the organization must receive broad-based public support through contributions. Donations to public charities are subject to more generous deductibility limits than donations to most other qualified charities.

A *supporting organization* is a public charity that supports one or more other public charities. For example, a supporting organization might be created to operate a research facility attached to a hospital. As long as the supporting organization is organized and operated exclusively to support one or more public charities, it is considered a public charity, whether its funds come from the general public or from only one donor. We'll discuss supporting organizations later in this chapter.

A *private foundation* is an organization created for charitable purposes that does not qualify as a public charity. Private foundations are typically funded by a single contributor or a single family and do not seek support from the general public. Most of the time, private foundations are run by the donors and their families. As such, they are subject to close scrutiny by the Internal Revenue Service and heavy excise taxes on certain conduct deemed unacceptable by the government. Contributions to most private foundations are subject to lower deductibility limits than apply to contributions to public charities. Some private foundations, however, are treated as public charities. We'll discuss private foundations later in this chapter.

◌ℜ *Are there specific requirements that I should be aware of before I make a charitable gift?*

Yes, there are. If you wish to take an income and gift tax deduction for your lifetime gift or an estate tax deduction for a gift of property from your estate at death, your gift must meet specific requirements:

- The gift must be to a qualified charity, which we discussed earlier.
- The gift must be a *completed* gift—that is, it must be *irrevocable*—once you give it, you cannot take it back.
- There must be a clear intention by the donor to make a gift, often called *donative intent.*
- The gift must be in an appropriate form.
- There must be "delivery" of the gift, either actual or constructive.
- There must be acceptance of the gift.

◌ℜ *What kinds of property can we give to charity?*

Although we primarily think of gifts in terms of cash, charitable gifts can take many forms. They can take the form of *intangible property*, such as stocks, bonds, securities of all types, and promissory notes. They can take the form of *tangible property*, such as jewelry, furniture, clothes, collections, boats, recreational vehicles, and motor vehicles. They can take the form of real estate, both vacant land or land with structures.

Even though charitable gifts come in many forms, there are reasons why some types of gifts are more appropriate than others. For example, the IRC restricts the deductibility of some forms of gifts, so if you are interested in taking an income tax deduction for a charitable gift, you should make sure that the gift will qualify for such treatment. Also, charities are often cautious in accepting some types of gifts because they may have problems attached to them that would subject the charities to liability if they were to accept the gifts. In this respect, charities do not have to accept all gifts.

If you intend to make a gift that may be unusual in form or that may be subject to a liability of any kind, you should consult your tax advisor to make sure the gift will be tax deductible and otherwise appropriate for acceptance by the charity.

CR *I don't know much about making charitable gifts. What is the best way to make one?*

There are numerous possibilities for making charitable gifts, ranging from outright gifts of cash or property to the charity; to delaying, or deferring, the contribution through conduits such as gift annuities or charitable remainder trusts; all the way to setting up your own family foundation (and they can take several forms); and all of these can be made during your life or after your death. Only you can decide which strategy is best for you and your family, based on your own unique circumstances and objectives, as recommended to you by your advisors.

OUTRIGHT LIFETIME
GIFTS TO CHARITY

Securities

CR *I want to make a $100,000 donation to my favorite charity.*

I have some highly appreciated stock worth $100,000 that the charity suggests I donate. I really like this stock; it pays a great dividend. I am reluctant to give it away. Does it make any difference whether I donate the stock or give $100,000 in cash to the charity?

The charity is giving you good advice. Give your stock to the charity and use the $100,000 in cash to purchase the same stock again. While you might incur some transaction costs when repurchasing the stock, you will be better off by contributing the stock. The stock has substantial unrealized capital gain that will be taxed if you sell it. As far as your assets are concerned, nothing has changed. You have $100,000 less cash and the same position in the stock. The difference is that your basis in the stock is now its fair market value; you have eliminated the unrealized capital gain. The unrealized capital gain follows the stock to the charity, but since the charity pays no taxes, this gain is never taxed.

I have some other stock that has lost value since I bought it. Should I give that to charity, too?

No. In this case you should sell the stock and use the capital loss to offset any capital gain or ordinary income tax, then donate the sale proceeds to the charity. You will get the same charitable income tax deduction you would have received if you had donated the stock, but in addition you will get another deduction for the capital loss.

Real Estate

I want to leave my house to my church. Should I just put that in my will?

That is the simplest way to transfer the house to the church at your death, but you won't get an income tax deduction that way. Instead, give the church a remainder interest in your home now. With this technique, you continue to live in the home and maintain it, and after you die the house automatically passes to the church. You get an income tax deduction now for the present value of the remainder interest. The result is the same as leaving the property to the church in your will, but you get the added benefit of a current income tax deduction.

🔊 *I have a piece of appreciated property that the local school board wants. I wouldn't mind selling it to the school board cheaply, but I'd like to get back at least what I paid for the property. What would you suggest?*

The transaction you describe is called a *bargain sale*. In a bargain sale, the property owner sells the property to a qualified charity for less than fair market value. The difference between the fair market value and the sales price to the charity is the "bargain" part of the arrangement, and it is considered a gift to the charity.

For example, if your property is currently worth $500,000 and you paid $300,000, you can sell the land to the school board for $300,000 in a bargain sale. You are entitled to a charitable deduction of $200,000. Your deduction for the year is limited to 30 percent of your contribution base, but you can carry forward the unused deduction for another 5 years. The downside is that even though you broke even on the sale, the tax rules require that you recognize some gain (in this example, $120,000) on the sale. This gain, however, may be offset by your charitable deduction.

🔊 *How did you calculate the amount of the gain on the bargain sale?*

The rules require that your cost basis in the property be divided *pro rata* between the portion you give to the charity and the portion you sell. Once the cost basis is allocated between these portions, you determine if there is any gain on the sale portion. In this instance, you calculate your gain as follows:

$$\frac{\$200,000}{\$500,000} = 40\% = \text{ratio of contribution portion to fair market value}$$

$$\frac{\$300,000}{\$500,000} = 60\% = \text{ratio of sale portion to fair market value}$$

$$\frac{\$300,000}{\times 60\%} = \$180,000 = \text{cost basis allocated to sale portion}$$

$$\frac{\$300,000}{-\$180,000} = \$120,000 = \text{capital gain on the sale}$$

Your contribution represents 40 percent of the fair market value and the sale price is 60 percent of the fair market value, so 60 percent of the $300,000 basis is allocated to the sale portion. Your resulting capital gain is $120,000.

CR *My father owned a gas station when I was growing up. I still own that real estate, and it is pretty valuable today. Can I give it to my church?*

You can, but the real question is whether the church wants it. Real estate used for a gas station or a similar use may be contaminated with environmental pollutants. The cost of cleaning up the property could be expensive, and your church may not have the funds to do so.

Tangible Personal Property

CR *I am a painter, and a local art museum has asked me to donate one of my paintings to it. I have the painting for sale for $10,000. Do I get a $10,000 charitable deduction if I give my painting to the museum?*

I'm afraid not. Since you created the painting, your deduction is limited to your cost basis—the cost of the paint, frame, and other materials. This result may change in the future, as Congress is considering legislation that would increase your deduction to as much as the painting's full fair market value.

Life Insurance

CR *I am currently giving a modest amount to my favorite charity on a regular basis, and I would like to make a more substantial gift. Is there a way I can give more to my favorite cause but stay within my budget?*

One way to leverage your gifts is to purchase a life insurance policy on your life and to give it to your charity. You can either make regular contributions to the charity so the charity can make the premium payments or simply make the premium payments directly to the insurance company. The premium payments are treated as charitable contributions (see the next question on the contribution limits for these gifts). When you die, the policy's death benefit will go directly to the charity, providing them with a substantial sum.

   We have a life insurance policy with a cash value that we don't need any more. We love the university that we both attended, and the school has a capital campaign going on. Should we cash out the insurance policy and give them the money?

No, you should give the policy to the university. If you cash out the policy, you will likely recognize taxable income on some of the cash value. If you give the policy to the school instead, you will avoid recognizing the income. You will receive an income tax deduction for the lesser of your basis in the policy (the total of all your premium payments, less policy loans) or the fair market value of the policy. If the policy has been in force for several years, it is more likely that your deduction will be for your basis in the policy.

    You also get a charitable income tax deduction for premium payments on the policy in future years. If you make the premium payments directly to the insurance company, your gift is considered "for the use of" charity and is therefore limited to 30 percent of your contribution base. On the other hand, if you contribute the premium payments to the charity, your gift is subject to a more generous 50 percent limitation. Therefore, it may be best to give the cash to the charity to pay the premiums instead of paying the premiums directly.

Retirement Plans and Annuities

   Can I make a gift of my retirement plan to charity?

To make a lifetime gift from your retirement plan you must withdraw cash from the plan, and you must pay income tax on that withdrawal even though you are giving the money to charity. For this reason most people do *not* make lifetime gifts of retirement plans to charity. Congress is considering a law to allow taxpayers, in some circumstances, to transfer their retirement plan assets to charity without paying income taxes.

    Many people name a charity as the beneficiary of their retirement plan, so the remaining plan assets pass to charity at death. That way the retirement plan is available during your life if needed; and by naming a charity as beneficiary, the plan assets avoid both the estate and income taxes that would be due if you named someone else as beneficiary.

SPLIT-INTEREST
LIFETIME GIFTS TO
CHARITY

⊘ *I am not ready to give my assets outright to charity. Is there a way to retain the income from my assets and still get a charitable deduction?*

You can make a substantial contribution to charity while retaining the right to receive income from the asset using a charitable remainder trust (CRT). A CRT is a type of *split-interest transfer.* That is, the property is divided into two separate sequential parts: the present interest and the remainder interest. In the case of the CRT, you keep the present interest, and the charity receives the remainder interest after your interest terminates.

⊘ *We have assets that produce a small sum of income, but if we sold them, we would face substantial capital gain taxes. Is there a way for us to sell the assets to improve our cash flow and reduce the impact of capital gain taxes?*

Low-yield, highly appreciated assets such as stock, real estate, or even a family business present this common problem, especially for people ready to retire. If you are charitably inclined, an effective planning strategy is to give the asset to a CRT in exchange for an income stream, typically payable over the lifetime of the donor(s). You can use a charitable remainder trust to implement this plan.

In general you can use a CRT to accomplish any or all of the following goals:

- To benefit one or more charities and have the satisfaction of receiving recognition for the gift during your lifetime, instead of after you die
- To convert a low-income-generating asset into a higher-income-producing asset
- To defer capital gain tax when selling a highly appreciated asset
- To reduce or eliminate estate taxes on the asset you donate
- To receive a current charitable income tax deduction
- To diversify your portfolio

Charity Receives Remainder: *Inter Vivos* Charitable Remainder Trust

ଔ *What is an* inter vivos *charitable remainder trust?*

An *inter vivos* trust is one that the maker creates during his or her life. A *charitable remainder trust* is an irrevocable split-interest trust because it pays a percentage of trust principal to named individuals and then distributes what is left, the remainder, to charity. The "split" is therefore between *noncharitable beneficiaries* and a charity or charities as *remainder beneficiaries.*

You establish the CRT as the trustmaker and the donor. You transfer a low- or non-income-producing asset or assets into the trust. The trustee sells the asset and reinvests in an income-producing investment. As the noncharitable beneficiaries, you and your spouse receive payments from the trust for a stated period, usually for your life or for a term of years not to exceed 20. At the end of the trust term, the remaining property in the trust is paid to the charitable remainder beneficiaries that you named in the trust.

Because charities are the remaindermen, you receive an income tax deduction upon transferring assets to the trust. Also, the CRT is a tax-exempt entity, so it doesn't pay taxes on any gain it realizes when it sells assets or on its other income.

ଔ *Why must the trust be irrevocable?*

Charitable remainder trust arrangements must be irrevocable in order to meet the requirements of the Internal Revenue Code for charitable tax deductions.

ଔ *What are the best assets to contribute to a CRT?*

In general, highly appreciated, low- or non-income-producing assets such as publicly traded stock with low dividend payments and debt-free real estate are the best assets to contribute. With proper planning, you can, in some instances, fund a CRT with your family business, using the trust as part of your business succession plan.

Even if you don't have assets that fit this description, a CRT may still be a worthwhile planning tool for you. With a CRT, you make a substantial gift to charity at death but receive an income tax deduction now. These benefits alone make a CRT an effective planning tool for many people who desire to support charitable causes.

❦ *Is a CRT the same as a "capital gain avoidance trust" that I hear people talk about?*

Frequently, financial professionals refer to a CRT as a "capital gain avoidance trust." In most instances, this is a misnomer. If anything, it is a *capital gain deferral trust*. Because a CRT is tax-exempt, the trust assets are not reduced by capital gain tax when the trust sells the appreciated assets contributed to the trust by the trustmaker. But, as explained later in this chapter, the capital gain tax on the sale is not necessarily eliminated but, in many cases, deferred and spread out over a number of years. Nonetheless, the noncharitable beneficiary usually receives more income over the trust term than if he or she had sold the asset and invested the after-tax sale proceeds.

❦ *Why should I consider establishing a charitable remainder trust?*

While there are a number of financial benefits for creating a charitable remainder trust, your primary reason should be a commitment to charitable giving.

A CRT is, first and foremost, a gift to charity. With a charitable remainder trust, you can convert your tax dollars into charitable gifts to your favorite causes and organizations and, in addition, receive financial and tax-saving benefits.

❦ *What are the tax benefits of setting up a CRT during my lifetime?*

An *inter vivos* CRT can provide you with several tax benefits:

- First, when you transfer money or property to a CRT, you get a current charitable income tax deduction for the present value of the charity's remainder interest in the property.
- Second, the estate tax on assets that you transfer to a CRT is eliminated or substantially reduced.
- Finally, the CRT is a tax-exempt entity. As such, if you transfer appreciated assets to the CRT and the CRT sells them, the CRT pays no capital gain taxes.

Income Beneficiaries

ᑫ *Who can receive payments from a charitable remainder trust?*

You, your spouse, your children or grandchildren, a friend, or anybody else, and in any combination that the trustmaker desires.

If a trust includes life payments to an individual or class of individuals, those individuals must be living at the time the trust is created.

ᑫ *I want to name my wife, myself, and then our two children as beneficiaries of my charitable remainder trust. Can I do that?*

Maybe, but with certain tax consequences. Under current law, the present value of the amount the charitable beneficiary is expected to receive must equal at least 10 percent of the initial value of the property contributed to the trust. One of the factors used to determine the present value of the charity's interest is how long the charity must wait before the trust ends and it receives the trust assets. Therefore, if the joint life expectancy of the four of you is too long, the charity's interest will be less than 10 percent. In that situation, you cannot name all four people as lifetime beneficiaries. In most cases, your advisor can offer a way around this problem.

Another factor to consider is the gift tax consequence of naming your children as beneficiaries of your CRT. When you do this, you make an immediate taxable gift to your children. While you may not have to actually pay any tax at this time because of the availability of your gift tax credit, you may use up valuable portions of that credit. However, if you and your wife reserve the right to cut off your children's income interest at your deaths by will or living trust, then the gift to your children is not "complete" and, therefore, not taxable until your death as part of the estate tax structure.

A final factor to consider is the estate tax consequences of naming your children. When you die, technically, whatever is then in the charitable remainder trust becomes a part of your estate. If everything goes directly to the charitable beneficiary, your estate gets a 100 percent charitable deduction and there is no estate tax. Similarly, if your wife is the sole income beneficiary after your death, then you get a 100 percent marital deduction and again there is no estate tax owing.

However, if your wife is not living at your death or the children and your wife are the income beneficiaries, then you will not get the marital deduction, and your estate tax deduction will be limited to the net present value of what the charity is projected to receive after the expected lifetimes of the named beneficiaries. In this situation, estate tax will be owing if you have a taxable estate.

Charitable Beneficiaries

 formerly *Do we get to choose the charity that benefits from the CRT?*

Absolutely. You are free to select one or more charities as beneficiaries of your CRT. When you choose to benefit more than one charity, you also decide what percentage of the remainder goes to each charity. For example, you can specify that 20 percent goes to the United Way, 50 percent to your church, and 30 percent to your alma mater. Most people choose public charities as beneficiaries, but you can also name a private foundation or supporting organization as the beneficiary of your CRT.

formerly *I don't know which charity to name in my charitable remainder trust; do I have to decide right now?*

Although a CRT is an irrevocable trust, your selection of the charity is not an irrevocable decision. Provided your attorney drafts this option into the CRT document, you can change the charity as often as you wish before you pass away or before the term of the trust ends.

Payment Options

formerly *Do I have income choices for a CRT?*

There are two basic methods for determining the annual payment:

1. *Fixed percentage based on initial value of contribution:* The trust pays the noncharitable beneficiaries a fixed percentage of the fair market value of the trust assets contributed to the trust. This type of CRT is called a *charitable remainder annuity trust (CRAT)*. Regardless of the trust's investment performance, the payments will not change from year to year.
2. *Fixed percentage based on annual trust value:* The trust pays the

noncharitable beneficiaries a fixed percentage of the fair market value of the trust assets *valued annually.* This type of CRT is known as a *charitable remainder unitrust (CRUT).* With this option, the amount of the annual distribution will fluctuate, depending on the annual value of the trust assets.

Charitable Remainder Annuity Trust

CR *How does the charitable remainder annuity trust work?*

The *charitable remainder annuity trust* allows the maker to lock in a payout rate of not less than 5 percent and not more than 50 percent of the value of the assets that he or she contributes to the trust. Once the trust has been established, the trustmaker cannot change the percentage income amount; and even if the value of the trust changes in the future, the annuity amount will not change. Because the annuity amount must continue in the same amount regardless of whether the trust generates sufficient earnings to make the payment, the trustee of the CRAT may be required to use principal to satisfy annuity payments. This type of trust does *not* allow for additional contributions once it has been established.

CR *Can you give me an example of how a CRAT works?*

Table 3-1 shows an example of how a CRAT pays with a $1 million initial contribution and a payout rate of 9 percent. If the trust term ended in the 10th year, the charity would receive $850,000, because the trustee had to use trust principal to make up the difference in the years that the trust did not earn the required annuity payment. However, the noncharitable beneficiaries did receive a fixed income stream of $90,000 per year over the 10-year period.

CR *Why would I use a CRAT?*

Because the annuity amount paid is based on the value of the contribution to the trust, the amount of the annuity remains fixed regardless of whether the value of the assets in the CRAT increase, decrease, or generate income. Thus, donors know what the annual income stream will be under a CRAT. This arrangement does offer the security of a definite amount of income each year but doesn't provide protection against inflation.

TABLE 3-1   Charitable Remainder Annuity Trust*

Trust year	Trust value	Payout amount	Asset growth
1	$1,000,000	$90,000	$100,000
2	1,010,000	90,000	50,000
3	970,000	90,000	80,000
4	960,000	90,000	120,000
5	990,000	90,000	100,000
6	1,000,000	90,000	150,000
7	1,060,000	90,000	(20,000)
8	950,000	90,000	90,000
9	950,000	90,000	(10,000)
10	850,000	90,000	120,000

*Based on a $1 million initial contribution, a 9 percent payout rate, and a random rate of return.

Charitable Remainder Unitrust

ଔ *How does the charitable remainder unitrust work?*

The *charitable remainder unitrust (CRUT)* allows you to set a payout rate of not less than 5 percent and not more than 50 percent of the value of the assets that you contribute to the trust. The basic features of the CRUT are as follows:

- Each year, assets in the trust are valued and the payout rate is applied to determine the distribution, or unitrust payment. So, even though the percentage remains fixed, the actual amount that is paid each year will change depending on the annual value of the CRUT.
- If the CRUT does not generate enough income in a year to pay the unitrust amount, the trustee of the CRUT may be required to use principal to satisfy the payment.
- The CRUT allows for additional contributions once it has been established.

ଔ *Can you give me an example of how a CRUT works?*

Table 3-2 shows an example of a CRUT with a $1 million initial

TABLE 3-2   Charitable Remainder Unitrust*

Trust year	Trust value†	Payout amount	Asset growth‡
1	$1,000,000	$90,000	$100,000
2	1,010,000	91,000	50,000
3	969,000	87,000	80,000
4	962,000	86,000	120,000
5	996,000	90,000	100,000
6	1,006,000	91,000	150,000
7	1,065,000	96,000	(20,000)
8	949,000	85,000	90,000
9	954,000	86,000	(10,000)
10	858,000	77,000	105,000

*Based on a $1 million initial contribution, a 9 percent payout rate, and a random rate of return.

†Calculated at the beginning of the year. Amount rounded down to nearest 1,000.

‡Calculated at the end of the year.

contribution and a payout rate of 9 percent. If the trust term ended in the 10th year, the charity would receive $858,000, because the trust didn't earn enough to cover the required 9 percent payout. However, with a CRUT, the trustmaker could have contributed additional assets to the trust to make up the difference so that trust principal could remain untouched.

◌ *Why would I use a CRUT?*

Because the payment is calculated each year based on the value of the assets in the trust, there is the potential that the trust investments will outperform the payout rate, thus resulting in larger payments in the future. In this regard, the CRUT can be a hedge against inflation. Donors who believe that the assets of a charitable remainder trust will earn more than the annual payout choose a CRUT. However, you must also be willing to accept the possibility that the trust's investments may underperform, resulting in a decreased unitrust payment.

A CRUT also gives you the flexibility to make additional contributions to the trust later on. These additional gifts will entitle you to another income tax deduction and possibly increase the amount of the unitrust payments you receive.

Variations on the Charitable Remainder Unitrust

℞ *Are there any alternatives to the CRAT or CRUT?*

There is no alternative for a charitable remainder annuity trust. However, there are variations on the standard charitable remainder unitrust:

- Charitable remainder net-income-only unitrust (NIOCRUT)
- Charitable remainder unitrust with net income makeup provisions (NIMCRUT)
- Charitable remainder unitrust with "flip" provisions (flip unitrust)

℞ *What is a charitable remainder net-income-only unitrust?*

A *charitable remainder net-income-only unitrust* pays the *lesser* of the "net income" of the trust or the unitrust percentage stated in the document. For example, for a NIOCRUT with a 5 percent payout and an asset value of $100,000, the unitrust payout is $5,000. However, if the trust only earns $2,000 in net income that year, the noncharitable beneficiary receives only $2,000 for the year. If, on the other hand, the trust earns $8,000, then the trustee pays $5,000 to the noncharitable beneficiary and the additional $3,000 of earnings is added to the principal.

The intent in the NIOCRUT is to preserve principal when the earnings are not sufficient to fund the percentage payout. Therefore, the trustee is never allowed to distribute principal to the noncharitable beneficiary. In our experience, almost all clients find this type of CRT undesirable because of the income-only limitation and opt for another type of CRT.

℞ *I wouldn't mind a NIOCRUT if there was some chance I might eventually get back the unpaid amounts. Is that an option?*

The *charitable remainder unitrust with net income makeup provisions (NIMCRUT)* allows you to recapture some or all of the "lost" payments in later years. Like the NIOCRUT, the NIMCRUT pays annually the lesser of the fixed percentage or the actual income earned by the trust. However, in years when the net income is less than the fixed percentage, instead of using principal to make up the shortfall or just losing that shortfall, the NIMCRUT carries forward the shortfall in a "makeup" or "IOU" account. In future years when the net income of the trust exceeds the fixed percentage, the additional income is paid to the noncharitable beneficiary until the makeup account is exhausted.

For example, suppose that the value of your NIMCRUT's assets is $1 million with a 10 percent payout rate. The distribution would be $100,000, but the trust earns only $80,000. The distribution would be $80,000 and the trust would "owe" you $20,000, which it would make up to you (all or in part) in a year when its income for the year exceeded 10 percent. So if in the following year the trust earns $110,000 and its assets are still worth $1 million, the trust pays you $100,000 (the 10 percent payout rate) plus $10,000 to make up last year's deficit. Now the trust's makeup account is $10,000; in future years the trust may repay that amount as earnings permit.

Q You continue to use the term "net income." Isn't income, income?

Well, that depends. For federal tax purposes, the Internal Revenue Code defines what constitutes income and when a taxpayer receives income. Taxpayers use these rules to determine how much they owe the federal government in income taxes. For trusts, there is another set of accounting rules that define fiduciary income. Most states have adopted statutes that govern this issue. A trustee applies these statutes to the trust's receipts and expenses in order to determine how much income the trust has available each year to distribute to beneficiaries. In most cases, amounts received that are considered income for tax purposes are also considered fiduciary income. But this isn't always the case, and in some instances the law permits the maker of the CRT to alter the definition of income by customizing the trust document. By *net income* we mean those amounts received by the trust that are treated as income under the fiduciary accounting rules minus expenses of the trust that the rules require or permit us to subtract from that income.

Q What is a flip unitrust?

A *flip unitrust* (also called a FLIPCRUT) is really a NIMCRUT with provisions that allow it to "flip" to a CRUT upon the occurrence of a certain event. You create a NIMCRUT whose annual unitrust payment is the lesser of trust income or the fixed percentage. Because it is a NIMCRUT, the distributions are low or zero when the trust does not earn sufficient income to make the fixed percentage payment. The annual deficiencies are added to the makeup account. Upon the occurrence of a triggering event defined in the trust document, the NIMCRUT converts to a standard CRUT. As a CRUT, the trust must make payments to you based on the fixed percentage amount, regardless of the trust's income. Depending on the situation, you may or may not be paid the makeup account before the trust converts to a standard CRUT. For the most part, clients who do not need the income immediately will choose to use this flip unitrust arrangement.

ℭ *Are there some limitations to using a flip unitrust?*

The most important limitation is that the triggering event cannot be under the control of the trustmaker. The triggering event must be a specific date or the happening of an event that is not within anyone's discretion. For example, the triggering event cannot be "my retirement" because one presumably has control as to when he or she retires. The trustmaker can, however, define the triggering event as "reaching age 65" because you can't control reaching a certain age. Other options for defining the triggering event include:

- a specific date,
- the birth of a child or a grandchild,
- the death of a person,
- the marriage or divorce of a person, and
- the sale of an unmarketable asset.

Term and Payout Requirements

ℭ *How long can a CRT exist?*

It can last for the lifetime of one or more noncharitable beneficiaries or a term of up to 20 years. You can choose a combination of life and term, such as the "longer of the life of X-beneficiary or 15 years" or "for the life of X-beneficiary then to Y-beneficiary for 10 years."

The National Committee on Planned Giving, a national association of charitable professionals, conducted a study on the payout options selected on existing remainder trusts. They reported that

94 percent of trustmakers choose the life-expectancy payout option, 4 percent choose a fixed term, and 2 percent choose a combination of the two.

Is there a minimum and/or a maximum income percentage I can take from my charitable remainder trust?

Whether you chose a CRAT or a CRUT, the payout percentage must be at least 5 percent of the trust assets but no more than 50 percent. The percentage must also be low enough that, in conjunction with other factors, the present value of the remainder interest ultimately passing to charity is at least 10 percent of the fair market value of the property you contribute to the CRT.

How often can the payouts be made?

CRTs are required to make distributions at least annually. However, distributions can be made more frequently, including semiannually, quarterly, or monthly.

Tax Results

Charitable Income Tax Deduction

How is the income tax deduction computed?

The Internal Revenue Service (IRS) looks at the gift as a whole split into two pieces. One piece is the value of your stream of payouts, and the other piece is the value of the future gift to charity. The value of the two pieces must add up to the fair market value of the asset transferred into the trust. Just like a pie, the larger the one piece, the smaller the other. Therefore, the larger the value of the stream of payouts, the smaller the value of the remainder gift to charity. The present value of the future gift to charity is the value of the income tax deduction, and the present value of the future gift to charity must be at least 10 percent of the value of the transferred asset.

The value of the gift to charity and the equivalent deduction are based on a number of factors, some of which are:

■ your age or the age of another noncharitable beneficiary,

■ the fair market value of the asset contributed,

■ the trust payout rate,

■ whether the trust is a unitrust or an annuity trust,

■ the frequency of the payouts, and

■ an estimated return that the government establishes and calls the *applicable federal rate (AFR)*.

For example, for a trustmaker aged 65 who transfers a $100,000 asset to a unitrust and receives annual lifetime payments, assuming the AFR is 5 percent, the relationship between the payout and the tax deduction is as follows:

Payout rate	Tax deduction
5%	$46,093
7%	$35,346
9%	$27,776

Of course, while the tax deduction goes down, the payout rate increases, and the trustmaker receives larger payments from the trust.

☙ Can I use the full income tax deduction in the first year?

Possibly. In most circumstances your income tax deduction is limited to 30 percent of your contribution base (for most people, your contribution base equals your adjusted gross income for the year) but may be either 20 percent or 50 percent, depending on the type of charitable beneficiary you name and the type of asset you contribute to the trust. For example, if your charitable deduction for the transfer to your CRT is $75,000, your adjusted gross income for the year is $100,000, and the 30 percent limitation applies, then you can take a charitable tax deduction in the first year of $30,000 (30 percent of $100,000).

You don't lose the other $45,000 of deduction; you can carry it forward for up to 5 years. The rules governing the charitable income tax deduction are quite complex, so make sure your advisor takes the time to explain to you how your deduction is calculated. Also, you can read the book *Giving: Philanthropy for Everyone* (Quantum Press, 2003) for a detailed explanation of these rules.

Charitable Gift and Estate Tax Deductions

Are there any other tax consequences from creating a CRT?

That depends on who receives the annuity or unitrust payments from the trust. If you alone or you and your spouse are the only non-charitable beneficiaries of the CRT, there are no gift or estate tax issues for you to worry about. However, if there are other beneficiaries (your children, for example), you may owe gift taxes when you create the trust or possibly estate taxes at your death based on the actuarial value of the payments that the other beneficiaries receive after your death.

Taxation of Distributions

Are the payments I receive from the CRT taxable to me?

Yes. This is a sometimes confusing area with respect to CRTs. While a CRT itself is tax-exempt, the beneficiary pays income taxes on the annuity or unitrust payments based on the type of income earned by the trust. There is a four-tier accounting system that applies to CRT distributions and controls the tax consequences to the recipient. Professionals often refer to this system as *WIFO—worst in, first out.* The tiers of the system are as follows:

1. Distributions are classified as ordinary income to the extent that the trust has ordinary income in the present year or undistributed ordinary income from previous years.

2. Distributions are classified as capital gains to the extent that the trust has capital gains in the present year or undistributed capital gains from previous years.

3. Distributions are classified as "other income," typically tax-exempt income, to the extent that the trust has any other income in the present year or undistributed other income from previous years.

4. Distributions are classified as distributions of principal.

All current and prior years' undistributed income in each tier must be exhausted before you move to the next tier. In other words, the trust must exhaust its current and accumulated ordinary income

before any part of a distribution to the beneficiary will be classified
as capital gain.

*ᴄᴙ Do you mean that I do have to pay capital gain taxes? I thought
you said the CRT was tax-exempt?*

The trust is tax-exempt, but the noncharitable beneficiaries are not.
As the CRT earns income, that income is accounted for, but the
trust does not pay any tax on it. Rather, as the trustee distributes
cash from the CRT to the noncharitable beneficiary, that person will
pay tax on the income earned in the trust, as described in the previous answer.

If you contribute highly appreciated assets to a CRT and then
the trust sells them, there are no *immediate* taxes to pay. This provides you with the opportunity to diversify the investment portfolio
without immediate tax implications. As the trust makes distributions, however, the person receiving the distributions will pay the tax
attributable to the amount being distributed.

Trustees

ᴄᴙ What does the trustee of a CRT do?

The trustee makes all decisions regarding trust investments and is
responsible for all accounting and governmental reporting. The
trustee must administer the CRT properly and make the payments
to the noncharitable beneficiary. If the trust is not managed correctly, the trustmaker could lose the tax advantages and be penalized
by the IRS.

The trustee may receive reasonable compensation so long as
it is not excessive and not paid out of the beneficiaries' income
distributions.

ᴄᴙ Can I be the trustee of my own CRT?

As the trustmaker, you can be your own trustee, even if you are a
beneficiary. Many trustmakers who name themselves as trustee hire
a professional administrator to handle the accounting and paperwork.

However, because of the experience required with investments
and the responsibilities for accounting and governmental reporting,
some trustmakers prefer to select an institution (a bank or trust

company) as the trustee or as a cotrustee. Some charities are also willing to act as trustee for you if they are the remainder beneficiaries of the trust.

Before naming a trustee, it's a good idea to interview several candidates and consider their investment performance, services, and experience with these trusts. Remember, you are depending on the trustee to manage your trust properly and to provide you with income.

℞ *Is there any situation when I shouldn't act as my own trustee?*

You can always act as the trustee, but in some cases you should appoint an independent trustee to perform certain duties. For example:

- If a NIMCRUT owns an annuity policy, an independent trustee should have the responsibility of deciding when to make the withdrawals from the annuity.
- If the trust is designed to have income "sprayed" or "sprinkled" to income beneficiaries, an independent trustee should be given that responsibility.
- If the CRT holds a hard-to-value asset such as real estate, the independent trustee should be in charge of appraising the asset.

An *independent trustee* is someone who is not related to you, your spouse, or to any other income beneficiary and is not subordinate to or controlled by you or these other individuals, such as an employee.

Changing the Trust

℞ *Can I change the CRT once I've established it?*

The trust is irrevocable, which means that generally a trustmaker cannot change it once he or she establishes it. However, it is possible to retain certain rights that give the trustmaker flexibility in the future to make certain changes:

- changing the trustee or filling trustee vacancies,
- changing charitable beneficiaries, and
- revoking income interests for noncharitable income beneficiaries.

These rights must be stated, or *reserved*, in the trust document. It's also important to remember that, if the trustmaker is the trustee, he or she can control and change the trust's investments.

ᏫᏍ *Can I change my mind later as to which charity will get the property in my charitable remainder trust at my death?*

Yes. As the trustmaker you can retain the right, or give the right to another, to change the charity or charities that you initially named. However, the right to make this change must be reserved in the trust agreement.

Many CRTs are drafted without reserving this right, and even the IRS's charitable remainder trust form fails to reserve this right. *Proper drafting is crucial*; be sure to hire an attorney experienced in charitable remainder trust drafting.

Asset Protection

ᏫᏍ *Do charitable remainder trusts provide any creditor protection?*

Since the transfer of your property to a CRT is irrevocable, a creditor cannot seize the property after the transfer. Keep in mind that only transfers that take place well in advance of any legal action against you are beyond the reach of your creditors. Any transfer of property (to charity or to anyone else) may be considered a *fraudulent convey-ance* if the transfer occurs shortly before or during legal proceedings against you. Also, in many states, a creditor can acquire your annuity or unitrust payment stream to satisfy claims against you.

Uses and Advantages

ᏫᏍ *You said I receive more from the trust than if I sold the asset myself. Can you explain this for me?*

After you transfer the appreciated asset to the trust, the trust can sell it at full market value without paying capital gain tax on the gain because of its tax-exempt status. The trust thus has 100 percent of the proceeds to invest in income-producing assets. Since the trust principal has not been reduced by capital gain tax, the noncharitable beneficiary usually receives more income over the trust term than if he or she had sold the asset and invested the sales proceeds.

Here's an example:

> Max and Jane Brody (ages 65 and 63) are planning to retire next year. Ten years ago they purchased some stock for $100,000. It is now worth $500,000. They would like to sell it and generate income for their retirement. If they sell the stock, they will have a gain of $400,000 (current value, less cost basis) and will pay $60,000 in federal capital gain tax (15% × $400,000) in the year of the sale. That would leave them with $440,000 to invest. If they invest the after-tax proceeds and earn 7 percent annually, that's $30,800 in annual income. Multiplied by their life expectancy of 26 years, this would give them a total lifetime income (before taxes) of $800,800.
>
> If instead they transfer the stock to a CRAT with a 7 percent payout, the trustee will sell it for the same $500,000. But because the trust is exempt from taxes, the full $500,000 is available to reinvest. The trustee invests the proceeds and earns 7 percent annual return and pays the Brodys $35,000 (7% × $500,000) each year. Over their life expectancy, the trust will pay them a total of $910,000. That's $109,200 more than if the Brodys had sold the stock themselves. Plus, they can take a substantial charitable income tax deduction that will reduce their current federal income taxes.

ℭℛ *I like the idea of using a charitable remainder trust to contribute to charity, but I don't need the income right now. Can I delay the trust distributions?*

Yes, with a NIMCRUT it is possible for the trustee (who may be the trustmaker) to affect the trust's cash flow by investing in a way that produces more or less "net income."

Often a trustmaker will contribute non-income-producing assets to a NIMCRUT (or purchase such assets inside the trust) to minimize current income and maximize appreciation of the makeup account. Some time in the future the trustee sells the non-income-producing assets and purchases assets that generate income so that the trust begins making the fixed percentage payouts to the trustmaker and paying back the makeup account.

One asset commonly purchased by the trustee to minimize current income is an annuity. While the annuity policy itself may generate income, as long as that income stays inside the annuity, the trust itself has no income to distribute to the trustmaker. If, however, the trustee withdraws cash from the annuity and the annuity has appreciated in value, then that amount would be considered net income for purposes of the distribution. In this way the trustee regulates the amount of net income the trust has for distributing to the noncharitable beneficiary. Because this technique gives the trustee so much control over the trust's income, the IRS requires that someone other than the noncharitable beneficiary have the authority to decide whether to purchase the annuity or take money out of the annuity.

    I'm putting all the money the law allows into retirement savings accounts and pension plans, but I'd like to save even more. Can a charitable remainder trust help me?

Yes. CRTs and qualified retirement plans share one important feature: their tax-exempt status. Trustmakers often use a flip unitrust arrangement as a supplemental or private retirement account. Because a flip unitrust starts as a NIMCRUT, it allows for the deferral of income until a later time by investing in non-income-producing assets. Once the triggering event occurs, the trust changes to a standard CRUT, and distributions based on the fixed percentage begin, regardless of the trust's net income for the year. So, if you plan on retiring at age 62, you would define the triggering event as "upon attaining age 62." Each year, you make a contribution to the trust as you do to your retirement plans, take a tax deduction for a part of the amount contributed, and let the trust build up a nice nest egg for you until you're 62.

Disadvantages of the Inter Vivos CRT

    Are there any assets we shouldn't use in a CRT and why?

You must be careful in selecting the assets to give to your CRT, because some types of property create serious problems or cannot be used at all. For example, you should not fund a CRT with any asset that produces unrelated-business taxable income. If a CRT earns this type of income, it loses its tax-exempt status for the year and could substantially impair the tax planning benefits of the trust. Many family businesses, partnerships, and rental properties produce this type of income.

Other types of assets, such as stock options from your employer, mortgaged property, Series EE savings bonds, artwork, and hedge funds, are often not suitable for funding a CRT. Individual retirement accounts and annuities are not appropriate. You should discuss this with an attorney or financial advisor familiar with the CRT rules to determine whether a particular asset is appropriate for your CRT.

ℭ *If we have a CRT, how do our children benefit?*

The property you contribute to the charitable remainder trust will not go to your family at your death; whatever property is remaining in your CRT when the trust terminates will go to the charity or charities you named as beneficiaries. This result sometimes discourages clients from using a CRT, as most people don't want to disinherit their families. But in our experience, people overestimate the problem. It is important to realize that not all of the property would necessarily pass to your family in any event. For example, assume you own property worth $100,000 that you bought for $50,000 5 years ago and want to sell. If the property is sold outside of a CRT, you will pay $7,500 (15 percent) in federal capital gain taxes, leaving $92,500. Assume further that you are in a 50 percent estate tax bracket; then your estate will pay $46,250 in federal estate taxes, leaving only $46,250 for your family.

The tax and other financial and personal benefits of using a CRT frequently outweigh the economic loss to the next generation. You also have the option to replace the property contributed to the CRT with life insurance that will pass to your family estate tax– and income tax–free.

ℭ *Can you explain more about replacing the value of the gift we make to the CRT?*

Many parents are understandably hesitant to give away their property to charity and disinherit their heirs. But with proper planning, you can have a CRT that will benefit you and your favorite charity *and* still leave your heirs the inheritance you want for them.

As we explained earlier, one of the prime tax benefits of a CRT is the ability to sell appreciated assets without paying capital gain tax.

In most cases, that strategy results in greater cash flow to the trust-maker than selling the asset without a CRT. In addition to the cash flow from the CRT, the trustmaker receives a charitable income tax deduction, lowering his or her income taxes. The extra cash flow and the tax savings are often sufficient to purchase a life insurance policy to replace the value of the asset that you donate to charity. Essentially, you are redirecting your tax money away from the government and into a life insurance policy for your family.

The life insurance is owned in an irrevocable life insurance trust, also known as a wealth replacement trust. With an insurance trust, the insurance proceeds will not be subject to federal estate taxes at your death. We discuss life insurance trusts in greater detail in Chapter 5, Wealth Transfer Techniques.

Life insurance can be an inexpensive way to replace the asset for your children. The cost of this insurance is frequently less than the tax and other financial benefits you personally achieve by utilizing the charitable remainder trust. The combination of a CRT with a life insurance trust is quite popular and effective; you are able to achieve all the benefits of using the CRT, while creating two legacies: one for your charitable causes and one for your heirs.

Charity Receives Income: *Inter Vivos* Charitable Lead Trust

CR *I donate to several charities each year, and I want to set up a charitable giving program. I don't want to make the charities wait for the money until I'm dead. Is there an alternative form of charitable trust for me?*

You may want to consider an *inter vivos charitable lead trust (CLT)*, which is a good strategy for donors who give large amounts of money to charity each year. A CLT is often described as the reverse of a CRT because the interests going to the charitable and noncharitable beneficiaries in a CLT are the opposite of a CRT.

With a CLT, you transfer assets to the trust, which pays one or more charities an income stream for a period of time. The interest going to the charity is usually referred to as the *lead interest* and, like a charitable remainder trust, is either an annuity amount or a unitrust amount. When the period of time you specify ends, the remaining trust property returns to you or goes to other noncharitable beneficiaries, such as your spouse, children, grandchildren, or anyone else you name in the trust.

℺ *What are the best assets to contribute to a CLT?*

The best assets are those that generate a steady stream of cash and are appreciating in value. No single type of asset best fits this description; it's wise to work with your advisors to select the best assets to fund your CLT.

Payment Options

℺ *What are the payment options for CLTs?*

The Internal Revenue Code provides for two payment options for CLTs, namely:

1. *Charitable lead annuity trust (CLAT):* The charity receives an annuity, which is normally stated in the trust document as a specified percentage of the fair market value of the trust assets at the time of transfer to the CLAT. For instance, if the trust document entitles the charity to a 7 percent annuity and you transfer $1 million to the trust, then each year the trust will pay the charity $70,000, regardless of how much the trust earns or whether the trust's investments appreciate or depreciate in value.
2. *Charitable lead unitrust (CLUT):* The charity receives a fixed percentage of the value of the trust property, as it is valued each year. As the value of the trust property fluctuates from year to year, so does the amount of the unitrust payment.

Term

℺ *How long does the charity receive the payments?*

The charity receives the annuity or unitrust payments for the length of time that you specify in the trust document. The life or lives of a specified individual or individuals—or, more commonly, a term of years—can measure the term. However, unlike a CRT, if the term is measured by a specified number of years, that term need *not* be limited to 20 years.

Tax Results

Taxation of the Trust

CR *Is a CLT also a tax-exempt trust?*

Unlike a charitable remainder trust, income earned by a charitable lead trust is subject to federal income taxes. Depending on how you choose to structure the trust, either you or the trust itself will pay the taxes. Structured one way, the trust will pay income tax on its income each year. The trust will receive a tax deduction for the amount it distributes to charity each year, which reduces the trust's taxable income. Alternatively, the trust can be designed so that the donor is treated as the owner of the trust assets, and the donor must report all of the trust's taxable income, deductions, gains, losses, and credits on his or her personal tax returns each year.

Charitable Income Tax Deduction

CR *Is there a way to receive an income tax deduction today for the gift I make to the charitable lead trust?*

The deductibility of a gift to a CLT depends on how the trust is structured for income tax purposes. If the trust pays the taxes on its income, you are not entitled to an income tax deduction. But if you are responsible for paying the taxes on the trust's income, then you receive a current income tax deduction for the present value of the income stream going to charity. You do not, however, receive any additional tax deduction for the amounts the trust pays to the charity each year.

For example, if you create a CLAT for a term of 20 years that pays 6 percent of the initial value each year, then your tax deduction is about 85 percent of the value of the property you contribute to the trust. (It is important to note that for this example we used a 3.6 percent AFR.)

Put another way, when a CLT trustmaker receives the benefit of an immediate income tax deduction, he or she must also accept the burden of paying the income taxes on the trust's future income. For that reason, in most situations people choose to forgo the income tax deduction. There is still an indirect income tax benefit without the charitable deduction: the income generated by the property donated to the trust is taxed to the trust and not the donor. So, by transferring the asset to the CLT, the trustmaker reduces his or her taxable income. Most people who create a charitable lead trust are not looking to reduce their income taxes, but are using a CLT as an estate planning tool and to fulfill their charitable giving goals.

Q *I am retiring from my company and will be getting a very large payment for my stock. I am contributing annually to my church. Could a CLT help offset the income taxes on the sale of my stock?*

You could establish a charitable lead trust that gives you a current income tax deduction. The tax deduction will help offset the income you receive from the payment for your stock. You will have to pay the taxes on the trust's income in future years, but you will most likely be in a lower tax bracket then. When the CLT terminates, the remaining trust property can return to you or pass to your family to reduce your estate tax exposure. It's important that you work with professional advisors who will calculate the potential tax savings from this strategy before you proceed.

Charitable Estate and Gift Tax Deductions

Q *What are the gift tax consequences of a CLT?*

A CLT trustmaker makes one and, potentially, two gifts when he or she funds the trust. First, the trustmaker makes a gift of the unitrust or annuity interest to the qualified charity. This gift does not generate gift tax because the trustmaker receives an offsetting gift tax deduction for the value of the charity's interest.

Second, if the property remaining in the trust after the charity's interest expires returns to the trustmaker, there are no gift tax consequences. But if the property passes to someone other than the trustmaker, then the trustmaker has made a gift subject to gift taxes. The gift taxes are calculated by subtracting the present value of the income stream going to charity from the total value of the assets you transfer to the trust. The method for determining the gift tax consequences for a CLT is essentially the same calculation we described earlier for a charitable remainder trust, except that in the case of the CLT, the value of the remainder interest is the amount of the gift to your noncharitable beneficiaries.

CR *What are the estate tax consequences of a CLT?*

If the CLT trustmaker is not the remainder beneficiary of the trust and has not kept any "strings" of control over the trust, the CLT property will not be included in his or her gross estate and thus will not be subject to federal estate tax. If the trustmaker is the remainder beneficiary, the trust property will be included in his or her gross estate and will be subject to estate taxes.

Changing the Charitable Beneficiaries

CR *Is there a way to structure the trust to allow flexibility for me to change the charitable beneficiaries?*

Yes, there are several ways to control which charities receive the annual distributions. A simple way to create flexibility is to allow the trustee (someone other than the trustmaker) to distribute funds among a group of charitable beneficiaries named in the trust document. This will allow your trustee the flexibility, from year to year, to decide which charities benefit from the charitable lead trust.

Another way to preserve your options is to pay the charitable distributions to a private foundation that you and your family establish. The foundation then makes distributions to other public charities each year.

A third way to control which charities benefit from the trust is to have the trust make distributions to a donor-advised fund (DAF). This is a special type of fund created by a public charity to give donors some level of say as to which public charities receive donations from the fund from year to year. We describe private foundations and DAFs later in this chapter. In most instances, the CLT trustmaker cannot control who receives distributions from the foundation or DAF, but the donor's family can have that power.

Uses and Advantages

CR *How does a CLT work as an estate planning tool if my children are the remainder beneficiaries?*

Because your children have no rights to the assets in the CLT until the CLT terminates, the value of the gift is substantially reduced for gift tax purposes. Depending on investment performance, your children, or other beneficiaries, may actually receive more than the gift tax value of the trust property.

As an example, let's say you establish a charitable lead annuity trust that you fund with $500,000 and that will pay your favorite charity 5 percent of this initial value for the next 15 years. At the end of the 15 years, whatever is left in the trust goes to your children in equal shares. During those 15 years, the trust's average investment return is 7 percent. Assuming the applicable federal rate (AFR) is 3.6 percent, the value of the gift to your children for gift tax purposes is about $214,000. But because the trust earned more than it paid out to the charity, your children receive a little over $750,000 when the 15 years is up. In this example your children actually receive tax-free over three times more than the gift tax value of the transfer. Plus, you gave $375,000 to charity through the trust.

As long as you do not retain any control over the trust or the right to receive any of the trust property at the end of the 15 years, the trust property is not subject to estate taxes when you die. As you can see, a CLT can be a powerful tool to avoid estate taxes and greatly enhance your children's inheritance even while making a substantial donation to charity.

◌ঽ *How do I know how much my children will ultimately receive from the CLT?*

You don't. Of course, we can make projections, as we did in the earlier question, but how much your children actually receive is a function of how well the trust's investments perform over time. The investments inside the trust must have a rate of return greater than the AFR for the month the trust was funded. For example, if you create a CLT when the AFR is 6 percent, the total return on the assets inside the trust must exceed 6 percent for the trust to succeed as a wealth transfer device. This is known as *leveraging* a gift; that is, property you give away through a split-interest trust earns more than the government anticipates (the AFR), and your beneficiaries receive more than the gift tax value of the transfer.

But if the investments in the trust do not have a total return greater than 6 percent, then your children will receive less than the expected amount and the trust did not fully achieve its estate planning purpose. For that reason, it is essential that your CLT trustee have professional investment counseling to ensure that the trust meets your goals.

❧ What are the advantages of a CLT?

The primary advantages of a CLT are:

- The trustmaker is benefiting charitable causes he or she considers worthy.

- The trustmaker can give property (the remainder interest) to family members while minimizing or even eliminating the gift tax on the transfer.

- Although most CLT donors opt to forgo the income tax deduction, they are still indirectly lowering their income taxes through the trust.

- Depending on how the CLT is structured, it can also completely avoid estate tax.

Disadvantages

❧ Are there any disadvantages to using a CLT?

The major disadvantages of a CLT are:

- The donor must give up the charitable income tax deduction to avoid paying taxes on the trust's income.

- Unlike a charitable remainder trust, the CLT is not a tax-exempt entity.

- The rules governing charitable lead trusts are somewhat complex, and the CLT document must meet detailed IRS requirements. The trust must file an annual tax return. In operating the trust, the trustee must comply with a number of complicated rules and limitations on self-dealing, taxable expenditures, excess business holdings, and jeopardizing investments.

TESTAMENTARY GIFTS TO CHARITY

Testamentary Charitable Remainder Trust

❧ Can I arrange to have a charitable remainder trust created for my children at my death?

You can have a CRT created at your death through your will or living trust and funded with all or part of your property. This is called a *testamentary charitable remainder trust (T-CRT)*. The payments must be scheduled to begin as of the date of your death, although they may be deferred until the end of the taxable year in which the funding is completed, which must be within a reasonable period of time for administration and settlement.

As with a lifetime CRT, with a T-CRT a portion of your estate's assets is invested, after your death, to pay a stream of payments to noncharitable beneficiaries for life or for a fixed number of years. At the end of the trust term, the remaining balance is paid to charity. The payment stream will be either as an annuity or as a unitrust payment, as described earlier for the *inter vivos* CRT. In either case, the set percentage cannot be changed once the trust is established. At the end of the trust term, the remainder interest in the trust can be distributed to any charitable beneficiary or beneficiaries or class of beneficiaries you desire. A T-CRT becomes effective only upon your death, so while you are alive and competent you can amend the terms of the trust if you desire.

Although you don't receive an income tax deduction for a T-CRT and the value of the interest given to the noncharitable beneficiaries will be subject to estate tax, your estate is entitled to a charitable estate tax deduction for the present value of the remainder interest that will go to charity.

ॐ *Why should I consider establishing a testamentary CRT?*

A T-CRT reduces federal estate tax, and you retain total control over your property until your death. Testamentary CRTs are becoming more popular, especially for people with large retirement plans and individual retirement accounts because of the restrictions on giving the proceeds of these plans to charity during life and the income tax consequences of leaving them to heirs. We also discuss these trusts in Chapter 6, Retirement Planning.

Testamentary Charitable Lead Trust

ॐ *Is there a way to create the CLT upon my death?*

You may create a *testamentary charitable lead trust (T-CLT)* in your will or revocable living trust rather than create one during your life.

A T-CLT becomes effective only upon your death, so while you are alive and competent you can amend the terms of the trust if you desire.

As with a lifetime CLT, with a T-CLT a portion of your estate's assets are invested, after your death, to pay a stream of payments to charity each year for a fixed number of years. At the end of the fixed number of years, the remaining balance is returned to your family, often estate tax–free. The payment stream will be either an as annuity or as a unitrust payment, as we described earlier for the *inter vivos* CLT. In either case, the set percentage cannot be changed once the trust is established. At the end of the trust term, the remainder interest in the trust can be distributed in any manner and to any beneficiary or beneficiaries that you desire—often your children or grandchildren. We sometimes refer to this as a "delayed inheritance" since the family will not receive assets for the fixed period of the trust.

℞ *What are the benefits of a testamentary CLT?*

The first obvious benefit of a T-CLT is that none of your assets are removed from your control or use during your lifetime when you may need or simply desire to use them. In addition, a *testamentary charitable lead annuity trust (T-CLAT)* is a very efficient way of significantly reducing estate taxes. This works because, for purposes of the estate tax, the present value of a stream of annuity payments transferred to charity by way of the charitable lead trust is deducted from your estate. With proper planning, the value of those annuity payments can equal the full fair market value of the assets transferred to the trust.

For example, it is possible to structure the T-CLAT so that if $500,000 in assets is transferred to the trust at your death, the present value of the total annuity payments is $500,000. In that case, there is no estate tax due on those assets. It is important to note that this "zeroing-out" of the federal estate taxes only works with an annuity trust and not with a unitrust. At the end of the trust's term, the remaining assets in the trust pass to noncharitable trust beneficiaries, such as your children or grandchildren, free of estate and gift taxes. This technique can work no matter how large or small the amount passing to the T-CLAT; we have seen millions of dollars pass to family members tax-free through this planning tool.

It is important to note that the same rules discussed earlier apply as to whether a T-CLAT is an effective method of transferring wealth. The assets in the trust must have a total rate of return greater than the applicable federal rate at the time of the trustmaker's death in order for the T-CLAT to succeed as a wealth transfer tool.

ALTERNATIVES TO TRADITIONAL PUBLIC CHARITIES

Private Foundations

CR *What is a private foundation and how do they operate?*

A *private foundation* is a special type of charitable organization, usually formed by an individual or family with a strong interest in philanthropy. The individual or family who creates the foundation is typically its only donor; foundations rarely engage in fundraising activities. Most foundations use the income from their investments to make grants to public charities. In fact, most foundations are required by law to give at least 5 percent of the value of their investments annually to public charities. A board of directors or trustees (usually the donor family) manages the foundation and selects the charities that receive its distributions.

CR *What are the benefits to the family of a private foundation?*

An individual who has a strong charitable desire but wants more control over his or her charitable gifts is a good candidate to be a founder of a private foundation. Along with the added control come several other important benefits:

- Founders can involve their children, and later their grandchildren, in their charitable activities while they are alive in order to watch and to mentor them.

- Founders can establish a long-term family tradition of charitable giving that carries their name, beliefs, and legacy far into the future.

- Founders can develop a systematic method of charitable giving, rather than writing a series of ad hoc checks each year to charities.

- Founders can avoid unnecessary estate, gift, and capital gain taxes on their wealth.

ભ *What are the disadvantages of a private foundation?*

Because of abusive practices engaged in by some private foundations in the past, the Internal Revenue Service monitors private foundations fairly closely and requires extensive IRS filings. Also, a private foundation pays a minimum income tax. There are a variety of activities that, if engaged in by the private foundation, trigger rather severe penalties.

The Internal Revenue Code limits the amount that a taxpayer can deduct each year for a charitable donation; these percentage limitations are lower for a private foundation than they are for other types of qualified charities.

Supporting Organizations

ભ *What is a supporting organization?*

A *supporting organization (SO)* is a special type of charity created under the Internal Revenue Code that operates to support the activities of one or more traditional public charities. It can support the charities financially and by running programs that expand or complement those of the supported charities. For example, a donor might create a supporting organization to build and operate a cancer treatment center as part of a local hospital.

An SO must either be controlled by the supported charity or operate in connection with the supported charity. In other words, it does not have complete freedom to go off and "do its own thing." An SO is typically set up by a private founding donor who agrees to operate the SO in such close association with at least one charity that it essentially becomes an extension of that charity. In most cases, the founder names numerous charities as potential benefactors of the SO, and the board that governs the SO decides which charities from the list should benefit each year. The founder chooses the governing board for the SO, and the founder and his family can operate the SO in conjunction with nonfamily members whom the founder selects.

ભ *Can others contribute to our supporting organization?*

Absolutely. There is no limitation as to who and how many donors can make tax-deductible contributions to an SO. So long as the SO qualifies under the IRC and the IRS's regulations as a supporting organization, anyone contributing to it will get the same tax deduction, and be subject to the same rules for deductibility, as someone making a contribution to a traditional public charity.

∞ *Do we have to support every charity that we named in our supporting organization?*

No. You are only required to support at least one charity each year. That support must be of such a nature or of such importance to that supported charity that it will be attentive to the SO's activities to ensure that the SO is operated in accordance with its organizational documents and the laws governing supporting organizations.

∞ *Is there a limit on how many charities you can name in a supporting organization as supported charities?*

Currently, there is no limit as to the number of charities that can be named in the organizational documents of a supporting organization. Naming a large number of charities is one way to soften the prohibition against naming additional public charities as supported charities once the SO is formed.

Another way to broaden the number of charities that can receive support from an SO is to name one or more *community foundations* as supported charities. By their very nature, community foundations underwrite a wide range and number of charitable activities. Therefore, an SO that names a community foundation as one of its supported charities and works with the community foundation potentially has the same range of philanthropic activities to choose from as the community foundation itself has.

∞ *If I create a supporting organization, will I have to give up control?*

Ironically, we find that the founder and the founder's family have the greatest flexibility in operating the SO if they give control of the SO to persons outside the family. Under this structure, the founder and his family do not make up a majority of the trustees or directors, and the founder names the independent trustees or directors who are highly likely to have the same goals as the family trustees.

Since the only restrictions on whom the founder can name are other family members and other persons under the founder's control,

the founder can vest control of the SO with friends and close associates who are likely to carry out the objectives of the founder and the
founder's family. The key here, however, is that *they are not legally
obligated to do so.*

℞ How does a supporting organization differ from a private foundation?

An SO is controlled or supervised by one or more supported charities. As a consequence, Congress felt it unnecessary to require of the
SO as much reporting as it does of a private foundation.

An SO qualifies as a public charity rather than as a private foundation. Accordingly, the tax deductions for contributions to an SO
have the same higher percentage limitations applicable to any other
public charity; tax deductibility of contributions to private foundations is more restrictive. An SO is not subject to the income taxes
and excise taxes that pertain to private foundations.

The primary disadvantage of an SO over a private foundation is
that the founder of an SO vests control outside of the family, whereas
the founder of a private foundation and his or her family has absolute control over the private foundation's activities, subject to the
restrictions contained in its organizational documents and the IRC.
Furthermore, there are no limitations imposed in advance on which
charities the private foundation can support so long as each is a publicly supported charity and recognized as such by the Internal Revenue Service.

Donor-Advised Funds

℞ I like the flexibility and control of private foundations and sup-porting organizations, but I don't have enough money to justify the time and expense of setting one up. Is there some alternative for me?

You may wish to set up a *donor-advised fund (DAF)*. A DAF is an
account you create at your local community foundation (or at other
larger public charities). You make contributions to the account (and
receive an income tax deduction), and the funds you contribute are
later distributed to one or more public charities based on your recommendations to the community foundation. The community

foundation acts as an administrator and intermediary, holding and investing your contributions, and over time distributing the funds to local charities. Technically speaking, the foundation is not obligated to honor your requests for distribution of the funds, but in our experience, foundations are very cooperative and eager to assist donors in their charitable endeavors.

DAFs are excellent planned-giving tools for donors who do not have enough wealth to justify creating private foundations or supporting organizations but who want to have some input in how their donations are utilized. The paperwork for the donor is minimal, and the initial contribution can be as low as $5,000.

ACTION STEPS

We respectfully present the following action steps to summarize the concepts that we discussed in chapter 3 and to suggest steps that you can take to prepare for meetings with your estate planning team of professionals.

❑ *Know what you want to accomplish.* People make charitable gifts for a number of reasons. Sometimes the motivation is purely philanthropic, and the donor is not concerned with any personal benefit from the donation. Other times the donor, while still pleased to make a charitable gift, is more interested in the tax and other benefits. It is important for you to identify your motivations and your goals, include them in your list of estate planning goals, and communicate them to your advisors.

❑ *Talk with your advisors and your charity.* Most charities and professional advisors have a wealth of information about charitable giving that they are happy to share. They can direct you in your charitable giving and present opportunities that you probably don't know exist.

❑ *Know who you're giving to and the purpose of your gift.* Unfortunately, there are numerous unscrupulous organizations passing themselves off as legitimate charities. Investigate any organization before you donate money to it; and understand its mission, management, and how your donation will be spent. Most charities will allow you to specify the purpose of your gift, and in our experience donors receive more satisfaction when they give for a specific purpose. For example, donating to the building fund at your church is certainly worthwhile, but knowing that your gift paid for three new pews will make you feel good every time you sit down in church. For donors who want more control over their charitable gifts, consider using a donor-advised fund or setting up a private foundation or a supporting organization.

❑ *Recognize the tax benefits of charitable gifts.* Charitable giving affects your taxes and your personal finances. Whatever your motivation is, the federal tax laws encourage charitable giving, and there's no reason not to take advantage of them to reduce your taxable income. Make sure that you always discuss charitable giving intentions with your tax advisor who can help you maximize the tax benefits of those gifts.

❑ *Integrate charitable planning into your financial and estate plans.* Our experience is that combining your charitable inclinations with your financial plan and estate plan benefits you, your charities, and your family in extraordinary ways. Using charitable gifts to minimize federal estate and gift taxes through charitable lead trusts and other techniques is a common, but somewhat complex, planning strategy. Of course, this requires a team of skilled financial and legal advisors to make the plan work.

❑ *Use charitable planning to secure your retirement.* It may sound odd at first, but for people with highly appreciated assets, charitable giving through a charitable remainder trust may be the best way to improve cash flow. Moreover, proper charitable planning can help secure your family's inheritance even while you make a substantial gift to your favorite cause.

❑ *Work only with qualified advisors.* Charitable planning requires advisors who are skilled in properly drafting legal documents and running complex calculations based on various assumptions and scenarios. If none of your current advisors are experienced in charitable planning, then you must find an advisor who is. Ask your existing advisors to recommend a new team member with charitable planning expertise. If they cannot suggest someone, your favorite charity probably can.

PART
TWO

Money

The tax laws in this country change frequently. The most recent changes occurred in 2003 when Congress lowered the income tax rates. For estate taxes, the major shakeup came in 2001, when Congress passed and President Bush signed into law the Economic Growth and Tax Relief Reconciliation Act of 2001 (2001 tax act). This law substantially affected estate planning and its tax, retirement, and financial planning components. The act is complex, but it is important to understand two simple facts from the start:

1. Most of the tax-relief provisions are phased in gradually through 2010. This lag gives Congress the opportunity to slow down or even to eliminate the scheduled tax cuts and repeals.
2. The act has a built-in self-destruct mechanism; all of the tax breaks the act provides will automatically disappear on December 31, 2010, unless Congress acts to extend or to make permanent the tax breaks.

After the 2001 tax act's repeal on December 31, 2010, the gift and estate tax laws will return to their status just prior to enactment of the 2001 tax act. Commentators have called the 2001 tax act complicated, hilarious, and even patently dishonest. Whatever we may believe about the law, one thing is clear: Flexibility in planning, now more than ever, is the key. Everyone will need to reevaluate his or her plan regularly to keep up with the changes in the law.

One unfortunate aspect of the 2001 tax act is its impact on the tax coffers of states that impose an estate tax (versus an inheritance tax), and this includes the majority of states. Before the 2001 tax act, these "gap tax" states collected an estate tax equal to the state death tax credit allowed under the federal estate tax laws. The 2001 tax act reduced the amount of this tax credit, which in turn reduces the amount of estate taxes these states will collect. In 2005, the credit disappears completely and will be replaced by a tax deduction that is less beneficial to your estate and the states. Many states are already suffering from this revenue cutback and have "decoupled" their estate taxes from the federal estate tax to offset the revenue loss. The result? Some estates will pay higher combined federal and state death taxes than anticipated, and estates that owe no federal estate tax could now owe state estate taxes. Despite the reductions in the federal estate tax, people will need to plan for federal and state death taxes more than ever before.

In Part Two, our contributors explain the challenges and opportunities that the new laws create for individuals and families. They provide a wealth of ideas to assist you as you plan during the years to come.

In chapter 4, our contributors have taken the logical course of starting with the basics of the federal transfer tax system. In particular, they explain the estate and gift tax rates and the credits and exemptions under the current law. Chapter 4 also looks at the impact of state death taxes. Proper use of the available credits and exemptions is crucial to successful estate planning. It is particularly important for married couples to use marital and family (credit shelter) trusts in estate planning to avoid estate taxes where possible. Above all, chapter 4 identifies ways for everyone to plan with flexibility in case the law does change again before 2011.

Because many people have estates whose value is sufficient to cause concern about federal gift and estate taxes, in chapter 5 our contributors present advanced strategies for reducing or even eliminating these taxes. Most of these strategies are based on making lifetime gifts or selling assets to heirs. Depending on your needs and financial situation, one or more of these techniques may be effective in your estate plan. But these techniques are complex and should not be implemented without counsel from a skilled estate planning attorney.

The topic of retirement is an important one today for a large segment of our population. Younger individuals want to know when to start and how to save for retirement, and people in or near retirement are concerned about whether they have saved enough. For many, their retirement plans are their most valuable asset, and they want to know how to pass those funds to their heirs in the most tax-efficient manner possible. In chapter 6 our contributors provide an excellent overview of retirement planning: goal setting, accumulation strategies, distribution planning, and coordinating retirement plans with estate planning. Our contributors explain the basic features and benefits of the various employer-sponsored plans and individual retirement accounts available for tax-deferred retirement savings. They also offer some creative alternatives to qualified retirement plans for individuals who already take full advantage of those plans but are looking for additional ways to save for retirement.

Recently the federal government revised, and thankfully simplified, the rules for distributions from qualified retirement plans. Still, our experience is that few people are able to understand these rules well enough to make appropriate choices about their plan distributions without professional assistance. Our contributors also unravel the mysteries of these distribution rules in this chapter. Retirees and anyone close to retiring should pay close attention to this discussion.

The laws will continue to change, but the planning concepts and strategies that our contributors so artfully present in Part Two are relevant today and, with the assistance of a skilled planning professional, will allow the flexibility you need in your estate plan to respond to those changes.

chapter 4

Tax Basics

ESTATE TAX REPEAL— REAL OR NOT?

❧ *Why are we discussing the federal estate tax? Hasn't it been repealed?*

On June 7, 2001, President Bush signed the Economic Growth and Tax Relief Reconciliation Act of 2001 (EGTRRA, or 2001 tax act) which makes comprehensive changes to the U.S. tax laws. Some of the changes include gradually reducing the top estate tax rate; gradually increasing the estate tax applicable exclusion; and reducing the state death tax credit and eventually converting it to a deduction. The act also "repeals" the estate tax, but only for the estates of individuals who die in the year 2010. In 2010, the estate tax will essentially be replaced by a new income tax. Some time prior to December 31, 2010, Congress must vote to extend these changes. If it does not extend the changes, the act "sunsets" on January 1, 2011, and the law reverts back to the estate tax law in place prior to EGTRRA.

❧ *What do estate planning professionals think about the future of*

TABLE 4-1 Summary of the Estate, Gift, and Generation-Skipping Transfer Taxes

	Stage 1: Continuation of the unified estate and gift tax system							Stage 2: Estate tax repeal	Stage 3: Return to pre-2001 tax act
	2003	2004	2005	2006	2007	2008	2009	2010	2011
Estate tax:									
Top marginal rate	49%	48%	47%	46%	45%	45%	45%	Repealed	55%*
Applicable exclusion	$1M	$1.5M	$1.5M	$2M	$2M	$2M	$3.5M	Repealed	$1M*
Gift tax:									
Top marginal rate	49%	48%	47%	46%	45%	45%	45%	35%	55%
Applicable exclusion	$1M	$1M	$1M	$1M	$1M	$1M	$1M	$1M	$1M†
Generation-skipping transfer tax:									
Top marginal rate	49%	48%	47%	46%	45%	45%	45%	Repealed	55%
Exemption	$1.06M	$1.5M	$1.5M	$2M	$2M	$2M	$3.5M	Repealed	$1M
State death tax credit	25%	Repealed‡							

*Following December 31, 2010, the 2001 tax act is scheduled to sunset with all rates reverting to what they were under the law in existence just prior to its enactment. Since the applicable exclusion amounts under prior law were scheduled to increase to $1 million in 2006, that is the amount they will be in 2011 following the sunset of the 2001 tax act.

†Beginning in 2010 the $1 million gift tax applicable exclusion amount is scheduled to be indexed for inflation.

‡Beginning in 2005 there will be a deduction for death taxes actually paid to any state with respect to property in the estate of a decedent.

the estate tax? Do they think Congress will permanently repeal the federal estate tax before 2010?

Those who try to tell you they *know* what will happen to the estate tax are kidding you and themselves. We can only make educated guesses based on recent events.

The barrier to repeal is that the estate tax is an important revenue source for the government even though the federal estate tax affects less than 5 percent of the population. Since the 2001 tax act was passed, the stock market has declined, unemployment has risen, and the federal government (and many state governments) is running up large deficits. Congress will have to replace the lost tax revenue, most likely through an income tax increase that would affect far more than 5 percent of the population. Most professionals think that our politicians will not have the luxury of leaving the 2001 estate tax changes intact. The economic reality of funding the federal government suggests further changes in the estate and gift tax laws, and so a permanent repeal seems unlikely at this time.

In the end, trying to predict what our governmental leaders will do in years ahead is a fool's errand. The smart thing to do is to plan now as if you were going to die this year, then keep your eye on Congress and review your estate plan regularly.

Also, remember that there are many nontax-related reasons to plan your estate. For example, you may want to protect your assets and the assets you leave to your loved ones from lawsuits, divorce proceedings, bankruptcy, and future creditors. Proper estate planning would also address these objectives.

ଔ *What is the law now?*

Table 4-1 is an overview of the taxes and deductions through 2011. Three things become apparent when you review this table:

1. The tax-relief provisions are phased in between 2003 and 2010. The 6-year lag between 2004 and 2010 provides future Congresses with many opportunities to reduce or to entirely eliminate the scheduled tax cuts and the repeal.

2. As we mentioned above, the 2001 tax act has a built-in provision that will cause it to disappear on December 31, 2010, unless Congress proactively extends the law.

3. Rather than simplifying the estate and gift tax system, the 2001

tax act made it far more complex because it created three distinct estate and gift tax systems, as noted in Table 4-1.

In the next two sections we discuss the taxes and the credits, exemptions, exclusions, and deductions as they stand now, and later in this chapter, we will present suggestions for planning through this legislative maze.

◌ঽ *When I die, what will be the tax consequences to my family?*

When you die, your estate and/or the beneficiaries of your estate could be subject to a number of taxes imposed by the federal and state governments. Specifically, your estate or heirs may have to pay:

- a federal estate tax on the full value of your net wealth,
- a generation-skipping transfer (GST) tax on property passing to your grandchildren,
- a state inheritance or estate tax, and
- income taxes on some parts of their inheritance.

THE TAXES

Federal Estate and Gift Tax System

◌ঽ *What are estate taxes?*

The *federal estate tax* is a tax assessed on the net value of all property transferred at a person's death. *Net value* is the gross value of your assets—including home, business interests, bank accounts, investments, personal property, individual retirement accounts, retirement plans, and death benefits from life insurance that you owned on your life—less your debts. The tax is paid from your assets, and then the remaining property passes to your family.

◌ঽ *If my assets are going to be taxed when I die, why can't I just give it all away while I'm alive?*

You can, but understand that the federal government also imposes a gift tax. The *gift tax* is a tax on the value of property an individual gives away during his or her life. The gift tax applies to the transfer of property by gift, whether direct or indirect, and whether the transfer is outright or in trust. The person making a gift is called a *donor.* The person receiving the gift is called the *donee.*

㊃ *Why is there a gift tax?*

The reason for the tax is simple. If there was no gift tax, then you could simply give away all your assets before death and avoid any estate tax at death. In essence, you have a choice: either hold on to your property until you die and subject your property to estate taxes, or give your property away while you are alive and subject the gift to the gift tax.

Of course, the decision is more complicated than that. But that's where professional advisors come into play; it's their job to help you make smart estate planning decisions.

㊃ *What are the estate and gift tax rates?*

Lifetime gifts and transfers at death are taxed at the same rates until 2010. Table 4-2 shows the maximum estate and gift tax rates for the years 2004 through 2011. Table 4-3 is the tax schedule for 2004. Because the maximum rate drops several times through 2009, the Internal Revenue Service (IRS) will issue a new rate schedule with each rate decrease.

TABLE 4-2   Maximum Federal Estate, Gift, and Generation-Skipping Transfer Tax Rates under the 2001 Tax Act

Year	Estate tax rate, %	Gift tax rate, %	GST tax rate, %
2004	48	48	48
2005	47	47	47
2006	46	46	46
2007	45	45	45
2008	45	45	45
2009	45	45	45
2010	0[*]	35	0[*]
2011[†]	55	55	55

[*]Repealed.

[†]After the 2001 tax act terminates on December 31, 2010, all rates revert to what they were under the previous law.

TABLE 4-3   2004 Federal Estate and Gift Tax Rates

Cumulative transfers	Tentative tax
Not over $10,000	18% of such amount
$10,000 to $20,000	$1,800 + 20% of excess over $10,000
$20,000 to $40,000	$3,800 + 22% of excess over $20,000
$40,000 to $60,000	$8,200 + 24% of excess over $40,000
$60,000 to $80,000	$13,000 + 26% of excess over $60,000
$80,000 to $100,000	$18,200 + 28% of excess over $80,000
$100,000 to $150,000	$23,800 + 30% of excess over $100,000
$150,000 to $250,000	$38,800 + 32% of excess over $150,000
$250,000 to $500,000	$70,800 + 34% of excess over $250,000
$500,000 to $750,000	$155,800 + 37% of excess over $500,000
$750,000 to $1,000,000	$248,300 + 39% of excess over $750,000
$1,000,000 to $1,250,000	$345,800 + 41% of excess over $1,000,000
$1,250,000 to $1,500,000	$448,300 + 43% of excess over $1,250,000
$1,500,000 to $2,000,000	$555,800 + 45% of excess over $1,500,000
$2,000,000 or more	$780,800 + 48% of excess over $2,000,000

Even though the tax rates are the same for transfers during life or at death, the economic effects of making taxable gifts during life and those of transferring property at death can be substantially different.

Generation-Skipping Transfer Tax

ca *What if I want to make gifts or leave property to my grand-children instead of my children? Are there any additional tax consequences?*

Yes. In most cases, gifts to your grandchildren are subject to a special tax known as the *generation-skipping transfer (GST) tax*. This tax is *in addition to* gift tax imposed on the transfer. One of the goals of the federal transfer tax system is to levy a tax as property passes from one generation to the next. Congress enacted the GST tax so that the government does not lose tax revenue at one generation when you make a gift to your grandchild.

The GST tax rate is a flat tax at the highest estate and gift tax rate in effect when the transfer is made. Table 4-2 shows the maximum GST tax rates between 2004 and 2011.

State Death Taxes

Cʒ *I read that my heirs will pay a state death tax when I die in addition to the federal estate tax. Is this true?*

In almost all cases, this is true. Some states have an *inheritance tax*. With an inheritance tax, the recipient of the property pays the tax based on the value of property and the recipient's relationship to the decedent. For example, the decedent's child would pay less inheritance tax than a nonrelative would pay on the same amount of money.

Most states impose what is commonly known as a *sponge* or *pickup estate tax* that is directly tied to the federal estate tax. The Internal Revenue Code provides a credit against the federal estate tax for state death taxes paid by an estate. The maximum amount of the credit is based on the value of the taxable estate. For example, in 2003 a taxable estate of $1 million was entitled to a state death tax credit of up to $18,280. So, a state that uses the sponge tax imposed a tax of $18,280 on that estate. The result of this system is that if an estate doesn't owe federal estate taxes, it doesn't owe the state either. And if an estate does owe federal estate tax, it simply sends part of that tax money to the state instead of the federal government (hence the nicknames *sponge* and *pickup*). In essence, the federal credit is a revenue-sharing program with the states. This tax system also simplifies the estate planning process—taxpayers need only plan for one estate tax. But this system is rapidly coming to an end.

Cʒ *Does the 2001 tax act affect state death taxes?*

To offset some of the revenue lost by other provisions of the 2001 tax act, Congress repealed the state death tax credit effective in 2004. The repeal of this credit, along with the increases in the applicable exclusion amount, will drastically reduce the amount of estate tax that these states will collect in the future. To recover this lost revenue, several states have recently revised their laws to "decouple" their estate tax from the federal tax. By decoupling the state death tax from the federal tax, a state can charge whatever amount of tax it chooses.

Several states now impose an estate tax on estates whose value is more than $675,000, even though only estates valued at more than $1.5 million will pay federal estate tax in 2004. Residents of these states must plan for two death taxes, and they will find that their estate plans are more complicated now than in the past. There is no clear solution to this new planning issue, and each state will likely have a slightly different death tax system in the future. It is very likely that all states will soon replace the pickup tax with another form of death tax to replace the lost revenue and perhaps even impose higher death taxes to make up for budget shortfalls.

You should contact your tax advisor soon to determine if you are living in one of the states that has decoupled its death tax from the federal estate tax. If you are, your estate plan may need revising. Even if your state has not done so yet, you can expect a change in your state's death tax laws in the near future.

CREDITS, EXEMPTIONS, AND EXCLUSIONS

Unified Credit

CR *I've read several articles about estate planning and they've used terms like "unified credit," "applicable credit," "estate tax applicable exclusion," and "estate tax exemption." What's the difference?*

The 2001 tax act made an already complex tax system even more difficult to understand, so professionals struggle to find the easiest way to explain the system to their clients. Conceptually, all four of these terms refer to the amount of assets that one may transfer to his or her loved ones (other than a spouse) free of federal estate and gift taxes.

CR *What is the unified credit?*

The *unified credit*, or *applicable credit*, is a tax credit that reduces or eliminates a taxpayer's estate and gift taxes. Once the value of a decedent's estate is determined and all of the appropriate deductions are taken, the remaining net value is the *taxable estate*. A tentative tax on that amount is calculated, and then the credit is applied. This credit reduces the amount of the final tax due.

This credit is called a *unified credit* because it can be used against taxable transfers during life (gift tax) and against transfers at death (estate tax). So when a person makes a taxable gift, the taxpayer calculates the gift tax on the transfer, then applies his or her available unified credit to the tax. However, as Table 4-4 shows, since passage of the 2001 tax act, a taxpayer cannot fully expend the unified credit during life. While the unified credit increases through 2009, a taxpayer can use only $1 million worth of the unified credit against lifetime gifts. The credit is not as "unified" as it was once.

CR *Can you give me an example of how the unified credit works?*

Table 4-4 shows the unified credit and the applicable exclusion it equates to each year from 2004 through 2011. Here is a simple example of how the credit works for the estate of a person who dies in 2004:

Taxable estate	$1,500,000
Tentative tax due (from Table 4-3)	555,800
Unified credit	555,800
Tax due	$ 0

TABLE 4-4   Unified Credits and Equivalent Applicable Exclusions

	Estate tax		Gift tax	
Year	Unified credit	Applicable exclusion	Unified credit	Applicable exclusion
2004	$ 555,800	$1,500,000	$345,800	$1,000,000
2005	555,800	1,500,000	345,800	1,000,000
2006	780,800	2,000,000	345,800	1,000,000
2007	780,800	2,000,000	345,800	1,000,000
2008	780,800	2,000,000	345,800	1,000,000
2009	1,455,800	3,500,000	345,800	1,000,000
2010	0	0	345,800	1,000,000
2011	345,800	1,000,000[*]		

*After the 2001 tax act terminates, all rates revert to what they were under the previous law, which means that the applicable exclusion will be $1 million for the unified estate and gift taxes.

If the taxable estate is equal to or less than $1.5 million in 2004, the unified credit wipes out the tax. If the taxable estate is greater than $1.5 million, the tax due is the difference between the tentative tax and the unified credit.

Applicable Exclusion and Unified Credit

CR *What does the term applicable exclusion mean?*

The *applicable exclusion* is the amount that the unified credit equates to in terms of how much an individual can transfer free of estate and gift taxes. Put another way, the applicable exclusion is the value of a person's estate that is sheltered from estate taxes by the unified credit. For example, from Table 4-4, the unified credit in 2004 is $555,800. This credit will shelter up to $1.5 million from estate and gift taxes, so we say that you can leave $1.5 million tax-free. When counseling their clients, most advisors refer to how much individuals can pass to their heirs tax-free in terms of the amount of the applicable exclusion.

Unlimited Marital Deduction

CR *What is the marital deduction?*

The *marital deduction* is an unlimited deduction for estate and gift tax purposes on the value of property that spouses can transfer to each other. This allows you to give an unlimited amount of money or other assets to your spouse during your life and at death with no gift tax or estate tax on these transfers. A limited marital deduction is available only if the spouse receiving the gift is a U.S. citizen at the time of the gift or at the time of the donor spouse's death unless the assets are put into a qualified domestic trust (see chapter 2).

There are a few limits on the types of property spouses can give to each other, but those are rarely applicable. It is also possible to make the gifts or bequests in special trusts that meet certain requirements of the Internal Revenue Code. We will discuss the rules for these trusts later in this chapter.

Gift Tax Exclusions

CR *How much can I give away during my lifetime before I have to pay gift taxes?*

That depends not only on the amount of the gift, but also the nature of the gift. A few types of gifts are tax-free under exceptions carved out in the Internal Revenue Code. For gifts that don't qualify for one of these exceptions, a taxpayer can give away up to $1 million without paying federal gift tax.

Gift Tax Annual Exclusion

> *My advisor suggested that I make annual-exclusion gifts to my family. What are those?*

The *annual exclusion* allows you to make tax-free gifts of $11,000 each year per donee. These gifts are often referred to as *annual-exclusion gifts*. As an example, let's say that you have three children. You can give them as much as $33,000 every year. If you're married, your spouse can give them the same amount, for a total of $66,000. To qualify for the annual exclusion, the gift must be a gift of a *present interest*, meaning that the donee can control, use, and enjoy the gift immediately. That usually means the gift must be an outright gift, although gifts to some trusts qualify as present-interest gifts as well.

The annual exclusion is indexed to inflation, but given the current low inflation rate, it will probably take 4 to 5 years before the amount of the annual exclusion increases to $12,000.

> *Is there a gift tax deduction available for gifts to a non–U.S. citizen spouse?*

Yes, the donor spouse is entitled to an annual deduction for gifts to a spouse who is not a U.S. citizen. This amount is $112,000 in 2003 (indexed annually for inflation). The gift must qualify as a present-interest gift (described above) and otherwise meet the rules for the marital deduction.

Medical and Tuition Payment Credits

> *Are there any other ways to make tax-free gifts?*

You can pay someone else's medical bills or tuition without paying gift tax, no matter how much you pay. For this rule to apply, you must pay the health care provider or school directly; you can't give money to a donee to pay for or reimburse him or her for these expenses. This exclusion applies to just about any medical expense, but for educational expenses, it only applies to tuition; room and board, books, and other educational expenses don't qualify.

Gift Tax Lifetime Unified Credit

ର Are there any other credits available to be applied against the gift tax?

There is a lifetime unified credit available to offset the tax on taxable gifts. Table 4-4 shows the gift tax unified credits and equivalent applicable exclusions for the years 2004 through 2011. Under EGTRRA, the dollar amount of the credit is fixed at $345,800. This is the equivalent of giving $1 million tax-free. Unlike the unified credit for the federal estate tax, the unified credit for the gift tax *will not increase or phase out under the current law.*

If a person makes lifetime taxable gifts, the total amount of the gifts reduces, dollar for dollar, the amount of that person's federal estate tax applicable exclusion. For example, if an individual who dies in 2004 has not made any taxable gifts, that person's federal estate tax applicable exclusion amount is $1.5 million. If, however, that individual made $500,000 worth of taxable gifts before dying, then his or her estate is entitled only to a $1 million estate tax applicable exclusion.

Annual Exclusion in Conjunction with the Gift Tax Applicable Exclusion

ର Can you give me an example of how the gift tax applicable exclusion and annual exclusion work together?

Yes. Let's say that you have two daughters, Christy and Connie; and a nephew, Richard. In 2004, you pay Richard's tuition expenses directly to his university in the amount of $15,000. Also in 2004, you make cash gifts to Christy and Connie in the amount of $40,000 each.

Richard's tuition payment is not a taxable gift. You can apply your gift tax annual exclusion of $11,000 to the $40,000 gift that you made to each of the girls. Thus, you make taxable gifts in 2004 of $58,000 ($80,000 − $22,000). You must file a gift tax return but you will not pay any gift tax because you will use $58,000 of your $1 million lifetime applicable exclusion.

Generation-Skipping Transfer Tax Exemption

C§ Does the law provide for any generation-skipping transfer tax exemptions or exclusions?

Yes. Each individual has a GST tax exemption of $1.5 million that he or she can use to exempt property, dollar-for-dollar, from the GST tax. So an exemption of $1.5 million exempts $1.5 million in property from the tax. Under the 2001 tax act, the GST tax exemption will gradually increase to $3.5 million in 2009. You can use this exemption on lifetime gifts to grandchildren, and any GST tax exemption remaining when you die is available to exempt from GST tax all or part of the value of transfers to your grandchildren.

Annual outright gifts to grandchildren that qualify for the gift tax annual exclusion are not subject to GST tax, thus they do not use up any of the GST tax exemption. If you pay your grandchild's tuition bill or medical expenses, those gifts are also exempt from the GST tax.

State Death Tax Credit

C§ What's happening to the state death tax credit?

As part of the 2001 tax act, Congress made two drastic changes to the state death tax credit. First, Congress reduced the amount of the credit—the credit in 2004 is 75 percent less than it was before the new law. Second, the credit will disappear entirely in 2005 and will be replaced with a deduction.

These changes have serious implications for states and taxpayers. States using the sponge tax are now collecting far less money than before, and the state sponge tax will disappear for most states in 2005 when the federal credit expires. Many states, faced with deficits and increased demands for services, have recently decoupled their death tax from the federal estate tax and now impose an estate tax on estates that are too small to incur federal estate tax.

When the state death tax credit expires and is replaced by a tax deduction in 2005, the situation will only become worse. A tax credit reduces your tax liability dollar-for-dollar, while a tax deduction only reduces the amount subject to tax. Thus, estates will no longer be able to completely offset their state death taxes against the federal estate tax. It is possible that estates that would not have been subject to federal estate tax under the previous law may now have to pay state estate tax and that larger estates may incur higher overall death taxes even though the federal estate tax is decreasing. As we mentioned earlier, it is important for individuals to contact an estate planning attorney to discuss the implications for their particular situations.

Calculating the Federal Estate Tax

CR *You said that there are deductions taken into account to determine my taxable estate. What are those deductions?*

Your estate includes everything you owned or had a right to receive at the moment of your death. The logical flip side to this rule is that your *taxable* estate is reduced by all your debts. For example, if a decedent had a $250,000 home and a $200,000 mortgage, the asset is reported at $250,000 on one schedule of the tax return and a $200,000 deduction is taken on another schedule, so that the estate is only taxed on the $50,000 equity interest. Other deductions include funeral expenses, unpaid medical bills from the last illness, and costs of estate administration such as accountant, attorney, and trustee fees.

CR *Are there any other estate tax deductions I should know about?*

Perhaps the two most important estate tax deductions are the unlimited charitable estate tax deduction, which was discussed in detail in Chapter 3, Planning for Loved Ones and Charity, and the unlimited marital deduction, which was explained earlier in this chapter.

CR *How are the federal estate and gift taxes calculated?*

The estate tax computation begins with determining the fair market value of all assets either owned or controlled by the decedent as of the date of death. This amount is called the *gross estate*. The value of property transferred to a surviving spouse and qualified charities, as well as estate administration expenses and other allowable deductions, are subtracted from the gross estate to determine the *taxable estate*. The amount of gifts made after 1976 is added to the taxable estate. The resulting sum is multiplied by the applicable tax rate from the estate tax rate schedule to determine the *tentative tax*. The tentative tax is then reduced by the sum of the gift tax payable on the post-1976 gifts, plus the applicable credit amount for the year of death. Credits are also available for state and foreign death taxes paid, tax paid on transfers from a person who died within 10 years before or 2 years after the decedent, and gift tax paid on gifts made before 1977 included in the gross estate.

◯ঽ *Can you give me an example of that calculation?*

As the previous answer shows, the estate tax calculation can be quite complex. Let's take a fairly simple example. Donna dies in 2004 and the value of her estate—which consists for the most part of her house, retirement account, and life insurance—is $2 million. Her debts, funeral expenses, final medical bills, and the cost of administering her estate total $150,000. In her will, Donna donates $200,000 to a local charity and leaves the rest of her property to her son. The calculation to determine the estate tax in this scenario is as follows:

Donna's gross estate	$2,000,000
Debts & expenses	– 150,000
Charitable bequest	– 200,000
Taxable estate	$1,650,000
Tentative tax (Table 4-3)	623,300
Unified credit in 2004	– 555,800
Tax due	$67,500

After taxes, Donna's son inherits a little over $1.5 million. Note that if Donna had survived until 2006, her estate would not have owed estate taxes; the 2006 unified credit of $780,800 would have wiped out the $67,500 tax.

Paying Estate Taxes

◯ঽ *When must estate taxes be paid?*

Depending on how much you own when you die, your estate may have to pay federal estate taxes before your assets can be fully distributed. The executor of an estate must file a federal estate tax return, Form 706, within 9 months after the decedent's death if the estate exceeds the available estate tax applicable exclusion in the year of death. In almost all cases, estate taxes are due in full at that time and must be paid in cash. Since few estates have this kind of cash, assets must often be liquidated. But estate taxes can be substantially reduced or even eliminated—if you plan ahead.

ᴄᴙ *How are estate taxes paid?*

Generally, we find that there are four methods of paying estate taxes:

1. *Pay cash:* If the estate has the cash available, heirs can use it to pay the estate tax bill.
2. *Sell assets:* The estate can sell marketable assets to raise the cash, although sometimes the full value of the assets is not realized, because the estate does not have time to hold out for the best price.
3. *Borrow funds:* If there is not enough liquidity within the estate and the heirs qualify, they can borrow the needed funds from a lender. The principal plus interest would eventually need to be repaid. For small-business owners, in some instances the IRS accepts payment, with interest, over several years.
4. *Purchase life insurance:* Individuals can purchase life insurance through a life insurance trust that receives the insurance proceeds and either lends cash to or purchases assets from the estate, thereby giving the heirs cash to pay the estate taxes. (See Chapter 5, Wealth Transfer Techniques, for a complete discussion of the irrevocable life insurance trust.)

ROLE OF INCOME TAXES IN ESTATE PLANNING

ᴄᴙ *Do income taxes affect my planning?*

Even though the estate and gift tax system is separate from the income tax system, there are income tax issues that can impact your heirs, and your estate planning professional will raise these issues during the estate planning process. The two income tax issues are:

1. *Basis:* Your cost basis in your property affects your heirs and can be an important consideration in estate planning.

2. *Income in respect of a decedent:* There are special income tax rules for property known as income in respect of a decedent (IRD). Because of the income tax rules for IRD, these types of assets require special planning.

Step-Up-In-Basis System

☙ *How does what I paid for an asset affect my heirs?*

Let's first review what *gain* is. Let's assume that you have an asset such as a stock that you originally purchased for $5,000 (your cost basis), and it has grown in value to $25,000 today. You have a $20,000 *unrealized gain* (it's unrealized until you sell it). When you sell the asset, you must recognize and pay tax on the $20,000 gain. If you owned the stock for 1 year or less, the tax on the gain would be taxed as ordinary income. If you own the stock for more than 1 year, it's a long-term capital gain, and the $20,000 gain is taxed at the current capital gain tax rate, which is now 15 percent for most taxpayers.

Under current law, the *step-up-in-basis system*, your heirs receive a basis adjustment on property that they inherit from you. Their basis in the property is the fair market value of the property on the date of your death. Let's look at an example of this. At your death, your original $5,000 cost basis in the stock would be "stepped up" to the fair market value of the stock on the date of your death, in this case $25,000. If your heirs sell the stock for $25,000, they would owe no tax. If they sold it for $35,000, they would owe tax only on the $10,000 profit in excess of $25,000.

This basis step-up can be a boon to taxpayers who inherit appreciated property. However, the 2001 tax act provides that in 2010, the one year when the estate tax is repealed, a *modified carryover basis system* replaces the step-up-in-basis system for property acquired from a decedent. This means that, with some exceptions, the basis for property acquired from a decedent dying in 2010 will be equal to the decedent's basis before death or the fair market value of the property at death, whichever is less. This modified carryover basis system does not come into effect until 2010, and Congress will in all likelihood change it or return to the original system before then. But, if it does become law, we can count on it being an accounting nightmare for heirs, because heirs will have to know the decedent's basis information when they sell inherited property.

CR *Does this same step-up-in-basis system apply to property that I gift during my lifetime?*

No. Generally for gifts of property made after 1976, the donee takes the basis of the donor, with some increase in the basis if the donor paid gift tax on the transfer. This is known as *carryover basis*. To determine a loss, the donee's basis is the carryover basis or the fair market value of the property when the gift was made, whichever is less. This rule prevents donees from being able to take a tax deduction when they sell gifted property at a loss.

Let's assume that you give the stock to your daughter today. Under the current law, because you are making the gift during your lifetime, your daughter "steps into" your shoes and takes your original $5,000 cost basis in the stock. When she eventually sells the stock, she will owe tax on the $20,000 in built-in gain, just as you would have had you sold it.

Understanding step-up in basis and the effect that it has on your heirs and on your estate is critically important if you have highly appreciated assets. Many people hold assets until death rather than sell them to avoid the capital gain tax on the sale. But, this strategy ensures that the assets are included in the estate at death and, therefore, the estate tax may be higher than the capital gain tax, depending on the size of the estate, the year of death, and other factors. Only by working with a competent estate planning professional will you know whether keeping the asset until death is the better tax strategy.

Income in Respect of a Decedent

CR *What is income in respect of a decedent?*

Income in respect of a decedent (IRD) is income that has been earned but not realized by an individual until after death. These assets, referred to by professionals as *IRD property*, do not provide heirs the favorable step-up-in-basis income tax treatment.

Probably the two most common assets that get hit with this additional IRD income tax are tax-deferred annuities and retirement accounts such as individual retirement accounts, 401(k)s, and similar types of pension accounts. Generally, IRD is taxed when it is received. For example, assume that Joe died and named his cousin Sam as the beneficiary of his pension plan. When Sam withdraws the money from the plan, he will pay income taxes at his ordinary income tax rate. In contrast, had Joe left Sam his house, stocks, or any other non-IRD asset, Sam would not pay income taxes on his inheritance. Keep in mind that this income tax is *in addition to* the normal estate taxes!

Recipients of IRD property are entitled to an income tax deduction for the estate taxes paid on the IRD property. Even so, *the total tax bite can reach as high as 80 percent.* We will discuss strategies for reducing or eliminating the negative economic impact of IRD property in Chapter 6, Retirement Planning. For now, it is important to understand that IRD property in your estate at the time of your death can generate estate tax for you and an income tax for your heirs.

BASIC TAX PLANNING STRATEGIES

Tax Planning under EGTRRA (2001 tax act)

CR *If we assume that Congress will not extend the 2001 tax act or pass new laws, how do we plan our estates?*

Estate planning is more important and arguably more complicated than before the passage of the "repeal" of the estate tax. For now, you and your advisors must plan for three distinct tax scenarios—in the event that you might die:

1. *Before 2009:* You have to consider how future increases in the estate tax applicable exclusion affect your plan and whether the results still meet your goals. Plan for the amount of the exclusion to gradually increase, the estate taxes to gradually phase out, and for your heirs to inherit property under the step-up-in-basis system.

2. *In 2010:* No federal estate taxes will be due, but your heirs must cope with a cumbersome carryover basis system.

3. *After 2010:* Plan for estate, gift, and GST taxes at a maximum rate of 55 percent and an estate tax applicable exclusion of somewhere between $1 million and $1.5 million per person. Under prior law, the applicable exclusion of $1 million was indexed for inflation, so we can only estimate what the actual number will be in 2011.

If you had a crystal ball to tell you what the law will look like when you die, planning would be easy. Obviously no one does, so planning is more problematic. Perhaps the best approach is to plan your estate based on the assumption that there will be an estate tax of some form when you die, but select a planning strategy that works well even if the estate tax is repealed. There should be an emphasis on flexibility.

Above all, keep in mind that estate planning is not just about taxes. Estate planning will always be about the disposition of your estate the way you want, when you want, and to whom you want, while protecting you and your loved ones in the event of your disability. Notwithstanding all the changes in the tax laws, the need for sound estate planning will always exist.

Let's say Congress does repeal the estate tax permanently. How would that affect my estate plan?

A repeal of the estate tax would significantly affect a great many estate plans. While the effects will vary greatly from person to person, there are some consequences we can expect to affect most people.

First, a repeal of the estate tax would make capital gain tax planning much more important. Even if the next generation inherits assets without the burden of an estate tax, they will have a carryover basis in the assets; that is, they will inherit the decedent's basis along with the asset. There are some exceptions to this rule, but many heirs will be forced to pay a large capital gain tax on the asset's eventual sale. It will be more important to keep track of the cost basis of all your assets.

Also, as we discussed earlier, the states will most likely increase or impose their own estate taxes. Many states are already revising their inheritance and estate tax laws to make up for the revenues lost under the 2001 tax act. If the federal estate tax is permanently repealed, we can expect all states to pass new death tax legislation. And, with most states scrambling for funds, it would not surprise us if some states were to view the repeal of the federal estate tax as an opportunity to increase their estate or inheritance taxes.

Finally, it is important to realize that none of the proposals offered in Congress repeals the gift tax. As the law stands now, the gift tax applicable exclusion of $1 million stays constant indefinitely.

CR *So how can I reduce or eliminate my estate taxes?*

In the balance of this chapter, you will discover that there are a variety of planning techniques to reduce or even to eliminate the federal estate taxes on your wealth. Which of these techniques are suitable for you depends on a number of factors; but we would prefer that you not think strictly in terms of tax reduction. Instead, focus on how you want to use your wealth to benefit your loved ones and charitable causes after your death. We find that most people can achieve their nontax objectives as well as reduce their taxes by using four basic planning techniques:

1. Use your estate tax applicable exclusion to take care of your spouse, children, or other loved ones after your death.
2. Take advantage of the unlimited marital deduction to provide for your spouse and to defer estate taxes.
3. Remove assets from your estate before you die by giving assets away to loved ones or to charity.
4. Purchase life insurance to pay remaining estate taxes or to replace assets lost to estate taxes.

Basic Planning for a Spouse and Children

CR *What are some of the estate tax issues when planning for a spouse?*

With the unlimited marital deduction, there is generally no estate tax due when the first spouse dies. Even the richest man in the United States can leave everything to his wife with no estate tax at his death. The estate tax bite will come, however, when the surviving spouse dies. Then the property inherited from the first spouse plus property he or she acquired thereafter is subject to estate tax at its full value. Through proper planning, however, the estate tax can often be reduced or even eliminated at the second death. The key to this goal is proper use of the estate tax applicable exclusion and the unlimited marital deduction.

CR *In 2004, my husband and I have combined wealth of $3 million. If we leave everything to each other and then at the second death leave everything to our two children, there will be no* *estate tax since my husband and I can each shelter $1.5 million from estate taxes. Right?*

No, this is not true. Many married couples fall into this trap. This is known as the simple "I love you" will or trust. The estate tax on a bequest to a surviving spouse is eliminated through the marital deduction, not through the applicable exclusion that shelters the $1.5 million estate tax.

Let's say that your estate is worth $1.5 million, you leave everything to your husband, and you die first. There are no estate taxes due at your death because of the marital deduction, but your estate tax applicable exclusion went unused. When your husband dies later, there is only his applicable exclusion available to offset the tax on your combined $3 million estate, and depending on the year of his death, that may or may not be sufficient to shelter the full amount. For example, if one of you were to die in 2004 and the other in 2006 and you left everything to each other using just the unlimited marital deduction, there would be no federal estate tax due on the first death because of the marital deduction; but there would be $460,000 in federal estate tax due at the second death in 2006 because the estate tax applicable exclusion in that year would only shelter $2 million of the combined $3 million estate (see Figure 4-1). By leaving everything to each other, you "wasted" the applicable exclusion of the first spouse to die, and that could have sheltered at least $1.5 million of the combined estate.

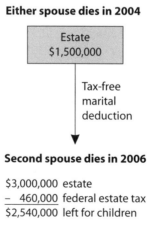

Either spouse dies in 2004

Estate
$1,500,000

Tax-free
marital
deduction

Second spouse dies in 2006

$3,000,000 estate
− 460,000 federal estate tax
$2,540,000 left for children

Figure 4-1   Results of no plan

So how do my husband and I leave everything to each other to reduce or to eliminate the estate tax on the death of the survivor of us?

The tax law allows you and your husband to use both of your estate tax applicable exclusions to shelter up to $1.5 million each (in 2004). The best planning approach is to minimize or even to eliminate the taxes at both deaths by fully using both exclusions. To take maximum advantage of the applicable exclusion, both spouses must have a minimum of the applicable exclusion amount in their estates (e.g., $1.5 million in 2004) and have family trust provisions in their wills or revocable living trusts. In this way, regardless of the sequence of their deaths, both applicable exclusions will be used to reduce the overall federal estate tax burden. In the most basic two-trust plan, on the first spouse's death, an amount of cash and property equal to the then applicable exclusion amount passes to the family trust. Assuming the first spouse dies in 2004, the amount of the applicable exclusion, $1.5 million—which also happens to be the full amount of that spouse's estate—would pass to the family trust. The result is no estate tax on the property passing to the family trust because of the applicable exclusion. On the death of the surviving spouse in 2006, the family trust, no matter what its value, passes free of federal estate tax to your children. The surviving spouse's $2 million applicable exclusion will shelter all of his or her estate.

Figure 4-2 demonstrates the benefits of this planning technique using both estate tax applicable exclusions.

By using both applicable exclusions, your estate tax liability went from $460,000 to zero.

Family Trusts

I like the tax results from using a family trust, but I feel as if I'm disinheriting my wife. Is that what you're suggesting I do?

Certainly not. There are many ways to design the *family trust* (also called a *credit shelter trust*) to provide for your wife and children. Typically, the surviving spouse has substantial rights to the income and principal of the family trust. The family trust can be drafted liberally to allow many benefits for your wife, although she cannot have unrestricted access and control over the family trust. Your attorney will draft your family trust after he or she fully understands your planning goals.

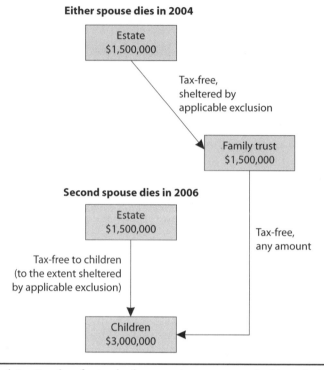

Either spouse dies in 2004

Estate
$1,500,000

Tax-free,
sheltered by
applicable exclusion

Family trust
$1,500,000

Second spouse dies in 2006

Estate
$1,500,000

Tax-free,
any amount

Tax-free to children
(to the extent sheltered
by applicable exclusion)

Children
$3,000,000

Figure 4-2   Results of using both spouses' estate tax applicable exclusions

℞ *What are the maximum rights my husband can have in my family trust?*

The maximum rights a spouse can possess in a family trust are the rights to:

- receive all of the income;
- receive the greater of 5 percent or $5,000 of the trust's principal each year;
- receive distributions in the trustee's discretion for health, education, maintenance, and support; and
- control who receives the property (with a few limitations) at death.

If you give your husband greater rights than these in the family trust, he will be deemed to control the family trust at his death, pulling the full value of the trust property into his estate for tax purposes—the very outcome you sought to avoid by using the family trust.

Is there an income tax on the family trust's income?

Yes, the income earned on the assets in the family trust is subject to income tax. The trust pays the taxes if the income is retained in the trust. If the income is distributed to the surviving spouse or to the children, they must pay income taxes on the amount received at the rates in their respective tax brackets. The trust receives a deduction for the amounts distributed so that the trust income is only taxed once.

Do the assets in the family trust receive a step-up in basis upon the death of either spouse?

On the death of the first spouse, all of his or her non-IRD assets receive a basis adjustment to fair market value, including those assets going to the family trust. Since assets held in the family trust are not included in the surviving spouse's gross estate (they pass to the beneficiaries of the family trust free of estate tax), they do not receive a step-up in basis at the death of the surviving spouse.

When does the family trust end?

Typically, the family trust terminates when the surviving spouse dies. The remaining trust property is then distributed to family members or held in further trust for their benefit, depending on the instructions that the trustmaker included in the document.

Marital Trusts

To take advantage of the marital deduction, do I have to leave property outright to my husband?

That's not necessary. In fact, more and more clients do *not* leave property outright to their surviving spouses but transfer property at their death to marital trusts. There are several advantages for creating a marital trust for a spouse, the most important of which are:

- You can name a cotrustee to serve with your husband and to provide him with asset and financial management assistance.
- By leaving assets in a marital trust, you may provide your husband with creditor protection if he is sued subsequent to your death.

■   The assets left in a marital trust can be protected from a later, perhaps unsuccessful, second marriage of your husband. Additionally, your husband may be able to more comfortably refuse to give away assets or to loan money to other family members or friends by stating that the assets were left in trust and cannot be used for other purposes.

○ঽ *Are there any requirements for the marital trust to ensure that it qualifies for the marital deduction?*

Yes. We describe the various types of marital trusts in some detail in Chapter 2, Planning for Loved Ones. To quickly summarize those requirements, in order to qualify for the marital deduction, the surviving spouse *must* have the following rights:

■   The spouse must have the right to all of the trust's income, paid at least annually, for life.

■   The spouse must be the *only* lifetime beneficiary of the trust; none of the income or principal can be paid to anyone else while the spouse is living.

■   The spouse must be able to direct the trustee to convert non-income-producing assets to income-producing assets.

If these criteria are met, the trust qualifies for the marital deduction. Of course, these are the minimum requirements. There is no limitation with respect to maximum rights.

○ঽ *So how do the different forms of marital trusts vary from one another?*

The major differences among the various marital trusts have to do with the spouse's level of control over and above the rights required by law to qualify the trust for the marital deduction. The amount of control one spouse wants to give to a surviving spouse is dependent on personal goals and desires as much as it is on the tax requirements.

For example, for spouses who wish to give as much control over the marital trust as possible, they would probably use a *total control trust*. With a total control marital trust, the spouse has the right to withdraw as much of the trust property for any reason without any restrictions. The downside of giving this much control, however, is that the trust will not be protected from the surviving spouse's creditors.

Our estate is currently valued at $6 million, owned 50-50 by us. How do my husband and I take advantage of both applicable exclusions and the marital deduction?

Both of you must create wills or revocable living trusts with marital trusts for the benefit of each other and family trusts for your benefit and that of your children. Both trusts will direct the amount of the applicable exclusion to the family trust. Because the applicable exclusion amount will change from time to time over the next 5 years, in order to be effective in the year that you may die, your attorney will not draft your will or trust with a specific dollar amount to be allocated to the family trusts. Rather, he or she will allocate "the current maximum applicable exclusion" to your respective family trusts. The balance of each estate will go to the marital trusts.

We'll assume that your husband dies first in 2008. His family trust would be funded with $2 million, which is the applicable exclusion amount in that year. The balance of his estate, $1 million, will be funded to the marital trust for you. The $2 million in the family trust is sheltered by his estate tax applicable exclusion, and the $1 million in the marital trust qualifies for the marital deduction. Thus, you pay no federal estate tax on your husband's death.

If your will or trust is drafted properly, upon your subsequent death, none of your husband's family trust assets—principal or appreciation—will be included in your estate for federal estate tax purposes, so they will pass estate tax–free to your children. Your estate will consist of your individually owned property ($3 million) and the property remaining in the marital trust, which we will assume will remain at $1 million. Your applicable exclusion will shelter all or part of the $4 million. For example, if you died in 2009, $3.5 million of your $4 million estate would pass tax-free to your children. If you died in 2010, the one year in which there is no estate tax, then the entire $4 million would pass tax-free. Figure 4-3 presents this example and assumes that you die in 2009, which means that your children would pay an estate tax of $225,000. After both deaths, your children would receive $5,775,000 of the combined $6 million estate, a far different amount than if you and your husband had not taken advantage of both estate tax applicable exclusions

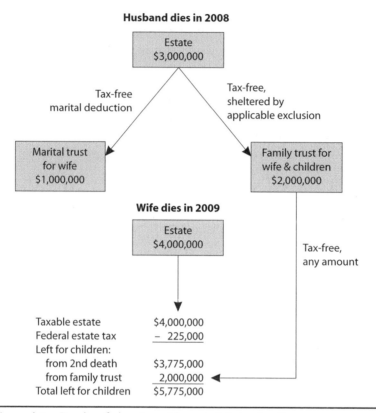

Figure 4-3   Results of planning with marital deduction & estate tax applicable exclusions

and the marital deduction. Without this basic planning, the estate tax at the second death would be $1.125 million versus $225,000—$900,000 more! There are other, more advanced planning options to reduce or even eliminate the $225,000 estate tax due in this example. We discuss most of these alternatives in the balance of this chapter and in Chapter 5, Wealth Transfer Techniques.

℞ *I'm afraid my wife will remarry and that her new husband could take advantage of the money I leave her. Can I set up a marital trust that provides that the trust will terminate and pass to my children if she remarries?*

You can do that, but with substantial adverse federal estate tax consequences. If you include the remarriage provisions that you desire, the marital trust would not qualify for the marital deduction. For the trust to qualify, your wife must receive all of the marital trust income for life under all circumstances. Terminating her income interest in the trust prior to her death disqualifies the trust for the marital deduction. You might consider using a *qualified terminable interest property (QTIP)* trust in which you, not your wife, control who gets the trust property when she dies, so that you can direct the balance to your children. The QTIP trust is widely used in estate planning in second marriages where spouses wish to provide for each other first and then to ensure that children from previous marriages are taken care of. It is the only form of marital trust that gives the first spouse to die control over the disposition of the trust property after the death of the surviving spouse.

Does the marital trust property receive a basis step-up when my spouse dies?

Yes, it does. Regardless of which type of marital trust you use, the property held in the trust will be subject to federal estate taxes when your spouse dies. As a result, the property in the marital trust will automatically receive a basis adjustment, assuming your surviving spouse dies in any year but 2010.

Planning with Community Property

We live in a community property state. Does that affect our estate plan?

Married couples living in a community property state receive a special income tax benefit known as the *double step-up in basis*. With community property, each spouse owns one-half of each marital asset. When one spouse dies, not only does the deceased spouse's interest in the property receive a basis increase, but the surviving spouse's basis in his or her half increases to fair market value as well. This can be a tremendous advantage if a married couple owns highly appreciated assets such as stock or real estate that they held long term or a family business that they built from the ground up.

In contrast, couples living in separate property states with jointly owned property only receive a step-up on the half of the property owned by the deceased spouse.

CR *What if we move from a community property state to a separate property state after we prepare our estate plan? Is there anything we need to do?*

If you have highly appreciated assets, which would benefit from the double step-up in basis, you will want to take steps to make sure that the property maintains its identity as community property. It would be wise to speak to your estate planning attorney before you leave the community property state so that he or she can speak to an attorney in your new state to coordinate the preservation of community property status of these assets.

Updating Existing Plans for the 2001 Tax Act

CR *We created our estate plan in 1999, before the most recent federal estate tax law changes. With all the changes in the law, do we need to change our plan?*

First, we believe that everyone should sit down with their estate planning professionals regularly to review their estate plans. Changes in the laws, your personal situation, and your finances make estate planning an ongoing process.

The 2001 tax act made a number of significant changes to the estate and gift tax laws, and most of them are positive for taxpayers. Still, you need to understand how these changes affect your plan and whether your plan needs revising in response to these changes.

Almost all estate planning documents contain a formula instruction describing how to allocate the decedent's assets between the family trust and the marital trust. The most commonly used formula allocates the largest amount possible (without triggering estate taxes) to the family trust and leaves the balance of the decedent's property to the marital trust. As the applicable exclusion amount increases through 2009, the formula will push more and more assets into the family trust, and less, and finally nothing in 2010, into the marital trust.

Strictly from a tax perspective, this is a good thing. But this result may be contrary to your other planning goals. You may prefer to leave a larger sum in the marital trust for your spouse's exclusive benefit after your death.

There are a variety of ways to draft the formula instruction in your estate plan to avoid "overfunding" the family trust. Your attorney can place a limit on the amount passing to the family trust, expressed as a dollar amount or a percentage of your wealth. You may prefer a more flexible approach, allowing your surviving spouse or a trusted friend some discretion in how much of your estate to place in each trust. The important point for you to understand is that estate planning is not a one-time event. It is an ongoing process that keeps up with the laws, your family situation, your personal goals, and your finances. If you haven't reviewed your estate plan in the past few years, by all means, do so soon.

TECHNIQUES THAT DON'T WORK

Q̃ I've just learned, through the Internet, about a type of trust that totally avoids all income, gift, and estate taxes and is totally private—even the IRS can't find out what's in the trust. I'm thinking about putting my assets into this kind of trust. What do you think?

Using such a "trust" is the same as handling radioactive material and not worrying about getting radiation poisoning. Be aware that various types of trusts—known as "Rockefeller trusts," "constitutional trusts," "common law trusts," and the like—are not the kinds of trusts that reputable estate planning attorneys produce. They are documents that unscrupulous people produce, and they are becoming more prevalent. Indeed, use of these fraudulent trusts has become such a problem that the Internal Revenue Service is taking an aggressive stand against them. Individuals who have such trusts will come under IRS scrutiny. And it appears that the IRS has never lost a case when challenging any of these trusts. A bogus document does not become legitimate simply by calling it a trust.

Q̃ But some of these claims sound a little like those described previously in this book. How can I distinguish a fraudulent or abusive trust from a legitimate trust?

Typically, fraudulent trusts are offered by nonattorneys who promise clients that they are creating a special "secret, elite trust," only known about and used by the wealthy and powerful, in order to eliminate *all* taxes. They are usually promoted with promises of tax benefits and no meaningful change in the makers' control over their assets, even though the trusts are irrevocable and all the makers' assets must be assigned to the trusts.

Typically, promoters make one or more of the following claims as to what the trust can do:

- It can eliminate all estate and gift taxes.
- It can allow income tax deductions for personal expenses paid on behalf of the maker by the trust.
- It can allow depreciation for the maker's house and furnishings.
- It can give a stepped-up basis for property transferred to the trust.
- It can reduce or eliminate self-employment taxes.
- It can reduce or eliminate income taxes, including capital gain taxes.
- It can shelter all assets from the claims of creditors, even though the maker has full use of the assets.

Most often not one of these claims is true. Typically, these trusts employ a method of hiding the true ownership of the assets they hold. These arrangements can utilize more than one irrevocable trust, each holding different assets of the taxpayer. Sometimes a foreign or charitable type of trust is involved, although with a charitable trust, there is personal use of the assets in some manner.

These abusive trusts usually have the original owner of the assets maintaining control over the assets after they are transferred to the trust. The owner retains true control over the financial benefits of the trust. The trust may have a trustee, who will often be the promoter or a friend of the maker, who simply carries out the instructions of the maker. Sometimes, the trustee gives the owner checks that are presigned by the trustee.

ℭℛ *What are the consequences of setting up such abusive trusts?*

Currently, the IRS is characterizing pure-equity trusts, constitutional trusts, and all other such trusts as "abusive trust arrangements." Under a program called National Compliance Strategy, the IRS is currently investigating these types of trust arrangements and subjecting the promoters and involved taxpayers to civil penalties and criminal charges. A national coordinated enforcement initiative is being made to catch and punish the users of these abusive trust schemes.

The IRS easily attacks the validity of these trusts by using long-standing legitimate laws applicable to trusts. Substance over form always controls taxation. For example, if personal expenses (education, personal travel, maintenance of residence) are being deducted, the IRS characterizes the whole operation as a "sham transaction." In addition to being fraudulent, many of these trusts are sold by fly-by-night operations. Remember, when the IRS starts investigating the taxpayers who made these trusts, the promoters will be long gone with no forwarding addresses, leaving their defenseless victims to fend for themselves against the IRS.

ACTION STEPS

We respectfully present the following action steps to summarize the concepts that we discussed in chapter 4 and to suggest steps that you can take to prepare for meetings with your estate planning team of professionals.

☐ *Estimate the value of your estate.* Prepare a list of your major assets with estimates of their values. Don't forget values of retirement plans and life insurance death benefits. Note on the list how each asset is titled, that is, how you own it—sole ownership, trust ownership, joint tenancy, community property, and so forth. Also add up your major debts. If you anticipate receiving an inheritance at some point, try to estimate its value, too. If you are married, combine the totals of your individual estates.

☐ *Estimate your current estate tax liability.* If you're up for a challenge, calculate the federal estate tax that would be due using the tables in this chapter, assuming you died today. Better yet, find an attorney, accountant, financial planner, or life insurance expert to do the number crunching for you.

☐ *Make tax-free gifts.* Depending on your financial situation, making annual tax-free gifts to loved ones may be the best strategy for you to minimize estate taxes. In addition to giving away the annual exclusion amount, you can pay for medical and schooling costs without paying gift tax. A financial planner can help you determine how much you can afford to give away while maintaining your lifestyle. If you were considering any of the options from Chapter 2, Planning for Loved Ones, for paying for your children's or grandchildren's education, you can discuss those options with the financial planner at the same time.

☐ *Avoid leaving everything to your spouse without planning.* Leaving all your property to a surviving spouse may seem like the right thing to do, but for tax planning, it's usually a mistake. Work with an estate planning attorney who can demonstrate the importance of using your estate tax applicable exclusion to minimize estate taxes at the second death.

❏ *Discuss the structure of your family trust with your estate planning attorney.* As long as you don't give your spouse too much control over this trust, you are generally free to structure your family trust any way that you wish.

❏ *Stay away from scams and shams.* Avoid disreputable planners who make promises that sound too good to be true. Representations about income tax avoidance, constitutional trusts, pure-equity trusts, and the like are signs that you need to end the meeting and find a legitimate advisor.

❏ *Locate a qualified estate planning advisor.* Pick your professionals carefully. Your primary advisor can be an attorney, financial planner, accountant, life insurance agent, or any other advisor skilled in estate planning. The point is that you must have competent advice to design and to implement your estate plan. If the advisor is not an attorney, he or she will be pleased to recommend a qualified one to assist you in designing and overseeing the implementation of your plan.

❏ *Review your plan regularly.* Laws change, families change, and circumstances change. You should review your estate plan every year or so to make sure it keeps up with these changes. Some advisors have a systematic process for reviews at regular intervals; others may want you to take the lead in scheduling follow-up visits. Either way, a good advisor will notify you if there are changes in the law. You should contact your advisor promptly if there is a significant change in your personal, financial, family, or business affairs.

chapter 5

Wealth Transfer Techniques

INTRODUCTION TO LIFETIME TRANSFERS

ℭ *Should I consider making gifts to my children and other heirs?*

While love and affection are significant motivations for making gifts, there are also tax advantages in doing so. By making gifts annually, you are removing assets and any future income and appreciation on those assets from your taxable estate. To the extent that your estate is taxable, you will save estate taxes for your beneficiaries on the value of the gifts and related appreciation that will occur until your death.

There are a number of questions you should ask yourself in deciding whether to make gifts to your children and others, regardless of how much in taxes it might save your estate: "How much can I afford to give away and still maintain my lifestyle?" "Am I prepared to give up control of my assets while I am alive?" "What will my children do with it—will they save it or spend it?"

ℭ *I would like to make gifts to my children and grandchildren to reduce estate taxes, but I am afraid I may need those assets before I die. Do I have any options?*

Before you give away assets, you should determine how much you can afford to give away. Take into consideration your current standard of living, your projected living needs, and the amounts you might need for emergencies and long-term health care.

We once represented an 83-year-old widow who had a $4 million estate, all in municipal bonds, paying 5 percent at the time. She lived a simple life, needing only $50,000 a year to meet her needs. Anyone could logically see that she had four times the amount of income that she needed to live on from her bond portfolio, and the bond portfolio was more than enough for a "rainy day fund." Still, she worried that she might need all of it some day and would not consider making gifts. She died several years later, quietly in her sleep. Her family paid more than $2 million in what could have been unnecessary federal estate taxes.

Deciding whether to make gifts can be an emotional issue, and we all know that fears and doubts can often overcome even the most logical plan. As estate planning professionals, our first priority is to design a plan that will protect your quality of life. We never encourage clients to bankrupt themselves or to jeopardize their security for the benefit of their heirs. Your financial advisor or estate planning attorney can help you calculate just how much, if any, he or she believes that you can comfortably afford to give. Later in this chapter we will explore planning tools that allow you to make gifts of your property to family members while retaining some benefits from the property. For the charitably inclined, we described in Chapter 3, Planning for Loved Ones and Charity, techniques for making gifts to charities that allow the donor to reserve rights to the income.

 formerly *What is the simplest gifting plan that my husband and I might implement?*

The simplest strategy is to give away money or property worth up to the annual exclusion amount each year. Since you are married, you and your husband could give away double the annual exclusion amount per donee. In 2004, the annual exclusion amount is $11,000 for individuals and $22,000 for married couples.

Let's assume that you have two married children and three grandchildren; that makes five potential donees. And assuming that you like your children's spouses, there could be seven donees. This means that you and your husband could give away up to $154,000 annually. Over 10 years, that's $1.54 million—$1.54 million that won't be subject to federal estate or gift taxes, potentially saving your heirs hundreds of thousands of dollars in unnecessary estate taxes.

○꒓ Can I use part of my gift tax exclusion to make gifts during my lifetime?

If you want to remove more than the amount of the annual exclusion from your estate, you can use all or part of your gift tax applicable exclusion amount. For example, if you make a $100,000 gift to a single donee, you must file a gift tax return. On the return, you would report a taxable gift of $89,000 ($100,000 – $11,000). Your $1 million gift tax exclusion will be reduced by $89,000.

○꒓ If I use all or part of my $1 million gift tax applicable exclusion, how does it affect my estate tax applicable exclusion?

Keep in mind that even though the Economic Growth and Tax Relief Reconciliation Act of 2001 (EGTRRA, or 2001 tax act) delineated the gift tax applicable exclusion and the estate tax applicable exclusion as separate exclusions (chapter 4, Table 4-4), they are applied in a unified manner. For example, in 2006 the estate tax applicable exclusion is $2 million and the gift tax applicable exclusion is $1 million. If you give assets valued at $1 million to your child in 2006 and then die in that same year, the estate tax applicable exclusion of $2 million is reduced by the $1 million gift you made. Thus your estate has only a $1 million applicable exclusion remaining to reduce estate taxes. If you don't make any gifts and you die in 2006, you can't add the two exclusions—you do *not* have $3 million to use as an applicable exclusion; you have only the $2 million as an estate tax exclusion.

While the gift tax applicable exclusion is constant at $1 million through 2010, the estate tax exclusion increases gradually through 2009. So between now and December 31, 2009, you can transfer up to $1 million gift tax–free during your lifetime and then pass the difference between the amount of gift tax exclusion you use (up to $1 million) and the amount of the estate tax exclusion at death.

Also, remember that the 2001 tax act does *not* repeal the gift tax. The gift tax remains in effect after 2009, evidently to make sure that taxpayers do not give away too many of their assets to avoid the estate tax when it returns in 2011.

ᖇ *Since there may not be any estate tax in the future, does it make sense to make gifts in excess of the gift tax applicable exclusion?*

Though we think it is unlikely that Congress will permanently repeal the estate tax, the fact is that the chances of that happening are better now than ever before. For that reason, except for clients with substantial wealth or other compelling circumstances, we do not generally recommend at this time that clients incur gift taxes, that is, make gifts in excess of $1 million.

Having said that, we still believe that making lifetime gifts is an important strategy to avoid future estate taxes, whatever they ultimately turn out to be. Viable reasons still remain to shift wealth to younger family members. And, since "what Congress giveth, Congress can taketh away," there is no guarantee that an estate tax or something similar will not be re-enacted before you die. In this chapter, you will discover techniques for making lifetime gifts (without paying gift tax) that have the potential for transferring in excess of $1 million to your family.

Lifetime Gifts versus Gifts at Death

ᖇ *Why would I want to use my exclusion on gifts during my lifetime rather than saving it until my death?*

Using your gift tax exclusion on gifts during your lifetime is much more tax-efficient than using your exclusion to reduce estate taxes at death. When you make a gift, all future appreciation in the value of the gifted property accrues outside of your estate and is not subject to estate tax at your death. For example, assume that you make a gift of $1 million to your children today. If you live for another 20 years and that property appreciates at 7.2 percent, it doubles in value every 10 years. At your death it would be worth $4 million. The assets you gave away appreciated $3 million after you made the gift. That $3 million will *not* be part of your estate for estate tax purposes and will have passed to your children without the imposition of either estate or gift tax.

On the other hand, had you not made the gift, then the $4 million of property remains in your estate and is subject to estate tax. If you are in the top estate tax bracket when you die, your estate could incur close to $2 million in estate taxes.

⋈ *Can I use my annual exclusion to make gifts in trust?*

The annual exclusion amount is only for gifts of a "present interest" in property. Gifts to trusts are generally "future-interest" gifts that do not qualify. However, there are sound ways to qualify gifts to irrevocable trusts for the annual exclusion.

Making Gifts in Trust to Qualify for the Annual Exclusion

⋈ *How do I qualify gifts in trust for my annual exclusion?*

To qualify gifts to a trust for the annual exclusion:

- You must give up control over the gifts that you make to the trust. This requires that you create an irrevocable trust.
- You must create a present interest for your beneficiaries. To do this the trust must contain "demand-right" language or instructions, which means that the beneficiaries of your trust must have the current right to withdraw the money or property that you gave to the trust. If the beneficiaries do not request that the money or property be given to them within a pre-set period of time, the trustee can maintain the money or property in the trust and manage it per your instructions in the trust.

Gifts to accounts subject to the Uniform Gifts to Minors Act (UGMA) or to the Uniform Transfers to Minors Act (UTMA) also qualify as annual exclusion gifts.

A Primer on Irrevocable Trusts

⋈ *What is an irrevocable trust?*

An *irrevocable trust* is a trust that cannot be changed or amended by its maker after it is signed. Irrevocable trusts are used to make gifts to others—the trust beneficiaries—"with strings attached."

When making gifts in trust, you transfer property to someone that you have chosen to serve as trustee, accompanied by a set of written instructions on how the property is to be managed and used for the benefit of your trust beneficiaries. These instructions are the strings attached to the gift. Gifts in trust enable the donor to control the use for which the gifts were intended.

∞ Why would I want to create an irrevocable trust?

If one of your goals is to reduce your estate taxes, an irrevocable trust may be the way to plan. Irrevocable trusts can be used to make annual exclusion gifts and taxable gifts. They can be used to make gifts of specific types of property, such as a residence, and they can be used to make gifts of principal in general while allowing the maker to retain the income for a period of years. To keep the trust's assets out of your taxable estate and to keep the trust's income out of your taxable income, you have to give up the power to revoke or to amend the trust, and you also have to give up the right to subsequently designate—outside of the trust's instructions—to whom or in what amounts trust income and principal are to be paid.

∞ Why would I want to set up a trust in which I relinquish total control?

You don't really give up "total" control. You establish the ground rules in the trust document, through your instructions, and you appoint the trustees to carry out those instructions.

∞ What's the difference between an irrevocable trust and a revocable living trust?

The major difference is reflected in the name—you cannot retain in an *irrevocable trust* the power to "revoke" it or to change its terms. If you could, the trust property would be treated for tax purposes in the same way as your revocable living trust property: It would be included in your taxable estate.

A *revocable living trust* is very much like a will in that it can be easily changed or amended, canceled, or revoked at any time without any requirement or reason for doing so. An irrevocable trust is nothing more than a complete and absolute gift that is made with strings attached. You can place the contingencies, requests, and prohibitions you wish into your irrevocable trust terms, but you cannot retain the right to change or alter it after you execute it.

☞ Can creditors attack my irrevocable trust?

You may not create a trust and place your assets beyond the reach of your existing creditors to defraud them in the case of an existing obligation or requirement. If, however, in good faith you place assets into a trust in which you are not a beneficiary or potential beneficiary, and you are subsequently sued by a future creditor, such a creditor will generally be prohibited from accessing the trust or the gifts you made to it.

In some states, including Alaska, Delaware, Nevada, and Rhode Island, it is possible to create a trust that allows the maker to have some rights in the trust and to still prevent creditors from taking the assets in the trust. These asset protection trusts are highly specialized and should be drafted only by highly skilled estate planning attorneys. We discuss asset protection trusts in greater detail in Chapter 11, Asset Protection Planning.

☞ What types of investments can an irrevocable trust own?

An irrevocable trust may own all types of assets. You can specify or list which assets it can own, refer to the state statute that lists those assets, or combine both in your trust instructions.

☞ Can an irrevocable trust ever be changed or revoked?

A trustee who is not the maker or a beneficiary of the irrevocable trust can be granted authority under the terms of the trust instrument to make limited amendments to the trust agreement. These amendments are generally limited to technical items arising from changes in the law or inadvertent drafting errors.

An irrevocable trust can be revoked only under special circumstances. These circumstances usually arise when the trust's purpose cannot be accomplished, such as when the trust is for a disabled child and the child has a medical recovery or when a change in the tax law makes the trust useless. To revoke an irrevocable trust, the trustee petitions a court having jurisdiction over it, after giving notice to all affected persons. The court may grant to the trustee and the beneficiaries the right to terminate the trust and to distribute the assets as provided in the trust instrument; however, courts rarely authorize termination.

A Primer on Demand Trusts

❧ *What is a gift of a present interest?*

To qualify for the annual exclusion, the gift must be a gift of a present interest. A *present interest* is defined as the unrestricted right to the use, possession, or enjoyment of property or the income from property. In other words, the recipient must be able to touch, feel, taste, and, above all, be able to use the gift immediately.

For example, if you give one of your children $11,000, whether in cash or by transferring assets into the name of the child, so that you have no further control over the assets, you've made a gift of a present interest that qualifies for the annual exclusion. But suppose you give the cash or assets to an irrevocable trust with instructions to hold the cash or assets until your child turns age 50. In this case, you have not given a present interest; you have made a gift of a *future interest*—your child won't actually enjoy the gift until age 50.

❧ *What are demand trusts?*

A *demand right* in estate planning is normally a right given to beneficiaries of an irrevocable trust to demand up to an amount that is the lesser of the beneficiary's share of the contribution made to the trust or the annual exclusion. The beneficiary can then "demand" his or her share of the contribution within a certain period of time after you make the transfer to the trust (usually 30 to 45 days). Because you have given the beneficiary the option of receiving the gift immediately with no further restrictions, the demand right qualifies the gift as a gift of a present interest for purposes of the annual exclusion. Accordingly, trusts that give beneficiaries this right are known as *demand trusts*.

Of course, your purpose in setting up your irrevocable trust will be undermined if your beneficiary—your child or grandchild—actually exercises his or her power to withdraw what you give to the trust. While the demand right must give your beneficiary the legal right to demand a withdrawal, in the usual family situation, all that is required is to explain to the beneficiary that your overall estate plan, and the family's best interests, will be served by his or her not exercising the demand right. However, it is important that there is no agreement preventing the beneficiary from exercising a demand right; the beneficiary must have the legal right to make the demand if he or she so desires.

ℭℛ *What's a Crummey Trust?*

A *Crummey trust* is another name for a demand trust. There is nothing crummy or shabby about a demand trust. The name "Crummey" comes from a U.S. Tax Court case in the 1960s that approved the use of a demand right to make a gift to a trust eligible for the gift tax annual exclusion.

ℭℛ *Does the trustee have to give my beneficiaries notice of this right?*

Obviously, a beneficiary cannot exercise a right that he or she doesn't know about. So, for the gift to qualify for the annual exclusion, it is vital that all of the trust beneficiaries receive notice of each gift and of their right to withdraw their share of the gift from the trust. It is the recommendation of most attorneys that the trustee send written notices without fail each time a trustmaker makes a gift to the trust. In addition, the trustee generally obtains a written acknowledgment from the beneficiaries that they received the notice, so there is a record that each beneficiary was advised of his or her rights. In our view, sending out notices each time a gift is made is a small price to pay to have the assurance that you can readily meet your burden of proof.

ℭℛ *Can a demand right be given to a minor beneficiary?*

You can give a demand right to a minor beneficiary through his or her guardian. In most states, a minor's parent is the natural guardian of the minor, so the notice usually goes to the minor's mother or father. If you have a minor child and make gifts to an irrevocable trust for the child, your spouse, as natural guardian, has the legal authority to exercise or not to exercise the demand right on the child's behalf.

ℭℛ *Are there any gift tax consequences of a demand trust on the beneficiaries?*

In addition to the annual-exclusion gift limitations, there is another limitation that may apply to demand trusts. This limitation is called the *5-and-5 limit*. Whenever a beneficiary of a demand trust declines to withdraw the gift made to the trust by the donor, the event is known as a *lapse*. Upon a lapse, that beneficiary is, for federal gift tax purposes, making a gift to the other trust beneficiaries of the amount allowed to lapse. The result can be that the beneficiary is involuntarily using up part of his or her gift tax applicable exclusion. This adverse result applies only to lapse amounts greater than $5,000 or 5 percent of the value of the trust.

It is for this reason that some planners advise limiting gifts to demand trusts to no more than $5,000 per beneficiary per year. Skilled attorneys can design trusts to get around the 5-and-5 limit in most instances.

LIFETIME GIFTS
TO FAMILY

Irrevocable Life Insurance Trust
(for wealth creation and replacement, or liquidity)

Purposes of the ILIT

CR *Doesn't my life insurance go to my children tax-free when I die?*

Life insurance does go to beneficiaries free of *income* tax. However, if you own the policy or have incidents of ownership over a policy on your life when you die, the proceeds will be included in your estate and will be subject to estate tax.

The way to avoid estate tax on your insurance proceeds is to have the policy owned by someone else. If the policy is owned by your children, directly, or by an irrevocable trust for their benefit, the proceeds of the policy will not be included in your estate.

CR *What are incidents of ownership?*

If the insured has any rights or privileges as to the life insurance policy or can access its cash value in any way, the insured has *incidents of ownership* in the policy. The Internal Revenue Code (IRC) provides that if the insured retains any rights in the policy, the proceeds will be included in his or her gross estate. Therefore, the insured cannot retain any rights in the policy, such as the right to borrow the cash value or to change the beneficiary of the policy.

ℂℜ *What's the role of life insurance in estate planning?*

Life insurance can:

- Provide liquidity for your heirs to pay estate taxes, debts, and administration costs
- Create an inheritance for your children and grandchildren
- Fund charitable bequests or serve as a substitute for your family for other assets that you donate to charity

ℂℜ *What is an irrevocable life insurance trust?*

An *irrevocable life insurance trust (ILIT)* is an irrevocable trust that is created to own and to be the beneficiary of life insurance policies on the trustmaker's life. Properly drafted, it does not allow the insured to retain any incidents of ownership in the policies.

ℂℜ *Why would I want to have an irrevocable life insurance trust?*

The primary benefit of an ILIT to own life insurance is that the policy's death benefit is not subject to federal estate tax when the insured dies. As we explained in a previous answer, if an insured dies with incidents of ownership over a life insurance policy on his or her life, the death benefit is subject to federal estate taxes. With an ILIT, the trust, not the insured, has all incidents of ownership, so the policy is not subject to federal estate taxes when the insured dies.

Moreover, since an ILIT is an irrevocable trust, it provides all the other benefits normally associated with them, including asset protection and dynasty planning.

ℂℜ *Who actually owns the life insurance policies?*

The ILIT, through its trustees, is both the owner and the beneficiary of life insurance policies on the trustmaker's life.

ℂℜ *Why can't one of my children own the insurance policy rather than using an ILIT?*

If you are using life insurance to provide liquidity to pay estate taxes when you die, you are strongly advised to place ownership of the policy in an irrevocable life insurance trust. Compared with the alternative of outright ownership of the policy by children, the irrevocable trust offers flexibility and safety in a number of ways:

- Minor children cannot own a policy.

- Adult children do not always act in a coordinated, timely, and responsible manner when called on to pay premiums to keep the policy in force.

- Even when adult children are responsible, a misfortune such as a lawsuit, bankruptcy, divorce, or death may put the policy at risk.

- If one of your children predeceases you, that child's interest in your life insurance policy will pass to someone else in accordance with the provisions of his or her estate plan or state law. The new owner may not be a family member and could possibly change the beneficiary designation or make other modifications that you would not find acceptable.

- Assuming the policy is kept in force by the children until your death, there is no assurance that all the children will act in concert to use the proceeds to provide the liquidity needed for paying the taxes on yours or your spouse's estate.

- Outright ownership of a policy by children precludes the use of generation-skipping transfer taxes and thus may unnecessarily subject unexpended proceeds to estate tax in the children's estates.

Features of the ILIT

℘ *Can you explain how the ILIT works? How do we make gifts to it and how will the trust pay the life insurance premiums?*

Here are the steps to follow to set up an ILIT and to pay the policy premiums on the life insurance it will own:

1. You and your advisors design the terms of your ILIT for the benefit of its beneficiaries.

2. Your attorney drafts the trust document, which you sign.

3. Thereafter, the trustee purchases a life insurance policy on your life, or you transfer an existing policy to the ILIT. (If you transfer an existing policy to the trust, you must live 3 years from the

date of the transfer to keep the policy proceeds out of your estate.)

4. You make gifts to the trust to cover the amount of the policy premiums.

5. The trustee sends a notice to the trust beneficiaries stating that you made a gift and that they have the right to withdraw their share of it.

6. If they do not withdraw their gift within a specific time (usually 30 to 45 days), the trustee will keep the gift in trust and manage it pursuant to the trust terms.

7. The trustee uses the gifts to the trust to pay the policy premiums.

You do not own the policy; the trust does. After your death, the death proceeds are not subject to income or estate tax, and the terms of the trust dictate when and how the proceeds will be paid to your beneficiaries.

◌ℜ *What provisions should I include in my ILIT?*

To a great extent, the terms of your ILIT will be dictated by your personal planning goals rather than by tax objectives. But in our experience, a well-drafted ILIT will almost always include the following terms:

■ The trustee will have the power and responsibility to pay the insurance policy premiums.

■ The trustee will have the right to engage in legal proceedings, if necessary, to collect policy proceeds.

■ The trustee will have the authority to purchase additional policies.

■ The trustee will be authorized (but not directed) to voluntarily lend trust principal to the trustmaker's estate or the maker's spouse's estate or to purchase assets from the estate of either the trustmaker or the maker's spouse.

■ The trustmaker will be prohibited from having any rights over the life insurance policies during his or her life.

■ The trust beneficiaries will be given the present right to take annual exclusion gifts upon notification by the trustee of these rights of withdrawal.

■ The trust will authorize the trustee to pour over the life insurance proceeds to the maker's living trust or estate if for any reason the proceeds are included in his or her taxable estate.

- The trust will contain the maker's instructions for disposition of the life insurance proceeds after his or her death.

Can I provide in the ILIT that after my death the proceeds will stay in my trust and be used to care for my family?

You can provide for your family in a number of ways. You can state, for example:

> I want my trustee to pay my wife all of the trust income, and whatever she needs from the principal in the trustee's discretion.

> I want my trustee to provide for the needs of my wife and children.

> I want my trustee to provide for the needs of my wife, children, and grandchildren.

> I want my trustee to provide for the needs of my wife, children, grandchildren, my parents, and my wife's parents.

Is there any way for my beneficiaries to use the cash value of the life insurance before my death?

Yes. You can give the trustee the flexibility to make loans or distributions from the cash value of the policy. The trustee can then distribute or lend the funds to the trust beneficiaries in accordance with the standards you specify in the trust document. Only certain types of insurance have cash value, and some severely restrict the terms of loans. Your professional advisors can help you make and provide for these choices.

My husband set up an ILIT and made me the trustee. How important is it that I send out the demand letters?

The purpose of setting up an ILIT is to make gifts to the trust with no gift tax liability and to remove the proceeds of the life insurance from the insured's estate.

Making sure that the beneficiaries of the trust have actual notice of the gifts made to the trust is critical. Only when beneficiaries have proper notice can they decide whether to leave the gifts in the trust or to demand that the trustee distribute the gifts to them. The Internal Revenue Service (IRS) looks for evidence that ILIT beneficiaries participated in a prearranged understanding with the trustmaker not to remove or demand the gifts. Without proof that the beneficiaries had notice of the gifts, the IRS could successfully argue that the beneficiaries had no meaningful opportunity to demand the gifts.

☞ *Who is responsible for collecting my life insurance proceeds?*

Your ILIT trustee will collect the policy death benefits and then distribute them to the beneficiaries or hold the proceeds in the trust for their benefit according to the terms you specified in the trust document.

☞ *On the basis of your experience, do you have any particular cautions concerning ILITs?*

Yes. Do not write the checks for life insurance premiums to the insurance company. If you do, you may defeat your planning. Write your checks to your ILIT trustee; then let the trustee deposit the money in the trust checking account and write the check on the trust's account to the life insurance company.

Trustees of the ILIT

☞ *Can I be the trustee of my ILIT?*

The trustmaker-insured should never be the trustee of an ILIT. This would give the insured incidents of ownership sufficient to bring the insurance proceeds into his or her estate, thus voiding the benefits of the ILIT. Also, it is recommended that the spouse of the insured *not* be the sole trustee of an ILIT of which he or she is a beneficiary, since the trustee's power to distribute assets to himself or herself could cause the assets to be included in the spouse's estate.

☞ *Can I terminate my ILIT trustees?*

You can provide instructions in your trust document as to how trustees are to be hired and fired. You cannot directly retain the hiring and firing rights, as doing so would place the trust property back into your taxable estate.

CR *Who do you recommend to serve as trustee?*

In our experience, the best trustee for an ILIT is a professional trustee, such as a bank or other corporate trustee; or an accountant. You can have a family member serve as trustee alone, but a better approach is to name a trusted advisor, such as your accountant, as a cotrustee to assist your family member in paying life insurance premiums, filing any required income tax returns, and sending required notifications to trust beneficiaries.

Many trustmakers include provisions in their trust agreements for a family member to serve as trustee during the trustmaker's life. After the insured dies, when sophisticated trust administration and investment management is needed, the trust provides that a corporate trustee be appointed successor trustee or cotrustee with the family member.

Tax Aspects of the ILIT

CR *I'd like to set up an ILIT, but I don't want to lose the opportunity to give money to my children so that they can use it now, while they need it. Can I do both?*

You can make gifts to an ILIT and make other gifts to your children if you want to. Let's examine how this might work.

The amount you give to the trust is a function of the annual premium on the life insurance that your advisors have suggested would be right for you and your family. If the annual premium divided by the number of trust beneficiaries is less than the gift tax annual exclusion for each beneficiary, you can make additional gifts to your children of the difference between the per-beneficiary premium amount and the annual exclusion amount.

CR *Should I use my gift tax applicable exclusion for life insurance premiums in excess of my annual exclusion, or should I use it for other purposes?*

The answer depends on your other circumstances. However, using your gift tax exclusion to purchase life insurance is generally a wise decision, since the death proceeds are usually far greater than the total amount of premiums to be paid over your lifetime. This is especially true if you do not live a long life.

When life insurance premiums use up a person's gift tax exclusion, professionals refer to the transaction as "leveraging the exclusion" because the life insurance proceeds are far greater than the gift tax exclusion expended.

Cℛ *The amount of premium for my insurance is greater than the $5,000 that can lapse each year without causing a gift tax problem for my beneficiaries. How do I pay the premiums without creating a tax problem for my loved ones?*

There are three main ways to get around the limitations of the $5,000 or 5 percent limit that we explained earlier in this chapter.

1. Use some of your $1 million lifetime gift tax applicable exclusion.
2. Your attorney can draft the ILIT document to create a separate trust share within the ILIT for each beneficiary. It is impossible to make a gift to oneself, and since there is only one beneficiary of each separate share, each beneficiary cannot be deemed to have made a gift that is in excess of the $5,000 or 5 percent limit. However, when the beneficiary dies, some part of the trust will be includable in the beneficiary's estate.
3. Your attorney can draft the trust to use "hanging powers." This is a somewhat complicated technique, but provided that your beneficiaries don't die prematurely, hanging powers can avoid the adverse estate and gift tax consequences for your beneficiaries.

It is important to seek the assistance of a skilled attorney to draft the correct provisions into your irrevocable life insurance trust.

Cℛ *I have a piece of real estate worth $5 million that should be worth $10 million by the time I die. I've heard that the transfer costs of a gift during life are less than those of a bequest at death. Could an ILIT produce an even more attractive result?*

Transferring the property now will be less expensive than holding on to the property until you die, especially if the property appreciates in value. If you make a $5 million gift of real estate to your children today, the gift tax will be approximately $1.9 million in 2004. Alternatively, if you do not make the gift and the real estate appreciates to $10 million by the time of your death, the estate tax on the property will be between $3 and $4 million. For most people, the thought of paying several million dollars in estate or gift taxes is unacceptable.

However, it may be possible for you to avoid this dilemma. For far less money, you might be able to purchase an insurance policy through an ILIT that would produce a death benefit large enough to pay the estate taxes. The life insurance policy allows you to leverage your gifts to the ILIT and to transfer the real estate to your children at a much lower out-of-pocket cost than paying either estate or gift taxes from your other wealth.

℞ *Must my ILIT file a federal income tax return?*

An ILIT is a separate entity for tax purposes. For this reason, the ILIT trustee should obtain a federal taxpayer identification number. An ILIT must file federal income tax returns if its gross income is $600 or more in any year. This rarely happens while the insured is alive, because the cash value, or inside buildup in the policy, is not taxable income until withdrawals in excess of the policy payments are made.

℞ *Can my ILIT pay my estate taxes directly to the government?*

That's a bad idea. If your ILIT trustee is legally obligated to pay your estate taxes or other debts of your estate, then the death benefit becomes subject to estate tax. A properly drawn ILIT will allow the trustee to lend money to, or buy assets from, your estate. In this way, cash is moved from the ILIT to your estate to pay taxes, debts, and administrative expenses without causing the life insurance proceeds to be included in your estate.

Disadvantages of the ILIT

℞ *Are there disadvantages to using an ILIT?*

While ILITs are a safe and attractive means of transferring assets and providing liquidity, their main disadvantage is their irrevocability. If circumstances change beyond what you envisioned in your trust instructions, the results could be less than you expected since you are incapable of changing the terms.

℞ *My investment counselor says I should not lock my life insurance*

into an irrevocable trust. But my estate planning attorney says I would benefit from an ILIT. Why am I getting two different opinions?

Different opinions come from different perspectives and often from different bases of knowledge. That is the reason why a team of professional advisors coordinating their efforts is so valuable; you can get a variety of views on the same issue, and new insights and planning can take place.

The correct answer for you depends on your personal goals and objectives. Furthermore, the two positions are not mutually exclusive. You can own some life insurance in your name so that you can access its cash value as you deem appropriate. Such a policy will increase the size of your estate for calculating estate taxes, but that is the price of total access and control over the policy.

However, if your primary purpose in purchasing insurance is not to access cash, but to pay estate taxes or to provide benefits federal estate tax–free to your loved ones in the event of your death, an ILIT is the best way to accomplish those goals.

Perspective changes the way an issue appears. For example, when you look at an elephant, it makes a world of difference if you look at it from the front, the rear, above, or below. From all directions, it is an elephant, but your viewpoint may dramatically alter the action you take to avoid being trampled by the elephant. This is true with the directions given to you by professional advisors. The most important advisor is the one who coordinates the others on your team to offer all the perspectives and to get all the advisors to see from one another's viewpoint so that you have the best estate plan for your needs and goals.

The Insurance

ᑫ *Is it a good idea to transfer existing life insurance policies into my ILIT?*

It is rarely a good idea to transfer existing policies into an ILIT if the maker is insurable. If the insured owns the policy, he or she has an incident of ownership in it. The IRC provides that if the insured transfers any incidents of ownership in existing policies and subsequently dies within 3 years of the transfer, the entire proceeds are included in his or her estate.

Furthermore, transferring an existing policy to an ILIT constitutes a gift. The value of the policy for gift tax purposes is "the interpolated terminal reserve value, plus unused premium." The interpolated terminal reserve value includes not only the cash value of the policy but also, among other things, the value of having an insurance company legally obligated to pay a death benefit upon the insured's death. By having the ILIT trustee acquire a new policy, the insured will not be making a gift of an insurance policy with an interpolated terminal reserve value.

⊂⅁ Can my trustee purchase term insurance for my ILIT?

Yes, your trustee is free to purchase term, whole life, variable life, universal life, or any other form of life insurance for your ILIT. There are reasons for the purchase of each, and your trustee should coordinate the necessary decisions with the trust's insurance advisor and attorney.

⊂⅁ Our attorney has advised us to establish a joint ILIT funded with a "second-to-die" insurance policy. What's that?

As we discussed earlier, in most situations with a married couple, no estate taxes are due when the first spouse dies; the estate tax liability arises only after both spouses are deceased. Given that fact, in many cases the couple does not need the life insurance to pay a death benefit until both have died. A *second-to-die life insurance policy* is a perfectly designed product for these situations. As the name implies, a second-to-die policy insures two lives, and only pays when both insureds are deceased. Second-to-die life insurance is far less costly than life insurance on the life of any one spouse or policies purchased separately on each spouse's life.

⊂⅁ Why should I go to the time and expense of establishing an ILIT, only to find out that I am uninsurable?

Most people are justifiably reluctant to go to the time and expense of establishing an ILIT until they know whether they are insurable and at what cost. For this reason, they frequently sign insurance applications before their trusts are drafted and signed. This exposes the insurance proceeds to taxation if the insureds die within 3 years.

One option to avoid this dilemma is to have someone else sign the insurance application as the proposed owner. Adult children, close relatives, or a business partner all have a potential insurable interest in the trustmaker and could sign the application.

Once the insurance underwriting is completed, and you complete and sign your ILIT, the policy can be reapplied for by the ILIT trustee without concern for the 3-year rule.

CR *How much should I rely on a life insurance illustration at the time that I purchase the insurance policy owned by my ILIT?*

A life insurance illustration is not the policy. The total cost and benefits of a policy today will depend upon such variables as investment yields, administrative expenses, mortality costs, and the number of policyholders who will cancel their policies in the future. Ultimate policy performance has little to do with the illustration.

Policy illustrations are useful only as road maps to assist buyers in understanding how their policies might perform. Not all life insurance companies and their agents always fully disclose the optimistic assumptions made in the illustrations. Consequently, you should work with a competent insurance professional, whose credentials are known to you, along with a qualified estate planning attorney, and, if appropriate, a financial advisor and an accountant. If there is any doubt about the illustration, always seek a second opinion.

CR *If I have been told that I am uninsurable, is it still possible for me to purchase life insurance?*

Many times the factors that one insurance company uses to determine noninsurability are not the same factors another life insurance company will use in making its underwriting decisions. It is likely that there will be some life insurance companies willing to insure you even though you have been rated uninsurable by another company's underwriters.

Certain life insurance needs can be met with a *joint life insurance policy* (also called *survivorship, last-to-die,* or *second-to-die* life insurance) since the insurance company's risk is minimized by insuring two—or more—lives under one policy. Even though one of the lives is rated uninsurable, policy coverage may nevertheless be obtained by underwriting that life with a healthy one.

Ↄ *What is "wait-and-see" life insurance?*

Wait-and-see life insurance is an alternative to an irrevocable life insurance trust. A husband and wife each purchase life insurance on the other's life. The husband's living trust owns the policy insuring the wife's life, and the wife's living trust owns the policy insuring the husband's life. Figure 5-1 depicts the following example.

Assume the husband dies first. The full death benefit on the husband's life will be paid to the wife's living trust for her use.

The insurance policy on the wife, which is owned by the husband's revocable trust, is allocated after the husband's death to his family trust rather than to the marital trust. The family trust is then the owner and the beneficiary of the policy.

The family trust, which is the trust that receives the amount of the applicable exclusion, is sheltered from estate tax on the death of the husband and on the wife's subsequent death. When the policy on the wife is allocated to the husband's family trust, it is generally valued at its cash value (called the *interpolated terminal reserve value*) rather than its death-benefit value. For example, if the cash value of the policy is $100,000 and the death benefit is $1 million, it is the $100,000 value that is counted toward the husband's applicable exclusion. If the applicable exclusion amount on the husband's death is $1.5 million, his family trust would hold the insurance policy on the wife's life, valued at $100,000, and other assets worth $1.4 million.

When the wife subsequently dies, the $1 million death benefit from the policy on her life will be paid to the husband's family trust as the beneficiary of the policy. Because the family trust is not subject to estate taxes on the wife's death no matter what its value is, the life insurance proceeds and the remainder of the assets held in the husband's family trust will not be subject to estate taxes on her death. The result is that one spouse's life insurance proceeds are not subject to federal estate tax. However, when the husband died, the proceeds of the policy on his life were payable to the wife's living trust. To the extent that these proceeds were not spent by the wife during her life, they *are* included in her estate at her death.

Another benefit of wait-and-see life insurance is that after the first spouse's death, insurance companies sometimes offer the surviving spouse the option of increasing the death benefit of the policy owned by the family trust on his or her life. The surviving spouse can make the decision at that time as to whether more life insurance is needed.

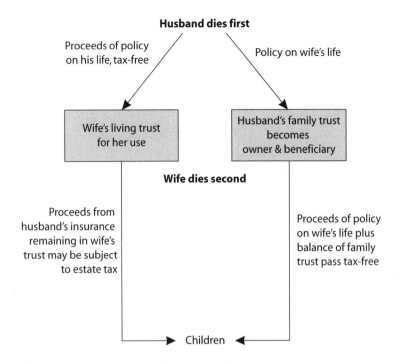

Figure 5-1   Wait-and-see life insurance

---

cx *What are the disadvantages of wait-and-see life insurance?*

It is possible that the value of the surviving spouse's policy will be greater than its cash value. For example, if the surviving spouse is not insurable because of health reasons, and death is imminent, the IRS rules would require a valuation of the policy that would approach its death benefit value.

Once the policy is in the family trust, the premiums will still need to be paid. Since all the assets in the family trust are estate tax–free, it is not wise to use these assets to pay the premiums unless there are no other assets available.

Generally, if a spouse has no other assets, he or she will want to have access to the assets in the family trust. However, with a wait-and-see life insurance trust, the spouse can have no direct access to the family trust. If the spouse does have access, the entire death benefit, on the second spouse's death, will be included in his or her estate and will be taxed.

If the cash value of the policy grows to more than the applicable exclusion amount, there will be estate tax due on the first spouse's death. Even if the cash value is less, it is still eating up the very valuable applicable exclusion. With an irrevocable life insurance trust, if it is established and maintained properly, none of the applicable exclusion need be used.

With wait-and-see life insurance, only one spouse's death benefits escape federal estate taxation. The death proceeds of the first spouse to die will be included in the surviving spouse's estate, to the extent they are not used, when that spouse dies. With an ILIT, all life insurance proceeds are estate tax–free.

Finally, a drawback of wait-and-see life insurance occurs if both spouses die before the policy on the first spouse to die is contributed to the family trust; that is, the second death occurs before the policy can be legally transferred to the family trust. In this case, the death proceeds from both policies will be included in the spouses' respective estates, and estate tax will be due. Had the policies been in an ILIT, none of the proceeds would be included in either spouse's estate.

Grantor Retained Interest Trust
(for income-producing and/or appreciating assets)

CR *What is a grantor retained interest trust?*

A *grantor retained interest trust* is a special irrevocable trust that allows the trustmaker (the grantor) to make gifts of property while retaining the property's use and enjoyment or by retaining an income interest in the property for a term of years.

CR *What is the purpose of a grantor retained interest trust?*

Grantor retained interest trusts are used primarily by people who want to transfer income-producing assets and future appreciation to their children at discounted values for estate and gift tax purposes but would like to continue to enjoy the benefits of or to receive cash flow from the assets for a period of time.

❧ *How do these trusts work?*

The maker of the grantor retained interest trust transfers assets to the trust and retains an interest in the assets for a period of years. At the end of the term of years, the assets pass to the trust's remainder beneficiaries. Because the beneficiaries will not have use or enjoyment of the asset or the income flow from the asset until some future time, the amount of the gift is the fair market value of the property transferred to the trust, minus the value of the maker's retained interest.

For estate tax purposes, as long as the trustmaker lives to the completion of the term of years, the value of the asset at the time it is transferred to the trust plus all future appreciation are removed from the trustmaker's estate. If the trustmaker dies before the expiration of the term of years, the value of the asset at the trustmaker's date of death is included in his or her estate. In effect, the individual's estate is no worse off than if he or she had never established the grantor retained interest trust and had never given away the asset.

❧ *What happens to the assets in trust at the end of the term of years?*

At the end of the trust term, the trustmaker has no further interest in the property. At that point the trustee either distributes the remaining trust property to the beneficiaries designated in the trust document or keeps the property in the trust for their benefit.

❧ *Why would I use a grantor retained interest trust?*

If you have an asset that is appreciating in value, good estate planning may indicate that you give away the asset to eliminate the potential estate tax that could result if you retain the asset and it continues to appreciate. However, this asset may be providing you with housing or income that you currently cannot or do not want to give up. Furthermore, the gift tax cost of giving the asset away may also be too high.

A grantor retained interest trust can offer an excellent solution. Through this trust, you can give the asset to your remainder beneficiaries while retaining possession and enjoyment of, or the income from, the asset for a term of years. At the end of the term, the asset can be distributed to the trust's remainder beneficiaries at its then fair market value without any further gift tax cost to you.

◌ৼ How does a grantor retained interest trust reduce the value of a gift?

Since possession and enjoyment of the asset or the income from the asset is not received by the remainder beneficiaries until the future, the present fair market value of the gift is discounted for gift tax purposes. The amount of the discount depends on several factors:

- The present fair market value of the asset
- The retained interest term of years
- The age and life expectancy of the trustmaker
- The value attributed to the possession and enjoyment or the percent of income retained by the trustmaker
- An assumed rate of return on the trust assets, called the applicable federal rate (AFR), that the IRS publishes monthly

Basically, the higher the value of the interest retained by the trustmaker, the less the value of the remainder interest passing to the beneficiaries; consequently, the gift amount and the applicable gift tax will be lower. As long as the trustmaker outlives the term of the trust, the present value and all future appreciation of the trust property is removed from the trustmaker's estate at a lower gift tax cost.

It is important to understand that at the time the maker transfers the property into the trust, he or she is making a gift of the value of the remainder interest to the beneficiaries and must file a gift tax return in that year. However, the beneficiaries do not take possession of the gift until the end of the retained interest term. The rationale for allowing a lesser value for the remainder interest than the fair market value of the asset is based upon what a disinterested buyer would pay for that interest, knowing that the buyer could not take possession of the asset until after the termination of the retained interest. In theory, that buyer would not pay 100 cents on the dollar, but would pay a lesser, or discounted, amount.

◌ৼ How do I determine the number of years that my retained interest should last?

The number of years for the term is a subjective decision, based on a number of factors. The longer your retained interest, the greater the value of that interest and the lower the value of the remainder interest—the value of the gift you make. But the risk is in setting the period too long, because if you die before the end of the trust term when your interest in the trust terminates, the trust property is included in your gross estate, and you lose the tax benefits of the trust. So obviously, your age and health are the key factors. We wouldn't recommend that a 90-year-old person retain an interest in the trust for 15 years, but that might be an acceptable risk for a person who is 60 years old and in good health.

Ultimately, you and your advisors will select the term based on a reasonable assessment of your longevity and your other planning goals, knowing it is a calculated risk because none of us knows when we will die. Some clients who are concerned that they may die before the end of the term purchase life insurance to guard against that risk.

CR *Can I use my gift tax annual exclusion for the gift to the children with a grantor retained interest trust?*

No. A gift to a grantor retained interest trust is a gift of a future interest because the beneficiary does not enjoy the gift until some time in the future when the term ends. The annual exclusion is only available for present-interest gifts.

CR *Can we use our gift tax applicable exclusion so that we do not have to pay any gift tax?*

Yes. In fact, the gift to a grantor retained interest trust *must* first be applied against your $1 million gift tax exclusion. You will not have to pay any gift tax unless you made prior gifts and either exhausted your exclusion or the value of the gift to the grantor retained interest trust exceeds your remaining exclusion.

CR *Is appreciation in the value of the asset still subject to federal estate tax?*

Transferring an asset to a grantor retained interest trust freezes the value of the asset at its fair market value at the time of the transfer. As long as you survive the term of your retained interest, all appreciation in the value of the asset after you transfer the asset to the trust is removed from your estate.

In fact, this tax-free transfer of the appreciation is the greatest benefit of using a grantor retained interest trust. As you read about the various types of trusts in the balance of this chapter, you will see examples with some very impressive results. But, there is an important caveat you should understand: For a grantor retained interest trust to be an effective wealth transfer tool, the assets owned by the trust must generate a total return (income plus appreciation) greater than the government-assumed interest rate, the AFR, mentioned earlier.

℞ *Are there any income tax issues I should know about regarding a grantor retained interest trust?*

The grantor retained interest trust is considered, for income tax purposes, a "grantor trust" under IRC rules. This means that all income, deductions, and credits of the trust are treated as if there is no trust, and those items are attributable directly to you, the grantor-trustmaker. So, for income tax purposes during the trust term, the trust is "transparent" and there is no special tax reporting you must do. This is not necessarily bad if you have the resources to pay the tax on the income because by doing so, you are allowing the assets in the trust to grow tax-free. The tax payment is, in essence, an additional gift to the remainder beneficiaries without any gift tax consequences.

℞ *Will my beneficiaries lose the step-up in basis on the asset if it is in a grantor retained interest trust?*

Yes. Your beneficiaries assume your original cost basis in the asset in the trust. They will pay tax on the appreciation of the asset in excess of your original basis, at the capital gain rate at the time they sell the property.

℞ *Does a grantor retained interest trust offer any creditor protection?*

You give away assets that you place in a grantor retained interest trust. If there is no fraudulent intent to hinder or delay the ability of known creditors to collect, the assets in the trust are out of the reach of your creditors. However, your retained interest could be reached by your creditors. Thus, a creditor could capture the income or could use or rent the property during the term, but once the term expires, the property then passes free of the creditor's claims to the remainder beneficiaries.

If the remainder beneficiary's interest is not retained in trust after expiration of the term, the property could be subject to claims of the remainder beneficiary's creditors. This is why it is always a good idea either to have the assets continue to be held in the same trust or to have them transferred to a separate trust, that you create, for the benefit of the remainder beneficiaries. Those beneficiaries could even serve as trustees or cotrustees of either trust at that time.

℞ *Are there any restrictions on who can be the trustee of a grantor retained interest trust?*

During the initial term, the trustmaker may be the sole trustee of the grantor retained interest trust, with complete control over the trust and the trust property. If desired, the trustmaker may also designate a cotrustee to serve.

After the initial term, the trustmaker cannot be a trustee of the grantor retained interest trust. However, the trustmaker may designate in the trust agreement a chain of trustees to serve in the event of his or her disability during the initial term and during his or her lifetime after the initial term.

℞ *Is there only one type of grantor retained interest trust?*

The most common grantor retained interest trusts are the:

- Qualified personal residence trust (QPRT)
- Grantor retained annuity trust (GRAT)
- Grantor retained unitrust (GRUT)

Qualified Personal Residence Trust

℞ *What is a qualified personal residence trust?*

A *qualified personal residence trust (QPRT)* is an irrevocable trust to which the trustmaker (grantor) transfers his or her personal residence. The beauty of the QPRT is that while you give away the future value of the house, you retain the right to live there for a specified number of years. During this period, virtually nothing changes for you: You reside in the home just as you have always done. At the end of the term, however, the title to the house is transferred to your remainder beneficiaries, usually children, in the manner that you determine at the time that you create the trust.

CR *What residences qualify for a QPRT?*

A *personal residence* is the trustmaker's:

- principal residence,
- another residence used for personal purposes (e.g., a vacation home); or
- an undivided fractional interest in either of the above.

To qualify for a QPRT, the structure must be occupied by the trustmaker as a residence. Other structures on the property such as guest houses, pool houses, stables, and similar structures also qualify.

CR *Can you give me an example of how a QPRT saves federal estate and gift taxes?*

Yes. Let's assume that Mary Smith has a home worth $1 million. Mary is 60 years old and picks a term of 10 years for her retained interest. If the adjusted federal rate is 6 percent, the gift of the remainder interest in the home to the children is $465,830. Mary's accountant must file a gift tax return in the year that Mary transfers the home into the trust showing that Mary made the gift. Assuming that Mary lives the retained term of 10 years and the home appreciates at 7 percent per year, the home will be worth almost $2 million when the children receive the property. The entire value of the home is out of Mary's estate for estate tax purposes. Thus, Mary has only used $465,830 of her gift tax applicable exclusion amount and has reduced the size of her estate by $2 million, while being able to use the home for an additional 10 years.

CR *If my house has a mortgage on it, can I transfer the house to a QPRT?*

Yes, but transferring mortgaged property to a QPRT is rather cumbersome. Each mortgage payment is, in part, another taxable gift to the remainder beneficiaries. It would be preferable to pay off the mortgage before you transfer the property to the QPRT.

CR *Who's entitled to the income tax deduction for the property taxes?*

Because the QPRT is a "grantor trust" under the IRC during the initial term, the trustmaker is treated as the owner of the property for federal income tax purposes. If the trustmaker pays the real estate taxes on the residence, he or she is entitled to the income tax deduction for those taxes.

ℭ Who pays expenses of the house during the trust's initial term?

During the initial term of the trust, the trustmaker pays the normal and customary expenses of repairing and maintaining the house. The trustmaker does not pay these expenses directly, but transfers cash to the trust, which in turn pays the expense.

ℭ What if my husband and I want to live in our residence after the initial term has expired?

If you want to continue to live in the house after the initial term has expired, you can rent the property back from your children. Attorneys customarily include a provision in the QPRT document allowing you to rent the home after its initial term. You should sign a rental agreement, and the rent should be the fair market rental price. The lease payments are amounts out of your estate and are not considered additional gifts to your children. Thus, this technique can further your estate planning goals.

ℭ What if I want to sell the home during the retained term?

A carefully drafted QPRT will allow for the flexibility of selling the home. The following are several possible options after you sell the home:

- *Purchase a replacement home of equal value:* If you purchase a replacement home of equal value, the new home is owned by the QPRT; nothing further needs to be done.
- *Purchase a replacement home of greater value:* If you purchase a replacement home of greater value, you have made an additional gift to the trust, and another gift tax return will be filed showing the amount of the gift.
- *Purchase a replacement home of lesser value:* If you purchase a home of lesser value, the excess sales proceeds are paid to you in the form of an annuity during the remaining term of the retained interest. This annuity is determined in accordance with an IRC formula.

■ *Do not purchase a replacement home:* If you do not purchase a replacement home, then you will be paid an annuity from the full amount of the proceeds from the sale of the home for the remaining term of the retained interest, pursuant to the same formula as stated in the above situation. At the end of the trust term, the liquid or other investable assets in the trust will become the property of the remainder beneficiaries in the same manner as if the residence was still an asset of the trust.

You must purchase a new home with the sales proceeds within 2 years or you will be forced into taking the annuity option.

☞ *My husband and I own our home jointly. Can we create a QPRT together for our home?*

You have a couple of options. You can retitle the home in the name of the youngest and/or healthiest of you, who establishes the QPRT and transfers the home to it. Another possibility is to divide the home into equal tenants-in-common interests and then each of you places your interest in your own QPRT. This technique in many cases reduces the value of the home (and thus the amount of the gift) based upon the "fractionalized" ownership between the two of you. The concept of discounting a fractionalized interest in property is somewhat complex but can be best summed up with a simple question: Would you buy half a house?

☞ *It seems like the QPRT could be a gamble on my part, because if I die during the QPRT term, the residence will be brought back into my estate and could create estate tax. Is there a way to pro-tect against that risk?*

To reduce your risk, you could purchase a term life insurance policy to protect against any estate tax that may be due should you die dur-ing the term of the QPRT. The policy should be purchased in an irrevocable life insurance trust to keep the death proceeds out of your estate.

☞ *Can you summarize the advantages and disadvantages of the QPRT?*

Certainly. The primary advantage is that a QPRT allows you to transfer your residence to beneficiaries at significantly lower tax costs than an outright gift or bequest. There are two drawbacks of a QPRT:

1. The first is that you must outlive the retained interest term, otherwise the full value of the home is brought back into your estate.

2. Second, your children do not receive a step-up in basis on the home, but they take your basis in the property. This means that when the children sell the home, they will, in all probability, pay capital gain tax on the sale.

Grantor Retained Annuity Trust and Grantor Retained Unitrust

Q *I like the idea of transferring assets to my children now, but I still need the income from those assets to live on. What can I do?*

Consider making gifts through a grantor retained annuity trust or a grantor retained unitrust. With either trust, you, as the grantor-trustmaker, transfer assets into the trust and retain an income interest for a specified period of time. At the end of the term, the trust assets will pass directly to or remain in trust for the remainder beneficiaries named in the trust agreement.

Q *What is a grantor retained annuity trust?*

A *grantor retained annuity trust (GRAT)* is an irrevocable trust into which the trustmaker transfers appreciating or income-producing property in exchange for the right to receive a fixed annuity for a number of years. When the term of the trust ends, any remaining balance in the GRAT is transferred to the remainder beneficiaries.

Q *What are some of the advantages and disadvantages of a GRAT?*

It is possible to produce significant transfer tax savings with a GRAT if the average rate of return from the property in the GRAT exceeds the applicable federal rate (AFR) used to value the grantor's retained interest. If the return generated exceeds that rate, the additional return accumulates for the remainder beneficiaries without additional gift taxes.

A disadvantage of a GRAT is that if the trust property does not generate a return greater than the AFR in effect when the trust was created, the trust will not achieve its goal of transferring wealth to the remainder beneficiaries tax-free. And as is the case with all types of grantor retained interest trusts, to avoid having the trust property returned to your estate, you must survive your retained interest.

∾ *Can you give me a simple example of a GRAT?*

Yes. Let's assume that you are 55 years of age and own stock in a corporation that you would like to give to your children. The stock is valued at $1 million and is increasing in value consistently at 9 percent. You would like to retain an income stream of $60,000 a year from the stock for 10 years and then let your children have the stock. Let's further assume that the current AFR is 6 percent. According to the governmental tables, the amount of the gift is $557,930, which is the value of the stock ($1 million) less the present value of the annuity interest you retained over the 10-year term, taking into account your life expectancy. Provided the stock continues to grow at 9 percent over the term, your children will receive almost $1.5 million after 10 years, which is also the amount you will have removed from your estate.

∾ *What is a grantor retained unitrust?*

A *grantor retained unitrust (GRUT)* is a trust in which the grantor retains a qualified unitrust interest, consisting of an irrevocable right to receive a fixed percentage of the fair market value of the trust assets valued annually. While the fixed percentage is set, the amount the grantor receives each year fluctuates as the value of the trust property changes from year to year.

∾ *How do GRATs and GRUTs differ?*

In a GRAT, the grantor retains the right to receive either a fixed dollar amount *or* a fixed percentage of the value of the property transferred to the GRAT, based solely on the *original value* of the assets as of the start of the trust. In a GRUT, the grantor retains the right to receive a fixed percentage of the value of the trust assets, based upon the *annually recomputed value* of the assets of the trust.

Another difference between the two is that the trustmaker of a GRAT can only transfer property to the trust once; the trustmaker of a GRUT can make as many contributions to the trust as he or she wants, but each additional contribution is a taxable gift.

GRATs and GRUTs are similar in one respect: the trust must make the annual payment to the grantor regardless of how much or how little income the trust earns.

ଔ *Why would I use a GRAT rather than a GRUT?*

In most situations, a GRAT results in a lower gift amount but transfers more wealth to the remainder beneficiaries. The payments from a GRAT are fixed, so all investment return not distributed to the trustmaker as annuity payments inures solely to the benefit of the remainder beneficiaries. With a GRUT, as the value of the trust's assets grow, so do the annual payments, so the trustmaker and the remainder beneficiaries share in the excess investment return. As a result, GRATs are typically more effective in transferring wealth to the next generation.

Because a GRAT has a fixed payment, the assets need to be valued only once, when the trust is formed. A GRUT's payout is based on a percentage of the value of the assets as determined each year. This means that if you are funding the GRUT with hard-to-value assets, such as real estate or nonpublicly traded stocks and partnership interests, an appraisal must be performed each year. This can be expensive and administratively complex.

For these reasons, in our experience, clients rarely use GRUTs.

ଔ *I like the idea of using a GRAT, but I've already used up my gift tax applicable exclusion. Is there anything else I can do?*

It is possible to create a GRAT without making a taxable gift. With a GRAT, the trust must make the annuity payments solely from the trustmaker's initial contribution and the investment return it earns on those assets. If the annuity amount exceeds the trust's investment return for a number of years, the trust will exhaust its resources, leaving nothing for the remainder beneficiaries. When this happens in real life, the consequences are disastrous. But when it only happens on paper, the results can be very positive.

To calculate the gift tax value of the remainder interest in a

GRAT, you calculate the present value of the annuity stream (based on the AFR) and subtract that figure from the fair market value of the property contributed to the GRAT. So if the value of the property going into the trust is $500,000, and the present value of the trustmaker's annuity interest is $500,000, the amount of the gift to the remainder beneficiaries is zero. Of course, this is only the gift tax value of the remainder interest. Assuming the trust's investments perform adequately, there will in fact be property left in the trust for your remainder beneficiaries at the end of the annuity term.

To achieve this result, the GRAT is structured a little differently than the traditional GRAT. If the trustmaker dies during the annuity term, with most GRATs, the annuity payments cease. In this new form of GRAT, the payments continue for the original term even after the trustmaker dies (the payments go to the trustmaker's estate). This feature ensures that the value of the remainder interest is reduced to zero. Also, in most cases the term of the trustmaker's retained interest is quite short—2 or 3 years—and the annuity is rather high. The result is that the trustmaker gets back the full value of the assets he or she originally transferred to the trust. The remainder beneficiaries receive the appreciation on those assets. Again, this appreciation is not a taxable gift to the beneficiaries. After the annuity term ends and the grantor has the property back, many grantors start the process over again, rolling the property into a new short-term GRAT.

Family Limited Partnership
(for income-producing investments and family businesses)

Features of an FLP

○ス *What is a family limited partnership?*

A limited partnership is a common business entity that consists of at least one general partner and one limited partner. A *family limited partnership (FLP)* is a limited partnership in which all the partners are family members or entities owned by family members.

General partners have full control to manage the partnership, regardless of their percentage of ownership. With this control comes personal liability for partnership debts and obligations. General partners are almost always the senior family members or entities controlled by them.

Limited partners have no right to participate in managing the partnership business and have limited liability for partnership debts. Limited partners are often children and grandchildren of the general partners.

In forming the FLP, senior family members transfer investment assets to the FLP in exchange for general and limited partnership interests. Thereafter, these assets are managed by the general partners for the benefit of the entire partnership.

◌ *How would my husband and I transfer assets to our children through the FLP?*

You and your husband would transfer investment real estate and marketable securities to a family limited partnership in exchange for 100 percent of the partnership interests. The two of you would retain a small general partnership interest and, through a systematic gift-giving program, transfer limited partnership interests to your children. Your children would own 98–99 percent of the FLP, and all appreciation on the value of their partnership interests would accrue outside of your estate for estate tax purposes. However, by virtue of the small general partnership interest that you and your husband continue to own, the two of you would retain total control over the assets in the partnership.

◌ *Can an FLP provide me with an income?*

As the general partner, you can authorize distributions of partnership assets, and you are entitled to receive a reasonable fee for management. The compensation amount must be reasonable, considering the responsibility you assume as the general partner and the time required for you to manage the partnership and its investments. Trust company fees for managing a trust of similar size are often used as a guideline in setting the compensation of a general partner. Excess compensation or distributions to you could damage the integrity of the partnership for transfer tax purposes.

◌ *How does the FLP reduce our income taxes?*

The FLP does not pay income taxes on its profits. A limited partnership is a "pass-through" tax entity. Income, losses, and deductions flow through to each partner on the basis of his or her percentage of ownership. In most families, the children are in lower income tax brackets than their parents are, so the results are a lower tax for the parents and a lower tax for the family unit.

Estate and Gift Tax Results of FLPs

ల *Why are discounts so important in making gifts?*

The federal estate and gift tax is a tax on the transfer of property during the owner's lifetime or at his or her death. The tax is based on the fair market value of the property transferred. *Fair market value* is the value at which property would change hands between a willing buyer and a willing seller, both having full knowledge of all relevant facts and neither being under any compulsion to buy or to sell. In determining the fair market value, a buyer will demand certain discounts in the sale price of property that he or she cannot immediately sell or that the buyer cannot control.

ల *Can you give me an example of how the discount works in an FLP to reduce estate and gift taxes?*

The value of the limited partnership interests is subject to a discount in calculating their fair market value. The following example shows how an FLP usually works.

Joyce and Arnie Riley want to give their children and grandchildren family securities and real estate worth $1 million and not pay gift tax to make the transfer. They form the JAR Limited Partnership and transfer the assets to JAR. Each of them is a general partner with 1 percent interest and also a 49 percent limited partner. Joyce and Arnie want to give away the 98 percent limited partnership interests as follows: to each of their four children, a 22 percent interest; to each of their two grandchildren, a 5 percent interest.

The Rileys hire a valuation expert to value the partnership interests. Because the limited partnership interests have no control and are generally not marketable under the partnership agreement, the appraiser discounts the value of the 98 percent limited partnership interests by almost 40 percent. For gift tax purposes, the amount the Rileys are giving away is $588,000.

❧ *How do I determine the amount of the discount that I can take?*

The amount of the discount must be determined by a qualified appraiser. There are many factors that are unique to each FLP that have a bearing on the appropriate discount, and only a valuation expert can properly determine what that discount should be.

❧ *Can you combine the FLP with other tax reduction strategies?*

Coupling an FLP with one or more of the other planning techniques discussed in this chapter can bring about powerful results. One tool often used with an FLP is an irrevocable grantor trust (IGT) that we describe later in this chapter. For example, let's assume Margaret, a widow aged 75, has two children and one grandchild, and an $8 million estate. Even if we only assumed a 5 percent growth factor, her estate is growing at $400,000 a year.

Initially, Margaret sets up an FLP and contributes $5 million in assets. She is the general partner with a 1 percent general partnership interest as well as a limited partner with 99 percent ownership. A qualified appraiser values the FLP and finds that a 35 percent discount is warranted. That means the value of the FLP is now $3.25 million.

She transfers 10 percent of her limited partnership interest to an IGT, with her children and grandchild as the beneficiaries. Next, Margaret sells the remaining partnership interests to the IGT, taking back a note. Because of the FLP discount, Margaret has sold the assets to the trust for far less than their value outside the FLP. This results in lower interest payments as compared with selling the assets to the IGT outside of the FLP, allowing more of the assets' return to accumulate for her beneficiaries.

Advantages and Disadvantages of the FLP

❧ *Can you summarize the advantages of using an FLP to give assets to our children and grandchildren?*

Some of the advantages of using an FLP are as follows:

- As general partners, you can still receive income for managing the assets.
- For estate tax purposes, the fair market value of the gifted FLP

interests and all future appreciation on the FLP assets are removed from your estate.

- For gift tax purposes, significant valuation discounts on the limited partnership interests are available.

- Discounted values of the gifts leverage your ability to give away more. Even greater leverage is available if you transfer the limited partnership interests to a grantor retained annuity trust or sell them to an IGT.

- With appropriate buyout provisions in the partnership agreement, assets remain in the family for future generations.

- Limited partners are protected from the FLP's creditors' claims.

- You can protect yourself against the general partners' liability by using an entity with creditor protection, such as a corporation or limited liability company, as the general partner.

- You can amend the partnership agreement.

- The income and losses of the partnership pass through to the partners, thus you have the potential of shifting income to partners in lower tax brackets.

CR *What are the disadvantages of the family limited partnership?*

There are several disadvantages of an FLP:

- Setting up a family limited partnership is expensive.

- The currently favorable state law, which offers strong asset protection, could change.

- Business owners must have the partnership's property appraised periodically to calculate the value of the limited partnership interest gifts.

Like many opportunities in life, your family limited partnership has the potential for enormous benefits to you and your family, but it is also expensive and carries a degree of uncertainty in terms of what future tax laws may say. However, no one knows what form the tax laws will take in the future; we cannot avoid planning because of that uncertainty. As to expense, you have created a wonderful estate for yourself and your family, and the potential estate tax savings to your family may far outweigh the expense of the FLP.

Limited Liability Company

Features of the LLC

Ⓡ *What is a limited liability company?*

The *limited liability company (LLC)* is a fairly recent entity that has become a very popular business form. The owners are referred to as *members*. It is a hybrid business form that combines the best characteristics of the limited partnership and the corporation:

- A member's ownership interest in an LLC is a percentage interest in the LLC, not an interest in the specific property of the LLC.

- An LLC requires fewer formalities than a corporation to create and maintain, but it provides its owners with the same level of liability protection as a corporation.

- The LLC can elect to be taxed as a partnership or a corporation.

- All members of an LLC enjoy limited liability—regardless of whether or not they participate in the day-to-day affairs of the business. There is no requirement that any member have unlimited liability, as is the case with the limited partnership.

- Any person or entity that can legally enter into a contract may be a member of an LLC. This includes any domestic or foreign corporation, partnership, limited partnership, trust, estate, another limited liability company, and natural persons.

Ⓡ *Can I use a limited liability company instead of a family limited partnership to transfer family wealth to my children?*

The LLC and the FLP have similar benefits, meaning that both offer asset protection and both offer valuation discounts. However, with the FLP you need to have two classes of partners: one or more general partners and one or more limited partners. Since only the limited partners have asset protection, to protect the general partner, the general partner is usually an entity such as an irrevocable management trust, a corporation, or an LLC. You can quickly see that the FLP structure is more complicated than the LLC, which only needs one or more members, who can serve as managers. Under Wyoming law, the manager is not even required to be a member. Many clients prefer the LLC because of its simplicity.

Whether an LLC or FLP is a better choice as a wealth transfer technique depends on the laws of your state pertaining to each. Many people choose to establish their FLPs or LLCs in states different than the ones in which they reside because the laws in their states are not as favorable as in others.

☙ *What are the income tax consequences?*

Most LLCs elect to be taxed as partnerships. As such, the LLC is a pass-through tax entity and does not pay income taxes on its profits. Just like the FLP, the income, losses, and deductions flow through to each member on the basis of his or her percentage of ownership, so the results are lower income taxes for the parents and for the family unit.

Estate and Gift Tax Results of the LLC

☙ *What are the estate and gift tax consequences of giving the LLC to our children?*

As with an FLP, an LLC can offer substantial valuation discounts. An LLC operating agreement will provide that a member (owner):

- cannot sell his or her ownership interest without the approval of the manager of the LLC;
- cannot give away his or her ownership interest without the approval of the member manager;
- cannot take any income from the LLC without the approval of the member manager.

These restrictions, and others inherent with an LLC, discount the value of an LLC interest. These discounts offer substantial estate and gift tax savings to parents and grandparents who establish LLCs. Although, we never recommend that clients establish LLCs solely for these discounts, they're icing on the cake; and the clients have great asset protection during their lives while maintaining control of the family real estate and investments.

SALES TO FAMILY MEMBERS

Irrevocable Grantor Trust

ℭℜ I like the GRAT idea. Are there any other techniques like that?

Yes, there is a similar technique known as an *irrevocable grantor trust (IGT)*. An IGT is an irrevocable trust that you create for the benefit of one or more beneficiaries of your choosing, usually the next generation. Instead of giving an asset to the trust and receiving an annuity from the trust, with an IGT you *sell* assets for fair market value in exchange for a promissory note. For a number of years, the IGT makes interest-only payments on the promissory note to you, then pays off the principal of the note to you in one balloon payment. The promissory note will not appreciate in value; it will always be worth its face amount. Therefore, the assets you sell to the IGT appreciate outside of your estate during the term of the promissory note.

ℭℜ So this is a sale? There is no gift involved?

No, there is a gift at first. For this strategy to work, it must be done in a businesslike manner. When you are selling property and taking back a note, you are in essence loaning money to the buyer. A bank would never lend money to someone who owned nothing, and neither should you. So that your loan to the trust is considered commercially reasonable, you should make a gift of some property or cash to the trust for "seed money." That way the trust has adequate collateral to support the note. Many estate planners feel that seed money of approximately 10 percent of the loan should fend off any IRS arguments that the loan lacks substance.

ℭℜ How does an IGT work?

The trustmaker establishes the IGT, but he or she cannot be either a beneficiary or a trustee of the trust. The trustmaker funds the trust with the gift of seed money. The trustmaker and the trustee then enter into a purchase-and-sale agreement for assets that the trustmaker expects will appreciate substantially in the future, such as

stocks or a closely held business interest. The trustmaker then transfers the assets to the trustee and takes a promissory note from the
trustee as payment.

Using the income and appreciation generated by the purchased
property, the trustee makes the interest payments to the trustmaker
as required under the note. When the note matures, the trustee pays
the trustmaker in full, often with the property the trustee originally
bought from the trustmaker. In the meantime, the property has been
significantly appreciating. The appreciation, minus the interest payments to the trustmaker, eventually passes to the trust's beneficiaries
estate tax– and gift tax–free. In this way, the trustmaker froze the
value of his or her estate by transferring to the next generation most
of the appreciation and income from his or her assets.

℟ What interest rate do I charge the trust?

The IRC considers loans to have a gift element if the loan does not
bear an adequate rate of interest. In fact, each month the IRS publishes a table of interest rates, and certain loans are classified as
"below-market" loans if they do not charge an interest rate at least
equal to the rates in the table. Needless to say, a below-market loan
has negative gift and income tax consequences for both parties.

In most cases you will charge the minimum rate necessary to avoid
below-market treatment. This rate is lower than rates commercially available, so you are not typically charging the trust a high rate of interest.

℟ My assets are highly appreciated. Won't I pay capital gain tax on the sale?

Under the IRC, a trust is usually a separate taxpayer and pays
income tax each year on all trust income that is not distributed to
trust beneficiaries. When the trust is a separate taxpayer, a sale to the
trust is no different than a sale to any other third party, so you would
recognize gain on the sale of appreciated assets to the trust.

But this is where the "grantor" part of an IGT comes into play.
With a grantor trust, the income of the trust is still taxable, but to
the trustmaker of the trust, not the trust. In effect, the trustmaker is
treated as the owner of the trust property for income tax purposes.
The logical effect of this rule is that a trustmaker-grantor cannot sell
property to himself or herself, so the trustmaker does not recognize
gain when selling an appreciated asset to the IGT.

When an attorney drafts the trust document to cause the trust-maker to be liable for income tax on the trust income, the trust is known as a *grantor trust*. Different advisors have different names for these trusts, such as *irrevocable grantor trusts* or *intentional grantor trusts* or *intentionally defective grantor trusts*. Whatever the name, the technique is essentially the same.

ᘐ *So why would I want to be taxed on the income?*

With an IGT, you are essentially paying income taxes for your beneficiaries, thus permitting a tax-free buildup of wealth inside the trust for their benefit. Your tax payment is the equivalent of an additional gift to the trust, but since the law requires you to pay the tax on a grantor trust, the payment is not a gift.

As a practical matter, you were paying the income taxes generated by the property before you sold it to the trust, and in all likelihood most of the trust's income is being distributed to you as interest payments (which are not subject to tax), so your income tax situation is no worse than before.

ᘐ *Are there any advantages to using an IGT over a grantor retained annuity trust if my purpose is to transfer assets out of my estate while retaining an income stream from those assets?*

There several advantages to using an IGT over a GRAT:

- First, under the IRC rules, the interest rate that you charge the IGT to avoid the below-market loan rules is less than the AFR used to determine the value of the annuity paid by a GRAT. Like a GRAT, the investment performance of the IGT assets must outperform this interest rate to achieve its wealth transfer goals. This means that an IGT has a lower investment performance hurdle to beat.

- Second, with an IGT, you receive the full estate tax benefit of the transaction even if you do not survive the entire term of the promissory note. With a GRAT, the benefit is lost, in whole or in part, if you do not survive the trust term.

- Finally, if you ever need the assets for your support, they will be returned to you when the promissory note is paid, and the note can always be prepaid. With a GRAT, you never receive more than the annuity payment.

  Then why would I ever want to use a GRAT instead of an IGT?

The primary reason is that there is some uncertainty associated with an IGT that is not associated with a GRAT. A GRAT is specifically authorized by the IRC. An IGT as an estate planning technique is not specifically sanctioned in the IRC. Tax practitioners, reading the IRC, believe that an IGT is a permitted strategy to cause asset appreciation to accrue outside of the trustmaker's estate. However, this strategy has not yet been tested in the courts. Accordingly, if the IRS challenges the technique, there is a risk that the appreciation on the assets transferred to an IGT could be pulled back into the trustmaker's estate.

    Also, if the trustmaker dies before the promissory note is repaid, there is some income tax uncertainty. When the maker of an IGT dies, the IGT becomes a taxpaying entity, separate and apart from the trustmaker. This raises the possibility that the trustmaker's estate must pay capital gain tax on the original sale of appreciated assets to the IGT.

Self-canceling Installment Note

  What is a self-canceling installment note?

A *self-canceling installment note (SCIN)* is a promissory note given by a buyer to a seller that calls for installment payments of principal and interest over a set period of time. It also provides that if the seller dies before the note is fully repaid, the remaining payments are automatically canceled and the buyer owes nothing further.

    The unpaid balance owed to the seller at the time of the seller's death is not included in the seller's taxable estate. Thus, if a parent sells an asset to a child in exchange for a SCIN and dies soon after the sale is completed, the parent's taxable estate will not include either the value of the asset sold, the appreciation on the asset, or the balance of the note owed by the child at the time of the parent's death.

  How would a self-canceling installment note help in our family planning?

A SCIN helps in several ways. It:

- keeps the assets sold under the SCIN in the family;
- shifts future appreciation on the asset out of the seller's estate;

- provides periodic payments to the seller for a term of years; and
- in many cases, allows the seller to recognize the gain on the sale over time, as the seller receives the payments.

ℭℛ *What are the main disadvantages of a self-canceling installment note?*

A SCIN must provide for a "risk premium" to compensate the seller for the possibility that the seller may die before receiving all the payments. The installment payments are therefore greater than those under a note having the same terms but without the self-canceling feature.

The risk premium may be either an increase in the principal amount of the note over the property's fair market value or an increase in the interest rate to be paid by the buyer on the unpaid principal. The amount of the premium is largely based on actuarial tables promulgated by the IRS, but if the seller's health is especially poor, an even higher risk premium may be required. If the risk premium is insufficient, the IRS will consider that a gift has been made by the seller to the buyer.

Private Annuity

ℭℛ *What is a private annuity?*

A *private annuity* is an agreement under which an owner transfers an asset to a buyer in exchange for the buyer's unsecured promise to make fixed periodic payments to the seller—the annuitant—for the rest of his or her life. When the seller dies, the buyer's obligation to make payments ends. The buyer's obligation to make the annuity payments is personal and is not tied to or secured by the property transferred or its income.

ℭℛ *How is the amount of the annuity payment determined?*

The amount of the annuity payment the buyer must pay to the seller is determined by the fair market value of the asset, the life expectancy of the seller (based on governmental actuarial tables), and the applicable federal rate (AFR) for the month in which the annuity is created.

CR *Why are private annuities used as an estate planning strategy?*

The primary benefit is that the annuitant removes an asset from his or her estate while receiving a fixed income stream for life. In most cases, the buyer is a member of the seller's family, so the seller is transferring property to a family member without incurring estate or gift tax on the property.

The ideal situation for a private annuity is when:

- the transferor is in a high estate tax bracket or is unmarried,
- the property is capable of producing income and/or is appreciating rapidly,
- the buyer is capable of paying the promised amounts,
- the parties trust each other (the private annuity must be unsecured), and
- the buyer has other assets and sources of income.

Private annuities are often used for clients with a shortened life expectancy due to a serious illness. In this situation, the buyer is someone the client wishes to transfer wealth to without incurring estate or gift taxes. As long as there is at least a 50 percent chance that the seller will live for 12 months after the transaction, the governmental mortality tables can be used in calculating the annuity amount.

There has been a resurgence in the use of private annuities as a planning tool in the past few years because the AFR has dropped sharply—from 8 percent in July 2000 to 3 percent in July 2003. A 70-year-old transferring a $500,000 asset in July 2000 received an annual annuity of $67,272. The same transaction generates a payment of only $46,828 in July 2003. The lower annuity payment makes it easier for children to make the payments and to keep more of the asset's income and appreciation.

CR *How does a private annuity differ from a self-canceling installment note?*

Unlike a SCIN, a private annuity carries no upper limit on the amount a buyer may have to pay to fulfill his or her obligations. That is, the buyer must make the annuity payments until the seller's death; there is no fixed term of repayment as with a SCIN. If the annuitant turns out to have the longevity of Methuselah, the private annuity will backfire and will cost the buyer far more than what he or she saved in federal estate tax.

SPECIAL TECHNIQUES
FOR FAMILY MEMBERS

Spouses

Demand Trust

◌ℜ *Is there a way to make gifts to my husband during my lifetime without those gifts being included in his estate at his death?*

You can achieve this goal by establishing an irrevocable demand trust naming your husband as the beneficiary while he is living and your children as the remainder beneficiaries after his death. The trust will provide your husband with the right to withdraw up to $5,000 or 5 percent of the value of the trust each time you make a gift to the trust. However, since your goal is to keep all of the trust assets free from estate tax liability upon both your and your husband's deaths, your husband allows the withdrawal right to lapse. The trust contains instructions for the trustee to make discretionary distributions of income and principal to your husband, as he needs over his lifetime, for his health, education, maintenance, and support.

If you transfer $5,000 into the trust annually for 20 years and the trust's investments grow at the rate of 7 percent, the value of the trust will be around $500,000 at that point. That amount will be exempt from estate tax when you die and when your husband subsequently dies. So by creating this trust for your husband, you have created a tidy little nest egg for him and have provided a substantial sum that will pass estate tax–free to your children.

We take care to limit his withdrawals to $5,000 or 5 percent of the trust value (the 5-and-5 rule) so that the trust property is not subject to federal estate tax when your husband dies. In the early years of the trust, the withdrawals will be no more than $5,000, but after 12–15 years, when the value of the trust exceeds $100,000, he can withdraw 5 percent of the value of the trust.

CR *Can I transfer to the trust each year more than the $5,000 you used in your example? Can I put the full annual exclusion amount into the trust?*

Without additional planning, it is not possible to transfer annually more than $5,000 or 5 percent of the value of the trust without adverse tax consequences. To increase your annual gifts right away to the annual exclusion amount, you must use a portion of your gift tax applicable exclusion and transfer an amount that multiplied by 5 percent equals the annual exclusion. For example, in 2004 when the annual exclusion is $11,000, you would have to use a portion of your gift tax exclusion and make an initial gift of $220,000 to the trust ($220,000 × 5% = $11,000). Once you've put that $220,000 into the trust, you can continue to contribute $11,000, each year to the trust instead of only $5,000 without using up any more of your $1 million gift tax exclusion.

This technique is referred to by some attorneys as "superfunding" the trust. Table 5-1 reviews the results of this superfunded example at several different terms of years, assuming a 6 percent growth and a 10 percent growth.

You can further leverage these results by giving property subject to valuation adjustments or discounts, such as units of a family limited partnership.

CR *Who can I name as the trustee?*

As the trustmaker, you can generally name anyone other than yourself as the trustee. Often the beneficiary spouse is the sole trustee. Your husband could be the sole trustee only if distributions are limited to the four ascertainable standards: health, education, maintenance, and support. If you choose, you may name cotrustees to serve with your husband.

CR *Who pays the income taxes on the trust income?*

Depending on how the trust is structured, either you as the trustmaker or your husband as the beneficiary will be liable for the income taxes on the trust's income. Since most couples file joint income tax returns, it doesn't matter much which of you is primarily liable. The result is that the trust is income tax–neutral; in other words, you

TABLE 5-1   Results of a Superfunded Irrevocable Demand Trust*

Year	Growth at 6%	Growth at 10%
5	$ 345,418	$ 410,468
10	527,975	734,935
20	1,099,211	2,099,075
30	2,122,208	5,637,303
35	2,905,722	9,152,804

*Assumes an initial gift of $220,000 and annual gifts of $11,000.

would have paid taxes on the property's earnings outside of the trust anyway.

ℭ Can my husband and I create a trust for each other?

Each of you may create a trust for the other. However, your attorney must take care that the terms of each of the trusts differ materially. This is to avoid a common-law doctrine called the *reciprocal trust doctrine*, which states that if two trustmakers create identical trusts for the other, the trusts are disregarded and the property is included in the trustmakers' estates.

Using two trusts can be a very, very powerful planning strategy as you can essentially double the amount of the gifts. Our clients appreciate these trusts because the beneficiary spouse (as sole trustee of his or her respective trust) can retain control over the trust's investments, can use the assets in the trust for retirement or for a rainy day, can protect the assets from creditors, and can protect the trust assets from any estate tax liability upon his or her death and on the trustmaker spouse's death.

ℭ What if I create a trust for my husband and then we get a divorce?

You have great drafting flexibility in specifying the terms of the trust. The trust can mandate that your husband's interest terminates in the event of a divorce or separation. The assets in the trust would flow immediately to your named remainder beneficiaries, who could be your children, grandchildren, or anyone else.

Lifetime Qualified Terminable Interest Property Trust

CR *I understand that my husband and I can both leave $1.5 million to our kids at our deaths without the payment of estate tax, but what happens if one of us has more assets than the other? I have assets worth $3 million, and my husband's assets are substantially less than $1 million. If my husband predeceases me, his estate tax applicable exclusion won't be fully utilized. What alternatives for estate tax planning do we have?*

We frequently see this problem with married couples. There are two potential solutions. The first and perhaps simplest solution is for you to give property to your husband so that if he dies first he has enough assets to fully use his applicable exclusion. Often, however, the wealthier spouse is uncomfortable making such a "simple" gift, especially if the assets were inherited from family or were earned prior to the marriage.

There is a second solution that may be more appropriate in such instances. It is called an *inter vivos* or *lifetime, qualified terminable interest property (QTIP) trust*, a trust very similar to the QTIP trust that we discussed in Chapter 2, Planning for Loved Ones, and Chapter 4, Tax Basics. The major difference between these two QTIP trusts is that the earlier QTIP trust is a testamentary trust (not created until your death), whereas you create the lifetime QTIP trust for your husband now.

CR *Can you explain how the lifetime QTIP works?*

Yes. The idea is that you, as the wealthier spouse, make a gift to your husband in trust and in an amount necessary to permit him to use his full estate tax applicable exclusion at death. The trust will be under the control of a trustee that you select and will pay all its income to your husband during his lifetime. At his death, the assets of the trust can either pass directly to your children, or can provide income to you for your life and then pass to your children at your death.

For example, if you create a lifetime QTIP trust for your husband and put $1 million of your assets into the trust, for estate tax purposes, the lifetime QTIP trust is considered to be your husband's property. When your husband dies, his applicable exclusion will shield the trust property from estate taxes. Because of the marital deduction, the gift you made to the trust is not taxable, so your applicable exclusion is fully available to transfer wealth to the children at your death. As a result of this planning, you have used both exclusions and passed $3 million estate tax–free to your children. If during your husband's lifetime, the value of the trust grows beyond his applicable exclusion amount, when he dies, some estate tax may be due. Even so, your combined estate tax liability should be less than if you had not established the trust.

Children and Grandchildren

UGMA/UTMA Accounts

ℚ *How can I make gifts to my minor child?*

All states have laws permitting you to set up an account at a bank or brokerage firm for the benefit of your minor child and to make irrevocable gifts to the account while your child is a minor. Gifts to these types of accounts automatically qualify for the annual exclusion for gifts. During your child's lifetime, the custodian can use monies from the account for the child's health, education, maintenance, and support. However, you cannot use the funds in the account to relieve your obligation as the parent to support the child. These accounts are generally known as UGMA or UTMA accounts, references to the names of the Uniform Gifts to Minors Act and Uniform Transfers to Minors Act that authorize and regulate the accounts.

ℚ *Are there any disadvantages to using these accounts?*

Establishing an UGMA or an UTMA account can lead to unintended or unwise consequences, among them being the following:

- Depending upon which state you live in, your child will automatically take control of the account upon reaching the age of 18 or 21, regardless of whether the child is emotionally mature enough to manage it.
- If you are custodian of the UGMA or the UTMA account, all the assets in the account will be includable in your estate if you die before they are distributed to your child.

- The assets in the account will count against the child if he or she applies for financial aid for college.

By using a trust that is set up specifically for minors, rather than using an UGMA or an UTMA account, you can still make gifts that qualify for the annual exclusion and can control how or when assets will come under the control of the young beneficiary.

ℭ *What type of trust do I create to make gifts for my minor child?*

You, or you and your spouse together, can create an irrevocable demand trust for your minor child. As we discussed earlier in this chapter, you must follow a couple of strict procedures for making gifts to a demand trust in order to qualify your gifts for the annual exclusion:

1. The trustee must immediately notify the minor beneficiary— through the child's legal guardian—that the trustmaker made a gift to the trust and that the beneficiary has a specified period of time (typically 30 to 45 days) to withdraw the gift from the trust.
2. After the withdrawal right lapses, the gift stays inside the trust and is governed by its terms.

An irrevocable demand trust is an important part of proper estate planning for anyone who wants to put money aside for a minor child, does not want the property to be taxed in the parent's or grandparent's estate, yet wants to retain some control over the child's use of the property after the child reaches the age of majority.

Section 529 Plans

ℭ *What is a 529 Plan?*

Internal Revenue Code Section *529 Plans* or other types of college savings plans are great tools for parents and grandparents to save for children's higher education. They are created, regulated, and administered by each state, which includes hiring an investment manager. The child can use the money to pay for his or her tuition, fees, books, and some living expenses. Each state has slightly different rules for its specific plan, so you need to read the details of your state's 529 Plan. You can use almost any state's 529 Plan since most do not have residency requirements. Some states allow tax-deductible contributions and most states do not tax the earnings within the plan; and the 2001 tax act made earnings in the 529 Plan federal income tax–free when used for college.

If the child for whom you originally established the account does not use the money for college, you can change the beneficiary to another family member such as the child's brother, sister, or even cousin.

If the child does not use the money for college, there will be tax and a penalty on the 529 Plan earnings when distributed. An exception to this is if the child receives a qualified scholarship and does not use the money in the plan for college. In that case, the child can use the money in the 529 Plan for any reason without penalty, but the child will have to pay income tax on the earnings.

◯ঽ Can you explain why 529 Plans are better than savings accounts that I have already set up for my children?

The two major reasons are that the investment earnings in and the distributions from a Section 529 Plan are not taxed if they are used to pay higher-education expenses. This means the plans are even better than tax-deferred accounts. A third reason is that funds that you have contributed to the plan are considered to be out of your estate. This makes them a very useful estate planning tool for parents or grandparents.

◯ঽ What happens if my son decides not to go to college?

The 529 savings plans provide a few options for this situation. There is a 10 percent penalty (in addition to income tax) on funds that your son withdraws but does not use for college expenses. Alternatively, you can still retain the account's tax-free status by transferring it to another child or certain other relatives if your son decides not to attend college. In fact, if you set up a 529 savings plan, you can change the beneficiary of the account at any time and can control the distributions.

◯ঽ Is there anything else I should know about these plans?

You can only contribute cash to 529 Plans. The plans generally have a minimum contribution requirement and a maximum contribution limit, which vary from state to state. And, of course, because of the great leveraging power of the tax-free growth of the funds, the best time to start contributing to these plans is while your children are young.

CR *Am I making a taxable gift when I put money in the plan?*

Congress included some special gift tax rules for Section 529 Plans. You can fund the plan with 5 years' worth of annual exclusion gifts in 1 year without triggering any gift tax filing or incurring gift tax. For example, in 2004 the annual exclusion is $11,000, so you can put up to $55,000 per child into the 529 Plan. There is a catch, however: You must outlive this gift by 5 years for this to be treated as a completed gift. Otherwise, the incomplete portion of the gift is added back to your estate. For example, Theresa sets up a 529 Plan for her grandson and puts in $55,000. Unfortunately, she passes away 2 years later. Because Theresa did not outlive the 5 years, the result is that $22,000 is considered to be a completed gift, which is free of estate and gift tax. The remaining $33,000 is considered to be an incomplete gift and is added back to Theresa's estate.

Irrevocable Trust

CR *I am currently holding stock in a privately held company that is planning a public stock offering within the next year. I want to make gifts of some of this stock now, but my children are still young, and I don't think it would be prudent to give them assets that will, hopefully, explode in value. Is there any way that I can accomplish this strategy?*

Making gifts of the stock now, while the value is low, is an excellent strategy. It would make sense to take this pre–initial public offering stock and put it into an irrevocable trust that could control the stock both before and after the public offering. This would allow you to keep the assets invested until the children reach a certain age or cross whatever milestones that you require. The gain on the sale of this stock will be taxed at the trust's capital gain tax rate, which is the same as it is for individual taxpayers, so you would not suffer any adverse tax consequences by using a trust. Overall, this appears to address all of your objectives for making a gift of this appreciating asset.

Irrevocable Grantor Trust

ᘓ *We are interested in using a private annuity but are concerned that our children are not responsible enough to handle the investments and to make the annuity payments to us. Do you have any suggestions?*

In this instance, you can establish an irrevocable grantor trust (IGT), which we discussed earlier in this chapter, for the benefit of the children; give assets to the trust utilizing your gift tax applicable exclusion to avoid a gift tax, and then sell other assets to the trust as buyer of the private annuity.

ᘓ *Can you explain how this combined IGT and private annuity would work?*

Yes. You first establish the IGT and then make a gift of cash to the trust using a portion of your gift tax applicable exclusion. The IGT buys assets from you in exchange for the annuity. If the assets that you sell to the trust do not generate sufficient income to make the annuity payment, the trustee of the IGT uses whatever portion of the cash gift that is necessary to make the payments.

As the maker of the IGT, you pay the taxes on the income that the trust assets generate. You receive your annuity payment under the private annuity agreement tax-free because you are paying the taxes on the earnings of the IGT. At your death, the private annuity ends and the children receive the balance of the trust assets based on the provisions you established in the trust.

Dynasty Trust

ᘓ *What is the most effective way to protect family wealth for generations?*

The strategy that protects wealth for generations is referred to as multigenerational, dynasty, or generation-skipping transfer tax planning.

ᘓ *What is dynasty planning?*

As the name implies, *dynasty* or *multigenerational planning* involves extending the benefits of your estate plan to your children and grandchildren; a multigenerational plan is a family wealth management plan that also sustains your values and traditions after your death.

To appreciate the power of dynasty planning, you need to fully appreciate the effect that estate taxes can have over time. Let's take the example of Thomas. Thomas dies in 2004 with an estate of $2 million. After death taxes and final expenses of $500,000, his daughter, Cindy, inherits $1.5 million. Cindy invests that money at 7 percent for 20 years, spends some of it during her life, and still dies with an estate of $5 million. Her estate is subject to an estate tax of 50 percent, leaving $2.5 million for Thomas' grandchildren.

If Thomas had engaged in dynasty planning, there would have been no federal estate tax on the $5 million at Cindy's death, doubling the amount available to his grandchildren and future generations. The estates of Thomas and Cindy paid a combined $3 million in federal estate taxes. Proper planning could have eliminated 85 percent of those taxes.

Because this type of planning is so powerful, Congress enacted the generation-skipping transfer (GST) tax, as we explained in Chapter 4, Tax Basics. The GST tax is a confiscatory tax system to curtail multi-generational planning, however, the law also provides that every person may transfer up to $1.5 million (2004 amount) of property without paying the GST tax. The key to multigenerational planning is using this $1.5 million GST tax exemption to its fullest extent.

∝ Are there reasons other than taxes for doing dynasty planning?

Besides the substantial transfer tax savings that will accrue over time to your family, there are several other strong reasons for dynasty planning. Dynasty planning is about helping to shape the lives of your progeny and passing on your beliefs to them. This long-range planning can provide for your descendants' education, encourage participation in worthwhile causes, support family entrepreneurism, and discourage behavior that you find unacceptable. By keeping the family wealth in trust, you can also shield it from divorce proceedings, lawsuits, predators, and poor money management skills.

∝ I think that the estate tax will be permanently repealed, so I'm unwilling to undertake this type of planning. Am I wrong?

We all know that the tax laws change regularly—and, these days, frequently. As the law stands today, the estate tax will be repealed for exactly 365 days, then return with its full vigor in 2011. All recent efforts in Congress to make the repeal permanent have died in the Senate.

Still, you could be right. Over the history of this country, Congress has repealed the estate tax three different times. But it has also passed legislation imposing an estate tax four times. Will there be a repeal in the future? Possibly. Will there be a *permanent* repeal? History suggests not. Your estate might not pay estate taxes, but in all likelihood your children's estates will. The possibility for major changes in our tax laws arises anew every 2 years when we have a congressional election.

The point here is that instead of leaving control of your family's finances to Congress, you can take charge now and ensure favorable results. You can either choose to affirmatively plan for the future or just hope for the best. We strongly recommend the first course of action.

ℭ How does dynasty planning work in a typical estate plan?

Your estate planning attorney drafts your estate planning documents with tax provisions to establish a pool of assets from your estate that equals your available GST tax exemption. In most cases, that pool is further divided to create a separate trust for each of your children. The assets in each share provide for the health, education, support, and maintenance of each child. The trusts are designed so that they are not included in the estates of your children when they die. At a child's death, the trust continues according to the terms you specify for successive generations within your family bloodlines.

ℭ Must my dynasty plan end with my grandchildren, or can it continue beyond that?

How long your dynasty plan can last depends on state law. Many states limit the duration of trusts. This limitation is known as the *rule against perpetuities*. This rule can be enormously complicated, but the upshot is that in most states a trust can only exist for 90 or so years before it must end. Some states have abolished the rule against perpetuities altogether. If you establish a trust in any of those states, it can go on indefinitely and never terminate.

Your attorney will explain the particular law in your home state.

If your state has this rule, but you are interested in establishing a trust that is not subject to this rule, it is possible to "move" your trust to a state that has repealed the rule against perpetuities. This is technically known as changing the *situs*, or *location*, of your trust.

Trusts that are intended to last indefinitely should be drafted with flexibility to allow for changing circumstances and changes in the law. In most cases, these trusts are managed by professional corporate trustees.

◌ *If I set up a dynasty trust, how will my beneficiaries have access to the money if they need it?*

The trust will generally provide that each generation of beneficiaries will have access to the trust funds for their "health, education, maintenance, and support" needs, which may sound limiting but in reality are quite broad, encompassing virtually everything a human being would ever need, including homes and trips to Europe.

Beyond that, you can decide the standards, manner, and purposes for distributions; the instructions for which you include in the trust document. You could authorize distributions for the down payment on a house, for college expenses or weddings, for "seed money" for start-up businesses; or you could prohibit distributions to beneficiaries with addiction problems. It is in these instructions that you have the greatest opportunity to mold future generations.

Some clients choose to provide a guaranteed income to their beneficiaries by creating a total return unitrust. This is a trust whose payout is based on a fixed percentage of the value of the trust, as determined each year. With a unitrust, the level of payment will not vary with current interest rates or annual trust earnings, but rather will be a function of the value of the assets owned by the trust.

◌ *Can I include GST tax planning in the demand trust I set up for my wife?*

The short answer is "yes." The disadvantage of doing this is that if the assets in the trust are largely expended for your wife's benefit, some of your GST tax exemption will be wasted. However, for clients who primarily see the spouse's demand trust as a wealth transfer tool and don't expect to spend the assets unless true economic hardship falls upon them, dynasty trust planning is a viable option. In most instances, the trust will purchase life insurance with the annual $5,000 gifts to maximize the benefits to your descendants.

∝ What about GST tax planning for my life insurance trust?

An irrevocable life insurance trust (ILIT) is one of the best dynasty planning tools available. This ILIT is structured much like the demand trust you create for your spouse, but instead of having only one beneficiary, all your living descendants are beneficiaries from the start. For each beneficiary, you can transfer $5,000 to the trust annually. So if you have a wife, two children, and four grandchildren, you can make annual gifts of $35,000 to the trust. Each year you will also allocate $35,000 of your GST tax exemption to the trust so that the trust is permanently exempt from the GST tax.

Your trustee will use that money to purchase a sizable life insurance policy, probably a second-to-die policy on you and your wife. The result is usually a pool of several million dollars to provide for your descendants for as long as the trust lasts. Over time, the trust can grow to an enormous sum.

An ILIT is perhaps the best way to "leverage" your GST tax exemption. For example, over the course of 20 years, you might allocate $700,000 of your exemption (20 × $35,000) to the trust, but when the life insurance policy pays off, there will be several million dollars in the trust. That money and its future earnings can be distributed to your children, grandchildren, and future descendants without any estate or gift tax liabilities.

TRANSFERS TO CHARITIES

∝ How can we avoid the estate and income taxes on our individual retirement account at our deaths?

Because qualified retirement plan proceeds are subject to both federal estate and income taxes, your heirs will lose much of your IRA to taxes after you're gone. One simple solution is to name your favorite charity as the beneficiary of your IRA and to use some of the distributions from the IRA to purchase a life insurance policy held in an irrevocable life insurance trust. As beneficiaries of the ILIT, your loved ones will receive the proceeds from the life insurance estate tax– and income tax–free.

> *I have heard that we can completely eliminate or zero-out our estate taxes. How would we do this?*

In addition to the basic tax planning strategies of using the marital and family trust, some families are able to completely eliminate estate taxes by incorporating some of the charitable planning techniques that we discussed in Chapter 3, Planning for Loved Ones and Charity.

Specifically, a charitable lead annuity trust (CLAT) can transfer substantial amounts of wealth tax-free. For example, Joe has a securities portfolio valued at $5 million and he wants to transfer the entire value without any gift taxes. He sets up a CLAT in May 2004. The trust provides the XYZ University with $350,000 per year for 20 years. At the end of the 20-year term, the portfolio goes to Joe's son, Albert. The exact amount of the annuity payment or the term of years in each case will vary, depending on the applicable federal rate. This transfer will completely escape a gift tax. In addition, it is possible for Joe to avoid any estate tax liability by structuring the same type of transfer in his estate planning documents so that such a transfer occurs at his death.

> *I own 100,000 shares of ABC Corporation stock that have appreciated greatly since I purchased them. I need to sell the stock to purchase a condominium and for my retirement income. Would a charitable remainder trust make sense in my case?*

Your situation is ideal for a charitable remainder trust (CRT). You can put some of the stock into a CRT and sell the balance to produce the funds for the condominium purchase. If the transaction is carefully structured, the charitable income tax deduction for the CRT will offset the capital gain tax you owe on the stock sale.

For example, let's say your stock is worth $1 million and you paid $200,000 for it. That's an $800,000 capital gain, so you'll pay $120,000 (15 percent) if you sell it all now. Instead, you transfer 50 percent of the stock to a charitable remainder unitrust (CRUT). The CRUT will sell the stock without paying capital gain taxes and will provide you with an income for the rest of your life. You also get an immediate $200,000 income tax deduction for your gift to the CRUT. You sell the remaining 50 percent of the stock and recognize the gain on the sale. But your charitable tax deduction from the CRT offsets the gain from the stock sale, so in this example you essentially sell the stock tax-free. Now you have the cash to buy the condominium, have a nice income stream from the CRUT to fund your retirement, and support your favorite charity.

ଡ *Most of my portfolio is invested in one stock that produces very low yield income. I am not as brave with investments as I used to be and would also like more income now that I've retired. I'd like to diversify my investments, but I don't want to pay capital gain tax. What can I do?*

If you want to spread out and lower the investment risk—and also increase the amount of income that the low-yield securities generate— you can do so with a charitable remainder trust. Let's look at an example of how this works.

April and Jim own stock that they have accumulated over many years during Jim's employment at the issuing company. The value of the stock is now $220,000. His total basis in the stock is $20,000. They receive about $2,000 every year as a dividend. If they create a CRT and donate the stock to it, the CRT may sell the stock without a capital gain tax and therefore will have the entire $220,000 to invest. The CRT may be designed to pay to April and Jim a 7 percent annual annuity from the trust. That would be a total of $15,400. That income will continue until both of them pass away. At that time the remainder of the funds will be paid to the charity of their choosing.

The alternative to April and Jim using a CRT would be for them to sell the stock themselves. This would create a rather substantial $200,000 capital gain ($220,000 sale price − $20,000 basis = $200,000 capital gain). With the federal capital gain tax rate currently at 15 percent, April and Jim would have to pay a $30,000 capital gain tax. If they invested the remaining $190,000 at 7 percent, they would receive an annual income from the investment of only $13,300.

With the CRT, April and Jim not only receive $2,100 more income annually, they also receive an income tax deduction for their gift to the trust and create a substantial gift for their favorite charity.

◌ℛ *My wife and I really like the idea of giving to charity to reduce estate and capital gain taxes, but if we give assets to charity, we don't have much left to give our children and we don't like that idea. Is this where we might use life insurance to create an estate?*

Yes. You would create an irrevocable life insurance trust, also referred to in these situations as a *wealth replacement trust*, to own a second-to-die life insurance policy on your joint lives, which will not pay the death benefit until both you and your wife have died. The premiums on this type of life insurance policy are less than if the policy were on your life alone. As we explained earlier in this chapter, once you establish the ILIT, you donate cash to it sufficient to pay the premiums on the policy.

If the ILIT is properly drafted and operated, the insurance policy death benefit is not included in either of your estates at your deaths. It passes to the ILIT and, hence, to your children, free of all estate taxes.

In addition to achieving the goal of creating an inheritance for your children to replace the one you gave to charity, you are making your annual gifts without any gift tax consequences and you have further reduced the size of your estate for estate tax purposes by the amount of the gift to charity and by the cumulative amount of the annual gifts.

ACTION STEPS

We respectfully present the following action steps to summarize the concepts that we discussed in chapter 5 and to suggest steps that you can take to prepare for meetings with your estate planning team of professionals.

❑ *Finish your basic estate plan before starting on the advanced strategies.* Before you can utilize an advanced planning technique, you first need to have a basic plan in place and fully implemented.

❑ *Determine whether you need advanced planning.* Typically, advanced planning is most effective for individuals whose wealth cannot be fully sheltered by the applicable exclusion. If that is not your current situation, advanced planning is probably not necessary. Even if your estate warrants advanced planning, you must commit to fully implementing and maintaining the plan before proceeding, and you must be willing to accept losing a certain amount of control over the assets subject to the plan.

❑ *Meet with a life insurance professional.* For many people, life insurance is a simple, cost-effective way to accomplish many estate planning goals. Any life insurance you purchase should be owned through an irrevocable life insurance trust (ILIT). If you currently have life insurance, meet with your agent to review the policy, then meet with an estate planning attorney to see about transferring the policy to an ILIT.

❑ *Evaluate your current advisors.* Advanced planning requires a team of advanced planning professionals. In many cases, you will need to supplement your existing team or build a new one to meet your advanced planning goals. To find the type of advisors that you need, ask friends, family members, and existing advisors. If those individuals aren't helpful, the trust department at a local bank is a good source, and, of course, the contributors to this book would welcome the opportunity to work with you (see Appendix E, Geographic Listing of Contributing Authors).

❑ *Understand the contents of any plan presented to you.* No matter how much you trust your advisors, you must understand and feel comfortable with the plan before you begin implementation. No one expects you to become an accountant or tax attorney, but you must generally comprehend the structure of the plan, how the plan affects you and your loved ones, and how it meets your goals. Most advanced planning tools cannot be changed after they are put into place. Make sure that you understand the tax and other benefits of the plan as well as its potential downsides. Don't be shy about asking questions, and keep asking questions until you feel comfortable with the plan. If you don't like the plan, tell your advisors what you don't like and ask them to make changes. This is your plan, your money, and your family. Don't settle for anything less than total satisfaction.

❑ *Follow through and regularly review your plan.* An estate plan that is not implemented does you no good. For some advanced planning tools, implementation is a fairly long process, and you must commit to seeing the process through. It's best if you and your advisors make a list of the necessary tasks and who is responsible for carrying out each task. And we cannot emphasize enough that good planning requires regular monitoring. Every year or so you must sit down with your advisors to ensure that your plan is working as you intended and to make any necessary adjustments.

chapter 6

Retirement Planning

IMPORTANCE OF
RETIREMENT PLANNING

What is retirement planning?

Retirement planning is formulating a game plan for when you will no longer be bringing home a paycheck. It's deciding how you want to live out your dreams for yourself and your family after retirement and planning so that those dreams come true.

Why is retirement planning important?

Most of us will have to provide for ourselves after we retire. Social Security was never intended to be a sole source of retirement income. Many of our parents could count on comfortable pension plans and other benefits from their employers to live on, but those benefits are not the norm for most of us today.

Retirement used to be a brief period of maybe 10 years or so. Now, Americans are living longer, healthier, more active lives; it is common for people to be in retirement for almost as many years as they worked. It is important to plan as early as possible for retirement to achieve financial security in your later years.

○R Doesn't Social Security take care of me?

Retirement planning is important for everyone who wants to maintain their financial independence after they stop working. Studies show that a retiree will need approximately 75 percent of his or her final annual income to maintain a lifestyle close to that achieved prior to retirement. While Social Security is a good starting point for a retirement plan, studies from the Employee Benefits Research Institute show that Social Security, even when combined with other retirement programs, will provide only about 42 percent of what the retiree needs. The balance must come from investments, savings, pension, annuities, and earnings from work. (EBRI Retirement Income Research: 2003 Findings. "Income of the Elderly Population: 2001," June 2003, *Notes*.)

○R I'm 35, and I have a good job. Is it too soon for me to start planning for retirement?

Heavens, no! If your employer offers a qualified retirement plan, you should start contributing to it. If not, then you should investigate other retirement savings tools and put away a sum of money each year. Starting as early as possible gives you two big benefits:

1. The younger you are, the more time you have to save for retirement and the more time your money has to grow.
2. By starting early, you develop a habit of saving regularly, which most Americans do not do.

Let's look at an example of the first point. To accumulate $1 million by the time you turn age 65, you need to save $8,174 a year (assuming an 8 percent rate of return). If you wait 10 years to start saving, you'll need to save $20,234 a year to get to $1 million.

By starting early, you can take advantage of the *compound interest* that accrues on your savings. Compound interest is one of the most important tools in accumulating a retirement nest egg. Compound interest literally works every day, 7 days a week, 365 days a year. By leaving investments in place over time, the principal earns interest, the interest earns interest, and, for tax-deferred investments, the tax savings earn interest. This is called *triple compounding*.

Even if you only deposit $2,000 each year at 8 percent interest, at the end of 30 years you will have accumulated $226,566. Table 6-1 demonstrates how much a person can accumulate by age 60, beginning at various ages, saving $10,000 per year, earning 8 percent, and the

TABLE 6-1   Effects of Compounding on Savings*

Starting age	Number of years to age 60	Amount accumulated	
		Deposited January 1	Deposited December 31
25	35	$1,861,021	$1,723,168
30	30	1,223,459	1,132,832
35	25	789,544	731,059
40	20	494,229	457,620
45	15	293,243	271,521
50	10	156,455	144,866
55	5	63,359	58,666

*Assumes $10,000 is invested each year with an 8 percent return.

difference between depositing the $10,000 at the beginning of the year versus the end of the year. It is obvious from this table that the younger you can start your savings program and the earlier in the year you can put the money into the plan, the greater the long-term rewards.

℞ *What are the benefits of using tax-deferred retirement plans or investments?*

First and foremost, they allow you to save more for retirement. For example, your contributions to a personal individual retirement account (IRA) are tax-deductible on your income tax returns; and amounts that your employer withholds from your pay as your contributions to an employer-sponsored plan are not taxed at the time. Let's say you put $10,000 a year into these tax-deferred retirement plans, and you are in a 35 percent income tax bracket (federal and state tax combined). When you contribute $10,000, you save $3,500 in income taxes ($10,000 × 35%). So, it cost you $6,500 to save $10,000. Another way to look at this is that you are contributing $6,500 and the government is contributing $3,500.

Factors to Consider in Retirement Planning

℞ *What issues should I consider in creating my retirement plan?*

You should consider the following seven factors as you are preparing your retirement plan:

1. Your current income and how much you can save
2. Your estimated income needs for retirement, which requires you
    to consider:
    a. where you would like to live—metropolitan area, retirement
        area, the beach in Mexico, the south of France;
    b. what you want to do—work at a new career, golf, do volun-
        teer work;
    c. what sort of lifestyle you want to maintain—frugal daily
        budgeting to splurging on lavish trips to Europe or building
        the dream retirement cottage at the lake.
3. Your sources of income during retirement
4. Your options for accumulating retirement funds using tradi-
    tional, non-tax-deferred methods
5. Your options for accumulating retirement funds using tax-
    deferred arrangements
6. Your options for distributions from your retirement plans
7. Investment planning strategies after you are retired

Your answers to these questions and your other financial and
personal goals will help you create the best retirement plan for your
situation.

ℛ Can I handle my retirement planning on my own?

The answer for the vast majority of people is "no." Retirement planning is as complex as it is important. Unless you can honestly call
yourself an expert in financial planning, investments, asset allocation, tax laws, and pension laws, you are going to need professional
help in developing and maintaining your retirement plan.

You should seek out a financial professional who specializes in
retirement planning to answer your questions about retirement, to
counsel you as you create your retirement plan, and help you to feel
a great deal more comfortable about your future.

Your financial advisor will consider the effects of the following
on your plan:

■ *Inflation:* During periods of inflation, prices rise, which means
  that your dollar buys less. Although the government's fiscal policies

have essentially kept inflation under control, ultimately life's necessities will most likely cost more in the future.

- *Taxation:* As tax laws and tax rates change over time, and as Congress and the Internal Revenue Service (IRS) often amend the laws and regulations governing retirement plans, it is vital to consider how those changes will affect your plan. It is also crucial to take into account your current tax situation as well as your potential tax situation during retirement.

- *Time horizon to retirement:* Your current age and the number of years you have until you retire will potentially dictate changes to your plan. If you want to retire at an early age, chances are that you will have to save more now or to set your income goals lower than if you retired later or to accept the fact that your money will not last throughout your retirement.

- *The investments:* The types of investments you select will likely have the greatest impact on your plan. It is important that your investments are diversified, chosen to meet the level of risk you can tolerate, and reviewed and adjusted over time as necessary.

☙ *What are my options for accumulating retirement funds?*

We will describe the following tax-advantaged methods in this chapter:

- Employer-sponsored qualified retirement plans
- Personal individual retirement accounts
- Employer-sponsored nonqualified plans
- Annuities
- Life insurance
- Charitable remainder unitrusts

The Relationship between Retirement Planning and Estate Planning

☙ *How does retirement planning relate to my estate plan?*

At times, retirement planning can be contrary to estate planning. The goal of retirement planning is to build up a retirement fund during your working years to support your lifestyle after you retire. You and/or your employer fund these accounts, often with pre-income tax dollars, and the earnings are exempt from federal and state income tax until you withdraw them. This provides years of compounding tax-deferred dollars, which will result in increased retirement savings—but also greater wealth accumulation and estate planning challenges for you and your family. Congress and the IRS do not intend retirement accounts to be passed to our heirs, so they created rules and regulations to ensure that we deplete those funds before we die or pay estate and income taxes on them after our death. Estate planning is also based on creating wealth but with the intent of preserving as much of it as possible to give to your loved ones during life or at death.

For people who have significant retirement plan balances, proper coordination with estate planning goals can be the difference between a plan that effectively transfers wealth and one that causes a tax debacle for heirs. The beneficiary you name for your retirement plan determines who inherits the funds on your death. Tax-deferred retirement accounts are considered IRD (income in respect of a decedent) assets, so your heir will be responsible for paying the income taxes on the balance of the funds that they inherit. Retirement accounts are also subject to federal estate tax, so careful integration of your retirement plan with your estate plan is necessary to ensure taking advantage of the estate tax avoidance techniques available to you.

Estate planning and retirement plan distribution planning are inextricably tied together to eliminate or to reduce the income and estate tax burden on your heirs. It requires skilled knowledge of both retirement planning and estate planning to successfully reconcile the contradictions so you can accomplish your goals without violating the tax rules.

ℭ *What goals should I have to make my retirement plan part of estate planning?*

Retirement planning will be one of the crucial steps in the estate planning process. For most people, retirement funds will constitute the largest asset in their estates, so it is critical that individuals plan for the after-death disposition of those funds to their loved ones in the most tax-efficient method possible.

EMPLOYER-SPONSORED QUALIFIED RETIREMENT PLANS

CR *I've heard about qualified and nonqualified retirement plans. Could you please explain the difference between the two?*

A *qualified plan* is an employer-sponsored retirement plan governed by the Employee Retirement Income Security Act of 1974 (ERISA) and the Internal Revenue Code (IRC). If the employer-sponsored plan meets the strict guidelines of ERISA and the IRC, the employer receives a tax deduction for contributions it makes on behalf of the employees; and employee-participants are able to defer income tax on all plan contributions and earnings. Participants do not pay income tax on the plan benefits until they receive distributions from the plan.

There are also plans that employers can use, namely, the savings incentive match (SIMPLE) plans and simplified employee pension (SEP) plans, that do not fall under ERISA control as "qualified" but are still income tax–deferred plans created under the IRC.

Professional advisors refer to *nonqualified plans* as plans that are also employer-sponsored but do not have to adhere to the provisions of ERISA and the IRC. Employers can tailor these plans to meet the goals and objectives of individual participants, but in return for this flexibility, the employers and participants forgo many of the tax benefits associated with qualified plans. We briefly discuss nonqualified plans later in this chapter under "Alternatives to Qualified Retirement Plans."

A complete discussion of all the employer-sponsored qualified and nonqualified plans is outside the scope of this book, but you will find detailed information on these plans in *Strictly Business: Planning Strategies for Privately Owned Businesses* (David K. Cahoone and Larry W. Gibbs, editors, 2002). In this chapter, we will briefly describe a few of the more popular plans—plans that smaller employers are likely to offer their employees.

CR *What are the advantages of employer-sponsored qualified plans?*

■ Employers realize current income tax deductions for contributions they make to qualified plans on behalf of participants.

Participants are not currently taxed on amounts they contribute to the plan or on amounts their employers contribute on their behalf.

- Participants can usually contribute far larger amounts to one of these plans than to the employer-sponsored SEP or SIMPLE plans or to their own personal IRAs.

- ERISA protects participants' funds from the claims of creditors and bankruptcy.

CR *What tax benefits are available to participants of employer-sponsored qualified plans?*

The two major tax benefits common to the employer-sponsored qualified, SIMPLE, and SEP plans are:

1. Participants make contributions on a tax-deferred basis, meaning that they do not pay income taxes on the amount of their contributions until they later make withdrawals from the plans. This allows individuals to save more for retirement.

2. The plan or account is tax-exempt, meaning that income and capital gains accumulate tax-free prior to distribution. Compounding of untaxed income and gain can produce significant growth in value over time.

CR *I'm a participant in an employer-sponsored plan that vests 100 percent after my fifth year of employment. What does "vest" mean?*

When an amount in the plan *vests*, it means that those funds belong to you and you do not forfeit them if you leave the employer for any reason. A participant's rights to his or her accrued benefit resulting from an employer's contributions to a qualified plan must vest at certain rates during the years of his or her employment. For example, if the plan says that you are 50 percent vested at the end of the third year of employment, then you have the right to withdraw 50 percent of the funds in your account. Vesting schedules are designed to foster employees' loyalty to the company.

If the plan allows employee contributions, the contributions and the earnings on them must be 100 percent vested immediately.

❧ I've heard that we have to start taking money out of our employer-sponsored plans at a certain age. Do I have to take distributions at any particular time?

Soon after reaching age 70½, you must begin making withdrawals of at least a certain amount or you will incur penalty taxes.

Defined-Benefit Plans

❧ My employer currently provides me with a defined-benefit pension plan. What is a defined-benefit pension plan?

A *defined-benefit plan* is a qualified retirement plan established most often by a large corporation with many employees because it is fairly expensive to establish and to maintain. There are several versions of defined-benefit plans, but they are all similar in the most important features. With these plans, the benefit is defined as a specific dollar amount or a percentage of the employee's income before retirement. For example, the plan may state that all employees at the age of 65 with 25 years of service will receive 70 percent of their highest annual salary for the rest of their lives.

This benefit is a contractual obligation of the employer. The amount of payment does not vary based on the investment performance of the retirement trust fund. Defined-benefit plans use actuarial assumptions (age and life expectancy of employees, employee turnover, interest rates, investment projections, probable increases in compensation levels) to calculate the amount that the employer must contribute annually to the plan to adequately fund it. These plans are heavily regulated by the federal government, and federal insurance provides some assurance that employees will receive at least part of the promised benefit if the plan fails.

❧ Why doesn't my employer offer a defined-benefit plan?

This type of plan is becoming more and more rare. Because of their expense, complexity, and intense governmental regulation, only the largest of employers offer this type of plan, and usually only employers with a unionized work force. Most employers are instead opting to offer defined-contribution plans.

Defined-Contribution Plans

CR *What is a defined-contribution plan?*

With a *defined-contribution plan*, the employer does not guarantee a specific benefit at retirement as is the case with the defined-benefit plan. Rather, the plan calls for the employer to make certain contributions to the plan on the employee's behalf, and each employee has a separate account within the plan. A retiring or departing employee receives the balance of his or her account (subject to vesting rules), either in a lump sum or in some form of periodic distribution. The amount the employee receives is based on two factors, the amount contributed and investment performance. The best you can do is estimate your account value at retirement based on your estimated contributions over time and a reasonable assumed growth rate for the money in your account.

401(k) Plan

CR *My new employer has a 401(k) retirement plan. What is a 401(k) plan?*

A *401(k) plan* is a qualified employer-sponsored profit-sharing plan that includes a *cash-or-deferred arrangement* that allows you to contribute to your own retirement account. Employees may make contributions in either of two ways, both of which are free of withholding for income taxes:

1. *By elective salary reduction:* Each employee elects to reduce his or her pay by a certain dollar amount or percentage of salary. The employer withholds that amount from each paycheck and contributes it to the employee's separate 401(k) account.
2. *By bonus-or-cash option:* If the employer has included this option in the plan, the employer offers employees a bonus, typically at year's end, and each employee elects to defer all or a portion of the bonus to his or her 401(k) account or to take it in cash.

There could also be a provision in the plan that the employer will match a certain portion of the participants' contributions. The amount of both the employer's deposits and each participant's deposits are limited by law.

CR *What are the contribution limits for a 401(k) plan?*

In 2004, the tax-deductible limit on employee deferrals is $13,000 and the limit increases $1,000 each year until 2006 when it reaches $15,000. Thereafter, the $15,000 amount is indexed annually for inflation. Also, workers age 50 or over may contribute an additional $1,000 per year to the plan as "catch-up" contributions.

CR *I still have money in my former employer's 401(k). What are my options concerning these funds?*

Your options are dependent upon a combination of factors and the answers you get to the following questions.

1. Does your former employer's plan allow you to leave your current balance in the plan?
2. If your current employer has a plan, does it accept the transfer of money (rollover) from another plan?

Your options are:

- If your answer to the first question is "yes," then you have the options of leaving the money in your previous employer's plan or rolling the funds over to a new or existing IRA.
- If your answer to the second question is "yes," you have the options of transferring the account balance to your new employer's plan or rolling the funds over to a new or existing IRA.
- If your answer to both questions is "no," you can roll over the money to a new or existing IRA account.

You can accomplish all of these options without triggering any taxes.

Savings Incentive Match Plan

CR *What is a savings incentive match plan?*

A *savings incentive match plan IRA (SIMPLE IRA)* is a low-cost alternative for the employer that wishes to offer a retirement program to employees but cannot afford to sponsor a qualified plan. A SIMPLE IRA is an employer-sponsored individual retirement account that permits larger annual employee contributions than a personal IRA allows. The SIMPLE IRA plan also allows participants to defer a portion of their pay to their SIMPLE IRA accounts or to fund individual retirement annuities. Employers can also contribute by matching employee contributions or by making other elective contributions.

◌ʒ *How much can employees contribute to a SIMPLE IRA?*

The limit for employee elective salary reduction contributions is $9,000 in 2004 and $10,000 in 2005. Thereafter, it is $10,000 indexed for inflation.

Simplified Employee Pension Plan

◌ʒ *What is a simplified employee pension plan?*

A *simplified employee pension (SEP) plan* is an IRA or an individual retirement annuity that employers establish for employees. Under a SEP plan, the employer, and in some cases, the employee, contributes funds to the IRA, which the employee owns and controls. The maximum contribution is 25 percent of an employee's compensation or $40,000, whichever is less (2003; indexed annually for inflation). Employees are immediately 100 percent vested in the contributions and have the right to withdraw the funds at any time (subject to taxes and penalties).

INDIVIDUAL RETIREMENT ACCOUNTS

Traditional Individual Retirement Account

◌ʒ *What is a traditional IRA?*

The *traditional individual retirement account (IRA)* allows individuals to invest funds for retirement on a tax-deferred basis. Both contributions and earnings accumulate on a tax-deferred basis until the owner of the account withdraws them—allowing the triple compounding—and then the withdrawals are taxed at the individual's then current

TABLE 6-2 Traditional IRA Schedule of Maximum Annual Deductible Contributions

Year	Maximum contribution under age 50	Maximum contribution at & over age 50
2004	$3,000	$3,500
2005	$4,000	$4,500
2006 & 2007	$4,000	$5,000
2008	$5,000*	$6,000*

*Indexed for inflation beginning in 2009.

tax rate. Contributions to traditional IRAs are tax-deductible for the year that the owner makes the contributions.

❧ *How much of a tax-deductible contribution can I make each year to a traditional IRA?*

If you meet the adjusted gross income (AGI) requirements and you are not covered by an employer-sponsored retirement plan, the maximum deductible contribution you can make each year is the lesser of 100 percent of compensation or the amount shown for each year in Table 6-2. Congress gave taxpayers who are at least 50 years of age the ability to increase their contributions so that they might be able to build larger retirement accounts in the shorter time frame they have until retirement. One of the advantages of an IRA is its flexibility. Individuals may contribute whenever they choose and in whatever amounts they choose during the year, or they can contribute different amounts each year, as long as the total contribution in a single year does not exceed the published annual limit or 100 percent of earned income.

❧ *How much can I earn and still be able to contribute to an IRA?*

Assuming you aren't covered by a qualified plan at work, the AGI limits for making deductible contributions to a traditional IRA are shown in Table 6-3.

❧ *Can I contribute to an IRA on a tax-deductible basis if I'm covered by a plan at work?*

You can, but there are limitations. Your contributions are fully or

TABLE 6-3   Traditional IRA AGI Limits for Annual Deductible Contributions

Filing status	If AGI is:	the deduction is:
Single, head of household, or qualifying widow(er)	any amount	100%
Married filing joint or separate return, spouse *not* covered by a plan at work	any amount	100%
Married filing joint return, spouse *is* covered by a plan at work	less than $150,000	100%
	$150,000 to $159,999	partial
	$160,000 or more	0
Married filing separate return, spouse *is* covered by a plan at work	less than $10,000	partial
	$10,000 or more	0

partially deductible depending on your AGI. Table 6-4 shows the AGI ranges for the appropriate years.

Since you are covered by a plan at work, the AGI limits for determining the deductibility of your IRA contributions vary depending on the year that you make the contribution. If your AGI is equal to or less than the lower range, the contribution (within the limit shown in Table 6-2) is fully deductible. If your AGI equals or exceeds the upper range, you're not entitled to a deduction for your contribution. Contributions are partially deductible if your AGI falls within the lower and upper ranges.

ଔ *My wife is a stay-at-home mom right now. Can she still have an IRA?*

Normally, a person who does not earn compensation income cannot contribute to an IRA. However, you can create a *spousal IRA* for your wife if she doesn't work or if she doesn't earn enough compensation income to make the maximum annual contribution as shown in Table 6-2. To qualify for a spousal IRA:

■   You and your wife must be legally married

TABLE 6-4   Traditional IRA AGI Limits for Deductible Contributions by Participants in Employer-Sponsored Plans

| Filing status | Year | AGI range | |
		Lower	Upper
Married filing joint return	2003	$60,000	$70,000
	2004	65,000	75,000
	2005	70,000	80,000
	2006	75,000	85,000
	2007 & beyond	80,000	90,000
Single or head of household	2003	40,000	50,000
	2004	45,000	55,000
	2005 & beyond	50,000	60,000

- You must file a joint federal income tax return
- You must earn more income than your wife
- Your wife must be younger than 70½
- Your wife cannot contribute to her own IRA

In 2004, the maximum contribution to a spousal IRA is the lesser of $3,000 or the combined compensation income of you and your wife. That amount increases to $4,000 for years 2005, 2006, and 2007; and increases to $5,000 in 2008.

☞ Are IRAs protected from the claims of creditors?

Most likely your IRA is protected. Your state law determines if your IRA is exempt from creditors, and most states exempt traditional IRAs at least to some extent.

☞ Is it better to contribute to my employer-sponsored 401(k) or to a traditional IRA?

The short answer is that you should contribute the maximum amount allowable to every tax-deferred plan that you can within IRS rules. Beyond that rule, it depends on your goals and the recommendations of your advisors. Each plan has its pros and cons:

- You have a nearly unlimited choice of investment options for your IRA funds; your options are usually more limited with employer plans.

- You can usually contribute far larger amounts to an employer-sponsored plan than to an IRA.

- Some employer-sponsored plans allow you to borrow part of your account's value. IRAs do not permit loans.

- It can take several years for your employer's contributions to the employer-sponsored plan to vest. (All dollars that you contribute to the plan are always 100 percent vested immediately.)

Rather than think of IRAs and employer-sponsored plans as competitors, you should look at them as complements to each other.

Roth Individual Retirement Account

CR *What is a Roth IRA?*

The *Roth IRA* has many of the same guidelines that the traditional IRA has. Earnings grow inside the Roth IRA tax-free. However, unlike the traditional IRA, contributions to Roth IRAs are *not* tax-deductible. When you withdraw money from your Roth IRA, assuming you've met all the requirements for withdrawal, you do not pay income tax on the contributions (you already paid tax on those) and *you do not pay income tax on the earnings*. In other words, most withdrawals are tax-free.

CR *How much can I contribute each year to a Roth IRA?*

The contribution limits for a Roth IRA are the same as those shown in Table 6-2 for the traditional IRA. You may contribute up to those amounts each year to a Roth IRA, less any contribution you made to a traditional IRA for that year. Contributions to Roth IRAs are not deductible and must be in cash. If you are age 50 or over, you can also make the additional catch-up contribution shown in Table 6-2.

Your eligibility to make contributions to a Roth IRA is phased out as your AGI exceeds certain amounts. Those amounts are shown in Table 6-5. Provided that you are within the income guidelines, you can make Roth IRA contributions even if you participate in an

TABLE 6-5   Roth IRA AGI Limits for Annual Contributions

Filing status	If AGI is:	the deduction is:
Married filing jointly	less than $150,000	maximum amount per Table 6-2 schedule, less contributions made to other IRAs that year
	$150,000 to $159,999	reduced
	$160,000 or more	0
Single, head of household	less than $95,000	maximum amount per Table 6-2 schedule, less contributions made to other IRAs that year
	$95,000 to $110,000	reduced
	Over $110,000	0

employer-sponsored retirement plan. A married person filing separately cannot contribute to a Roth IRA if he or she earns more than $10,000 a year.

ℭ℞ *My wife and I are taking full advantage of our 401(k) plans. Should we consider using a Roth IRA for additional savings?*

The Roth IRA is a good choice for additional savings above those in a 401(k). The tax advantages of a Roth IRA, combined with your 401(k) plans, can work to your advantage, particularly if you have a few years to go until retirement. Most people who have qualified retirement plans at work are not eligible to make tax-deductible contributions to a regular IRA, so a Roth IRA is usually the only alternative.

Unlike 401(k) contributions, which are pretax when made and fully taxed at withdrawal, contributions to a Roth IRA are not currently deductible but do accumulate free of tax and are generally available without income tax at withdrawal. So, a Roth IRA allows you to pay tax now on the smaller contribution amounts in order to shelter the larger accumulated amount from tax later.

ℭ℞ *We have used the traditional IRA for many years. But now we are intrigued by the "tax-free" nature of the Roth IRA. Can we convert our traditional IRA to a Roth IRA? And if so, what are the costs and benefits of the conversion?*

To determine if converting your traditional IRA to a Roth IRA is possible and beneficial, there are many factors that you and your advisors should evaluate, such as age, income needs, and estate planning goals. First, to qualify for conversion, your modified adjusted gross income cannot exceed $100,000 in the year of the conversion, and if you are married, you must file a joint tax return with your spouse.

If you meet this first qualification and convert to the Roth IRA, the entire amount that you convert from the traditional IRA would be subject to income tax in the year of the conversion. If you have sufficient non-IRA funds available to pay the income tax in the year of conversion, then converting to the Roth could make sense.

One of the attractions of the Roth IRA, though, is that you are not required to take minimum distributions at any age.

Although both types of IRAs would be included in your estate, the traditional IRA would be subject to income taxes while the Roth IRA will provide tax-free income to your heirs. Your beneficiaries would receive more from a Roth IRA if sufficient time had passed since conversion.

The issue of conversion is complicated. A professional advisor who is knowledgeable in this area should do the number crunching for you to determine if this is the right decision for your situation.

DISTRIBUTIONS FROM RETIREMENT PLANS

Employer-Sponsored Qualified Plans

Withdrawals Prior to Age 59½

༄ *I am taking an early retirement from my employer and want to know when I can begin drawing from my retirement accounts without incurring a penalty?*

The general rule is that if you withdraw funds from your qualified retirement plan prior to your reaching age 59½, it will be considered a premature distribution, and the amount you take will be subject to a 10 percent penalty in addition to regular income taxes. There are a number of exceptions to imposition of the early-withdrawal penalty tax for qualified plans, and the exceptions can vary for the specific type of plan. Primary exceptions common to all types of plans are for distributions when:

1. The plan participant dies, and the distribution goes to a beneficiary or the participant's estate.
2. The plan participant becomes totally and permanently disabled.
3. Distributions are made to a participant who separates from the service of an employer after reaching the age of 55.
4. It is a qualified rollover to an IRA or another qualified plan.

In addition, some employer-sponsored plans also allow for distributions prior to age 59½ for the following reasons:

1. Distributions are part of a series of substantially equal periodic payments that begin after the participant no longer works for the employer.
2. Distributions are for medical expenses that exceed 7.5 percent of the participant's adjusted gross income.
3. Distributions are for health insurance premiums for the account owner or his or her spouse and dependents after the account owner has become unemployed.
4. Distributions are used for postsecondary education costs for immediate family members or grandchildren.
5. Distributions are made to the participant's former spouse or child under a qualified domestic relations order.

It is important for you to review the provisions of your plan to make sure that you know what the rules are before you make any withdrawals or roll the funds over to any other plan.

Distribution Options between Ages 59½ and 70½

℞ *Assuming I am either 55 and separating from service or have reached 59½, what are the payout options for most qualified plans?*

Generally speaking, there are four payout choices:

1. An annuity based on life expectancy
2. An annuity over a fixed period of time
3. A lump-sum distribution in cash
4. A lump-sum rollover to a traditional IRA or other qualified plan

If you are married, your choices are generally limited to a joint-and-survivor annuity for you and your spouse unless he or she consents in writing to another form of payment. Whatever you do, do not cash in your plan or you will trigger unnecessary taxation. At the very least, roll the monies over to an IRA to keep those assets growing tax-deferred until you need them and to provide you access to a wider range of investment choices. Once you make this election, it is usually irreversible, so it is imperative that you contact your financial and tax advisors to go over your alternatives and to determine which one is the best for you.

CR *I am recently retired; is there any reason to roll over my qualified retirement plan to an IRA?*

Some of the reasons why you might want to roll over your qualified retirement plan account to an individual retirement account are:

1. If you roll over your account from your company's retirement plan to an IRA, your financial advisor will most likely monitor the account investments more closely than you or your company will. This will also make it easier for your advisor to ensure that the investments in the IRA are balanced properly with the rest of your portfolio.
2. You will likely have more investment options with your own IRA than you have with your company's retirement plan—especially if your qualified plan is invested heavily in the company's stock.
3. The IRA will frequently allow you more flexibility in naming beneficiaries.
4. The IRA will give your beneficiaries more opportunities to stretch out the period of time over which they must withdraw

the funds, thus stretching out and potentially reducing their income tax liability.

Individual Retirement Accounts

Withdrawals Prior to Age 59½

CR *What are the rules regarding distributions from traditional IRAs?*

You can withdraw money from your IRA at any time and pay income tax on the amounts you withdraw. However, unless certain exceptions are met, withdrawals before age 59½ are subject to a 10 percent penalty. The 10 percent penalty is *in addition* to the income taxes due on the total amount of the withdrawals.

CR *When can I take my money out of my Roth IRA?*

You may withdraw your contributions from your Roth IRA tax-free at any time because you already paid the income tax on those contributions. You may withdraw the earnings from your Roth IRA account tax-free and penalty-free provided that the IRA has been in effect for at least 5 years *and* one of the following applies:

- You are age 59½.
- You are deceased, and your beneficiary or estate makes the withdrawal.
- You become disabled.
- You are a "qualified first-time home buyer" using the distribution (up to $10,000) in the purchase of a primary residence.

Distributions of earnings from a Roth IRA that has been in effect for at least 5 years for any of the above reasons are known as *qualified distributions*. Qualified distributions are not includable in gross income.

Distributions of earnings from Roth IRAs before any of the events specified above are met are deemed *nonqualified distributions*. Nonqualified distributions are taxable and potentially exposed to a 10 percent penalty.

Unlike the traditional IRA and the employer-sponsored quali-fied, SEP, and SIMPLE plans, there are no requirements to begin distributions from a Roth IRA at age 70½. An individual can con-tinue to defer tax on Roth IRA earnings for his or her entire lifetime.

CR *Is it possible to take penalty-free distributions from a traditional IRA before turning 59½?*

An *early distribution* from a traditional IRA is any distribution taken before the owner reaches 59½ years of age. *All* early distributions from a traditional IRA are subject to a 10 percent penalty unless an exception applies. Early distributions of *earnings* from a Roth IRA are also subject to the 10 percent penalty unless an exception applies. There are eight exceptions to this rule for both types of IRAs:

1. The owner dies before reaching age 59½, and the distribution goes to a beneficiary or the owner's estate.
2. The IRA owner becomes totally and permanently disabled.
3. Distributions are part of a series of substantially equal periodic payments.
4. Distributions are for higher-education expenses for the IRA account owner or his or her spouse, children, or grandchildren.
5. Distributions are for medical expenses that exceed 7.5 percent of the IRA owner's adjusted gross income.
6. Distributions are for health insurance premiums for the account owner or his or her spouse and dependents after the account owner has become unemployed.
7. Distributions are used by first-time home buyers for expenses up to a $10,000 lifetime cap.
8. It is a qualified rollover to another IRA.

Withdrawals between Ages 59½ and 70½

CR *How much can I take out of my IRA when I turn 59½?*

There is no governmental limit to the amount you can withdraw from an IRA once you reach age 59½, so you can take out whatever you want.

Required Minimum Distributions at Age 70½

CR *Exactly when do I have to begin withdrawals from my IRA?*

You are not required to take distributions from a Roth IRA. You *must* begin to withdraw funds from your traditional IRA the year you reach age 70½; however, you can postpone actually taking the withdrawal until April 1 of the following year. This date is known as the *required beginning date*. Each year after that date, you must take a *required minimum distribution (RMD)* from your IRA.

CR *I have heard that the rules dictating how much I have to withdraw from my IRA have been simplified. Is it true that under the new rules I will not have to take out as much as under the old rules?*

It is true that you will not be required to take out as much from your traditional IRA when you reach age 70½ as was required under the old IRS regulations. The new regulations are based on new mortality data showing that people are living longer than before. Since we'll live longer, the government has reduced the required minimum distribution so that we don't outlive our IRA funds.

The new rules are simpler, too. Now, you calculate your RMD using a life-expectancy table that the IRS publishes specifically for calculating RMDs. The table is based on the joint life expectancy of you and a hypothetical beneficiary who is 10 years younger than you. The actual age of your beneficiary is no longer a factor in determining RMD unless your only beneficiary is your spouse and he or she is more than 10 years younger than you. If your spouse is your beneficiary and is more than 10 years younger than you, you can use an alternate table that will allow you to take even less money out of your IRA to satisfy your RMD.

CR *How do I decide whether to use single-life expectancy or joint-life expectancy payment options?*

Under the new rules, you don't. The IRS has published, as part of its final regulations, two tables that control your RMD calculation:

1. *Uniform lifetime table:* You are required to use this table if you are single or if you are married and your spouse is *not* more than 10 years younger than you.

2. *Joint-life and last-survivor expectancy table:* You are required to use this table if your spouse is the sole beneficiary of your IRA, and he or she is more than 10 years younger than you.

CR *How do I calculate the minimum distributions based on life expectancy?*

Most individuals will use the IRS uniform lifetime table for unmarried account owners and owners whose spouses are *not* more than 10 years younger. You would divide the fair market value of your IRA as of December 31 by the appropriate divisor for your age as shown in the table. The result is your RMD.

For example, if you are 74 years old in 2004 and your wife is 65 or you named anyone other than your wife as beneficiary, the divisor on the uniform lifetime table is 23.8. If your IRA was worth $200,000 on December 31, 2003, divide $200,000 by 23.8, and the resulting $8,403.36 is your RMD.

If your wife were more than 10 years younger than you, say 60 and 74, respectively, in 2004, and your wife is the sole beneficiary of your IRA, you would use the joint-life and last-survivor life expectancy table. According to that table, the joint-life expectancy of a 74-year-old and a 60-year-old is 26.6 years, so your RMD for 2004 is $7,518.80, determined by dividing $200,000 by 26.6.

CR *I'm 75 and have been taking required minimum distributions from my IRA. Am I stuck using the old minimum distribution laws or can I use the new laws to reduce the distribution?*

You are allowed to recalculate your RMD using the new rule just as if you had never started to take required IRA minimum distributions yet.

CR *Is it important to take my IRA minimum distributions as required?*

The penalty for failing to take an RMD is one of the most severe imposed by the IRS. You will pay a 50 percent penalty on the amount of your RMD that you fail to take out each year. For example, if your

RMD for this year is $5,000 and you only take a $3,000 distribution, you'll pay a $1,000 penalty (50 percent of $2,000).

& *Can I take more than the required minimum distribution or take the money in any other option than just cash every year?*

You must take your RMDs from a traditional IRA under one of the following methods:

- *Lump sum:* You are free to take out the entire account balance and to pay taxes on it. In fact, some IRA agreements provide for a lump-sum distribution unless you elect otherwise before your required beginning date.

- *Annuity:* You can purchase an annuity from an insurance company with the account balance. You can purchase several different types of annuities that comply with IRS requirements, including a single-life annuity for your life or a joint-and-survivor-life annuity for your life and the life of another person you choose.

- *Life expectancy:* The distributions will be based on the uniform lifetime table or on the joint-life and last-survivor expectancy table.

- *Any period that is shorter than any of the above:* You can withdraw more than your RMD during any year and pay the taxes on the amount.

& *What would happen if I didn't name any beneficiaries?*

Your RMD would be calculated based on the uniform lifetime table.

& *I became 70½ this year. If I do not have to make a withdrawal from my IRA until April 1 of next year, why did my accountant have me take the distribution this year when I didn't need the money?*

You can postpone the first withdrawal until April 1 of next year, but you must also take your second withdrawal by December 31 of next year—two withdrawals in one year. Your accountant is advising you to voluntarily take that first withdrawal this year so that you don't have to take two RMDs in one year. That could push you into a higher income tax bracket, forcing you to pay more in total income taxes than you would pay if you had spread those withdrawals over 2 years.

BENEFICIARIES OF
QUALIFIED RETIREMENT
PLANS AND IRAs

℞ *What are the rules for distribution to beneficiaries after my
death, and why are they important for me to consider?*

We'll answer your second question first. The rules for distribution
are important because of their income and estate tax effects on the
recipients of the proceeds. If you own an IRA, a qualified retirement
plan, or an annuity at your death, there will be more than one tax on
its value. Like all other assets that you own at your death, these assets
are included in your taxable estate and are subject to federal estate tax.

Since you didn't pay the income tax on the proceeds in any of
these plans before your death, someone else has to pay it—and that
someone else will be your beneficiary when he or she receives distributions from the plan. Such distributions are referred to as *income in
respect of a decedent (IRD)* and can be quite expensive for your heirs.
Retirement account owners should plan to pass these proceeds to
their beneficiaries in a manner that allows the beneficiaries to stretch
out the withdrawals over the longest period possible, thereby deferring the income taxes. Also, the longer the plan assets remain in the
tax-deferred account, the greater the tax-free accumulation. Tax-free
accumulation and income-tax deferral combine to greatly increase
the value of the account for children or grandchildren.

Although recent changes in the regulations for postmortem distributions from retirement plans are mostly favorable to taxpayers, the rules
are still rather complex. First, there are three categories of beneficiaries:

1. Spouses
2. Individuals other than spouses
3. "Not individuals"

The rules are different for how each of these three categories of
beneficiaries can take distributions from the IRA after the death of the
account owner. Further, the rules are different depending on whether
the account owner died before or after the required beginning date.

Although some employer-sponsored plans may impose limits on
these options, the material that follows is generally applicable to traditional IRAs, Roth IRAs, and qualified retirement plans.

◌ℛ I thought you said I didn't have to take minimum distributions from a Roth IRA?

You don't, but the beneficiary who receives the account after you die does. Congress wanted to give you the flexibility to use Roth IRA funds as needed for retirement but didn't intend for them to be a tax-free investment vehicle that could last for generations. So, whomever you name as the beneficiary of your Roth IRA must follow the same rules as everyone else who inherits retirement plan benefits.

◌ℛ When can I change my beneficiary?

Under the new rules, you can change your beneficiary at any time while you are living. And, under the new rules, your final beneficiaries do not have to be determined until September 30 of the year after you die, which allows for some "clean-up" planning after you're gone.

Some employer-sponsored plans, such as the 401(k), pension or profit-sharing plans, and others, have restrictions on beneficiary options. If your plan will not let you do what you want, rolling your money into an IRA will usually give you more options. If your money is in an IRA and the institution serving as custodian will not agree to your wishes, move your IRA to one that will.

Spouse As Beneficiary

◌ℛ So what options does my husband have if I name him as my sole beneficiary?

As your sole beneficiary, your spouse will have two basic options after you die. He can elect either to be the owner of the IRA or to be the beneficiary of the IRA.

If he chooses to be the owner, he can keep your IRA or roll it over into a new or existing IRA in his own name. In either instance, he will be able to delay taking distributions until he reaches age 70½ and can name new beneficiaries. Your husband has this option regardless of whether you died before or after your required beginning date.

If he chooses to be treated as a beneficiary, then his required minimum distributions will be based on whether or not you died before or after your required beginning date:

- *You die before your required beginning date:* Your husband (as beneficiary) must withdraw the entire account either within 5 years of your death or over his life expectancy.
- *You die after your required beginning date:* Your husband must receive RMDs based on the longer of either his life expectancy or yours (even though you're dead, you still have an actuarial life expectancy). Alternatively, your husband as beneficiary can purchase an annuity contract meeting IRS requirements.

Some IRA custodians allow the surviving spouse to name a new beneficiary, but others will only follow the account owner's original instructions as to who should receive the account after the surviving spouse dies.

Generally speaking, the surviving spouse will receive smaller distributions from the account by choosing to be treated as an owner. The main benefit to electing treatment as a beneficiary is that the spouse can receive distributions prior to age 59½ without incurring a penalty for early distributions.

ᴑᴙ *Why would I not always name my spouse as the beneficiary of my retirement plan assets?*

IRA and retirement plan assets passing to a surviving spouse are exempt from federal estate tax because of the unlimited marital deduction. But you should not automatically assume that naming your spouse as the beneficiary of your retirement plan is always the best strategy. As we explained in Chapter 4, Tax Basics, leaving everything to your spouse wastes the estate tax applicable exclusion of the first spouse to die. If your estate does not have sufficient other assets to fully fund a family trust and to utilize your credit, the retirement plan assets could be used to make up the difference—if you don't name your spouse as the beneficiary of the retirement plan.

ᴑᴙ *As unmarried partners and the beneficiary of each other's IRA, can we use the spousal rollover option?*

As unmarried couples, you are not entitled to the tax-free rollover option. You would take the proceeds as any other nonspouse individual beneficiary of an IRA.

Nonspouse Individuals As Beneficiaries

CR My wife and I have children from previous marriages. Can we each keep our respective children as the beneficiaries of our own IRAs and company retirement plans?

Yes, you can name your children as the beneficiaries of your respective retirement plans. However, by law, a surviving spouse is entitled to receive survivors' benefits from a qualified plan when the participant dies. In other words, you are entitled to benefits from your wife's plan, and she is entitled to benefits from yours. This law prevents participants in qualified plans from disinheriting their spouses with regard to plan proceeds without the spouses' knowledge and consent. There are very strict requirements under the law for obtaining a signed waiver from a spouse relinquishing his or her rights to the plan proceeds, so talk to your employers about the necessary paperwork for each of you to sign a waiver. This law does *not* apply to IRAs, so you can each name your children as beneficiaries without additional paperwork.

CR If I name someone other than my husband as beneficiary of my IRA, how does that person receive the money?

Your beneficiary always has the option of taking a lump-sum distribution of the whole account. But if your beneficiary is looking to defer the distributions as long as possible from an IRA, here are the rules:

- *You die before your required beginning date:* Your beneficiary must either take distributions from the account based on his or her life expectancy, commencing December 31 of the year after your death; or withdraw the account balance within 5 years following the year of your death.

- *You die after your required beginning date:* Your beneficiary can take distributions over your remaining life expectancy or over his or her life expectancy, whichever period is longer; or can elect to withdraw the entire account balance within 5 years following the year of your death. For either of the life-expectancy options, distributions must commence by December 31 of the year following your death.

ᴑᴫ *Can I have multiple beneficiary designations on the same IRA?*

You can name multiple beneficiaries who will receive the IRA after your death, but there will be only one beneficiary on each plan whose age is used to calculate how the distributions will be paid after your death. When you name multiple beneficiaries, such as "Tommy Jones, Mary Jones, and Davey Jones," or collectively "my surviving children," the rules require that the life expectancy of the oldest beneficiary (the shortest period) is used in calculating the required minimum distribution for all of the beneficiaries after your death.

There is, however, a way around this limitation. During the "clean-up" period after your death, your beneficiaries can divide your IRA into separate accounts. That way each beneficiary can use his or her own life expectancy to calculate the RMD for his or her distributions. You can do this in advance for your beneficiaries by including instructions on the beneficiary designation form that the custodian should establish a separate account for each beneficiary after your death.

In most cases, using separate accounts is the preferable approach. Doing so allows your younger beneficiaries to take smaller distributions and to continue the tax-deferred growth of the assets in their accounts.

Estate

ᴑᴫ *Can my estate be the beneficiary?*

If you name your estate as beneficiary, the account balance must be paid out to your estate no later than 5 years after the year you die, and the benefit of tax-deferred investing is lost prematurely. Also, by naming your estate as the beneficiary, you needlessly force your IRA to go through probate and may be exposing it to the creditors of your estate.

Revocable Living Trust As Beneficiary

ᴑᴫ *How are required minimum distributions calculated if my trust is the beneficiary?*

After you die, the RMDs are paid to the trust over the life expectancy of the oldest beneficiary of the trust, usually your spouse. The trustee can withdraw more money if needed to follow your instructions, but the rest stays in the account and continues to grow tax-deferred.

ભ *My IRA makes up a large portion of my wealth. I want to leave the IRA to my kids, but I want to find some way of protecting the account from their creditors, rash spending, and so forth. What can I do?*

It often makes good sense to name a trust as the beneficiary of your qualified plans and individual retirement accounts. With a living trust, you can ensure proper distribution of the account proceeds, particularly if a named beneficiary should pass away before you. In a trust, you can select a trustee to manage the proceeds for beneficiaries who may need investment help, and you can include spendthrift provisions in the trust to provide creditor protection for your beneficiaries, such as against the claims of ex-spouses. Before you name your living trust as the beneficiary of your IRA or retirement plan, you must consult with an estate planning attorney to make sure that your trust qualifies as a beneficiary under the IRS rules.

In some cases, it may be best to name your spouse or other persons as the first (primary) beneficiary of your IRAs and retirement accounts and to name your living trust as the secondary (contingent) beneficiary. You should consult with your estate planning attorney and financial advisor before making your beneficiary election.

ભ *What makes a trust "qualified" to be the beneficiary of my IRA?*

For a trust to qualify as a beneficiary of an IRA, the trust must meet the following six requirements:

1. The trust must be valid under state law.
2. All beneficiaries of the trust must be individuals, as determined on September 30 of the year following the death of the plan participant or account owner.
3. The beneficiaries must be identifiable from the trust instrument.
4. The trust becomes irrevocable at the participant's or account owner's death.
5. In some cases the participant or account owner must send a copy of the trust (or certain information about the trust) to the plan

custodian or plan administrator on the required beginning date. He or she must also agree to provide a copy of any trust amendment within a reasonable time after making the amendment.

6. By October 31 of the year following the year in which the participant or IRA owner died, the trustee of the trust must either provide a copy of the trust agreement to the plan administrator or account custodian or provide it with a list of *all* possible beneficiaries of the trust as of September 30; and certify that, to the best of the trustee's knowledge, the list is correct and that the trust meets the requirements for a see-through trust.

Charity

Q Can I give my IRA directly to a charity while I'm living?

No. Your only option is to make a withdrawal from the IRA and give that to charity. You will owe income taxes when you make the withdrawal, but you will receive a charitable deduction that you can take against your income. Due to the limitation on charitable deductions, the deduction may not totally offset the income tax on the amount you withdraw.

For the past few years members of Congress have proposed changing the law to permit certain IRA owners to donate assets from their accounts to charity without incurring the income tax on the withdrawal. This change appears to be popular in Congress and with taxpayers, but nonetheless had not been made into law at the time this book was published.

Q I'm considering naming a charity as a beneficiary of part of my IRA. Is there any problem with this?

Under the old regulations, this plan posed adverse tax consequences for your noncharitable beneficiaries. Since a charity does not qualify as a beneficiary, including it as a beneficiary at your death would force your IRA to be distributed to all your beneficiaries within 5 years after the year you die.

Under the new regulations, this result can be avoided if the charity receives its share of the IRA *before* September 30 of the year following your death. That way, on September 30 (the day the IRA's beneficiary is determined for distribution purposes), the IRA has only persons as beneficiaries. So if you are going to name a charity as a beneficiary, your trustee or executor has to be certain that the payment is made to the charity within the required time frame.

ᗄ Can you tell me about using a charitable remainder trust as the beneficiary of my IRA?

Naming an *inter vivos* or testamentary charitable remainder trust (CRT) as the beneficiary of your IRA may have merit if you are charitably inclined. You can name your spouse or anyone else you might have named as the IRA beneficiary as the CRT's noncharitable beneficiary. At your death, the balance of the IRA is paid in a lump sum to the CRT. The noncharitable beneficiary receives the income of the CRT, and after his or her death, the remainder is paid without income or estate taxes to the charitable beneficiaries named in the CRT. With this approach, the required minimum distribution rules no longer apply to the CRT noncharitable beneficiary who will pay tax on CRT trust income only as he or she receives it.

ALTERNATIVES TO QUALIFIED RETIREMENT PLANS

Employer-Sponsored Nonqualified Plans

ᗄ Can you give me a summary of the nonqualified retirement plans that an employer might want to establish?

Nonqualified plans are not subject to the provisions of ERISA and, as a result, the contributions are not tax-deductible for the employer when it makes the contributions. Most employers use nonqualified plans because they can be "discriminatory" in nature, meaning that the plan design for any respective participant is not necessarily the same as that for another participant, so they provide a way for employers to benefit key employees. In summary, those plans include:

■ *Salary reduction plans:* Under these types of plans, the employee defers a portion of current compensation (which reduces current taxable income) and the company invests these funds to accrue benefits for the ultimate purpose of providing an income payout at the employee's retirement. The corporation will receive an income tax deduction at the time it pays the benefits to the employee at retirement and the employee will report those benefits as ordinary taxable income. In the interim, the growth on plan assets will not be taxed to the employee—if they are taxed at all, because the investments can be designed to grow tax-deferred.

- *Salary continuation plans:* Under these plans, the corporation promises to pay a stated benefit to the employee at retirement. The corporation will receive an income tax deduction at the time it pays the benefit to the employee at retirement and the employee will report the income at that time as ordinary taxable income.

Employers use these plans to reward key employees for their valued services while keeping them in "golden handcuffs." Each plan can be designed to meet the overall objectives of either or both the employer and the employee.

Demand Trust for Spouse

Q My wife does not work outside of the home and does not have a retirement plan. Is there anything we can do to provide for her without having to deal with all of those complicated IRA rules?

Yes. The demand trust for spouses can be very effective as a savings program for retirement. It differs from the traditional IRA and other tax-deferred retirement plans in that the gifts you make to the trust are with after-tax dollars, and the trust principal does not grow tax-deferred. On the plus side, however, it is much more flexible than the IRA and employer-sponsored qualified retirement plans in that there are no penalties for early withdrawals or requirements for mandatory minimum distributions at 70½, among other things.

In addition, the trust provides asset protection; and unlike the IRA and qualified plans, the trust proceeds are not subject to estate tax at your wife's death. (See also demand trusts in Chapter 5, Wealth Transfer Techniques.)

Q Can you explain how the demand trust works as a retirement plan?

Yes. You create the irrevocable demand trust for the benefit of your wife during her life and then for your children after her death. You make a gift of $5,000 to her trust every year for a certain number of years. As trustee, she invests the money. You owe no gift tax because your annual gift is under the annual gift tax exclusion amount.

You don't want to violate the 5-and-5 rule, so we limit the annual gifts to $5,000 in the initial years. In later years when the value of the trust exceeds $100,000, you can increase the gift to 5 percent of the value of the trust. Your wife has the right to withdraw the $5,000 gift, but it is anticipated that she will not withdraw it and instead let her right to withdraw lapse.

Your wife could have anything from the trust she ever needs for her health, education, maintenance, and support. If she is the sole trustee, she need only ask herself for the money.

Over time, these annual exclusion gifts can grow remarkably, particularly if the income tax liability of the trust is passed through to you as the trustmaker. In about 30 years, if the trust grows at the rate of 7–8 percent, the value of the trust would be about $1 million for your wife. And, whatever is remaining in the trust at her death passes estate tax-free to your children.

Annuities and Life Insurance

ᖇ *After putting the maximum into my retirement plan at work and contributing to my Roth IRA, I still pay a lot of taxes and I don't qualify for a traditional IRA. What other alternatives are available for additional retirement savings?*

There are a couple of investment vehicles that would help you control the amount of taxes that you pay and provide the opportunity for growth. Your options are an annuity contract and a life insurance policy. The unique features of these products are that your contributions to either would accumulate on a tax-deferred basis until after retirement.

ᖇ *How does an annuity work as a retirement planning vehicle?*

The biggest advantage of an annuity is the tax-deferred buildup, since there are no immediate income taxes as interest and growth are accumulating within the annuity. Over a period of time, this can become a rather substantial benefit.

Another advantage is that an annuity can be liquidated over a long, continuous period of time and can be guaranteed for a lifetime. In addition, at death, the annuity policy passes directly to a beneficiary, outside the probate process.

⟶ *Am I required to take minimum distributions from an annuity after age 70½?*

No. There is no IRS mandatory withdrawal rule for annuities. However, there is a penalty tax of 10 percent if you take distributions from a deferred annuity before reaching age 59½. There are some exceptions to this penalty, such as taking withdrawals if you become disabled before reaching the age of 59½.

⟶ *What advantages does a life insurance policy offer?*

In addition to the same tax-deferred benefits as investing in an annuity, you are afforded favorable tax treatment on taking money out of the contract. Under current tax and insurance laws, when you withdraw money from the cash value of a life insurance policy, you can withdraw the total of your cost basis (the premiums you paid) tax-free.

When you have completely recovered your cost basis, most policies will allow you to borrow from your policy at favorable interest rates. The terms of borrowing can vary among insurance policies, but the result is that you are able to get additional amounts out of the policy on a tax-free basis. Any loan amount outstanding at the time of your death is subtracted from the death benefit.

The death benefit paid to your beneficiaries is income tax–free, unlike the proceeds of retirement plans or annuities.

⟶ *But won't the life insurance be subject to estate taxes when I die?*

Normally, to avoid estate taxes on a life insurance policy, you must give up ownership and the right to withdraw the cash value or to take loans from the policy. But you may be able to retain the right to benefit from the policy indirectly by using the irrevocable demand trust for a spouse, which we discussed earlier. With this trust, the trustee purchases a life insurance policy on the trustmaker-spouse and later withdraws cash value or takes loans on the policy and distributes the cash to the beneficiary-spouse. Because you, as the insured, have no control over or beneficial interest in the policy, it is not included in your estate at death. The trust will also escape federal estate taxes when the beneficiary-spouse dies.

Charitable Remainder Unitrusts

☞ *What are the advantages of using a charitable remainder unitrust with net income makeup provisions or a charitable remainder unitrust with flip provisions over traditional IRAs, company 401(k) plans, and other retirement plans?*

There are many advantages for using a charitable remainder unitrust with net income makeup provisions (NIMCRUT) or a charitable remainder unitrust with "flip" provisions (flip unitrust) as a retirement planning tool over tax-deferred retirement plans:

- *Unlimited contributions:* There is no limit to the amount of money that the trustmaker can contribute to a NIMCRUT or a flip unitrust in any year as there is with the tax-deferred retirement plans.
- *Penalty-free withdrawals:* There are no penalties associated with an "early withdrawal." The unitrust payments are not subject to any penalty taxes.
- *Control:* The trustmaker and/or the trustmaker's spouse may be the trustee. There is no need for plan administrators—although there may be a need for a special independent trustee, depending upon the trust assets and the planned transactions.
- *Payment flexibility:* The trustmaker may contribute cash, stock, or other eligible property to the trust, receive a deduction, and defer capital gain tax on the sale of the assets in the trust.
- *Tax-advantaged payments:* Through careful investment of trust assets, the income payments from a NIMCRUT can produce primarily capital gains, which will reduce income taxes in the future.

☞ *Can you give me an example of how a flip unitrust works as a private retirement plan?*

Yes. Suppose a married couple, both age 40, wish to save $10,000 annually toward retirement. Their attorney helps them establish a joint flip unitrust with a 5 percent payout and they contribute $10,000 to the trust each year for 25 years, until they retire. The trust will switch to a standard unitrust when the oldest trustmaker reaches age 65.

They receive approximately $54,000 in charitable income tax deductions over the 25 years. Assuming an average growth rate of 10 percent and no distributions over 25 years and assuming that they convert the trust assets at retirement to 6 percent income-producing and 2 percent growth investments, the couple would receive a unitrust payment of approximately $64,000 the first year, and the payments could possibly be even higher in future years. At their deaths, the charity that the couple selected receives approximately $1.7 million.

TAX PLANNING FOR
RETIREMENT PLANS

Income Tax Planning for Spouses

CR *How does the spousal IRA rollover work?*

After the plan participant's death and if the surviving spouse is the beneficiary, he or she has the option of rolling over the assets of the retirement plan to another IRA. Although the spouse could roll over the retirement plan assets into his or her own existing IRA, it is usually best to establish a new, separate spousal rollover account.

CR *I am a 50-year-old widow. My husband, who was 62 when he died, named me as the beneficiary of his IRA. Should I exercise my right to roll it over into an IRA of my own?*

The answer to your question largely depends upon whether you expect to need the money from his IRA before you reach age 59½. If you roll over his IRA into your own IRA, then you will be subject to the early withdrawal penalties for any withdrawals you make before age 59½; but it allows you to extend the date by which you must begin to take withdrawals. If, however, you choose to remain the beneficiary of your husband's IRA and to make withdrawals from it, you are not subject to any early withdrawal penalties.

You can have the best of both choices with careful planning. Remain the beneficiary of your husband's IRA until you reach age 59½ so that you can withdraw funds as you need them; and after you turn 59½, elect to be treated as owner of the account. Alternatively, estimate how much you will need until you are 59½ and keep that amount in his IRA, but roll over the remainder to your own IRA. You should take this planning approach only after consulting with a qualified tax advisor.

○ঽ *Is there any advantage of doing a spousal rollover?*

One benefit of doing a spousal rollover is that it enables you to name your own beneficiaries.

Income Tax Planning for Nonspouse Beneficiaries

○ঽ *Is there a way to reduce the income taxes on distributions to my heirs?*

Yes. Instruct your custodian to set up separate accounts for your beneficiaries. This way, each beneficiary can calculate the lowest possible RMD for his or her age. The income tax impact could be less because each child would receive only his or her RMD.

○ঽ *At my death, my property will be divided between my family and my charities. Does it make any difference which assets are used to fund the different shares?*

When allocating assets to beneficiaries, it is important to consider income tax issues. Certain assets such as mutual funds and real estate receive a step-up in basis at death. This means that all the built-in capital gain goes away and the beneficiary receives the asset without any income tax liability. For other assets such as IRAs, tax-deferred annuities, and U.S. Savings Bonds, the built-in gain is not classified as capital gain but rather as income in respect of a decedent (IRD) which does not go away at death. To make matters worse, the IRD is taxed to the beneficiary as ordinary income rather than at the more favorable capital gain tax rates. Therefore, if you are making charitable bequests and have IRD assets, it is generally best to satisfy those bequests with the IRAs and other IRD assets and to leave to your noncharitable beneficiaries the assets that receive a step-up in basis. The charity will be exempt from paying income tax on the bequest, and your noncharitable beneficiaries will receive assets that do not have an income tax time bomb ticking inside them.

Estate Tax Planning

  ☙ *I thought my IRAs and other retirement plans would pass to my*
named beneficiaries at my death outside of my estate. Why do I
have to worry about estate planning for the retirement plan?

Although the balances in your IRAs and other retirement plans may
pass directly to your named beneficiaries outside of your probate
estate, these balances are still considered assets owned by you and are
part of your federal taxable estate. And, if you own an IRA, qualified
plan, or annuity at the time of your death, there will be more than
one tax on their value. Distributions from these plans trigger taxable
income to the recipients and are also included in your taxable estate.
Because the beneficiary you name for your retirement plans determines who inherits the funds on your death, estate planning and
retirement plan distribution planning are inextricably tied together.

    Careful integration of your retirement plan with your estate plan
is necessary to ensure taking advantage of the estate tax avoidance
techniques available to you. These issues can literally mean a difference of hundreds of thousands of dollars.

  ☙ *Where does the money come from to pay the estate tax on my*
IRA?

The value of the IRA is subject to federal estate tax, and the heirs
will have to pay the estate tax within 9 months after the IRA owner's
death. If your heirs are forced to withdraw money from the IRA to
pay the estate tax, that will trigger income tax on the withdrawal. In
effect, the heirs are being taxed on the money they had to take out of
the IRA in order to pay the estate tax. Taking money out of the IRA
for taxes leaves less money to grow tax-deferred for your heirs.

    There are various strategies available to reduce this tax impact.
One commonly utilized strategy is to begin taking distributions
from the IRA on an annual basis as early as possible after age 59½.
This move is a way of "prepaying" the tax, and the distributions are
then reinvested in a manner that avoids future income and estate tax
inclusion. This manner is accomplished by the formation of an irrevocable life insurance trust, which purchases a life insurance policy
(typically a second-to-die policy). The annual IRA distributions are
gifted, utilizing the gift tax annual exclusion, to pay the premiums

on the life insurance. After both spouses are dead, the proceeds in the life insurance trust replace the amounts your beneficiaries must pay the government in estate and income taxes on the IRA.

     If I'm married and my total estate, including IRAs and other retirement plans, does not exceed the applicable exclusion amount at my death, won't my retirement plans pass estate tax–free to my beneficiaries?

Not necessarily! If the primary beneficiary of IRAs and other retirement accounts is your surviving spouse, which is usually the case for income tax reasons, you may not get the full use of your combined applicable exclusion amount. This is because when you name your spouse as the beneficiary of your IRA and other retirement plans, those assets *bypass* the estate plan and go directly to your spouse. If you do not own enough assets outside the IRA and/or other retirement plan, the parts of the estate plan that are designed to "soak up" the applicable exclusion amount may not be fully utilized. The result may be estate taxes, depending, of course, on the size of the IRAs and other retirement plans and the value of the other assets in the estate.

    Also, many people do not factor in the future growth of the retirement accounts. It is the value of these accounts on the date of death that determines estate taxes, not the value when they are created. If you have sizable IRAs or other retirement plans and expect to live for a few years, these accounts may create an estate tax problem. You should consult a competent advisor to determine the extent, if any, of this potential problem and how you can plan to overcome it.

     I want to name my trust as the beneficiary of my retirement plan proceeds for estate planning purposes. How would this work after my death?

At your death, the plan proceeds are included in your estate for estate tax purposes. If the trust has been properly drafted, the beneficiaries of the trust will be considered the beneficiaries for purposes of determining the RMDs to the trust. The RMDs go to your revocable trust. Depending on the size of your estate and the nature of your other assets, the RMDs will go either to your family trust or to the marital trust or they may be divided between the two trusts, with a portion of each RMD going to one trust and the balance going to the other.

To the extent that the plan distributions pass to the marital trust, they escape federal estate tax under the marital deduction.

It is also possible that all or part of the retirement plan or IRA distributions may be used to "soak up" your applicable exclusion amount and to pass to your family trust.

For example, let's assume that you die in 2005, when the estate tax applicable exclusion will be $1.5 million per person. Let's say your estate consists of an IRA worth $600,000 and $450,000 in other property that is funded to your revocable trust. Your estate is worth a total of $1,050,000. For maximum estate tax savings, many estate planning professionals would call for placing all $1,050,000 into the family trust to utilize as much as possible of the $1.5 million applicable exclusion—which means that all the IRA proceeds are placed into the family trust.

◑ *Are there any tax disadvantages to using those proceeds to fund the family trust?*

Yes. For every dollar of plan benefit value that is allocated to the family trust, the trustee will be required to pay income tax on that dollar when the benefits are actually received by the trust. If the proceeds are taxed at the highest income tax bracket, which is a distinct possibility, a substantial part of the IRA will go to pay taxes. The result is an underfunded family trust—the full applicable exclusion amount will not pass to heirs at your spouse's death since the applicable exclusion amount will be reduced by the amount of income taxes paid. The greater the amount of retirement benefits allocated to the family trust, the less actual value available to your ultimate beneficiaries.

◑ *A large part of our estate is invested in a rollover IRA. How can we minimize the double hit of income and estate taxes?*

Some advisors might suggest that you take more than you need out of your retirement plan today, pay the income taxes today, and make gifts to your heirs now rather than leaving them a large retirement plan subject to both estate and income taxes.

CR *I have an annuity that I don't need for retirement income, so I plan to let it grow and pass it to my children at my death. Is this a good idea?*

Annuities are excellent vehicles for accumulating retirement income on a tax-deferred basis. However, if one attempts to use the additional wealth in an annuity as a bequest to the next generation, the results can be unattractive. Annuities are generally poor wealth transfer vehicles.

As with IRAs and qualified plans, annuities can be double-taxed at death. Annuities paid to beneficiaries are subject to income taxes to the extent of the gain over basis. They are also included in your estate for estate tax purposes. Therefore, in some cases, affluent people who have annuities and plan to pass them on to their children will find that after 20-plus years of growth, the net amount passing to their children is less than the annuity is worth today!

Consider annuitizing the annuity or setting up systematic withdrawals and buying life insurance in an irrevocable life insurance trust with the cash flow. In most cases, the results of this strategy can be very favorable.

CR *I want my wife to receive lifetime income from my IRA and want the remaining account balance to go to charity after my wife's death. How can I accomplish this?*

One method involves establishing a charitable remainder trust (CRT) and naming it as the beneficiary of your IRA account. Your wife is the noncharitable beneficiary of the CRT. At your death, when the IRA proceeds flow into your CRT, the assets do not belong to your wife; she has a right only to a unitrust or annuity payment each year. When the IRA proceeds are paid into the CRT, there are no immediate income taxes. However, the amounts paid by the CRT to your wife are subject to income tax as she receives them, just as income paid to them directly from an IRA would be.

If there are noncharitable beneficiaries of the CRT other than your wife, such as your children, there will be estate tax due. The estate tax is calculated on the present value of the income stream that the nonspouse, noncharitable beneficiaries will receive. Thus, the estate must have other assets from which to pay the estate taxes, as the estate cannot invade the principal of the CRT to pay the taxes.

This strategy takes a great deal of planning. As with any sophisticated planning device, it should be implemented only when it is appropriate to a particular situation and has been thoroughly analyzed by knowledgeable professionals.

○ℜ *Are there any downsides to using a CRT?*

Depending on the age of the person (or persons) you are naming as beneficiary, that person may benefit more over time from the IRA than the CRT. Both a CRT and an IRA are tax-exempt, but a fairly young IRA beneficiary may receive more money from an IRA over his or her lifetime than he or she could receive from a CRT. In the end, you must balance this possibility against your charitable desires, taking into account your overall estate plan. Also, this plan may require you to take larger required minimum distributions than naming your spouse as your beneficiary. A knowledgeable financial advisor or estate planning attorney can offer you guidance on which strategy better meets your goals.

ACTION STEPS

We respectfully present the following action steps to summarize the concepts that we discussed in chapter 6 and to suggest steps that you can take to prepare for meetings with your estate planning team of professionals.

❑ *Start saving for retirement now.* You should plan and start saving for retirement as early as possible—even if you can only afford to save a few dollars each month. Few people, if any, have ever said that they started to save for retirement too early. The earlier you begin saving for retirement, the earlier you can retire or the more money you can expect to receive when you do retire.

❑ *Contribute as much as you can to your retirement plan at work.* Next to health insurance, a tax-deferred, employer-sponsored retirement plan is the best benefit there is, so take advantage of it and contribute the maximum amount allowed, or at least as much as you can afford to contribute.

❑ *Set up a traditional individual retirement account (IRA) or Roth IRA if you don't already have one.* After employer-sponsored plans, IRAs are your best bet for saving for retirement. If possible, contribute as much as the law permits every year. If you're over 50, make the additional "catch-up" contributions.

❑ *After maximizing your contributions to a retirement plan and an IRA, consider alternative techniques.* Retirement planning strategies such as nonqualified plans, annuities, charitable remainder trusts, and spousal demand trusts can boost your retirement savings and can provide additional cash flow during retirement.

❑ *Find a financial advisor to manage your investments.* Our experience is that few people have the time and knowledge to manage their investments properly without professional help. To find a qualified financial advisor, ask friends, family members, and existing advisors. If those individuals cannot recommend someone to you, read Chapter 13, Finding and Working with Professional Advisors, for some ideas, and, of course, the financial advisor contributors to this book would welcome the opportunity to work with you (see Appendix D, Contributing Authors, and Appendix E, Geographic Listing of Contributing Authors).

❑ *Know your objectives.* Whether you are aged 35, 55, or 75, you should always have clear retirement objectives. This is another reason why you need a financial advisor—to help you define your goals and then to structure a plan for achieving them.

❑ *Coordinate your retirement planning with your estate plan.* For many people, their retirement plan is their most valuable asset. Retirement plans present particular problems in estate planning, and it takes careful planning to ensure that your loved ones receive the maximum benefit possible from your remaining retirement funds after you die. Only an advisor skilled in both retirement and estate planning can give you the guidance you need.

❑ *Learn your options before you retire.* If you are about to retire, you probably have many questions about your options under your employer-sponsored plan. Frankly, the choices you must make before retirement are difficult, and you should seek as much help as you can from the plan administrator and your advisors.

❑ *Learn your options* before *you reach age 70½.* Since data shows that we are living longer than before, you want to do whatever you can to ensure that you don't outlive your IRA funds. To that end, you need to understand the somewhat complicated options for taking your required distributions *before* you have to begin taking them so that you have everything set up properly to take the minimum amount required by law. This is where the trusted financial advisor and estate planning attorney can help you again.

❑ *Get a regular retirement plan checkup.* Having enough money to retire comfortably takes attention and effort. Meet with your financial advisor every few years to make sure you're on the right course to meeting your objectives with your retirement plan.

PART THREE

Control

It is apparent from the amount and nature of the research submitted for this section by our contributors that, after love, control is the essence of many clients' concerns in modern estate planning. In this entire section, there is one overriding theme: we want to maintain control of our personal and financial affairs as much as possible for as long as possible without interference from the courts and other interlopers. We are not speaking of our controlling family members "from the grave," so to speak. Rather, we are talking about our individual needs to preserve our dignity and independence as best as possible until our death. Because of the various important roles that control plays, Part Three contains more chapters than the previous two sections.

We begin in chapter 7 with a discussion of how estates are administered—and all estates must be administered in one of two ways: probate or trust administration. This may seem like an unusual topic to begin a discussion of control, but our contributors felt that if readers understood the consequences of failing to plan, they would be more apt to take control and to engage in estate planning. Your estate plan—or lack of a plan—will take on added importance for your heirs at your death. Our contributors explain with great clarity the events that occur after death so that you can better understand the relationship between proper planning and a smooth postmortem administration for your family.

Many clients are concerned about the effects that a physical or mental disability would have on their families. Most estate planning practitioners agree that disability planning is not only important but also essential. Typically, an individual's ability to create income is his or her most valuable asset. Without the ability to create income, a person could lose everything he or she has worked to build. In some ways, a lengthy disability is the worst tragedy that can befall us, and yet, during our working years, the odds of becoming disabled are significantly higher than the odds of dying prematurely. Statistics show that a 35-year-old male has a greater than 50 percent chance of being disabled for at least 90 days before age 65. Of those disabled, some will remain so for years, if not for life. Most people are ill-prepared to financially survive a short-term disability of even 6 months. In addition to the financial concerns, the personal aspects of disability planning include identifying who will take care of you if you are physically or mentally disabled; how and where you will be cared for; and who will make medical decisions for you if you cannot.

Chapter 8 outlines the best ways to minimize the effects of disability. Our contributors explain how well-drafted living wills and powers of attorney can serve to spare you and your family some of the anguish that typically accompanies a disabling illness. As we go to press with this text, the impact of the recently passed Health Insurance Portability and Accountability Act (HIPAA) provisions is just being felt. HIPAA was intended to ensure the privacy of patients' medical information and records. As with many laws, it also adds difficulty for individuals and their families. Without a form signed by a patient allowing medical information to be released to anyone or specifically identifying a "personal representative" to receive the information, family members cannot obtain medical information from medical caregivers and institutions. For example, without the proper authorization, children of patients cannot be given medical information about their parents in order to help their parents understand the medical opinions they receive or obtain health insurance records to decipher bills and payments for them. These financial and personal issues can be resolved with the proper disability planning outlined in chapter 8.

Chapter 9 explains the many benefits of trust-based estate planning, the primary benefit being to maintain control. During the last 10 years, living trusts have become the standard for good estate planning for the vast majority of individuals. Still, some readers may not fully understand the mechanics and benefits of living trusts. In chapter 9 our contributors succinctly and accurately describe how a living trust functions and its superiority to a will-based estate plan for most people.

Chapter 10 is of special importance to small-business owners. Typically, the business is your largest asset, and an exit strategy with a business succession plan is crucial to your estate and retirement planning goals. Business succession planning is often an emotional subject for owners, and our contributors offer some realistic questions and answers to help you come to terms with the emotional side of transferring your business.

For owners who want to sell their businesses to co-owners, children, or employees, this chapter offers important planning tips. Our contributors describe the various techniques to design and implement a business continuity plan through stock redemptions and buy-sell agreements, with a careful comparison of these different techniques and the circumstances in which one technique might suit an owner's needs more than the others. In particular, the chapter suggests some innovative ways to sell businesses to children through self-canceling installment notes, private annuities, and irrevocable grantor trusts.

For owners who can afford to give their businesses to their children, chapter 10 describes some important tools for accomplishing the transfer, including the pros and cons of transferring businesses to family members during life versus at death. Also, for business owners facing the common problem of how to provide an inheritance to children who do not work in the business, our contributors offer suggestions to resolve this dilemma. Successful business succession planning requires the assistance of a skilled business appraiser, and small-business owners should have some awareness of the procedures and methodologies for a proper appraisal. Our contributors also provide an overview of the valuation process in this chapter.

Asset protection is not a new concept, but it is a topic that has drawn more attention in recent years in response to increased risks. In today's litigious society, more and more of us are seeking ways to shield our assets from unreasonable claims and demands. We all want to protect ourselves and our families from uncertainty as much as possible. Chapter 11 explains why asset protection planning is an important part of estate planning to control and protect our assets, and it describes techniques available for accomplishing asset protection.

Liability and casualty insurance is the most common form of risk management and is a good start for asset protection. But for many people, it is no longer enough. The corporation, one of the oldest forms of business arrangements, was created in part to shield investors from liability. It appears from our contributors' research that clients today are more interested in the newer, less complex types of business entities, namely the limited partnership and the limited liability company. Not surprisingly, then, our contributors give little emphasis to the corporation and instead focus on these new, more user-friendly entities. Even if you do not own an active trade or business, you may find that these entities are attractive vehicles to manage your risk.

In response to the mounting litigation crisis that exists in this country, several states have enacted legislation to allow people to transfer assets into special trusts that provide legitimate asset protection. Our contributors give us an excellent overview of these self-settled asset protection trusts.

Asset protection has, regrettably, also become a fertile field for unsavory operators peddling fraudulent asset protection schemes. Their promises and solutions are not only unscrupulous, but in many cases illegal. Anyone interested in asset protection or tax planning should be aware that asset protection is a complex legal field, and we urge you to seek the counsel of reputable, competent advisors to assist you in developing an asset protection plan.

As the U.S. population grows older and medical science helps us live longer but not necessarily better lives, protecting and planning for our ourselves, our families, and our assets is taking on greater significance than ever before. Chapter 12 addresses one of the fastest growing segments of estate planning: elder law, or as we prefer to call it, planning for seniors. This planning includes Medicare and Medicaid benefits and long-term-care expenses. The baby-boomer generation faces the challenge of caring for their parents and at the same time trying to plan for their own senior years. With governmental social programs shrinking and retirement plans losing value, it is no surprise that more and more people are looking for guidance for themselves and their parents to plot the best course of direction for how to live in comfort, while maintaining control, in later years.

Our contributors do a masterful job of explaining the issues that make up what is commonly referred to as "elder law planning." They discuss in detail Medicare, the major governmental program for health care for seniors, including the types of medical care Medicare will and won't provide and some options to fill the Medicare "gap." They discuss the costs of long-term health care and offer an overview of the long-term health care options available.

For those who may need public assistance to meet their long-term-care needs, chapter 12 gives a summary of Medicaid eligibility requirements. Moreover, those looking to Medicaid and similar public programs for assistance will find that the key to qualifying for these benefits is proper planning that *must* occur far in advance of the need for long-term care. Our contributors offer guidance in planning for Medicaid eligibility and, most of all, stress the importance of starting this type of planning sooner rather than later.

Our contributors believe that long-term-care insurance is a wise investment for individuals who want to have more control over their choices during their senior years, and they provide relevant information on choosing a policy that will best fit your needs and pocketbook.

Some readers may feel that chapter 13 contains the most valuable information in the entire book. In our experience, one of the reasons people fail to plan is because of their inability to find a competent estate planning attorney with whom they can work. Chapter 13 suggests ways to find an attorney and describes the characteristics to look for in that professional. But estate planning usually requires more than an attorney. Usually, developing and implementing an estate plan requires a team of caring professionals planning in collaboration on your behalf. Chapter 13 recommends methods to find the other professionals whom most clients will need on their teams: financial planners, accountants, and insurance professionals. With the right team, you can be assured that your estate plan will meet your planning needs.

chapter 7

Administering Estates

_CR_ _What is estate administration?_

Estate administration is the legal process by which assets and obligations of the decedent are ascertained, so that the decedent's obligations can be paid and the asset distribution can be made to beneficiaries without fear of further claims against the estate. Will-planning utilizes the probate process to administrate, and living trust–centered planning uses the trust administration process.

_CR_ _Why should I be concerned about estate administration? After all, I'll be dead when that happens._

There are two reasons for you to be concerned. First, you may some day find yourself administering the estate of a family member. We often find that executors and successor trustees are unprepared for the task of winding up a decedent's affairs. Learning about the process now will make you feel more comfortable when the time comes for you to carry out your loved one's last wishes.

Second, we find that it helps for clients to understand this process while preparing their estate plans. Unless you have some appreciation for the estate administration process, it will be difficult for you to make informed decisions about the disposition of your assets and to select the most qualified people to serve as your executor and successor trustees.

IMMEDIATE ACTION STEPS AT THE DEATH OF A FAMILY MEMBER

CR *What immediate actions do we need to take on the death of a family member?*

The most immediate things to do for a person who has passed away are as follows:

- If you know that you are the trustee or personal representative for the deceased, inform the family of your position and check the deceased's estate planning documents for instructions regarding memorial services and/or special burial arrangements. Assist the family as needed with funeral arrangements, flowers, cemetery marker, announcement in the paper, special wishes for a memorial service, and notifying friends, relatives, employer, and others.

- Secure important papers and personal property, including jewelry, cash, and the keys to all the automobiles.

- Secure the decedent's charge cards.

- Make arrangements for pets if the decedent lived alone.

- Secure the home against vandalism and theft. Get someone to stay at the home during the memorial and funeral services.

- Contact the attorney who drafted the documents and set an appointment. If the trustee or personal representative cannot ascertain who the attorney is or if the decedent did not have an estate planning attorney, he or she should immediately retain an attorney with experience in estate administration.

Once you have taken care of these things, everything else can wait. Take time to spend with your family and to deal with the memories and emotions at hand.

Is there anything I shouldn't do?

It is almost as important to know what not to do at this time as what to do. There are important post-death tax planning options available that may be lost if you act without professional tax advice.

- Do not close bank accounts, withdraw monies, or pay bills from the accounts.
- Do not use a power of attorney.
- Do not let any personal property be divided up or removed from the decedent's home.
- Do not commingle your money with that of the decedent.
- Do not cash any retirement plan distribution checks or make any withdrawal elections, or otherwise take any action with regard to the decedent's IRA or pension benefits before you have consulted with an attorney and accountant.
- Do not change title to any of the decedent's assets.
- Do not make life insurance death claims.

NEED FOR PROFESSIONALS

Who should do the after-death administration work?

The attorney who drafted the estate plan (or another attorney who is experienced in after-death administration) and the decedent's financial advisor, accountant, and life insurance agent must work side by side to administer the estate properly. By utilizing the skills and knowledge of all these professionals, you can be assured that all work is successfully completed and that the decedent's estate plan is fully executed.

If there are problems with the plan, can they be corrected?

There are opportunities under the law to change the estate plan of a person by having potential recipients of the property "disclaim" their various interests. In other situations, elections under the estate planning documents may be made that would alter previously envisioned tax consequences. These potential opportunities should be carefully reviewed with legal counsel and family members who will be affected by the decisions.

ADMINISTRATION FOR A DECEDENT WITHOUT A WILL OR A TRUST

ଓ *What happens if an individual dies without an estate plan?*

When a person dies without a will or living trust, that person dies *intestate*. The decedent's assets are subject to a court proceeding called an *administration* that must be started by a family member, friend, or next of kin. An administration is much like probating a will, but there are additional steps. The court will appoint an *administrator,* or personal representative. For the most part, the administration proceeding request is initiated through a legal document called a *petition* that calls for the naming of an administrator. In the administration process, unhappy relatives or other interested persons, such as creditors of the decedent, can challenge the petitions of would-be administrators.

Once appointed by the court, the administrator generally must post a bond equal to the value of the gross estate. In addition to other duties, the administrator must prove where the decedent resided and who the decedent's heirs are, because the laws of the decedent's state of domicile will determine which heirs receive his or her property.

ADMINISTRATION FOR A DECEDENT WITH A WILL

ଓ *What is the probate process?*

In a nutshell, the *probate process* is a court proceeding that establishes the validity of a will and provides legal oversight to ensure accuracy in accounting for a decedent's assets, fairness in the treatment of heirs, and protection for the rights of the decedent's creditors.

Each state provides time limits and procedural steps to properly probate an estate. The process begins with the presentation of the will for probate. The probate process can take anywhere from a few months to many years, depending on the complexity of the estate and on whether there are any challenges to the validity of the will or its interpretation.

∽ What assets have to go through death probate?

Assets titled in the decedent's name alone must go through probate to pass to the heirs. As an example, if the decedent owned General Motors stock and only his name appeared on the certificate, the only way the surviving spouse or children can inherit the stock is through the probate process. The probate court issues an order assigning the ownership of the stock so that the stock transfer agent can retire the decedent's stock certificate and reissue a new certificate in the name of the heirs.

Assets that are titled in the decedent's name with others as joint owners with right of survivorship do not go through probate. Assets such as life insurance contracts titled in the decedent's name but that name specific individuals as beneficiaries also do not go through probate.

∽ Are probate assets readily available to the family?

One of the major problems with probate is that the assets are, for the most part, tied up until the process is completed. There are some statutory allowances available for a widow, dependent children, and other family members. These allowances are meager at best and certainly cannot compare to what a family is used to.

∽ What are the differences between an executor and a personal representative?

These terms refer to the person whom a court appoints to administer an estate. When the law refers to a "person," the term includes bank trust departments and other corporate fiduciaries.

Executor, or *executrix* (the legal term for a female executor), is the traditional term for a person named in a will and subsequently approved by the probate court to administer and distribute the property of a person who has died with a will. We inherited this term from England. *Personal representative* is the modern term for "executor" and is without gender. Many states have adopted statutes that replace the term "executor" with the term "personal representative."

For all but the most technical purposes, these terms can be used interchangeably.

ભ If a will names me as the estate's personal representative, am I empowered to act on its behalf?

No. Before you have any authority to act, you must file a petition with the probate court to request that it appoint you to act as personal representative. This will entail the court's acceptance of the will as valid.

Ultimately, the probate court will enter an order that gives you or some other person the power to act. It is the probate court's order that empowers you to act, not the decedent's will.

ભ Who will handle the distribution of out-of-state property?

If there is real or personal property located in another state, the personal representative may have to arrange for an ancillary administration in the probate court of the county and state in which the property is located in addition to the deceased's state of residence. Out-of-state intangible property such as bank accounts can usually be collected without opening an ancillary probate.

Certified copies of the will and other filings from the home state's probate court are sent to a law firm in the other state so that the firm can complete the probate process under its state's procedure. The heirs can receive their property when this out-of-state proceeding is completed.

ભ If I am named as the executor, what do I have to do with the decedent's assets?

As executor, you have the responsibility of gathering all the decedent's assets and reporting to the court by preparing and submitting an inventory. You recommend and the court appoints an appraiser to value real estate and any other asset that doesn't have a readily ascertainable value. The due date of the completed inventory is governed by state law.

You must then take possession of the assets, usually for several months, in order for creditors' claims to be filed and satisfied according to state law. After you have paid the decedent's debts, claims, and taxes from the probate assets, you will receive the court's order to distribute the remaining property to the decedent's heirs as provided in the will. You then must prepare a final accounting and submit it to the probate court for approval.

⚘ *What happens if my family can't find my will when I die?*

In most states, when the decedent's will cannot be located, it is presumed that the person destroyed the will prior to death and intended to revoke it. It is very important to store your original will in a safe place, such as a safe deposit box, or, better yet, your attorney's safe deposit box, as yours may be sealed on your death. Let your family members know where you put the original by keeping a copy of your will in a place where they will find it, with a note as to where they can find the original. The probate court will require the original to begin the probate process.

ADMINISTRATION FOR A DECEDENT WITH A LIVING TRUST

⚘ *Is it true that with a revocable living trust my spouse and family get all of my property without the necessity of lawyers performing any legal work?*

No. There is a common misperception that when you create a revocable living trust, the simple act of establishing the trust makes it possible to automatically pass on your assets without any further legal work or taxes.

A fully funded revocable trust does, indeed, permit you to avoid court-supervised probate administration of your assets after your death. Still, there is postmortem (after-death) legal work that is necessary and not avoidable even if you have established and fully funded a living trust. This is so because if you were the trustee of the trust while you were living, after your death all of the banks, brokerages, insurance companies, and other financial institutions that hold assets that belong to the trust need to be apprised of the death of a trustee and require legal and proper documentation to know who they are to take their instructions from now.

In addition, for living trusts that contain tax-planning instructions to divide the assets into two or more subtrusts (the marital and family trusts), the trustee will need professional guidance to accomplish that goal. The estate will likely also be required to file a federal estate tax return.

Organizing and accomplishing these various tasks is normally beyond the ability of the successor trustees, and the assistance of good legal counsel can save thousands of dollars and countless hours of frustration and confusion.

ଔ *I am a successor trustee for my brother. What will I have to do when he dies?*

The following are some of the duties you will have as the successor trustee:

1. Read and understand the trust document so that you will know who the beneficiaries are; what they are to receive and when; who, if anyone, are your cotrustees; and general matters regarding your trusteeship, administration, and investment powers.

2. Engage a skilled accountant or estate planning attorney for preparation of the decedent's final income tax returns and, if applicable, estate tax return, which is due 9 months from the date of death.

3. Have the attorney who drafted the estate planning documents prepare an affidavit of successor death trustee for you to provide to financial institutions so that they will know you are now in charge of the trust.

4. Order at least 12 certified death certificates.

5. Notify the decedent's professional advisors that you are now the trustee for the deceased trustmaker.

6. Notify life insurance companies, retirement plans, military affiliations and associations, and any others that will provide a death benefit. Remember, do not file a death benefit claim on the decedent's life insurance policies, individual retirement accounts (IRAs), or other retirement plans until you have verified the tax options with an accountant or attorney.

7. Collect all income due the deceased; keep a ledger of income received. Keep all check stubs and letters of explanation. *Never commingle trust assets with your personal assets.*

8. Collect and pay all contractual obligations, bills due, and taxes. Keep a ledger of accounts payable and keep a copy of all statements and all receipts.

9. Make assets productive during the estate-trust administration

process. Always exercise prudence, reasonable care, and skill when investing trust assets. If you lack the requisite skill or experience, use the decedent's professional advisors or, if necessary, retain a skilled investment advisor.

10. Make sure you keep any cotrustee and all the trust beneficiaries fully informed after the death of the trustmaker until the completion of the trust administration process. They are permitted to have a copy of the trust and supporting documents.

11. Begin (within the 9 months) to create and fund the subtrusts such as the marital, family, common, or other beneficiaries' trusts. Your accountant or estate planning attorney should counsel you on this process since effective estate and income tax savings results can be achieved if done properly.

⚘ What obligation does a trustee of a revocable living trust have to account to the decedent's beneficiaries?

Although the administration of a trust is usually accomplished outside the review of the probate court, certain rules still apply and these rules may be enforced by trust beneficiaries. Accordingly, the prudent trustee will notify, in writing, all the beneficiaries named in the trust, including any contingent beneficiaries, of the existence of the trust and the death of the trustmaker.

Unless otherwise prohibited by the trust document, it is wise to supply all beneficiaries with a copy of the trust and to inform them that they have the right to seek and employ legal counsel if that is their wish.

In most jurisdictions, the trustee will have a duty to report and account to the beneficiaries named in the decedent's trust at least once a year. This requirement may generally be waived by the consent of the beneficiaries or by express waiver granted in the decedent's trust instrument. However, good practice dictates a full accounting of all trust activity by the trustee to the named beneficiaries at frequent intervals to avoid any misunderstandings among them.

⚘ When should I begin making distributions from the trust?

As trustee, you must follow the trust's instructions. Those instructions usually require that the deceased's legitimate debts, income taxes, and death taxes be paid and that distributions be made to his or her beneficiaries. Since you may be personally liable if you make distributions to beneficiaries and then do not have enough money or property left in the trust to pay debts and taxes, you must determine which debts and taxes should be paid from trust assets. This may take some time. You also do not want to make distributions to beneficiaries until you consult with the estate administration attorney. Making a payment to a beneficiary without this consultation may impair after-death planning opportunities.

A well-advised trustee will spend trust funds only for the immediate needs of family members and to maintain the affairs of the decedent and consider partial distributions while always retaining assets sufficient to meet the contingencies for unsettled claims and undetermined taxes.

When it is appropriate to make distributions, following the terms of the trust, you will distribute the property in this order:

1. Items set forth on the memorandum of personal property.
2. Specific bequests of cash and property to individuals or charities.

You will distribute or hold all other property in trust, according to the trust's terms.

ACTIONS FOR PERSONAL REPRESENTATIVES AND TRUSTEES

Gathering Evidence of Assets and Liabilities

What techniques do you use to determine a decedent's assets?

If a decedent has a previously prepared schedule of assets, this job is much simpler. If there is no schedule of assets, we normally attempt to locate as many of the deceased's financial documents as we possibly can, such as:

■   statements from financial institutions (e.g., bank accounts, brokerage accounts, mutual fund accounts, IRA statements);
■   deeds and mortgages;

- stock certificates;
- evidence of ownership in a business (e.g., partnership agreement, limited liability agreement, etc.); and
- life insurance policies in the decedent's name.

Federal and state income tax returns can be helpful in ascertaining a decedent's assets. We may also contact the decedent's accountant and other attorneys, if possible, as they may have a clearer picture of the decedent's estate.

℞ *What other assets should I look for?*

Easily overlooked assets include:

- Income tax refunds
- Deposits (security deposits for rental property or utility deposits)
- Collections (coins, stamps, etc.)
- Corporate share certificates
- Time-share contracts for recreation properties in other states
- Life insurance benefits and disability insurance benefits that are incidental to credit card accounts and savings accounts
- Old life insurance policies for small amounts
- Property entrusted by the decedent to someone else
- Monies owed to the decedent
- Rights to reimbursements under medical insurance policies and long-term-care contracts

℞ *What about qualified plans and individual retirement accounts?*

That depends on who the beneficiary of the plan is. If the trust is the plan's beneficiary, it is an asset of the trust you must manage. Don't be hasty about making any plan withdrawals or cashing distribution checks. You will want to educate and inform yourself about the options that may be available as to plan distributions. We suggest that you sit down with the attorney and the accountant as well as any financial advisor to review the available alternatives.

℞ *You've covered real estate and bank accounts and personal property*

that were all owned by the trust. What should I do about life insurance policies?

How you handle life insurance policies will depend on how they were owned. If an irrevocable life insurance trust owned a policy, then only the trustee of that trust can receive the life insurance proceeds. But if the insured's living trust is the owner or beneficiary of the policy, it is your responsibility to see that the death benefit is collected. You will need a certified copy of the death certificate for each policy.

Call the decedent's life insurance agent to obtain the claim forms. Some life insurance agents will visit with you at your home or office and help you complete the claim forms and get them filed.

Paying Creditors

CR *When should I pay bills?*

The personal representative or trustee handling the estate must make a clear determination of the value of the estate before paying any of the estate's debts. Once the value of the estate is completely determined, if there are sufficient assets to pay all the claims, including any estate taxes that are incurred as a result of the death, claims are paid.

CR *How do I determine the creditors' claims?*

All states have time limitations on debts of deceased persons. These time limitations are typically called *statutes of limitations* or *bar dates*. You will typically need to gather information about known creditors' claims, and normally you will be required to give the known creditors written notice of the debtor's death. For unknown claims and creditors, you would publish a notice in the newspaper to unknown creditors according to your state statute about giving notice of the death.

Giving notice is vital to start the statute of limitations or bar date against the estate's creditors. The bar date for an estate is usually much shorter than it is for claims against living persons, 60–180 days from the date of the notice delivery or publication date versus 1–3 years. If you fail to give notice, creditors will have several years to pursue claims against the estate, the personal representative, and the heirs of the estate.

If the entire estate consists of trust assets, you and your attorney need to determine whether your state applies the shorter bar date to the applicable trust(s); some states may require that a minimal probate be opened to allow the trust to take advantage of the shorter claims' bar date. If so, you will need to weigh the advantages and disadvantages of each alternative and make a timely decision.

Now that I know what the creditors' claims are, how do I pay them?

You need to analyze all incoming claims. It is important to determine the validity of each claim, the type of claim, the priority of the claim, and the amount of the claim before you begin paying any claims or distributing assets or gifts to beneficiaries. In determining the validity of the claims, you must also determine whether you will contest any of the claims. You must be aware of your state law deadlines for contesting claims. These deadlines are often as short or shorter than the bar date for making the claim.

Most states have a "ladder" of priorities for claims against the deceased. Surviving spouse and family allowances, expenses of administration, taxes, and secured claims are usually at the top of the ladder, and various unsecured claims are on the lower rungs. The highest priority must be paid in full before the next priority. If there is not enough money for the next lower "rung," the creditors at that rung will only receive a percentage of the remaining money. Because creditors must be paid before beneficiaries, they will not recover anything either, unless they are also entitled to payment from one of the higher rungs, such as a family or homestead allowance.

Only when these tasks are completed can you begin the job of paying the claims. It can be very embarrassing and expensive if you make a mistake. You may be required to recover the unpaid debt from the money you have already paid to beneficiaries, or worse, in some instances from your own pocket if you are found to have violated your fiduciary duty.

Valuation of Assets

How will my estate be valued at the time of my death?

Generally, your estate will be valued at the fair market value of all the assets as of the time of your death. If a property is encumbered, the value will be its net equity. Certain property, such as farm property or real property used in a closely held business, may be valued for estate tax purposes according to special rules. *Fair market value* is generally defined as the price that would be paid between a willing seller and a willing buyer when neither party is under pressure to complete the transaction.

Some assets are easily valued, such as marketable securities listed on an established securities exchange. Other assets, such as real property or partnership interests, may require appraisals to establish value. Since the Internal Revenue Service (IRS) is not required to accept your appraisals, and in fact can hire its own appraisers in the event of a dispute, hiring recognized and qualified appraisers is important. *The cost of qualified appraisers is well worth any additional expense.*

℞ *Who will be responsible for valuing my assets after my death?*

Assets that have readily ascertainable values, such as certificates of deposit and bank accounts, do not have to be appraised in order to determine their value. Assets such as real estate or business interests should be appraised because their fair market values are sometimes subjective and potentially subject to IRS challenge.

In probate, the court will appoint either an appraiser recommended by the personal representative or a person from a list the court maintains. If you have done trust planning, your trustee will hire certified appraisers to value your property as needed.

DISCLAIMERS

℞ *What is a disclaimer?*

A *disclaimer* is an irrevocable refusal to accept an interest in property. The effect of a qualified disclaimer is as if no transfer was made to or from the person making the disclaimer. Most states have statutes that allow disclaimers and set forth how they are to be made.

℞ *I may receive an inheritance from my mother, but I would*

rather have it pass to my children. Is there a way that I can get the property to my children without incurring gift taxes?

This is a perfect situation for using a qualified disclaimer. If you disclaim your inheritance after your mother is deceased, the assets will pass as if you were deceased when your mother died. The recipient of those assets in this event will be determined by the terms of your mother's will or trust. If the document provides that in the event of your death, your share will pass to your children in equal shares, then your children will receive the assets that you have disclaimed. You will not be deemed to have made a gift to your children for gift tax purposes.

The disclaimer is an incredibly useful tool for leveraging the amount of gifts that you can make during your lifetime without gift tax liability. There is no limit on the amount you can disclaim, and all assets that you disclaim to your children will escape estate taxes upon your death. There may, however, be generation-skipping transfer (GST) taxes in your mother's estate if the amount going to your children is greater than the then available exemption for generation-skipping transfers.

Because of all the limitations and traps that exist for qualified disclaimers, it is critical that you consult an estate planning attorney immediately after you become aware of your right to any asset that you may want to disclaim.

ℭ *What is a qualified disclaimer?*

A disclaimer is qualified if it meets the requirements of the Internal Revenue Code. It is important that any disclaimer meet these requirements, or the disclaiming party will be deemed to have made a gift to the person receiving the property by virtue of the disclaimer. The requirements for a *qualified disclaimer* are as follows:

- The disclaimer must be in writing.
- The disclaimer must be delivered to the person who is attempting to transfer the interest, to his or her legal representative, or to the holder of the legal title to the property interest.
- The disclaimer must be delivered no later than 9 months after the date of the transfer creating the interest or 9 months after the person making the disclaimer becomes 21.

- The person making the disclaimer must not have accepted the interest or any of its benefits.
- As a result of the disclaimer, the property must pass, without any direction on the part of the person making the disclaimer, either to the spouse of the person making the transfer or to someone other than the person making the disclaimer.

That seems strange. Why would anyone refuse to accept an inheritance?

Yes, on the surface it seems highly unlikely that anyone would refuse an inheritance. However, disclaimers are exercised to redirect property to another person either for tax purposes or as a reallocation of assets for nontax purposes. Here are some examples:

- A surviving spouse might use a disclaimer to achieve certain estate tax results in the deceased spouse's estate. This might occur when there is too much value going directly to a surviving spouse and results in an underfunding of the family trust. By disclaiming a portion of the assets, the surviving spouse may be able to redirect some of the value of the assets to the family trust and thereby maximize estate tax savings for the family unit.
- A terminally ill child might disclaim property inherited from a deceased parent. The property would then pass automatically to his or her children without being included in the estate of the terminally ill child.
- A child whose estate is already substantial might disclaim an inheritance so that the property passes directly to his or her children, as long as it qualifies for the GST tax exemption.
- Elderly parents who inherit from a deceased child and who really do not need the inheritance might disclaim the inheritance so it passes to their other child—who will receive the parents' estate when they die anyway. This prevents the deceased child's property from being "trapped" or "caught" for a period in the parents' estates.

There are a variety of situations in which a disclaimer of an interest can be particularly useful in planning for family members. Individuals should obtain counsel before deciding to accept or to reject property to determine if disclaimers may be appropriate in specific situations.

INCOME TAXES
AFTER DEATH

A Decedent's Final Income Tax Return

Why must an income tax return be filed after the death of an individual?

The decedent earned income prior to death, and that income is subject to income taxes. Since the income was reported to the government (and taxes withheld) under the decedent's Social Security number, a final return is necessary. In the case of a married individual, the final return may be filed as a joint return with the surviving spouse.

Any income actually received on a cash basis as well as any expenses that were actually paid should be reported on a decedent's final return. The tax period between the beginning of a person's taxable year (almost always January 1) and the date of his or her death is treated as the tax period for which Form 1040 and the state income tax return must be filed.

Income Earned after the Decedent's Death

How is income that is earned after the decedent's date of death reported?

Any income earned after the decedent's death is reported on the estate's income tax return, on the trust's income tax return (if the decedent had a living trust), or on the returns of the beneficiaries who received the income.

FEDERAL ESTATE TAXES

When must a federal estate tax return be filed?

A federal estate tax return is required if a decedent's gross estate (including taxable gifts made by the decedent) is valued at or more than the applicable exclusion amount in the year of death. A federal estate tax return must be filed and the tax paid 9 months after the decedent's death. If it is impossible or impracticable to file the return within 9 months, a 6-month extension is available. Nevertheless, the tax is still due within 9 months unless an extension to pay the tax is authorized under the Internal Revenue Code.

ACTION STEPS

We respectfully present the following action steps to summarize the concepts that we discussed in chapter 7 and to suggest steps that you can take to prepare for meetings with your estate planning team of professionals.

❑ *Contact the decedent's attorney promptly.* As soon as practical, contact the decedent's estate planning attorney so that he or she can assist you (as executor or successor trustee) in winding up the decedent's affairs and administering the estate. Even if the decedent had a fully funded revocable living trust, an attorney will be very helpful—if not essential—in making sure that matters are settled correctly and promptly.

❑ *Avoid certain actions until you consult with the attorney.* Until you have been advised to do so by the attorney, do not close bank accounts, make any retirement plan election, pay any of the decedent's bills, or distribute any of the decedent's property.

❑ *Identify decedent's assets and debts.* Look through the decedent's tax returns and checkbook for indications of whom he or she owed money to, and examine all financial records to identify and list bank and brokerage accounts, real estate holdings, life insurance policies, retirement plans, and any other assets he or she owned; and debts owed.

❑ *Assemble records of decedent's assets and debts.* Evidence of what the decedent owned and owed is crucial to proper postmortem administration. Evidence of ownership includes statements from financial institutions, deeds, stock certificates, life insurance policies, partnership agreements, and any other documents that clearly state an ownership interest in an asset. Evidence of debts and liabilities include loan documents, copies of deeds of trust recorded by lenders, credit card statements, and any other documents that indicate the decedent owed money to another party.

❑ *Have the attorney prepare an affidavit of successor trustee.* If the decedent had a living trust, you will need an affidavit of successor trustee to show to banks, brokerage firms, and other entities before they will work with you. If there is a probate estate, you will need certified copies of the letters of administration or a similar court document to prove your authority.

❑ *Work with advisors to fund the subtrusts.* The decedent's estate plan may instruct you to create a marital trust and family (or credit shelter) trust with the decedent's property. This is a complex undertaking that you should not attempt to do without the assistance of an attorney and an accountant. Failure to fund these trusts correctly and promptly could needlessly subject the estate to federal estate tax.

chapter 8

Planning for Disability

REASONS TO PLAN
FOR DISABILITY

ભ *Why do I need disability planning?*

Advances in medical care have increased our life expectancies, but not necessarily our quality of life. It is not unusual now for people to become physically disabled or mentally disabled, or both, for an extended time.

Since World War II, relocation of families is commonplace: grown children move away to pursue careers or are transferred around the country; parents move to warmer climates to enjoy their golden years after retirement. As a result, many parents and children today reside great distances from each other.

Even when children reside in the same city as their parents, without proper authority, they may not be able to care for their parents.

Married couples assume that their spouses will be there for them but do not consider the consequences if their spouses also become disabled.

305

What happens if no competent spouse is available or no effective planning is in place? The courts will decide. A judge will appoint a guardian who will be responsible for making the living, financial, and health care arrangements for the incompetent person. The courts usually follow a system of priorities in making guardian appointments: spouse, adult children, parents, siblings, and so on, but there is no guarantee of that order.

If you have not chosen who your guardian will be, you may end up with a person you do not want. For example, the court might appoint your oldest child to be your guardian, but you might prefer another child. Without disability planning, the court will make all of the decisions for you in a process known as a living probate.

ℭℛ *What is living probate?*

Living probate is a generic term for court proceedings otherwise known as *guardianship* or *conservatorship*. Living probate occurs when a person is legally incompetent to manage his or her own affairs. Usually, a family member will start proceedings by filing a petition claiming that a relative is no longer competent and requesting the appointment of a guardian and/or a conservator. The court will then receive testimony and other evidence to determine whether the person is incompetent. In many states, these proceedings are public. If the court finds that the person is no longer capable of managing his or her affairs, the court supervises the disabled person's (*ward's*) assets or personal affairs, usually both, by appointing a conservator and/or a guardian. A conservator typically manages assets and makes financial decisions, and a guardian cares for the ward's personal matters. The same person is often appointed to both positions. The guardianship or conservatorship continues under court supervision for as long as the person remains incompetent.

ℭℛ *What is so bad about living probate?*

Living probate has many undesirable features:

- *Public.* Living probate is a court proceeding and, as such, everything is done publicly. The hearing to have a person declared incompetent is held in open court. Anyone who wants to listen in at the hearing is free to attend and can go to the courthouse and see in the records what is wrong with the person and what he or she owns.

- *Expensive.* Living probate is an ongoing proceeding, resulting in annual costs and attorney's fees. In addition, there may be accountant's fees, because at least once a year the conservator must return to court to give the judge a full accounting of the ward's assets and all receipts and expenditures.

- *Frustrating.* When a living probate estate is opened, the court takes control of the ward's assets. In certain cases, the conservator must get permission from the court for expenditures for the ward's needs. Permission is obtained only after the guardian calls the lawyer who prepares a petition, files the petition with the court, secures a court date, appears in court, gets a ruling, and reports back to the conservator.

- *Time consuming.* Because of the need for court approval to sell assets, pay expenses, and file annual accountings, the entire process is slow, cumbersome, and expensive.

ℛ *How can I avoid a living probate if I become disabled?*

You can drastically reduce the chances that you will ever have to go through a living probate by preparing a comprehensive estate plan that includes the following documents:

- Fully funded revocable living trust
- Power of attorney for health care
- Power of attorney for financial matters
- Living will or medical directive

The living trust should include a definition of disability so that family, your doctor, or other trusted individuals can make a private determination of your situation without the need of a court determination. The living trust names your "disability trustee" to manage the property in the trust in the event that you are disabled. If all of your property is in your trust and under the control of your disability trustee, there is no need for a court to appoint someone to manage your assets. The person named in the financial power of attorney has legal authority to manage property outside of your trust or to transfer it to the trust on your behalf.

The person whom you name in the health care power of attorney has authority to make medical decisions for you when you are unable to make them yourself.

In addition to these documents, a disability plan may also include disability insurance and long-term-care insurance.

After your disability plan is in place, you should review it periodically to make sure that it continues to meet your wishes.

ᗏ I have a small estate. Does it make sense for me to have disability planning?

If you have a modest estate, proper disability planning is even more essential to protect your assets from dissipation by living probate fees and costs. Without proper planning, your family will most likely have to initiate a living probate proceeding in order to get authority to manage your affairs.

ᗏ I have a will. Why do I need additional documents?

A will is not effective until after you die and it is submitted to, and accepted by, the probate court. To control your affairs after you become incapacitated and to avoid living probate, you simply must have these other documents.

ᗏ Does putting our assets in joint tenancy solve the living probate problem?

Placing assets in joint tenancy is not a satisfactory solution. With most joint-tenancy property such as real estate or brokerage accounts, the asset cannot be controlled without the assent of both joint tenants.

REVOCABLE LIVING TRUST

ᗏ How does a living trust avoid living probate?

When you set up a living trust, you fund your trust with your assets; that is, you transfer assets from your name to the name of your trust. The assets in the trust are controlled by you as the trustee. At your disability, the trust provisions empower another trustee—someone you named—to take over. There is no need for a court to take control when you become incapacitated, because your successor trustee assumes responsibility for your property. The concept is very simple, but this is what keeps you and your family out of court.

℞ *How does the revocable living trust ensure that I am taken care of if I become disabled?*

The revocable living trust protects you and your assets during any disability if it is properly written *and* funded. If the assets are not titled in the name of the trust, or there is no one with the power to transfer them to the trust, then no matter what the trust says, it cannot protect you. A well-drafted living trust includes the following provisions to take care of you during your disability:

- *Definition of disability.* You define in the trust document under what circumstances you want the successor trustee to take over managing the trust.
- *Who determines disability.* You provide in your trust who you want to decide if you are disabled. Advisors often recommend that two licensed physicians of the family's choice must certify that you are unable to manage your assets and make decisions. Some people prefer to select a person in whom they have a great deal of confidence and whose decision-making ability they trust.
- *Your successor trustees.* You name your successor trustees in the trust document in the event of your disability.
- *Guidance for your care.* The trust contains a set of instructions to guide the successor trustees. You should instruct your trustees as to your preferences for care, such as long-term care at home instead of a nursing home or similar facility. A well-drafted living trust also contains language about continuing your social, religious, and family activities as much as possible given the effects of your disability, how the bills are to be paid, and any other instructions that you feel are necessary.

The trust also provides instructions to guide the successor trustees in providing financial assistance to family members. In the event of a long-term illness, you might authorize your trustees to use your funds to assist your spouse and adult children who incur serious health problems or other financial emergencies during your illness.

⚭ *I don't want to place the entire decision-making burden on my wife if I become disabled. What can I do?*

Often, a spouse is not at his or her best at this point in time, because emotions may affect sound judgment. Adding one or more objective decision makers to the equation may ease that burden and provide support to the nondisabled spouse. You can utilize a panel of people to decide if a disability exists so that your wife does not have to make the decision alone. Members of this group may be your doctor, a specialist, your wife, and your children. There is no limitation to the number of people or their relationship to you that can serve on your panel.

⚭ *What types of financial powers can I delegate to my successor trustee that could help me during a period of incapacity?*

You can give your successor trustee power to transact the following types of activities if you are disabled or incapacitated:

- Buy, sell, mortgage, improve, or rent real estate.
- Purchase or sell stocks, bonds, or commodities.
- Vote ownership interests in stock.
- Open or close bank accounts or accounts at other types of financial institutions.
- Enter, open, or close safety deposit boxes.
- Write checks; withdraw or deposit money.
- Borrow money and pledge your assets as collateral.
- Operate, buy, or sell a business interest.

⚭ *What are the duties of a successor trustee once I become disabled?*

After the trustmaker has been declared disabled according to the provisions of the trust, the following are the primary duties of a disability trustee:

- Make sure the trustmaker is receiving quality care in a supportive environment. Give copies of health care documents (medical power of attorney, living will, etc.) to the physicians. Offer to help notify the trustmaker's employer, friends, and relatives.

- Notify the attorney who prepared the trust document in case the trustee or a family member needs to call with questions.

- Have the attorney prepare an affidavit of successor trustee, which provides the trustee the authority to exercise the fiduciary powers and control over the disabled trustmaker's assets.

- Secure and inventory all property, especially real estate and valuable tangible personal property. Secure the house and car keys, take care of any home maintenance items, and keep all insurance coverage in force.

- Transact any necessary business or financial transactions for the disabled trustmaker. For example, apply for disability benefits, pay insurance premiums, receive and deposit funds, pay bills (including mortgage, taxes, and other obligations) and, in general, use the trustmaker's assets to take care of him or her until recovery. Always act with the utmost honesty and document major decisions and actions. There should be absolutely no commingling of trust assets with the trustee's own assets. Keep a ledger of accounts payable and a copy of all statements and receipts.

- Collect all income due the disabled trustmaker. Keep a ledger of income received. Keep all check stubs and letters of explanation.

- If there are minors or other dependents, look after their financial care.

DURABLE POWERS OF ATTORNEY

Powers of Attorney in General

ℭℛ *What is a power of attorney?*

A *power of attorney* is a document by which a *principal*—the person giving the power—appoints another person—called an *attorney-in-fact* or *agent*—to perform specific acts on the principal's behalf.

There are two basic types of powers of attorney:

1. *general power of attorney*, which grants the agent broad powers to deal with all of the principal's assets and to take any action on his or her behalf; and

2. *limited* (or *special*) *power of attorney,* which allows the agent to perform only certain acts or to control specific property.

Traditionally, a power of attorney automatically terminates when the principal becomes disabled or dies. Although this is still true, states have passed legislation allowing a principal to grant *durable powers of attorney* (either general or limited) that remain valid after the principal becomes incapacitated. A power of attorney is durable only when it specifically states that it is to continue upon the legal incapacity of the principal. Durable powers of attorney are used in disability planning to allow the agent to act on the principal's behalf during periods of disability.

CR *When does my power of attorney become effective and when does it terminate?*

This depends on the terms of the document and your state's laws. Usually, your power of attorney is effective when you sign it. In the context of disability planning, of course, there is no need for the power until you are disabled, and some people are troubled about authorizing others to act for them while they are still capable of handling their own affairs. To address this concern, some states have laws authorizing "springing" durable powers of attorney. With a springing durable power of attorney, your agent is not authorized to act unless and until you become disabled.

If the power of attorney is not a durable power, it will terminate upon your incapacity. All powers of attorney automatically terminate when you die.

You may revoke your power of attorney at any time. The best way to do this is to destroy all copies. If the agent has already transacted business with a third party pursuant to the power, you should notify the third party that you have revoked the power of attorney.

Durable Power of Attorney for Financial Matters

CR *I'm starting to understand the importance of fully funding my trust. What if I become incapacitated before I get all my assets into it?*

Your estate planning attorney will prepare a *durable special* (or *limited*) *power of attorney* specifically for this purpose. The document is *special* or *limited* in that it limits the agent's power, in this case, only to transfer your property to your trust and grants no other powers. In this way, a trusted member of your family or an advisor can complete your funding for you if you are living but unable to do so.

○ Are there other types of powers I could give to my agent under a durable power of attorney for financial matters?

Typically, the first power is to allow the agent to be able to fund assets to your revocable living trust so that all of your assets are available to care for you and your family. It is becoming more common to give the agent additional powers, such as:

- to make gifts to family members;
- to make, change, or revoke beneficiary designations on and to manage life insurance policies, qualified retirement plans, individual retirement accounts, and annuities; and
- to file tax returns.

○ Why wouldn't I give these powers to my successor trustee rather than giving them to someone under a power of attorney?

You can certainly give these powers to your successor trustee, but you should also give them to that same person through a power of attorney. A trustee's job is to manage and use property *in the trust* for the benefit of its beneficiaries; a trustee has no authority to act unless the action relates to trust property. Your agent handles personal and financial matters such as applying for disability benefits, filing your tax returns, opening your mail, acting as your agent for lawsuits not related to trust property and performs any other tasks you assign to him or her in the power of attorney. You can instruct the agent to transfer certain assets to the trust, but other assets, such as retirement accounts, must remain outside the trust. If you want the trustee to have the authority to manage the property that must remain outside the trust, the appropriate way to convey those powers is through the power of attorney document.

Because many of these duties overlap, many people appoint the same person as successor trustee and agent of the power of attorney for financial matters.

Durable Power of Attorney for Health Care

CR *What is a durable power of attorney for health care?*

A *durable power of attorney for health care* is an important part of disability planning. It is a legal instrument by which you designate an agent to make health care decisions for you in the event that you are unable to do so for yourself. In the health care power, you can inform your agent of your preferences regarding medical issues that are important to you, such as home care, life support, and pain management.

Although a health care power does not affect your assets, it is an important estate planning tool.

CR *Last week my wife called the doctor for me to get my test results. The doctor said he couldn't discuss the results with her. Why not?*

As part of the Health Insurance Portability and Accountability Act of 1996 (HIPAA), in April 2003 the U.S. Department of Health and Human Services issued strict guidelines regulating disclosure of patient information. The regulations permit doctors to discuss a patient's situation with the patient's "personal representative," that is, someone authorized by the patient or by state law to make health care decisions for the patient. Thus, if the patient has not executed a power of attorney for health care, health care providers will likely refuse to share medical information with anyone except a court-appointed guardian.

These new regulations prevent your health care professionals from releasing information about your health to *anyone* without your written permission. With these new rules in place, it is crucial that all of us sign durable powers of attorney for health care.

CR *Who should be my health care agent?*

Here are some characteristics you may want to consider when deciding whom to name as the agent in your health care power of attorney:

- *The ability to engage or draw out busy health care professionals:* Communication is essential for gaining information; having a medical background helps with this process but is not essential.
- *The ability to command attention and respect:* A person with this quality is more likely to be included in decision making.

- *Leadership abilities:* A respected leader among family members can instill unity and confidence.

- *Time to devote to this task:* Busy executives or people with many responsibilities are not always capable of devoting the time needed.

- *Geographical proximity:* Having an agent who is nearby is advantageous, but this is not as important as the above characteristics.

Having more than one person acting simultaneously as an agent is not recommended in most cases. It is hard enough to get overburdened medical staff and physicians to spend time explaining options and care alternatives to one person. Forcing them to work with a committee is almost impossible.

It is also important for you to discuss your health care desires with your health care agent before disability occurs. Your agent needs to hear from your lips and see in your eyes that the choices you expect that person to make are truly your choices and that you believe your health care decisions are a matter of personal dignity and control. Having this knowledge will greatly ease your agent's burden of making difficult health care decisions.

LIVING WILLS AND MEDICAL DIRECTIVES

⚬ঽ *What is a living will?*

A *living will*, or *medical directive* or *physician's directive*, depending on what your state calls it, is a directive to your physician that states that you do not want "extraordinary means" employed to keep you alive should you be in a terminal condition or in a permanently unconscious state. This will not only relieve your family of the burden of applying to the courts to authorize stopping artificial life support but will also relieve your family from having to make this decision at all.

⚬ঽ *Why do I need a living will? Can't my husband make those decisions for me?*

In many cases, the answer is "no." Without written instructions from you to your physician to prohibit the prolonged use of artificial life support, your husband may not have the right to act on your behalf. A living will contains specific instructions from you as to what action you want taken or not taken if you are permanently unconscious or when death is imminent. It gives direction and purpose to your loved ones, instead of placing the entire burden on them to make these life-and-death decisions. A living will goes a long way to ease the burden and the guilt that a spouse or other family member may bear as a result of having to make this decision without any direction or instruction from you.

❧ Which is better, the health care power or the living will?

The documents serve two different purposes. A health care power of attorney authorizes the agent to take a wide range of steps on your behalf, from authorizing an emergency operation to arranging for long-term rehabilitation. Your agent acts as your advocate to make sure that you get quality medical care and that your treatment wishes are respected. You can certainly authorize your agent to order the cessation of life-sustaining treatment, and most powers of attorney do so if consistent with the patient's wishes.

Nonetheless, it is still a good idea to have a living will in addition to the power of attorney. A living will, in effect, communicates directly to your doctor. It saves your agent from the terrible task of deciding whether to end your life.

If possible, you would use a health care power of attorney *and* a living will or directive. If you do that, it is important that you make sure that they are both consistent with each other so that your wishes are carried out.

❧ How can I be sure that there is no hope for me to live before someone implements the instructions in my living will?

Many states provide that at least two physicians must examine you and must determine to a reasonable degree of medical certainty, based upon the medical technology then available, that you are either permanently unconscious or that death is imminent. In some cases, the physicians are required to notify certain members of the patient's family, and if any one of them feels that the diagnosis is incorrect, then there is a procedure by which the physicians' determinations can be reviewed by a court of law.

Where should I keep my original living will, and who should receive copies?

Your original living will should be kept in a safe place that is easily accessible at all times (not a safe deposit box, which cannot be opened at night or on weekends). Be sure someone in your family or a close friend knows where your living will is located and that he or she has ready access to it in case of an emergency. You may wish to give copies to family members, friends, and your attorney or clergy.

Because doctors are required to follow your directive and exercise the living will immediately upon the determination that death is imminent, it is not recommended that you provide your doctor with a copy of your living will until you are to be admitted to a hospital. Once the living will is provided to a hospital, it becomes part of your medical record. It is generally more comfortable if a family member waits a day or two to make sure that the doctor's determination of imminent death is correct before he or she and the hospital exercises the authority provided under the living will. Your family will generally know you best and will be able to determine what your desires are or are not at this time when it is most important.

How long is my living will valid?

As long as you signed it voluntarily, your living will is valid until you rescind it. If you decide at any time to revoke any portion of your living will, communicate this change to your attending physician immediately and retrieve and destroy all copies given to others. Then execute a new living will.

I'm a little confused as to exactly how the trust, the powers of attorney, and the living will all work together. Can you summarize and differentiate these for me?

Yes. First of all, the four documents that we've described must be designed and drafted in conjunction with each other to ensure that they are all consistent with each other. Beyond that, each document addresses different disability concerns and handles different issues, which are shown in Table 8-1. This may all seem at bit complicated, but these documents are necessary in order to form a comprehensive disability plan for you.

TABLE 8-1   Summary of Documents in a Disability Plan

Document	Purpose in disability plan
Revocable living trust	In this document, you name a successor trustee who has the fiduciary and legal authority and responsibility to manage your property during your disability. However, your successor trustee can only act with respect to trust property. The trust may not own all of your assets. This is particularly true with qualified plan funds, individual retirement accounts, and life insurance policies.
Durable power of attorney for financial matters	The agent that you appoint under this instrument performs many of the same functions as a successor trustee, but only with respect to property that is *not* a part of your living trust. In this document, you may give the agent the authority to place property in your trust. If you choose not to use a living trust as the foundation of your estate plan, then the agent you appoint will be responsible for all your property and handle all your nonmedical affairs while you are disabled.
Durable power of attorney for health care	This document appoints someone to make all medical and health care decisions for you when you are mentally or physically unable to do so. This may or may not include the authority not to connect you to or to disconnect you from life-sustaining machines in the event that you are permanently unconscious or when death is imminent.
Living will or medical directive	This is a statement, signed by you, telling your doctors what you want to occur if you are permanently unconscious or when death is imminent. In this document, you remove all decision-making authority from your agent under the durable power of attorney for health care with respect to these particular life-and-death decisions. If you would like to vest total discretionary decision-making authority in your agent under the power of attorney, then you would not sign a living will.

DISABILITY INSURANCE

⟨ℜ *What is disability insurance?*

Disability insurance is insurance that provides an income to an individual if he or she becomes disabled. The disability income paid is based on the amount of premium that the insured wishes to pay and the amount of income the insurance company will provide for that premium amount on the basis of the insured's age, occupation, and health status.

Disability income insurance replaces a portion or a percentage of lost income that is considered earned income. If a proposed insured is independently wealthy or has substantial unearned income, the insurance company will typically not be able to offer disability coverage.

⟨ℜ *How much disability coverage can I purchase?*

The maximum amount of disability insurance available must be carefully calculated. The purpose of disability insurance is to replace earned income lost because of disability. To provide an incentive for the insured to return to work, full income replacement is not permitted. On the average, insurance companies will allow the insured to replace approximately 60 percent of gross income before tax. The percentage is lower for higher incomes.

⟨ℜ *How important is disability income insurance?*

Most financial experts agree that disability coverage is not only important, but essential. For most people, their ability to create income is their most valuable asset. Without the ability to create income, they could lose everything they have worked to build.

⟨ℜ *When shopping for disability insurance, what are the key points I should look for to make sure I have complete protection?*

Some of the key points in a disability insurance contract are:

- Dollar amount of benefits
- Premium guarantees

- Length of time benefits will be paid
- Definition of disability
- Policy exclusions

℞ *If I own a business, is there some type of coverage for business expenses?*

A disabled business owner or professional may face continued business expenses but have inadequate business income to pay them. Business overhead expense (BOE) insurance is a reimbursement policy designed for just such a situation. The proceeds from a BOE policy can help keep a business or practice in operation by reimbursing normal business expenses until the insured recovers or all the total aggregate benefit amount is paid, whichever comes first.

℞ *If I purchase disability insurance coverage, what are the tax implications of any benefit payments I receive?*

If you purchase the policy individually, premiums for disability insurance are not deductible but the disability benefits received by you are exempt from income taxation.

For business-owned policies with premiums paid for by the employer on behalf of the employee, the situation is different:

1. The premium paid by the employer on behalf of the employee is not considered to be taxable income to the employee.
2. The premium paid by the employer is deductible by the employer (group or individual coverage) as long as the policy benefits are payable directly to the employee.
3. Benefits paid to the employee upon a disability are fully taxable as ordinary income to the employee during the year the benefit payment is received.

LONG-TERM-CARE INSURANCE

℞ *What is long-term care?*

Long-term care is assistance provided to individuals who are functionally impaired. *Functional impairment* means that a person needs care because of cognitive or other impairment and/or is unable to perform at least two of the six *activities of daily living* without assistance. These activities are bathing, dressing, toileting, eating, medicating, and transferring from a chair to a bed. As the name suggests, long-term-care insurance provides cash to pay for this type of assistance, whether in a nursing home or other setting.

‏ *Do I need long-term-care insurance?*

According to the U.S. Congressional Report on Aging, long-term-care expenses are the number one cause of impoverishment among retirees today. It is a good idea to look into long-term-care insurance while you are healthy and in control of your life. Long-term-care insurance can help you and your family maintain that control when you might otherwise lose it. This insurance can be a bit pricey, but the amount you save if you end up needing it is impressive. We discuss long-term-care insurance in detail in Chapter 12, Planning for Seniors.

ACTION STEPS

We respectfully present the following action steps to summarize the concepts that we discussed in chapter 8 and to suggest steps that you can take to prepare for meetings with your estate planning team of professionals.

❑ *Locate existing disability plan documents.* These might include a living trust, powers of attorney, a living will or a medical directive. As with every other part of your estate plan, it's important to periodically review your disability planning documents to see that they still meet your needs. It's also a good idea to sign new disability documents every few years; banks and doctors are sometimes hesitant to follow "stale" documents.

❑ *If you don't have a disability plan, create one now.* No matter what your age, it is essential that you have a well-designed disability plan in place. Even though you have family that you think could make these decisions for you, don't put that burden on them at a time when they will be too emotionally distraught to remember what you wanted. Carefully consider *who* you want to care for you and your affairs while you are unable to do so; and consider *how* you want to be cared for:

- Do you want to remain at home if possible?

- What type of facility do you want to stay in if it is necessary?

- Is there anyone else who is dependent on you and whom you want to continue providing for?

- Who do you want to decide whether you are incapacitated and how do you want them to determine that you are?

- What are your wishes concerning life-sustaining procedures when there is little chance of recovery?

- What other instructions do you want to give your caregivers?

❑ *Meet with an insurance professional about disability and long-term-care insurance.* We cannot stress enough the need for disability and long-term-care insurance. These two types of insurance are perhaps the best ways to secure your finances and your personal dignity in the event of serious long-term disability. If you currently have these types of policies, review them with your agent to make sure that they provide you with the coverage you need.

chapter 9

Living Trust-Centered Estate Planning

Q *What is living trust–centered estate planning?*

The definition of estate planning that the editors of *Love, Money, Control* coined many years ago and that many of the contributors to this book espouse in one form or another is:

> I want to control my property while I am alive and well; care for myself and my loved ones if I become disabled; and be able to give what I have to whom I want, the way I want, and when I want; and, if I can, I want to save every last tax dollar possible while minimizing professional fees and court costs.

Living trust–centered estate planning is planning to achieve those goals implicit in this definition by using the revocable living trust as the foundation document in the estate plan.

Q *What other documents should I expect to have in my estate plan?*

A proper estate planning portfolio using living trust–centered documentation will often contain:

- A section for personal and family information, including addresses and telephone numbers
- A list indicating the location of original documents such as the original trust, will, life insurance policies, and birth certificates
- A list of the names, addresses, and telephone numbers of professional advisors, trustees, and family advisors, such as attorney, accountant, insurance agent, and priest/rabbi/minister
- A list of all assets that you own including certificates of deposit, bank accounts, life insurance policies, annuity contracts, retirement accounts, and business interests
- Your revocable living trust agreement or, if you are married and it is applicable, a joint trust for both of you
- An affidavit of trust that contains pertinent facts about your trust that can be used to prove the trust's existence while preserving the privacy of its detailed provisions
- Your pour-over will (discussed later in this chapter)
- A memorandum to distribute your personal effects (what form this takes will depend upon the state in which you reside)
- Durable powers of attorney to appoint agents to fund your revocable living trust with any assets inadvertently or otherwise left out of the trust and to manage your other financial, personal, and legal affairs
- A durable power of attorney for health care to designate an agent to make medical decisions on your behalf and to authorize medical service providers to allow your agent access to your medical information and records
- A living will or advanced medical directive that expresses your wishes about the use of life-support systems and invasive medical procedures to artificially extend your life
- Memorial instructions that contain your burial or cremation wishes and information on the type of memorial service that you would like to have
- An anatomical gift form that allows you to make a gift of all or part of your body for medical or dental education and research, therapy, or transplant procedures
- Property agreements to sever and terminate your and your spouse's joint tenancy interests so that those interests can be transferred to your respective revocable living trusts
- Documentation of the assets that have been transferred to your revocable living trust

Though we discussed some of these documents in Chapter 8, Planning for Disability, we will discuss in more detail the most important of these documents again in this chapter.

THE REVOCABLE LIVING TRUST

ଓ *What is a revocable living trust?*

A *trust* is a contract between its maker and one or more trustees. In the contract, the trustmaker gives instructions to the trustee concerning the holding and administering of trust assets. These instructions specify how the assets are to be held and distributed during the maker's good health, upon his or her disability, and ultimately upon his or her death.

With a *revocable living trust,* a person can be (and usually is) both the maker and the trustee. A husband and wife will often be joint trustmakers and joint trustees of a joint revocable living trust.

The term "revocable" literally means "able to revoke" and in the case of a revocable living trust, refers to a set of powers that are typically listed in the trust agreement which specify that the trustmaker has the power to amend (change) or revoke the trust entirely. Upon revocation, the trustee is most often directed to return all trust assets to the trustmaker. In addition to having the power to amend or revoke the trust, the maker has the power to place assets into the trust, to remove assets from the trust, to make all investment decisions concerning trust assets, and to control and direct all payments and distributions from the trust.

A *joint revocable living trust* is a single trust created by a married couple that addresses each spouse's wishes as to his or her separate property or the couple's community property if they live in a community property state. Both spouses are the trustmakers, and both are most always the trustees. Joint trusts are almost always used for residents of community property states and sometimes in noncommunity property states, depending on the couple's planning needs and desires.

ଓ *It seems as though revocable living trusts suddenly popped up on the radar screens a few years ago, and now they are all we hear about. Where did they come from?*

Trusts have been around for at least two thousand years. History tells us that Roman Emperor Augustus had a trust in 63 B.C. We know King Richard I (the Lion Heart) used a trust arrangement to take care of his property and family when he left on the Crusades. More recently, the Rockefeller and Kennedy families and many other famous and wealthy persons in this country have had trusts at various times during the last 200 years. A huge body of statutory and case law governs trusts. They are tried and true estate planning vehicles.

Yet, it is only within the last few decades that trusts have become a viable estate planning tool for middle-income, middle-class America. For several centuries in the law, the thinking was that there had to be a "separation of identities" where trusts were concerned. In other words, a trust required three different persons: a trustmaker, a trustee, and at least one beneficiary. That requirement made living trusts too cumbersome, and only irrevocable trusts and testamentary trusts were used in estate planning. (We'll explain those trusts shortly.)

Fortunately, the law is a constantly evolving body. Over time, legal scholars (and, more important, judges and lawmakers) realized that "separation of identities" was not necessary for a trust to be valid. Thus, the same person could fill two and to some extent all three roles, or "wear all three hats." With this new approach, trusts are more flexible and useful in estate planning for everyone. Now a person can "make" a trust while living, serve as the trustee, and be one of the beneficiaries.

∝ *What is the difference between a revocable trust and an irrevocable trust?*

The trustmaker of a revocable trust can revoke, change, or amend the trust at any time and for any reason. A revocable living trust can be designed to control all of the maker's property, totally avoid the probate of the maker's estate, and maximize federal estate tax savings. This flexibility makes a revocable living trust an ideal foundation for almost all estate plans.

Irrevocable trusts, on the other hand, generally cannot be altered or amended without the approval of a court. Accordingly, irrevocable living trusts should be used only in certain circumstances after careful consideration and planning. Most often, irrevocable living trusts are used in conjunction with revocable living trusts to accomplish additional estate tax planning goals and to hold selected assets of the trustmaker for the benefit of the trustmaker's loved ones. If the trustmaker retains no rights in his or her irrevocable living trust and is not a trustee or a beneficiary of the trust, the assets of the trust can generally be excluded from the trustmaker's gross estate for estate tax purposes. This allows the trustmaker to lower and, at times, eliminate federal estate taxes.

❧ You keep referring to "living" trusts. As opposed to what— "dead" trusts?

Well, in a way, "yes." Living trusts are a form of *inter vivos* (during your life) trusts, created to be operational during your lifetime. You sign the trust agreement and place assets in it while you are alive.

A revocable living trust survives your incapacity and your death. It allows the trustee to manage and distribute the assets of the trust during any incapacity and after your death in the manner you specified in the trust agreement, without any court intervention. Within a revocable living trust, there may be one or more *testamentary trusts,* that is, trusts that are not operational until after your death. The family and marital trusts are common examples of testamentary trusts within a revocable living trust.

A trust created in a will is testamentary and does not come into existence until after your death. Since these testamentary trusts are not operational during your lifetime, you cannot place any assets in them during your life; the court has to do that after your death. Hence, your assets must go through the probate process before being placed in the testamentary trust. In some jurisdictions, testamentary trusts may be subject to court supervision until all assets have been distributed and all trust purposes have been completed.

❧ What is the difference between a living trust and a living will?

A living will is an important part of your estate plan because it allows you to preplan for very sensitive personal issues that affect you and your loved ones. A *living will* directs your physician to discontinue life-sustaining procedures if you are in a terminal condition or a permanently unconscious state. Each state has its own statutes that provide specific guidelines and language that can or should be included in your living will.

A *living trust* deals with your financial affairs rather than with health care issues. With a living trust, you can give instructions about what is to happen to your assets when you are no longer able to manage them yourself, whether due to incapacity or to death.

ℭ *I don't have a large estate. Wouldn't a will be just as good for me as the revocable living trust?*

A will can meet most of your estate planning goals, but a will is only effective on your death and cannot provide for you if you are mentally or physically unable to take care of yourself. Even for people who do not have taxable estates, the revocable living trust is a far better planning vehicle because it provides the following benefits that a will does not:

- *Avoids living probate.* If you become disabled or are unable to manage your financial affairs, your living trust can eliminate the need for a court-appointed guardian or conservator to take control of your assets. If you have transferred all your assets to your living trust, it will control how those assets are managed during your incompetency.

- *Avoids death probate.* Your assets can go directly to your beneficiaries after your death without court interference.

- *Is valid in every state.* The laws of every state recognize the validity of a living trust. It can freely cross state lines with you, without any need to redraft its terms to comply with local law if you decide to move to another state.

- *Discourages attack by discontented heirs.* You have more than likely heard the stories about bitter court contests over what was or was not left to an heir in a will submitted for probate. A living trust is not part of the public probate process, which invites and encourages disputes. It is also not governed by the archaic and complex rules surrounding a will. These features make a living trust less prone to successful attack by dissatisfied heirs.

- *Avoids probate in multiple states.* If you own real estate in multiple states, you can avoid the "ancillary" probate proceedings in each state as long as your real estate is titled in the name of your living trust.

- *Is private.* One of the most important benefits of a revocable living trust is the privacy it offers to surviving family members: it does not subject the family's financial affairs to the public probate process as a will does.

These are just a few examples of the goals you can achieve with a revocable living trust. When you remain mindful of the real priorities in estate planning, you will never choose a planning vehicle solely on the basis of the size of your estate, your marital status, or your age. Rather, you will choose the vehicle that operates best to meet your goals and objectives.

☙ *How do I most effectively avoid guardianship and probate?*

Through a fully funded revocable living trust, you can totally avoid guardianship and probate proceedings. You do so by including instructions in the trust document that specify how your successor trustee should manage the assets in the trust if you become disabled. You have the benefit of your assets, consistent with your directions, during any period of disability while avoiding the expense, delay, and lack of privacy imposed by a court-supervised guardianship proceeding.

Similarly, you leave instructions in the trust document for your successor trustee, indicating how the trustee should manage and distribute the trust assets after your death. Because those assets are titled in the name of the trust, you avoid the expense, delay, and lack of privacy caused by a death probate.

☙ *My partner and I are not married. Will living trusts help us protect our assets for each other?*

Because the law treats married couples differently from unmarried couples, and because society makes certain assumptions about the distribution of a spouse's property, you and your partner have special planning needs. Unless you prepare estate plans specifically leaving your property to each other, when one of you dies the surviving partner will inherit nothing from the deceased partner. Therefore, it is critical to ensure, through a competent attorney, that you and your partner have legally enforceable documents granting each other the powers and benefits you want.

In addition to your respective living trusts, consider writing a letter to those family members who might legally or practically presume that they will be in charge of you and your affairs in the event of your incapacity and after your death. Your letter should explain what you have done and why, and it should request that they not interfere with your wishes.

○ℛ *What are the benefits of a revocable living trust?*

Control, cost, convenience, and confidentiality are the four primary reasons that many people turn to trust-centered estate planning.

- *Control.* Perhaps the most important attribute of a revocable living trust is that it allows the trustmaker to retain control of his or her financial and personal affairs even in the event of disability. Studies show that people are likely to experience a lengthy period of disability before death. While a will has absolutely no effect until the will maker has died, a revocable living trust is effective as soon as the trustmaker signs it, so he or she can plan for disability and other issues that may arise during life. After the trust is properly funded, the trustmaker can continue to control the assets in the trust.

- *Cost.* The cost of administering the trust after the maker's death is generally much lower than the professional fees for administering that same property through the probate process.

  With a revocable trust, there is no need to retain an attorney to steer the estate through probate. The successor trustee is fully empowered to administer and distribute the trust property without court supervision. Further, properly funded living trusts avoid expenses dictated by and associated with probate law for notices, hearings, and other procedures. Of course, the successor trustee may seek the advice of an estate planning attorney and a knowledgeable accountant as needed, but in most cases the assistance required from professional advisors is minimal in comparison to those required for a probate administration.

  Similarly, there is no need to hire an attorney for living probate. With proper trust-centered estate planning, health care agents are appointed and successor trustees are designated and empowered to administer and care for the trustmaker. Living probate–related costs, including attorney fees, filing fees, and the like, are avoided, resulting in preservation of trust assets for the benefit of the trustmaker and his or her beneficiaries.

- *Convenience.* Though the results of administration of a probate estate or of a trust are the same—taxes are paid and distributions are made to the beneficiaries—the probate process is cumbersome and time-consuming in comparison to the process of administering a trust. The trustmaker's specific directions within the trust document address the contingencies of disability and death and appoint successor trustees to carry out those directions.

■ *Confidentiality.* Trusts are private. While wills and the entire probate process are open to the public, trusts remain confidential. For many, this in itself is a compelling factor in favor of using revocable living trusts.

Most of us have been raised to keep our financial matters private. It is unlikely that we would discuss our income or net worth with neighbors or at a social gathering. However, if you die with a will controlling your affairs, all of your sensitive financial matters are at once open to public scrutiny. Your will and the accompanying inventory of your estate, the value of your assets, and your outstanding debts will be filed with the probate court in the county where you resided at death. Anyone, such as an intrusive neighbor or potential suitor for your business, can simply contact the court, forward a small check to cover the expense of photocopying your estate file, and receive copies of all papers filed in your estate.

Since fully funded trusts are not subject to the rules of the probate court, the inventories, notices to beneficiaries, and accountings of all assets and debts of your estate are not filed with the court and hence are not open for public scrutiny.

ᗄ *I'm afraid I'll lose control of my assets if I don't own them anymore. Will I lose control if I transfer my assets to my revocable living trust?*

Among the provisions of your trust are your instructions for the trustee in regard to managing and distributing the assets for and to your beneficiaries—you dictate the terms which your trustee (the new owner of your property) *must* obey. There is no higher duty under the law than that owed by a trustee to a beneficiary.

As if that were not enough control, you can be the sole beneficiary of the trust during your lifetime. Your trust will contain instructions telling the disability trustee how to take care of you during a legal incapacity, and the trustee must follow your instructions and use your property for your benefit.

And finally, for the ultimate in control, you can be your own trustee while you are alive and competent. You make all the decisions to buy, sell, give away, acquire, and use the property, just as you always did prior to transferring them to the trust.

℣ *What is life like after I put all my assets into a revocable living trust?*

Life goes on just as it did before. It's kind of like putting all your assets into a big box with no lid on it. You can put property in and take it out anytime you want. You have complete control over what happens with all of your assets even when you yourself are no longer able to make decisions about them. Unlike you or me, the box doesn't die or become disabled, so court involvement is not needed to carry on your affairs after disability or death. At death, the lid goes on the box and the trust becomes irrevocable.

℣ *How long does it take to set up a revocable living trust?*

Typically, it takes about 2 to 3 weeks after the initial consultation for the attorney to prepare the trust documents. After the trust documents are signed, it is necessary to complete the funding documents that are used to transfer ownership of your assets to the trustee of your trust. This process can take from a few days to several months, depending on the number and types of assets and your level of diligence in seeing the process through to completion. These time frames can often be shortened greatly if an emergency situation exists.

℣ *When does my living trust become effective?*

A revocable living trust document and all the ancillary documents created as part of a living trust–centered plan become effective when they are properly signed. In order to receive the greatest benefits from a revocable living trust, however, you must retitle your assets in the name of the trust. If you do not accomplish this, any assets not placed in the trust prior to your death may have to go through the probate process before coming under the control of the trust.

℣ *Does my trust end when I die?*

Your living trust doesn't have to die with you. Assets can stay in your trust, managed by the trustee for the benefit of your heirs (including minor children and grandchildren) for generations.

℣ *Are assets held in a living trust protected from creditors' claims?*

Generally speaking, assets held in a revocable trust are not protected from the legitimate claims of the trustmaker's creditors. This is because the maker can revoke the trust and take back the trust property at any time. The law finds that it is inequitable to allow the trustmaker to have this control and full use and benefit from the trust property while denying creditors the power to compel revocation in order to satisfy their just claims.

If drafted with this goal in mind, your living trust can protect your beneficiaries from the claims of their creditors through spendthrift provisions that insulate the trust funds from their claims.

ભ *It's quite possible that my wife and I may relocate within the next few years. Will we have to replan our entire estate with an attorney in our new home state?*

The U.S. Constitution guarantees that "full faith and credit" must be given in any state to any living trust agreement that was valid in the state in which it was created and executed. Thus, if your trust is valid in the state in which you signed the document, it will continue to be valid should you relocate to another state. Your agreement will generally not need revision to carry out your wishes, regardless of where you live. It is always a good idea, however, to check with a qualified estate planning attorney to see if any aspects of *state* law in your new home state will affect your plan. This is especially true if you relocate to a community property state from a separate property state, or vice versa.

States do have different requirements with respect to pour-over wills, living wills, durable powers of attorney for health care, and other documents. It is imperative that you have an attorney in your new home state review those documents to make sure that they comply with the laws of that state.

ભ *I've heard that everyone should have a will. Does my living trust replace a will?*

Yes. A properly drafted and fully funded revocable living trust replaces a will. However, as a practical matter, a special will called a pour-over will should be a part of your living trust–centered plan. We discuss pour-over wills later in this chapter.

ભ *If revocable living trusts are such an outstanding planning tool, why don't attorneys recommend them to every client?*

There can be some disadvantages to using living trusts, although they are few in number and most of them depend upon the state(s) where you live. Even when there are disadvantages, the benefits of a revocable living trust usually *far* outweigh the drawbacks.

- *Expense.* One objection to revocable living trust–centered planning is that it is more expensive than a will. True enough in some cases. However, a living trust–centered plan is usually only *initially* more expensive than a will. The cost of a will plus the cost of the probate process that must accompany it almost always exceeds the cost of a funded living trust plus the cost of its private after-death administration.

- *Funding.* Some people find it annoying to have to change the ownership of their property to a living trust. This process to initially fund the trust can be time-consuming, but it only has to be done once. And if people think it is a problem to do it themselves while they are alive and well and know what they own and where the evidences of ownership are located, think of what a problem it will be for their spouses or children after they die and the family members have to do this for the probate court. Some people also find it annoying to have to fund the trust every time they purchase a new asset. In today's marketplace, living trusts are routinely recognized by financial institutions so that it is no more difficult to title a new asset in the name of the trust than it would be to title it in the individual's own name—it's just a matter of remembering to do it.

The choice is this: People can either "probate" their own estates themselves while they are alive or pay the courts and lawyers to do it for them after they are no longer around.

- *Tenancy-by-the-entirety property.* Tenancy by the entirety (a form of joint ownership available to a husband and wife in some states) offers creditor protection that couples lose when they transfer the property into their revocable living trusts. Generally, the creditor of one spouse cannot force the sale of such property to satisfy a debt, at least while both spouses are alive. For some couples, under certain circumstances, tenancy-by-the-entirety protection might warrant keeping the property outside of their living trusts until the first spouse passes away or until circumstances change.

- *Homestead.* In some states, homeowners may not be entitled to the creditor protection and property tax benefits afforded by state homestead laws if they place their homes in revocable living trusts. However, with proper planning there are often ways to maintain these benefits after placing the home in a living trust.

■ *Special assets.* Certain professional practices, small businesses, franchises, and retirement accounts require special handling for living trusts. In some states, real estate transfer taxes may be triggered upon transfer of real property to a trust (this is very rare); or title insurance companies may have particular requirements that are bothersome.

If debt-encumbered property is to be held in a living trust, written assurance should be obtained from the lender that the transfer will not trigger a "due-on-sale clause." (By federal statute, this cannot happen in regard to a personal-residence mortgage.)

This may seem like a long list, but these issues, when they do occur, are minor and rarely outweigh the substantial benefits of a funded revocable living trust. Today more and more state legislatures are sweeping away the few remaining and outmoded quirks of state law regarding the use of living trusts.

Your estate planning attorney, financial advisor, and accountant will guide you through any issues regarding funding your revocable living trust in your state with your particular assets.

TRUSTEE SELECTION

Duties of a Trustee

ભ *What is a trustee?*

A *trustee* is a person or a licensed corporation appointed by a trustmaker to oversee the operation of the trust. The person or corporation acting as trustee owes a special fiduciary duty of care to the beneficiaries of a trust. When the trustmaker appoints more than one person to serve as trustees together, those persons are known as *cotrustees.*

ભ *What is a successor trustee?*

A *successor trustee* is a trustee who takes over for a previous trustee when that trustee is no longer able to perform the duties of a trustee, for whatever reason. Usually the trustmaker names successor trustees in the trust agreement.

It is common to have two or three successor trustees named. Theoretically, there is no limit to the number of successor trustees you can have acting at the same time, but, as a practical matter, having too many may be costly and cumbersome.

ℂ What is the primary function of my trustees?

The primary job of your trustees is to follow your instructions. In law, a *fiduciary* is a person who is entrusted with the assets of another and who is obligated to carry out the direction set forth by the person entrusting those assets. That is why your revocable living trust should contain your very specific instructions as to how your trust assets are to be managed and distributed. Your trustee is merely an agent whom you appoint and who has the duty to carry out your instructions. Fiduciaries cannot derive personal benefit from the assets entrusted to them. Therefore, the instructions set forth in your revocable living trust must be followed by your trustee and cannot be changed by your trustee. Any deviation from your instructions will subject your trustee to personal liability.

In general, each state has statutes that detail the powers and duties of a trustee in carrying out the management of the trust estate. It may be necessary for the trustee to seek professional management or investment advice if such expertise is not within the trustee's experience. The following list includes some of the general duties of a trustee:

- Preparing a complete inventory and valuation of the trust assets
- Obtaining a federal tax identification number from the Internal Revenue Service (IRS)
- Paying applicable expenses (medical, funeral, etc.) and taxes (federal estate tax, if applicable, and inheritance tax)
- Dividing and allocating assets to the subtrusts created in the trust if required by the terms of the trust
- Distributing assets according to the directions of the trust
- Preparing accountings as may be required

ℂ You've mentioned successor disability trustees and successor death trustees. How many trustees do I have to name?

To answer this question, you must first understand in what instances, and for what stages of a trust, trustees are designed. Trustees need to be supplied upon the occurrence of the following events:

- Creation of the trust
- Disability, death, or resignation of a trustee
- The creation of subtrusts within a trust

Usually the trustmaker names himself or herself to be the initial trustee and, if married, the spouse as cotrustee. The trustmaker then designates in the trust document who should take over the trustee-ship upon the disability, death, resignation, or termination of either of them and then anyone who replaces either of them. The trust-maker can even name different trustees for the subtrusts (e.g., marital, family) that are created within the original trust document.

You should provide for a series of successor trustees to assume the duties after your death or disability. For example, if you and your husband are the initial cotrustees, your trust document might say something like this:

> Upon my death or disability, I want the following to replace me as cotrustee with my husband. If any one of them is unable or unwilling to serve, then the next one will serve.
>
> [successor #1], then
>
> [successor #2], then
>
> [successor #3]

You might continue with a series of successor cotrustees:

> If my husband is then unable or unwilling to serve, then the following will replace him:
>
> Set 1: [successor] and [successor], then
>
> Set 2: [successor] and [successor]

❧ *If I name more than one trustee, who controls?*

This depends solely upon your trust instructions. Some couples want each spouse to be able to act without the consent of the other. You can include a provision in your trust that allows either of you to act as trustee in the administration of the trust. Your instructions could specify that, after your death or disability, your spouse must agree to or that he or she must carry the vote of at least one other trustee to block a specific action or to institute a certain action. You can provide that after your spouse's death, certain actions require a majority vote, or you can provide otherwise.

CR *How difficult is it to remove or change the person or entity I designate to serve as a trustee?*

In the case of a revocable living trust, you retain the right to amend the trust during your lifetime, so you can easily change the trustees at any time by a simple amendment to the trust instrument.

CR *In general, should I allow my beneficiaries to remove a trustee that I have named in my trust agreement?*

It is not a good idea to have a trust that does not provide some method for removing a trustee. Without this power, your beneficiaries may have to take legal action if appropriate grounds exist for removing the trustee and the trustee refuses to resign. Matters change over time, and it is entirely possible that a particular trustee may become inadequate, incompetent, or both.

If the beneficiaries are not satisfied with a trustee's performance, the trust instrument should specifically grant them, or some other person, the power to fire the existing trustee and hire a new one under specific circumstances that you designate in the document. When this happens, the next person you named on your list of successor trustees in the trust agreement becomes the new trustee.

In the event that the list of named trustees runs out, it is customary to provide in the trust agreement that a court can be allowed temporary jurisdiction over the trust for the sole purpose of appointing a new trustee. Courts usually appoint corporate trustees under such circumstances. This method prevents the beneficiaries from "trustee shopping" (constantly hiring and firing trustees until they find one that meets their needs or does what they want), since continually going to court would be expensive and unproductive. At the same time, it does enable them to replace a trustee who is unsatisfactory with one who is more suitable.

Characteristics of Trustees

CR *What particular abilities, education, or training should my trustee have?*

The selection of a duly qualified and honest trustee is one of the most important decisions to be made in the creation of a trust. This is because the trustee is the person with the primary responsibility for carrying out the trustmaker's wishes to the best of his or her ability. As a result, someone who is familiar with the trustmaker and his or her desires regarding how assets should be invested and how and when assets should be distributed may serve a valuable role as a trustee. Guidance and specific instructions in these areas can be included in the trust instrument.

Because the trustee will be expected to make investment decisions and will be required to account for all financial transactions involving trust assets, it is helpful if the trustee has some degree of financial knowledge and ability. Many times a person having all the desirable characteristics of a good trustee may not be available. For this reason, a trustmaker may wish to consider appointing a set of cotrustees consisting of more than one individual or an individual and an institution. Using this "team" approach allows the individual strengths and abilities of the cotrustees to be combined to best carry out all aspects of the trust administration.

❧ What characteristics should trustees have?

Your trustees should possess the following characteristics:

- Be honest and trustworthy
- Have the ability to make and handle investments
- Be financially accountable for any mistakes they make
- To the extent possible, be situated in the area where your beneficiaries and your assets are located
- Have good relationships with the beneficiaries
- Be likely to survive you
- Be someone who, you feel confident, will manage your affairs wisely

❧ How can I assess potential trustees?

You should ask yourself a great number of questions when selecting trustees:

- Are they free of monetary problems of their own?
- Have they demonstrated financial managerial ability?
- Do they have any history of substance abuse?

- Do they know the beneficiaries well?
- Are they reliable?
- Do they have the required specialized skills to manage my assets?
- Have they demonstrated problem-solving ability?
- Are they the right ages?
- Are they likely to be available when needed?
- Will they seek and utilize professional assistance when circumstances require it?
- Will they accept the appointment?

Initial Trustees

Should I name someone as an initial cotrustee with me?

If you are married and each of you has his or her own trust, it is common practice to name the other spouse as a cotrustee. If you and your spouse have a joint trust agreement, typically both of you will act as its initial cotrustees.

If you are single and have adult children, you should consider naming one or more of them as trustees. If you do not have children, or you have children but would prefer that they not serve, you might consider a close friend, relative, or professional advisor.

If you would like professional money management, you can consider naming a corporate fiduciary. Of course, if you do, it will charge trustee's fees, but those fees may well be worth it if the services provided meet your needs.

Who to Name As Successor Trustees

Family Members As Successor Trustees

Can my husband be the sole trustee after my death?

You can name your husband as the sole trustee of the marital trust and the family trust after your death. However, there has been significant professional debate over naming a spouse as sole trustee of the family trust. If the family trust principal distribution to the spouse is *not* limited by the *ascertainable standards*—health, education, support, and maintenance—as required by the Internal Revenue Code (IRC), the risk of naming your husband as a trustee of the family trust is that the entire amount of the trust will be included in his estate at his death and subject to federal estate tax. We believe it to be a risky practice from a tax standpoint for a spouse to be the sole trustee of the family trust and would strongly recommend that you name a cotrustee to serve with him.

As for naming your husband as the sole trustee of the marital or qualified terminable interest property trust, there will be no estate tax problem. That trust will be included in your husband's estate no matter who is trustee.

◌ Wouldn't it be best if I named a family member as my successor cotrustee?

Although family members will usually serve for little or no compensation and are usually known, trusted, and loved by trust beneficiaries, if the trust is to remain in existence for any length of time after your death, they oftentimes may not be the best choice for a trustee. Family members often make decisions on an emotional basis rather than an objective one. They are often inexperienced and may not know what is required of them under the law. If they make mistakes, they may not have the financial resources available to cover losses to the beneficiaries. Lastly, they may die, become incapacitated, let power get the best of them, or run into their own financial difficulties.

◌ Can I have a financial institution act as a cotrustee with a family member?

Yes. A corporate trustee and a family member can act as cotrustees. In fact, this arrangement provides the best of both worlds. The family member knows what is going on with the beneficiaries and brings the family situation to the table. The corporate trustee knows how to invest and maintain records, can make objective decisions, and has financial resources.

◌ What if I do want family members as my successor trustees? How will they know what to do in order to make my plan work?

Many people choose to have their children or other family members, rather than institutions, serve as successor trustees on either death or disability. You should make them aware in advance of what will be required of them. If you do not, they may not act properly or may refuse to act when the time comes.

One problem with choosing family members as successor trustees is that most people have never served as a trustee before and don't understand what they will need to do to accomplish your objectives. Therefore, it is important that you select an estate planning attorney who will help educate your successor trustees as to what will be required of them when they serve in that capacity. The more you can prepare your successor trustees in advance, the greater the likelihood that they will be ready to act on your behalf in the manner that you desire.

○○ Why do you feel so strongly that having cotrustees is beneficial?

A combination of several individuals or professional trustees is beneficial for a great many reasons that center around qualifications and balance. Also, it is prudent to have trustees watching trustees for the benefit of your trust beneficiaries. Many people want to name as successor trustees loving family members who are probably not particularly adept with money or investments but who are trustworthy and personally close to the beneficiaries. In such instances, naming a trusted accountant or a corporate fiduciary as a cotrustee can shore up the individual's weaknesses while still making his or her many strengths available to your beneficiaries.

It is generally not a good idea to put one child in charge of another child's inheritance even if they get along famously. There are certain things you can do in estate planning that bring families together at death, while other things can pull them apart. Naming a child to be a trustee for a sibling is one of the things that can pull them apart. In most circumstances, *siblings should not be each other's trustees*.

○○ I want all four of my children to be involved in handling my estate after my wife and I are gone. Should I name all of them as cotrustees?

Probably not. Some people think that naming all of their children as successor cotrustees will make things simpler and easier after the parents pass away because all of the children will be involved. Usually, just the opposite happens. When there is more than one trustee acting, the trustees have to confer and discuss the administration of the trust. Even the process of discussing the trust administration can be cumbersome if the trustees are located in several different states, or worse, in other countries. Once they make a decision, the signatures of all four trustees will typically be required, at least for some actions. This means that documents may have to be forwarded in turn to each of the children. Even with modern express mail delivery, this can mean a delay of several days or weeks in completing the transaction.

Not only are there logistical problems when naming several cotrustees, but real conflicts among siblings as trustees can develop. It is not unusual for them to have differences of opinions on how the trust should be administered. While these differences are normal, they can sometimes blossom into hurt feelings and resentment among the children, creating irreparable rifts in the family, particularly when a few of them band together against others.

Can I name my adult son as the sole trustee of his own trust?

You could name your son as sole trustee of his own trust, but you would be wise to name at least one other person or institution as a cotrustee with him. A properly drawn trust is generally not subject to the claims of creditors unless the sole beneficiary is also the sole trustee. If your son is sole trustee of his own trust and gets into financial or legal difficulties, creditors can obtain and execute judgments against him. If your son is a cotrustee of his trust and resigns, a creditor would have a difficult task in asserting rights against the trust or the remaining trustee.

You should name a trustee team that will take into account each child's needs and your wishes for his or her success and happiness. You might not want to name the same trustees for a spendthrift child (who may need the direction of a corporate fiduciary or a certified public accountant) as you would for an accomplished professional or executive child who needs a cotrustee only to provide added creditor protection for his or her trust.

Institutions As Successor Trustees

What are the advantages of corporate trustees?

Corporate fiduciaries have several advantages:

- They act objectively and follow trust instructions without emotion.
- Managing trusts is their business; they do it professionally day in and day out.

- They have investment, tax, and estate administration expertise.
- They don't die or become incapacitated, and if they go out of business, their obligations will be assumed by another corporation.
- They are highly regulated by governmental agencies.
- They have the resources to cover their errors and mistakes.

Cℜ *What are the major disadvantages of corporate trustees?*

- They charge fees for what they do.
- Because they are supposed to make decisions on an objective and unemotional basis, they are often thought of as being "mean-spirited" and "uncaring."
- They are not always the best choice for an estate that consists mainly of real estate and/or a family business.

Cℜ *Are there corporate trustees that are not banks?*

Many brokerage firms have established or are establishing trust company subsidiaries. If you are comfortable with your broker, he or she may be able to continue to help in the investment decisions concerning your money after your death by using the brokerage firm's trust company. Your estate planning attorney or financial advisor will have information on trust companies and can help you choose the most appropriate institution for your family.

Professional Advisors As Successor Trustees

Cℜ *Can we appoint our attorney or accountant to be a successor trustee of our living trust?*

You can name anyone you want to be a successor trustee; however, most attorneys will respectfully decline this appointment. Attorneys are not in the business of acting as trustees, and you may be better served by using the attorney's services solely as an advisor.

Many accountants are willing to act as successor trustee for clients with whom they have close relationships. They usually know the family situation and are certainly capable of handling the financial affairs; however, your accountant may feel more comfortable having a corporate cotrustee serve with him or her to provide financial planning expertise and to share the fiduciary liability.

Should I name a bank or trust company as sole trustee over my wife's marital and family trusts?

Most spouses do not want to have their affairs managed by a corporate entity over which they have no control, but many trustmakers do want the benefits offered by professional trustees. You could name your wife as a cotrustee of your marital and family trusts with a corporate trustee and provide that she can terminate and replace it with another corporate fiduciary.

Why would I give my wife the right to fire a corporate fiduciary?

Experience has taught most practitioners that if a spouse—or any other beneficiary for that matter—is "locked in" to a trustee, it is more likely that the trustee will not be as responsive to the needs of the beneficiary. You can allow her to terminate and replace the trustee as she determines or under certain circumstances that you proscribe in your trust document.

You can specify the precise replacement or furnish a list from which the replacement can be selected and/or specify the characteristics of the corporate trustee that she has to use, such as one with a capital and surplus of $50 million.

Compensating Trustees

Is a trustee entitled to be paid for his or her services?

There is no rule that says trustees must be paid for providing services, but individuals or entities designated to serve as trustees are also not required to serve for free if they choose not to. In many instances, family members are named as trustees, and even if the trust provides for a reasonable fee for their services, the family members may waive their right to receive a fee. On the other hand, if the trust administration extends over a lengthy period of time, even family members serving as trustees may become resentful if forced to spend large amounts of time administering the trust without compensation.

Most corporate trustees, such as banks and private trust companies, have published fee schedules which usually include an annual fee based upon the percentage of assets under administration, plus certain minimum fees for trusts with assets valued at less than certain minimum amounts. Corporate trustees will gladly provide their fee schedules to potential customers.

ᛒ *I want to name my sister as a successor trustee of my trust, but she will not be a beneficiary. Can I provide that she gets a fee for her services as trustee; and if so, what should that fee be?*

Your sister need not be a beneficiary in order to be your trustee. Although in many cases a family member acting as trustee will waive the fee for his or her services, every trustee is entitled to be paid. You can specify the amount of the fee that your sister should be paid for the services she renders as trustee, or you can provide a formula for her payment based upon the fees charged for the same services by professional trustees in the locality. In addition, you can provide that your sister should be reimbursed for any necessary expenses she incurs for administering your trust.

TRUST PROTECTORS

ᛒ *What is a trust protector?*

A *trust protector* is a person or corporation that, depending on the terms of the trust, has authority to oversee the trustees, to change provisions of the trust, to veto acts of the trustees, and, in general, to ensure that the trust is being property administered.

You may want to provide a way to correct ambiguities or errors in the trust that could result in the trust failing to carry out your intentions. You may want someone to have the discretion to respond to changes in the law to ensure that your trust carries out your intent and secures the best tax treatment consistent with that intent.

You can view the trust protector as Superman flying in to save the day, or at least as a mild mannered mediator to intercede in disputes. The role of the trust protector can be to resolve or even avoid disputes without having to resort to protracted court battles.

ᛒ *Why would I want someone to have such powers?*

The answer is "control." Most trust documents provide for distributions to be made to the beneficiaries by age 35 or so. That is not usually too long a time frame to consider in designing an estate plan. With the development of certain concepts, however, trusts can now last much longer and now require some sort of fail-safe provisions to take into account the changes that can happen.

Another problem that you should consider is that bank trust departments can, and do, change hands. Your attorney may have drafted your trust to have the trust department of a local bank serve as trustee because of your attorney's familiarity with their policies or due to your wishes. Whether that relationship will remain after the local bank merges with a larger institution may be of concern to you. You may also feel secure in knowing that a close friend who serves as a trust protector can exercise certain powers without serving as a trustee. This way, their liability as a trust protector can be limited or removed.

What specific powers may I give my trust protector?

There are many powers you can give a trust protector, but no one trust protector would have all of the following powers:

- To modify or amend trust provisions to take advantage of tax or other legal changes that affect trust administration
- To correct ambiguities in the trust that otherwise might require court intervention to interpret
- To correct drafting errors that defeat your intent
- To delete or add beneficiaries (but be careful about giving such power to anyone)
- To amend administrative provisions of your trust that relate to the identity, qualifications, succession, removal, and appointment of a trustee
- To amend the date the trust ends by extending or shortening that date so long as they do not allow the trust to exist longer than the law permits
- To approve discretionary distributions of income or principal to a trustee-beneficiary that are not covered by what the IRC calls "ascertainable standards"
- To require accountings from the trustee or require the trustee to post a bond
- To unilaterally resolve any disputes between beneficiaries or between a beneficiary and a trustee without requiring court intervention
- To appoint, under limited circumstances, the assets of the trust to a new trust, or even to distribute the assets directly to the beneficiaries (this power is very aggressive but no current laws or regulations prohibit it)

ᘓ *This sounds too complex. Doesn't this just add an unnecessary layer of detail to my estate plan?*

Laws change and people change, and what you would want to accomplish with your estate plan may be different due to these changes. The purpose of designating a trust protector is not merely to add more "boilerplate" to your estate plan, but to help you consider how to respond to the changes you suspect could occur. The trick is to set up a means of handling those changes without undoing the rest of what you have set up in your estate plan. A carefully crafted set of instructions to a trusted advisor who can use his or her best judgment to meet the challenge of a new set of circumstances that arise when you are disabled or after your death is the reason for setting up a trust protector.

ᘓ *Is my trust protector a "fiduciary" like a trustee is?*

Your trust protector does not have to serve in a fiduciary capacity unless you want to impose that level of responsibility. You can impose a lower level of responsibility so the trust protector has only a "personal duty" or exercises "best judgment" as opposed to the higher level of a fiduciary responsibility, especially if the trust protector is a trusted family friend or advisor. This way, the trust protector will be less concerned about being sued in the event that he or she does what you wanted, especially if the action will make him or her unpopular with one of the beneficiaries.

ᘓ *Can I appoint someone in my family as the trust protector?*

You can, but appointing a family member as the trust protector may create unwanted tax consequences. One of the reasons that you set up a trust is to have it hold assets beyond the reach of your family members for both tax and nontax reasons. However, if the family member has too much control over the assets in the trust—such as the power to amend the trust—those assets may well become part of the family member's estate (and be taxed by the IRS) or they may become reachable by that family member's creditors.

For example, if your son is both a trustee and a beneficiary of your trust and he makes a distribution to himself for his own "health, education, maintenance, or support," he will not be treated as the owner of the trust assets. If, however, he can make a distribution of trust assets to himself for any reason, or for no reason, he would be considered as being not only a beneficiary of the trust, but he will also be considered the owner of the trust. If he is determined by the Internal Revenue Service as being the owner of the trust, all of the trust assets will be added to his estate and this may create unnecessary taxes that he will have to pay. Additionally, if he is the owner of the assets, these assets could become available to his creditors, a result you may have wanted to avoid.

As the exception to this, a trust protector could be given the limited power to replace a trustee since a beneficiary may well have the same right.

ℭℛ *Who are good candidates to serve as trust protectors?*

The possible candidates for this position are legion subject to the concerns addressed in the previous question. It could be your Uncle Ralph or Aunt Mary, or someone in the family who is a born diplomat. You can choose your attorney, who drafted the trust, your accountant, or your financial advisor.

If you choose someone who provides you with professional services, make sure that too much of his or her income during any calendar year does not come from you. This could inadvertently make the trust protector "subservient" to your wishes. Also, provide that the trust protector cannot have any personal financial interest in any trust property or in the outcome of any transaction or other trust business other than reasonable compensation for his or her services.

ℭℛ *What fees can my trust protector charge for work done as a trust protector?*

The fees your trust protector can charge depend upon what you and the trust protector agree upon. Since the duties of the trust protector will usually be more limited than those of a trustee, the fees they will receive should also be less than those of the trustee. Instead of setting an annual amount to be charged, it may make more sense to have the trust protector charge an hourly rate for the actual time they spend serving on behalf of the trust. The hourly rate could be the same as what a trustee would charge for their services. Alternatively, the more responsibility the trust protector assumes, the more they may want to charge for their exposure to liability to your beneficiaries for the actions they take on behalf of the trust.

FUNDING AND IMPLEMENTING A REVOCABLE LIVING TRUST

The Funding Process

ଔ *Is there anything I must do after I've signed my trust documents?*

Revocable living trusts are valid as probate-avoidance mechanisms *only* if they are properly "funded." For your property to avoid probate, all of your assets (if possible) should be owned by your trust or your trust should be the beneficiary of any property that requires beneficiary designations. But be careful when you fund your trust: Not all assets should be held in a revocable living trust, so professional advice is a must.

ଔ *What is meant by "funding" a revocable living trust?*

Funding a living trust means changing ownership of your assets to the trust or naming the trust as the beneficiary of assets such as qualified retirement plans and life insurance policies. Since the trust controls only the assets that are titled in its name or are paid directly to it by beneficiary designation, assets left outside the trust may have to go through probate at the time of your death.

Keeping your living trust fully funded is an ongoing process. As you acquire new assets, you must title them in the name of your trust so that they will not pass through probate. However, once you complete the initial transfer process, placing assets into your trust as you acquire them requires only a small amount of effort to reap huge benefits and safeguards.

ଔ *If all my assets are titled in the name of my living trust, how do they avoid probate upon my death?*

Assets titled in the name of the deceased must go through probate so that title can be changed from the name of the decedent to the name of his or her heirs. Assets titled in the name of a living trust are held, administered, and distributed according to the terms of the trust agreement and thus avoid the judicial probate process of retitling.

◌ ◌ *What activities are necessary to accomplish trust funding?*

Here is a summary of what is generally required in funding a trust:

- Gathering detailed and accurate information regarding how you currently own each of your assets
- Deciding how each asset should be owned, such as in the husband's trust, in the wife's trust, or in both and in what percentages
- Deciding who should be the beneficiary and contingent beneficiary under each insurance policy and each retirement plan (There are many variations, all of which have significantly different legal and tax implications.)
- Preparing the various documents required to change ownership or beneficiary designations to the trust
- Consolidating all the information about your assets in a user-friendly source for you and for your successor trustees on your death or disability

◌ ◌ *Can you give me an example of funding?*

Suppose you created the Jessica Valentine Living Trust dated November 24, 2004, and you are the initial sole trustee. The property that is currently titled in your name will be retitled to read:

> Jessica Valentine, Sole Trustee, or her successors in trust, under the Jessica Valentine Living Trust, dated November 24, 2004, and any amendments thereto.

In practice, using the full name may be cumbersome since it probably won't fit into computer software programs used by most brokerage houses, banks, or public agencies, so they often use an abbreviation like:

> Jessica Valentine, Trustee, u/a dtd 11/24/04

This is sufficient for purposes of holding title in the name of the trust, since it identifies the current trustees and refers to a particular trust document ("u/a" is an abbreviation for the words "under agreement").

This retitling of your assets enables your successor trustees to deal with the property, according to your instructions, in the event of your disability or death.

> *I am reluctant to transfer my assets out of my name and into the trust. By transferring them, won't I be losing control of them?*

Deeds and other types of transfer documents are required to show that ownership of an asset is held by a revocable living trust, but some people fear they are losing control in some way merely because there is a transfer occurring. In fact, the opposite is true. By transferring assets to a living trust, the trustmaker is able not only to continue controlling the assets as always but also to control their management through the terms of the trust in the event of his or her disability or death.

The trustmaker can add or remove property at any time and change or amend the trust at will. The trustmaker totally controls the trust and its assets. Therefore, there is no reason to fear the transfer of assets into a revocable living trust.

> *Once my assets are funded into my trust, can I sell any of them?*

Once you create your living trust with yourself as the initial trustee, you are not restrained in any way as to how you use, manage, invest, sell, or handle your trust assets. Accordingly, you control the assets that are titled in the name of the trust in the same manner that you controlled them prior to putting them into your trust. The only difference is that you now sign your name as trustee.

> *I've heard that funding a revocable living trust makes estate planning more difficult and time-consuming. Is this true?*

This view is often promoted by people as a reason to avoid living trust–centered estate planning. Interestingly, funding your trust is one of the major *advantages* of living trust–centered planning.

The argument that funding a living trust makes estate planning more difficult and time-consuming runs counter to both legal and common sense. If it is indeed so difficult to locate and transfer assets during your lifetime, how can the process be more easily accomplished *after* your death, *without* your assistance—without the help of the person who owned the assets and knew more about them than anyone else? Most people do not have their financial paperwork well organized at the time of their death or disability. This results in a legal "scavenger hunt" on the part of those left behind. The time it takes to locate assets is often a major cause of delay in the average probate estate.

It's only human to procrastinate. Few people look forward to the paperwork involved in retitling their assets into the names of their trusts. However, many people go through the funding process, usually with the assistance of an attorney or financial advisor, and most have accomplished the complete funding of their trusts with little, if any, hassle.

With your participation, problems that loom today can be easily solved. Without your participation, those same problems can cause lengthy delays, costs, and aggravation for your loved ones.

⧬ *How do I determine the method to use to transfer my various assets into my trust?*

Most assets have some sort of paperwork, such as stock certificates or bank account signature cards, that indicate the assets' owner for legal purposes. As a general rule of thumb, the same paperwork that originally conveyed those assets to your name will be used to reconvey them to your trust. Most law firms that regularly prepare living trusts can provide you with instructions that will assist you with the paperwork.

⧬ *Do I have to show my bank, broker, or anyone else a copy of my trust when funding it?*

Your trust is and should remain a confidential document. In a well-drafted estate plan, an *affidavit of trust* is used in lieu of your actual trust document. It is a summary of the essential elements of the trust, such as its name and date of execution, the names of the trustees and cotrustees, and what powers they have. The affidavit of trust suffices as proof of the trust without disclosing the private information contained within the actual trust document.

Because living trusts are so commonly used these days, when transferring assets to your revocable living trust, many transferring agents do not require any more information to make the transfer than the information contained in the affidavit of trust. They will require that all initial trustees sign the documents that change the title to the name of the trust.

Congress recently passed the Patriot Act to combat terrorist

activities. This legislation requires that banks, brokerage firms, and
other financial institutions request specific data from all of us when
we open new or change existing accounts or when we transfer funds
between accounts. As we publish *Love, Money, Control,* banks and
brokerage houses are just beginning to implement many of the new
requirements, so we cannot be certain what the transferring agents
may require. They may want information regarding your trustees, beneficiaries, and purposes of the trust in addition to what is in the affidavit of trust; or they may accept just what is in the affidavit of trust.

CR *If I create a revocable living trust, can I keep assets in my own
name and have them transferred to my trust at death without
going through probate?*

In some states, certain kinds of assets can be owned in your own
name and be transferred to your living trust at death without going
through the probate process. For example, many states allow you to
own bank accounts with a *payable-on-death (POD)* designation to a
named beneficiary. In these states, all bank checking, savings, and
money market accounts can be owned by you with the designation
payable on death to your living trust. Many states have also adopted
a *transfer-on-death (TOD)* designation for stocks and brokerage
accounts. Therefore, in these states, it would be a good idea for you
to own your stock or brokerage accounts with a TOD designation to
your living trust so that your trust will be funded with these
accounts at your death. Check with your attorney to see if your state
allows these types of designations. If it does, this may be one method
of funding part of your revocable living trust.

All states allow beneficiary designations on assets such as life
insurance, annuities, and retirement plans. As long as your living trust
is designated as the beneficiary, the proceeds from these assets will be
distributed to your trust at death without going through probate.

All other assets should be funded to the trust as we've described.

How *Not* to Implement the Trust

CR *What would happen if I didn't fund any of my property to the
trust?*

One of the reasons you prepare a living trust–centered estate plan is to avoid the probate process. If you do not transfer all your assets to the living trust, you are subjecting your heirs to the process and all its attendant problems that you were attempting to avoid.

Ultimately, if you do not transfer your assets into your living trust, you fail to take advantage of the many safeguards and benefits offered by a living trust–centered plan. You increase the expenses as well as the hassles that your loved ones may have to face through probate.

CR *My wife and I have a combined estate valued at well more than $1.5 million and growing. We own all our property jointly with right of survivorship, and we do not live in a community property state. We each recently created a living trust with marital and family trusts and a pour-over will. Do we have all the documents we need?*

You probably have excellent documents, but given your situation, they are currently useless from an estate planning standpoint. How assets are titled is critical to proper planning; you and your spouse could lose massive federal estate tax benefits if you continue to hold your assets jointly.

Property that you hold jointly with right of survivorship is not owned by you or your trust at your death but, rather, by the survivor of the two of you. All of your property will automatically pass to your wife if you should be the first to die. There is nothing in your trust, and, therefore, no property will go into your family trust, meaning that your estate will be unable to take advantage of your applicable exclusion amount. When your wife later dies, the entire value of all the assets that the two of you formerly owned as joint tenants is included in your wife's gross estate for estate tax purposes. She can transfer her entire applicable exclusion amount to your children free from estate taxation, but the rest will be taxed. Also, her assets will have to go through probate, so your joint estate will further shrink by the amount of the probate costs. You and your wife could avoid all these costs by properly retitling your assets to transfer them into your respective living trusts.

Allocation of Assets

CR *How does a married couple decide which assets will be funded into the husband's trust and which marital assets will be funded into the wife's trust?*

Your estate planning attorney's objective in funding trusts for a married couple is to allocate assets in a way that satisfies the couple's respective ownership needs and desires while minimizing the effect of income and estate taxes on the couple and their children. In addition, liability concerns are often addressed as part of the allocation of assets in the funding process.

❧ *How do we fund our trusts with our joint property?*

With jointly held property (joint tenancy with right of survivorship or tenancy by the entirety), the joint or survivorship aspect of your ownership must be terminated so that each of you owns a one-half undivided interest in the property as tenants in common. Each of you can then transfer your half of the property to your own trust. Even if you and your spouse are using a joint trust, it is necessary to go through this process.

❧ *What are the determining factors in funding the spouses' respective trusts?*

There are four main factors to be considered.

1. *The psychological factor.* Many spouses feel that all their marital assets are marital property and that both spouses have equal rights and ownership to all these assets. Others feel that some assets are more clearly associated with one spouse than the other. For example, a wife who has inherited property from her parents, such as a family vacation home, may feel stronger emotional and legal ties to that property than her husband does. Or a husband whose hobby is investing in the stock market may have a desire to maintain control over the couple's brokerage accounts. These and similar factors need to be taken into consideration when allocating assets between the spouses and their respective trusts.

2. *The predetermined ownership factor.* Another consideration is whether there are significant qualified retirement plan assets that by their nature have a predetermined ownership. Qualified retirement assets must be owned by the plan participant. If one spouse owns a substantial qualified plan, the other spouse's trust may be funded with more assets to offset the difference.

3. *The capital gain factor.* Yet another concern when allocating assets between the spouses is the age and health of each spouse. Is it likely that one spouse in particular will die before the other? If the couple owns appreciated property, the couple should consider a transfer of the appreciated property to the trust owned by the ill spouse in order to obtain a quicker step-up in basis for the appreciated property. However, the asset will not receive a basis step-up if the ill spouse dies within a year of the transfer.

4. *The liability factor.* Does one spouse have greater exposure to liability claims as a result of his or her occupation or of the type of property that he or she owns (e.g., rental real estate or a business that deals in hazardous materials)? If so, it is important to make sure that assets necessary for the family's basic needs are not jeopardized. For this reason, it makes sense to have the spouse who is not exposed to the claims own the bulk of the family assets if the marriage is stable and the spouses are comfortable with that arrangement.

Couples who have significant assets and are concerned with liability issues may also want to consider employing more sophisticated asset protection strategies such as family limited partnerships or asset protection trusts.

Responsibility for Funding

℞ *Who is responsible for funding my trust?*

Funding a revocable living trust is the responsibility of the trustmaker and his or her advisors. While the attorney who drafted the trust should take the lead in funding it, the trustmaker must help by furnishing evidence of ownership of all assets and by supplying any other necessary information. Doing so will make the process go faster and will reduce the cost of funding. Other advisors such as the accountant, life insurance professional, and financial advisor should also work with the attorney in their areas of expertise so that all funding is coordinated. In the past few years, many estate planning professionals have begun to outsource the paperwork in the funding process to one of several organizations that specialize in this work. If your attorney uses one of these companies, then he or she will oversee and direct that organization to ensure that all of your assets are funded properly.

○ℛ *What are the advantages of having my attorney do the trust funding?*

Most people who desire to fund their own trusts start with good intentions but fail to follow through and ensure that the funding is complete and correct. There are many benefits of having your attorney fund your revocable living trust. A good estate planning attorney will have a system in place for funding trusts quickly and accurately. If the attorney funds trusts on a regular basis, he or she will be able to identify possible problems with the assets before starting the process. Often the attorney will already have solutions or will have established relationships in the business community to solve any such problems. In addition, the attorney will be able to verify that all assets were in fact retitled and that each was done correctly.

To some people, convenience is the primary motivation for having attorneys fund their trusts. Most people have busy schedules, which make funding their own trusts a nuisance. The idea of having someone else complete their funding is appealing. In other instances, individuals may not want the responsibility or may have limitations that prevent them from funding their own trusts.

○ℛ *Can my financial advisor fund my revocable living trust?*

Many states have legal and ethical restrictions that prohibit or limit financial advisors' degree of participation in the funding process. For example, many states have ruled that people other than attorneys who advise clients on how assets should be titled are engaging in the unauthorized practice of law. Financial advisors and accountants, however, can often provide invaluable assistance in the funding process; but it is important for your attorney to see to it that each asset is placed in the proper trust, in order to ensure maximum estate, gift, and income tax results.

Transferring Specific Assets

Bank Accounts

○ℛ *Do I have to transfer my bank accounts to the trust?*

If you do not transfer your checking and savings accounts to your trust, they will become probate assets at your death. Unless your state allows POD or TOD designations, with some exceptions, you should transfer to your trust all bank accounts, money market accounts, certificates of deposit, and other accounts that you have at financial institutions.

For such transfers, most banking institutions simply require that you sign a new signature card showing the ownership of the account in the name of the trust. There do not have to be any outward changes with respect to the account. In other words, you can continue to use your same checks and there is no necessity for you to sign the checks as "trustee."

The exceptions to transferring all bank accounts are those accounts on which you may lose automated teller machine privileges or special senior citizen account privileges. You may decide to leave your checking account in your name to avoid losing these privileges or you may decide to move your accounts to a bank with more liberal policies. Your estate planning attorney can help you make this decision.

℞ *How should a safety deposit box be titled?*

Your safety deposit box should be rented by the trustee for the trust. That way, the successor trustee can access the box without any difficulty after your death or disability.

Retirement Accounts

℞ *Should I retitle my retirement account to the name of my trust?*

No. If you do this, all the income tax you have been deferring while putting money in the account will become due. Individual retirement accounts (IRAs), 401(k) plans, and other qualified plans should not be retitled to the name of your trust.

℞ *Can I change the beneficiary of my IRA, 401(k) plan, and other qualified retirement plans to my trust?*

The proper beneficiary for your qualified plan or IRA depends on your particular planning goals. Your spouse or your trust may be named. It is very important that your attorney advises you on the different alternatives you have when it comes to naming the beneficiaries of your retirement plans. One of the keys to an estate plan that will meet all your objectives is properly coordinating it with your retirement plan.

Publicly Held Securities

⚬ *How do I transfer my non-IRA brokerage account and mutual funds to my trust?*

The process is very similar to transferring your bank accounts. Your broker or financial advisor will establish a new account for the trust and will transfer your investments and mutual funds to the new trust account.

⚬ *How do I transfer publicly held securities when I have the certificates in my possession?*

If you hold the individual certificates, you need to contact the transfer agent and get a blank transfer form. You complete the form, have your signature guaranteed, and then send the form and the certificate to the transfer agent. It may be easier to have your stockbroker make the transfer or to have your broker put the stocks in a "street account" for you at the brokerage firm.

If you have a reinvestment account with the company, you can usually return the stock certificates to the transfer agent for deposit in your reinvestment account. Then you can transfer that account to your trust.

⚬ *Should I transfer my stock options to my living trust?*

The stock option plan may prohibit such a transfer. Because of the different types of stock options and the many different provisions of stock option plans, it is imperative that you work with your accountant, attorney, and the company to determine whether, when, and how you should fund your trust with stock options.

Closely Held Business Interests

⚬ *What factors do I have to consider for transferring business interests to a revocable living trust?*

You and your advisors will consider the following before transferring any business interests to your revocable living trust:

- The type of entity that you own an interest in is critical because there may be some restrictions on certain types of ownership interests being held by a trust.

- If you determine that your trust may legally hold your owner- ship interest, you have to determine whether there are any transfer restrictions contained in any agreement, such as a shareholders' agreement or a partnership agreement.

- If the trust becomes the owner of the business interest, most likely the trustee of the trust will "vote, manage, and control" the business interest that is in the trust.

As we have discussed throughout this book, it is important to select knowledgeable advisors. If you own business interests, you and your advisors will have to consider those interests in your overall estate planning goals as well as other techniques that you may use to reduce estate taxes. You may transfer your ownership interests to another type of trust agreement instead of the living trust. If you wish more information regarding planning for privately held busi- nesses, see *Strictly Business: Planning Strategies for Privately Owned Businesses*, David K. Cahoone and Larry W. Gibbs, editors (Quan- tum Press, 2002).

❧ *Do partnership interests present difficulties in the retitling process?*

Your attorney must review the partnership agreement to make sure that this type of transfer is permissible. Generally, transfers of part- nership interests require the approval of the general partner. Because revocable living trusts are now the standard for good estate planning, partnership agreements often allow transfers to a partner's revocable living trust—the partnership has no desire to have your interest tied up in a guardianship or probate proceeding any more than you do.

❧ *Can I transfer my limited liability company to my living trust?*

You need to review the limited liability company operating agree- ment to make sure that this type of transfer is possible. Usually, the consent of the other members or of the member manager is required for all transfers. If there is no provision for such a transfer or it is prohibited, the operating agreement can be amended to permit the transfer. As with partnership interests, in all likelihood the other owners will approve the transfer as there is generally no reason for them not to.

ℭ *Can I transfer shares of my corporation if the stock is subject to transfer restrictions?*

Closely held stock can present special challenges when funding a revocable living trust. Certain types of closely held stock may be subject to various state statutes or shareholders' agreements that restrict ownership of the stock. Any transfer in contradiction to an underlying agreement or in violation of state statutes may create unintended consequences. In most cases, the shareholders' agreement or other private restriction can be amended to allow the transfer.

ℭ *Can my S corporation stock be held in a revocable living trust without breaking the S corporation election?*

Yes. During your lifetime, your revocable living trust can own your S corporation stock because a revocable living trust is a permissible S corporation shareholder. With proper planning, your trust can continue to own the stock after your death without terminating the company's subchapter S election.

Real Estate

ℭ *How do I transfer my real estate to my revocable living trust?*

Title to real estate is transferred by means of a deed from the existing owners to the trust. Each state has very specific rules with respect to the drafting of deeds, and your estate planning attorney should prepare the deed to ensure that the title is properly transferred.

To avoid errors in transfer, it is advisable to have an updated title search performed to ensure that an accurate legal description is utilized and that the proper owners are identified. If an improper legal description is utilized, a cloud can be placed on the title of record, which can cost many times the cost of the title search to have corrected.

ℭ *I own real estate in several states. Can I put all of my real estate into one trust, or do I have to have a trust in each state?*

Putting real estate from several states into one trust is not a problem. In fact, this is one of the benefits of a living trust. By having your real estate in one trust, you avoid ancillary probate in multiple states. However, the mechanics of transferring real estate vary widely among the states. The use of counsel in the state where the property is located is necessary to confirm that the form of deed used will be acceptable to the title companies and that it will meet the various recording requirements of the particular jurisdiction. Your estate planning attorney should be able to find attorneys in the other states to perform this work.

ᐊᖫ *Can I transfer my house to my living trust without losing any federal tax benefits?*

A transfer to a revocable living trust is an income tax–neutral event. You can continue to deduct the interest on your mortgage on your income tax returns. In addition, you remain eligible for the $250,000 ($500,000 if married) capital gain tax exclusion if you otherwise qualify.

ᐊᖫ *Should I be concerned with state tax issues when transferring real estate to my living trust?*

Generally, *ad valorem* tax issues such as homestead exemptions remain unaltered, but you should always review this with your attorney. In some states, homestead exemptions may be affected by transfers to a living trust, but this is highly unlikely.

ᐊᖫ *If my residence is in my trust, am I able to refinance it?*

After property has been transferred to a revocable living trust, a problem sometimes arises when the owner wants to refinance the home or get a home equity loan. The lender may want assurances that the trustee has the ability to encumber the trust property.

There are two possible solutions to this dilemma. You could provide the lender with a copy of the trust agreement or affidavit of trust to assure the lender that the trustee has the power to encumber the property. Alternatively, if you want to keep your documents private, you could take the property out of the trust, allow the lender to secure the debt against the property, and then put the property back into the trust. The latter is often the easier course of action.

ᐊᖫ *We live in a community property state and want to transfer to*

our joint trust commercial real estate that has a mortgage with a due-on-sale clause. Is there any way to do this without notifying the lender?

Some community property states permit the transfer of property to a joint revocable living trust through a marital property agreement, which is used as a substitute for a deed. A petition would have to be filed with the probate court at the time of the first death, but the transfer of the real estate to the trust at that time is considered a nonprobate transfer. If these special circumstances do not exist in your state, you should obtain permission from the mortgagee.

◌⃝ *Can we lose the benefit of creditor protection if we transfer our real estate to a living trust?*

In some states there are safeguards against claims of creditors when property is held by husband and wife as tenants by the entirety. These safeguards may be lost if the property is conveyed into a living trust. Many states have homestead exemptions that protect the family home from the claims of creditors. The homestead exemption may be lost in some jurisdictions through trust funding. It is, therefore, important that you seek the advice of your attorney before transferring real estate to the name of your trust.

Vehicles

◌⃝ *Is there any advantage in placing cars, recreational vehicles, mobile homes, and boats into a living trust?*

Yes, the same advantage you will have in placing any property in a living trust. The reason for placing your property in a living trust is the combined benefit of disability planning and probate avoidance. If you title your vehicles in the name of your living trust, your disability trustee will be able to take care of them if you become disabled. Also, when you die, your death trustee will be able to pass the title of the vehicles to your heirs without going through the probate process.

Some states allow an individual to transfer motor vehicles to a spouse or children without the necessity of probate. Your attorney will guide you on whether you should transfer your vehicles to your trust.

Personal Property

CR *What about my personal belongings, furniture, and those types of items?*

Your personal property, furniture, furnishings, silverware, china, collectibles, and so on, are conveyed to the trust by a general bill of sale or assignment, which your estate planning attorney will prepare. In most cases there is no need to do a detailed inventory of your personal property.

CR *How do I transfer my art collection to my living trust?*

For collections of substantial value, such as antiques, stamp, coin, or art collections, and other high-value items, most practitioners tailor specific assignment documentation to convey the items to the trust.

Life Insurance and Annuities

CR *Should life insurance be owned by my revocable trust?*

That depends on the size of your estate and your estate tax planning needs. Ownership of life insurance by the insured's revocable trust will add to the estate value and increase the estate tax burden. In these cases, it may make sense to employ an irrevocable life insurance trust as the owner of the policies. In cases where the estate asset values are low, and there is little danger that the estate will be subject to estate taxes, your living trust should be the owner *and* the beneficiary of the policy. If you become disabled, this allows your trustee to control the policy and access the cash value if needed for your welfare.

CR *If I make my living trust the beneficiary of my life insurance policy, will the proceeds be subject to creditor claims in the same way they would be if my estate were the beneficiary?*

In virtually every state the proceeds will not be subject to the claims of your creditors if you name your living trust as the beneficiary of your life insurance. Your living trust should contain a spendthrift clause in order to fully protect the proceeds from the claims of creditors.

○ℝ *My IRA owns an annuity. Should I change the ownership of my annuity to my living trust?*

If the annuity is a "retirement-type" annuity, that is, one owned by a 403(b) plan, an IRA, or any qualified retirement plan, you should *not* change the ownership to your living trust.

○ℝ *Should I change the ownership and beneficiary of my regular annuity to my living trust?*

As long as your annuity is *not* owned by a retirement plan, you *may* change the ownership of the annuity to your living trust without adverse tax consequences. IRS regulations allow for tax-deferred treatment of an annuity of this type as long as it is owned by a "natural person." A properly drafted revocable living trust qualifies as a natural person. However, some older annuities issued before October 21, 1979, will lose their special step-up-in-basis feature if you transfer title to a living trust.

Naming your living trust as the beneficiary of the annuity will allow the proceeds to be distributed in accordance with the instructions in your living trust and will facilitate federal estate tax planning.

If you are married, you may *not* want to name your living trust as the beneficiary of the annuity. To do so will preclude your spouse from continuing the annuity as a tax-deferred investment after your death. This tax-deferred advantage is available only to a surviving spouse.

If you own this type of annuity, you should consult your attorney before you make any ownership or beneficiary changes.

POUR-OVER WILL

○ℝ *If I have a living trust, why do I still need a will?*

You need a special type of will called a *pour-over will* for several reasons:

1. The primary purpose of this type of will is to act as a safety net to "catch" any assets that you own at your death outside of the trust. The pour-over will merely states that all assets held by the decedent and which pass through probate will "pour over" to the trust-maker's living trust, which contains the tax planning provisions and instructions for managing and distributing your property.

2. The second purpose of a pour-over will is to appoint a guardian for minor children. Your revocable living trust governs how funds will be managed for a minor beneficiary and designates the trustee who will manage those funds, but guardians should be named in your will. Even when all assets have been transferred to the trustmaker's living trust, a pour-over will may have to be probated for the sole purpose of appointing the legal guardian of a minor child. However, this type of probate is usually relatively simple, without the costs and delay that a full probate of assets creates.

3. Finally, it is the only place in which you can revoke any previous will and codicils you might have executed so that they cannot interfere with your new estate plan.

CR *If I have a pour-over will, does it have to be probated when I die?*

If your living trust is fully funded so that your pour-over will controls no property, there is no need to probate your will except to appoint the legal guardian of minor children.

CR *Should my initial cotrustee also serve as my personal representative (executor) after my death?*

An executor is responsible for handling the probate administration of an estate, including distribution of all probate assets. It is important that the executor be someone who will follow the written instructions as set forth in the will. The executor is also responsible for distributing personal property items that have a high sentimental value even though they may not have a high economic value.

If you have a living trust–centered estate plan, the executor may not have as much responsibility as the executor of a will-based estate plan, but it is good practice to have your cotrustee also be your executor.

MEMORANDUM OF PERSONAL PROPERTY

CR *In what document do I give items of personal property?*

If your state allows it, you can use a *memorandum of personal property,* which is a separate document that gives specific items of tangible personal property to specific people. For example, if you wish to give the antique rocking chair to your daughter and the stamp collection to your son, then you write that in your memorandum. You can change your memorandum any time without your lawyer's assistance. For items with a high market value, the better course of action is to specify, in the trust document or will, who should receive the property.

MAINTAINING YOUR ESTATE PLAN

Miscellaneous Postsigning Matters

ଔ *Should I notify anyone after I have completed my living trust documents?*

You should inform your successor trustees that you have signed your trust and, in most cases, you should provide them with a copy of the trust documents and, later, with copies of amendments if you change your trust. In more sophisticated plans where tax planning has been accomplished, you should advise your accountant that you have done your planning.

ଔ *Where should I keep my estate planning documents?*

The best place to keep your original documents is where they will be safe but accessible, such as a home safe or office vault; and where you, your family, or your authorized agents can easily locate them after you are disabled or deceased.

It is also good for you to have a set of copies in your home or office, and your attorney should also keep a copy in case your sets are lost or destroyed.

Funding Review

ଔ *How can I ensure that my living trust stays fully funded?*

Most lawyers provide instructions and forms to assist trustmakers with their ongoing funding. Some attorneys even have formal, annual review or maintenance programs to ensure that funding is current. These review programs also help trustmakers keep their trusts up to date regarding changes in the law and changes in family and financial matters.

Tax Reporting

ભ *Will the changes in ownership of my assets to my revocable trust affect how I report my income taxes or make my income tax reporting more complicated?*

Transferring your assets to your living trust will not change how you report your income taxes and will not make reporting more complicated. Your living trust is your alter ego. You continue to keep your books and records in precisely the same manner that you did before the trust's creation.

Amending or Restating the Documents

ભ *If I want to change my distribution pattern, say, by reducing a gift to my niece, do I have to redo my entire trust?*

No. You simply execute an amendment to your trust revoking the section or clause pertaining to your niece and replacing it with your new wishes.

Changes of any kind do require formal, written documentation. A written *amendment*, or *restatement* if the complexity and number of changes are extensive, prepared by an attorney is generally necessary to properly change the provision of any trust document. If done improperly, an intended change can cause confusion and even litigation. You should not attempt to change your trust by yourself (e.g., by crossing out the old clause and writing in your new instruction).

ભ *Are amendments or restatements expensive?*

Sometimes they involve nothing more than word processing—for example, replacing the name of one successor trustee for another—which should cost you little. Others will involve sitting down and talking through things with your estate planning attorney and gaining the benefit of his or her wisdom, knowledge, and skill in this area. The more wisdom and knowledge and skill that's involved, the greater you can expect the expense to be in making an adjustment.

Reviewing and Updating Your Estate Plan

  Now that I have set up my estate plan, what do I need to do to maintain it?

Many estate planning attorneys encourage their clients to participate in a formal updating or maintenance program. A maintenance program is a systematized process whereby you pay a reasonable, minimal fee each year in return for the estate planning attorney keeping an eye on your circumstances. These programs ordinarily involve ongoing review of your plan with periodic amendments or other adjustments automatically included in the program; and there may also be included a process of educating your family members and successor trustees in the operation of your plan to be sure that, when the time comes, they will know what to do.

  If I am not in a formal updating program, how often should my estate plan be reviewed?

If you are not participating in a formal review program with your attorney, the rule of thumb is, generally, that a revocable trust should be reviewed at least every 3 years. However, because of the ever-changing landscape of the tax laws and legal structure, many people are finding it beneficial to participate in an annual review or maintenance program.

  What types of changes require that we review our estate plan?

The following sources of change require a review of your plan, if not an actual change to your plan:

- *Personal circumstances:* These will include additions to your family, changes in your health or the health of your children, marriages or divorces in the family, increases or decreases in wealth, or your retirement. These can all cause you to rethink how you have laid out your plan for incapacity and transfers to your loved ones at death.

- *External factors:* Tax and other laws change and courts change their interpretations of laws, which may affect how much, when, and how property transfers. Attorneys and financial advisors who focus their practices on estate planning are always changing the way they plan and developing and/or incorporating new strategies in their clients' plans in response to changes in the law and even changes in society. In order for your estate plan to take advantage of new methods of planning, it needs to be updated and reviewed regularly.
- *Assets:* Over time, people sell one asset and buy another and forget to fund the new assets into the trust. Periodically, the trust should be reviewed to ensure that it is still properly and fully funded.

It is the combination of these factors that might make it advisable for your plan to be reviewed every few years at the very least. On the other hand, a good estate planning attorney will build flexibility into your estate plan so that constant attention is not necessary. For example, once a trust is set up and funded, assuming your circumstances and the laws do not change, it may not need to be amended for many years.

℞ *If there are subsequent changes in the law or changes in my personal circumstances, how do I know my estate plan is still valid?*

The relevant words in your question are "estate plan." It is not as important to worry about the documents themselves as it is important for you to recognize that an estate plan is constantly changing. As the laws and circumstances in your life change, it may be necessary to amend your plan to reflect those changes. You should review your estate plan at least every 3 years and keep your attorney informed of any major change in your financial or family situation that would alter your plan, such as a death or divorce in the family. Overall, it is important that you and your estate planning attorney talk about these issues so that you are both comfortable that there is a process by which your plan will always reflect your current estate planning goals.

Your estate planning attorney should notify you of any change in the law that affects your estate plan and should explain how your plan is affected. The combination of review by you and your estate planning attorney will ensure that the plan is effective regardless of how long it may be in force.

You should discuss with your estate planning attorney how you will stay in touch with one another to ensure that your plan remains current with respect to any major changes in your life (you might win the lottery), your family situation, or the law. You may want to ask your attorney how he or she will contact you if there is any significant change in the law that might affect your plan and if there is any new development in estate planning that could improve your plan.

CR *How do I know if I have financially outgrown my current estate plan?*

Many people set up an estate plan today not realizing that as their assets grow, they may outgrow their current planning. Therefore, it is imperative that you select an attorney who will track the growth of your estate and counsel you on a regular basis in order to determine if you have outgrown your planning and if any additional planning is required.

CR *I created my trust 15 years ago. My attorney is now retired. Do I need to have my estate plan reviewed?*

Yes. There have been major changes in the federal estate tax rules, as well as in the retirement planning area. Even if you believe your family situation has not changed much and your assets are all funded into your trust, you should have the trust reviewed for potential changes that need to take place due to any changes in the laws that have occurred.

Action Steps

We respectfully present the following action steps to summarize the concepts that we discussed in chapter 9 and to suggest steps that you can take to prepare for meetings with your estate planning team of professionals.

❑ *Meet with an attorney to set up a revocable living trust.* A revocable living trust should be the cornerstone of almost every estate plan in order to:

- Avoid probate.

- Maintain your privacy.

- Protect you and your assets during disability.

- Provide a lasting legacy for your family.

You can customize your living trust to meet almost any goal or desire you have, so think carefully about what terms you want in your document.

❑ *Select your successor trustees.* You can select an institution or family members to succeed you as trustees during any disability and after you die. Each of these offers advantages and disadvantages. You should carefully consider:

- Who you want to name as your immediate successor trustee

- Who you want to act as trustee when you and your spouse are both gone

- Who will serve as trustees if you created trusts for children

- Whether you want cotrustees to serve in any of these situations to provide moral support or financial advice when necessary

If you are going to name family members, you should tell them in advance that you are considering them and ask them if they are willing to accept this important responsibility.

❑ *Make sure your trust is funded.* An unfunded living trust does you little good when it comes to avoiding living and death probate proceedings. Work closely with your advisors to ensure that all appropriate property is transferred to your trust.

❑ *Keep your trust funded.* Make sure that new assets that you purchase are funded to the trust, if appropriate.

❑ *Keep your trusts balanced.* For married couples, it is important that each spouse own enough property through a living trust to utilize his or her applicable exclusion at death. Periodically review the assets in each trust to make sure both trusts are adequately funded.

❑ *Keep your documents in a safe but accessible place.* We've heard about every place from leaving them on the coffee table to burying them in the backyard. A lockbox or a desk drawer in your home is your best choice. Tell several people where your documents are located.

❑ *Participate in an updating program if available.* Some attorneys offer an annual updating service to their clients. It can be money well spent. In today's hectic world, most of us forget about our estate plan soon after we sign it. By committing to a regular, ongoing review process, you can be assured that your documents will be fully funded, up-to-date, and ready to carry out your wishes when the time comes.

chapter 10

Business Succession Planning

THE EXIT STRATEGY AND SUCCESSION PLAN

Q *What is an exit strategy?*

According to Steven G. Siegel in his book, *Family Business Succession Planning* (National Law Foundation, 1999), only half of all family-owned businesses last more than one generation and very few last more than two generations. Pundits, commentators, and politicians often criticize the federal estate tax as the offending culprit; however, the statistics are similar in nations, such as Australia and Canada, that do not have an estate or succession tax. Estate tax "erosion" is certainly a factor; but in our opinion, it is certain *not* the primary factor. After years of experience working with small-business owners, we believe that the major causes are (1) the owners' failure to plan in advance for the succession of the business in the event of their death, disability, or retirement; and (2) their failure to train, motivate, and involve the next generation of owners.

No one lives forever, and most owners do not want to own and operate their businesses forever. An *exit strategy* is a long-range plan for how you want to divest yourself of the ownership of the business when any of certain events occur. Usually, these events are retirement, disability, and death. Your first decision, then, is whether you want the transition of your ownership to occur before or after your death. Business owners tend to invest the vast majority of their funds in one asset, the business. This can make preparing for retirement and planning for the business at death or disability quite complex.

I'm not sure I'm ready to think about exiting my business. Do I have to do it now?

Transitions are emotionally difficult under the best of circumstances. For many business owners, the business has been their life, a source of pride, and the source of their income. For some, planning their exit from the business is akin to planning their own funeral.

The business owner is not the only person who may resist a transition, whether the transition be to outsiders or to family members. Succession planning can affect the business owner's spouse, children, key employees, customers, vendors, colleagues, and friends. However, transitions are inevitable. The thoughtful business owner will eventually bring about the transition according to a plan. But for the ill-prepared, that transition may mean the death of the business as well.

What are common exit strategies?

The most common options for exiting a business are:

- Sell to co-owners who may or may not be family members.
- Sell to key employees who may or may not be family members.
- Sell to all employees through an employee stock ownership plan (ESOP).
- Give the business to family members.
- Sell the company to outsiders.
- Give the company to charity.
- Take the company public.
- Liquidate the business.

So what is a business succession plan?

A *business succession plan* details the steps for implementing your chosen exit strategy. Good business succession planning allows the smooth transfer of control and ownership of the business so that it can continue to operate without you. For example, if your exit strategy is to sell the company to outsiders and retire to a villa in Tuscany, good business succession planning will help you position the company for a sale, find the right buyer at the appropriate time, and create a smooth transfer of ownership.

ᘓᘓ *What issues do I have to consider in developing my succession plan?*

Most of the questions that you should consider for developing your succession plan fall into these five categories:

1. *Timing of your retirement:* You have to make this decision so that, depending on your choice of exit strategies, you have time to train successors or bring in co-owners or position the company for sale.

2. *Management succession:* You need to decide who will manage the business if you retire, die, or become disabled. Your decision is vital to the survival of the business. Realistically consider your ability to gradually transition your control to others while you are still working in the business. If you are unable to give up some control, you will also be unable to assess your successors' abilities before you turn the entire company operations over to them.

3. *Ownership:* You have to decide in advance if you want to transfer management only to others and retain total ownership or if you will transfer total or partial ownership as well. Your decision will be driven mostly by whether you need proceeds from a sale for retirement.

4. *Estate planning:* If your exit strategy is to transfer the business to your family at your death, you will have to carefully consider how you will divide the ownership among your children or how you will balance the fact that you are giving the family business to one child and nonbusiness assets to your other children. Your ability to plan for the family dynamics of this exit strategy will be the deciding factor for the success or failure of your succession plan. One aspect of estate planning you cannot ignore is how the heirs will pay the estate taxes without being forced to sell the business.

5. *Business valuation:* Whether your exit strategy is to sell the business, give it away, take it public, or liquidate it, you must determine an accurate fair market value of your business.

SPECIAL CONSIDERATIONS FOR TRANSFERS TO FAMILY MEMBERS

CR *What are my options for transferring the business to children?*

Basically you have two options:

1. Sell the business, during your life or after your death, to the child who is active in the business, and then divide the proceeds, along with your other property, among all of your children, as you desire. A sale during your life will freeze the value of the business in your estate by the amount of the purchase price. Increases in the value of the business following the sale are attributable to the child who purchases the business, not to you or your estate.

2. Give the business during your lifetime or at your death to the child who is active in the business and give your other property to the children who are not active in the business.

CR *Should I sell the business to my children or give it to them?*

In our experience, it is unusual for all of the business owner's children to participate in the family business. A lifetime or testamentary gift of the business to the participating children may be perceived as unfair by the nonparticipating children. A sale to children who work in the business may be perceived as fair, but a sale is possible only if the children have the financial resources to make the purchase.

CR *My son works in my business, but my two daughters do not. I want to treat my children equally. Should I leave my business to all three of my children, equally?*

This is a question common to all parents who own family businesses. They want to treat their children fairly, so think they need to treat them equally. However, "equal" is not always "fair," and vice versa. Asking your son to share the results of his hard work in the business with his two sisters who contribute nothing to that business is not going to be perceived by your son as being fair.

You need to give yourself permission to plan fairly, even though the result may produce an unequal economic benefit. There are many ways to create an economic benefit for your nonparticipating daughters to compensate for the transfer of the family business to your participating son, including the purchase of life insurance naming them as beneficiaries.

ভ *My husband and I want to retire and travel in the next few years while we are still healthy, but we are not really sure that our children are capable or even interested in running the business. What should we do?*

Consult with your children as a group and then individually. You will never know what a child wants and expects without asking. Assume nothing. Keep an open mind, and do not be critical or judgmental. Family participation in the business is not an option if no one in the family wants to continue the business. If one or more family members are interested in continuing the business, it is critical for you to realistically assess their qualifications, often with an impartial third party serving as guide and facilitator.

To maintain family harmony, choose your successors very carefully and groom them thoroughly. Talk with each of your children about the decisions you are making and the reasons for those decisions. Contain and attempt to control emotional reactions by fully disclosing the facts. Once you have chosen your successor or successors, begin a succession training program immediately.

ভ *What are some of the things we should consider in developing a succession plan for our daughter to take over the business?*

Some of the more important considerations in family business succession planning are:

- Are you certain that your daughter is capable of running the business?
- Does she want to run and own the business?
- If she doesn't currently work in the business, what will happen with your loyal key employees when you tell them that their new boss will be your daughter who may know little or nothing about the business?

- What is the structure of the family itself, its makeup, the number of individuals involved and not involved in the family business; the multiple agendas (hidden as well as direct) and road blocks that you and your advisors must identify and address?

I'm the founder of my company. How do I ensure that the company will pass to my children?

Here are some additional suggestions whether you are transitioning the business to family members or others:

- Consult your advisors to discuss your ideas before you make any final decisions.
- Start the process early so you have time to evaluate all of your options and choices.
- If you have children or nonfamily key employees currently working in the business, evaluate how each performs and who is best at each function (marketing, finance, etc.).
- If your children are not currently in the business but will make it their career choice, get them involved as early as possible to provide them with the necessary experience before you retire.
- If more than one child will take over the business, determine what the respective ownership should be and provide a means for one of them to buy out the other in the event of the death, disability, withdrawal, or retirement of one of the future owners or in the event of disagreement among them.
- Determine if you want children who are not involved in the business to receive any part of the profits of the business after you are gone.

The most important thing you can do to make a successful transition is to create your succession plan as early as possible so that your successors have time to be trained under your tutelage.

What techniques might I use if I am going to sell the company to family members or to nonfamily key employees?

You can consider several techniques, each with its own set of advantages and disadvantages as we discuss in this chapter. Whether you use these techniques alone or in combination, you need to evaluate them in light of your goals:

- Installment sale
- Irrevocable grantor trust
- Self-canceling installment note
- Private annuity

You could also consider a sale to all employees using an ESOP.

I am the sole shareholder of my business, and I would like to transfer it to my two adult children. My objectives are to sell it to them at a price that is as low as we can justify, and for me to have a stream of income from the business for the next 10 or 15 years. How should I structure this transfer?

A deferred compensation plan for your benefit prior to the sale can reduce the company's value. This will accomplish several goals. It will reduce the value of the business, since you are putting a large liability on the books. This will justify a lower sale price to your children, since the company is worth less. It will also allow the business to take a deduction for the payments made to you. The risk that you take is that these payments are general obligations of the company and will not have any priority in the event that the company files for bankruptcy or cannot afford to make the required payments.

SELL TO CO-OWNERS

You said that a sale to co-owners is a possible exit strategy. How do I implement this strategy?

You can structure a buy-sell agreement so that the company and/or your co-owners buy your interest when you are ready to retire. Buy-sell arrangements also include provisions for what happens to the business if you become disabled or die while involved in the management and operation of the business.

What is a buy-sell agreement?

A *buy-sell agreement* is a succession plan for business owners to use in the event of death, disability, disagreement, or retirement (often known as *triggering events*) to protect both the departing owner and the integrity of an ownership group. A buy-sell agreement documents the owners' decisions regarding:

- restrictions on the sale or transfer of ownership interests to parties outside the current ownership group;
- which triggering events will require that an owner sell, and the business or other owners buy, the owner's interest in the business;
- how the business interest is to be valued on the occurrence of a triggering event; and
- how payment is to be made (lump sum or installments).

ᙅ *What are the most important objectives of a buy-sell agreement?*

A buy-sell agreement should have several tax and nontax objectives, as follows:

Tax objectives:

- To minimize income tax for the seller (capital gain versus ordinary income)
- To maximize the tax basis for the buyer
- To fix the value of an owner's interest for estate tax purposes
- To provide cash to the owner's estate for paying estate taxes and other costs

Nontax objectives:

- To control the voluntary transfer of an owner's interest during his or her lifetime and avoid the introduction of outsiders into the ownership group
- To delineate a clear method of determining the value of the deceased or departing owner's interest, such as a specific sale price or a formula to determine the price
- To furnish the remaining owners or the company with the liquidity to fulfill the obligation and prevent forced liquidation of the company
- To create a market for an otherwise unmarketable business interest

- To provide for an orderly transition of ownership, management, and control

∝ *Where does the cash come from to buy out each other?*

In an increasing number of cases, life insurance is used to fund a buy-sell agreement because it can be effective in almost any type of buy-sell arrangement. It funds the buyout at the death of an owner by providing cash to the deceased owner's family to implement the buyout; and the policy's accumulated cash values can be used to fund the buyout on an owner's disability or retirement.

∝ *When is the best time to sign a buy-sell agreement?*

The best time to sign a buy-sell agreement is at the same time the business is formed, or early in the relationship, while everyone can still agree and when everyone is more likely to be insurable. The worst time to get an agreement signed is when problems or disagreements begin to arise or when the owners are too old or ill to be insured.

∝ *What are the different types of buy-sell agreements?*

Three agreements commonly used in buy-sell planning are:

1. Cross-purchase agreement
2. Entity-purchase (redemption) agreement
3. A hybrid of the two agreements

∝ *What is a cross-purchase agreement?*

A *cross-purchase agreement* is a buy-sell agreement in which the remaining co-owners agree to purchase the interest of a deceased or departing owner. Cross-purchase agreements are favored when there are relatively few, usually only two or three, business owners. A cross-purchase agreement can be overly complex and expensive if there are too many owners and the buyout is to be funded with life insurance because each owner must purchase a life insurance policy on every other owner.

∝ *What is an entity-purchase agreement?*

An *entity-purchase,* or *redemption, agreement* is a buy-sell agreement in which the business agrees to purchase (redeem) the interest of a deceased or departing owner. After redemption, the ownership percentage of the remaining owners increases. For example, suppose a company has three owners who each own a 33 percent interest. On redemption of the equity interest of owner A, owners B and C will each have a 50 percent ownership interest.

ℭ℞ *What is a hybrid agreement?*

A *hybrid agreement* is also called a *two-tier buy-sell agreement*. Both the individual equity owners *and* the company itself may have rights, duties, and/or obligations within the same agreement to acquire the interest of a deceased, disabled, or retiring owner. The hybrid agreement affords a "wait-and-see" opportunity for the remaining owners to individually purchase the equity interest or to shift the acquisition burden to the company. A hybrid agreement may also permit a partial redemption by the company and a partial acquisition by the remaining owners.

ℭ℞ *How do we decide which agreement to use?*

The appropriate arrangement for your business depends on several considerations:

- How many owners will have an interest in the company?
- Are all the owners employees of the company?
- Are the owners related to one another?
- Who will buy out the deceased or departing owner—the company or one or more remaining owners?
- How will the company or the remaining owners pay the obligation?
- Is it likely that the business will be sold during the lifetime of existing owners?

SELL TO KEY EMPLOYEES

ℭ℞ *How can I sell my business to key employees who may or may not be family members?*

An *installment sale* allows you to sell your business in exchange for an interest-bearing promissory note payable over 2 or more tax years. The installment sale works best if the cash flow from the business is sufficient to meet the debt-service requirements. An important factor is the human element: You are no longer involved in operating the business but are dependent on the success of the business to receive your retirement income.

❧ Can you give me an example of how the installment sale arrangement works for the sale of my business?

Sure. Let's say that Homer Fudge owns a family corporation with a tax basis of $100,000 and a fair market value of $1 million. Homer sells the stock of the business to his daughter, Coco, for $200,000 cash and a promissory note in the amount of $800,000. The note is to be paid in ten equal annual installments of principal of $80,000, plus interest at the market rate. Under the installment technique, Homer will recognize $180,000 of capital gain upon receipt of the $200,000 in cash. The capital gain portion is determined by dividing the total gain ($900,000) by the purchase price ($1 million) resulting in a quotient of 0.9. The 0.9 is then multiplied by the cash payment received ($200,000) in the first year. The balance of the gain, $720,000 ($900,000 total gain less $180,000 gain recognized in the first year), is recognized over the 10-year term of the promissory note at the rate of $72,000 per year (0.9 × $80,000 annual payment).

Homer will also report the interest he receives on the promissory note as interest income, taxed as ordinary income.

❧ How does an installment sale affect my estate and gift taxes?

If the amount your children or other key employees pay for the business (cash and installment note) is equal to the fair market value of the business, there is no gift. However, if the fair market value of the business is more than the total amount the buyer pays in cash plus the installment note, then you are making a taxable gift of the difference.

One of the biggest benefits of the installment sale has to do with estate taxes. Once you sell the business to your children or other key employees, it is no longer in your estate for estate tax purposes and the value of the promissory note is locked in at the time of sale. You own the promissory note, and its value will be included in your estate, but if the value of the business increases, the value in your estate will not go up. The value will be the same as at the time of sale, or even less if you are spending the note payments on a well-deserved, luxurious retirement. If the buyers pay the loan in full before your death, any proceeds from the sale that you haven't spent will be included in your estate.

CR *Can I secure the payment of the installment note with collateral or require the buyer to put money in escrow?*

If you accept collateral for the promissory note or otherwise secure its payment with other assets, there is no adverse tax effect. However, if you require the buyer to deposit funds into an escrow account from which future note payments are to be made, the funds will be considered a payment on the note upon deposit to the account and will cause early gain recognition, unless there is a substantial restriction on your access to the escrowed funds.

An alternative to using an escrow account is a standby letter of credit from a financial institution. This would satisfy your concern regarding the family member's ability to pay without causing acceleration of the gain recognition.

CR *Are there any disadvantages of an installment sale?*

Yes, there are disadvantages, depending on your point of view:

- Once you sell the business to children or other key employees, you have given up control (assuming you sold at least a controlling interest). For some, this is a very difficult adjustment to make. For others, they can hardly wait to be rid of the burden.
- The sale of the business results in the recognition of a capital gain.
- You may still have your largest investment tied up in one asset— a promissory note. If something goes wrong and you don't get paid, this could be disastrous to your financial well-being. If you sell the promissory note or otherwise dispose of it, this will accelerate the capital gain that you may be hoping to spread out over a longer period of time.

SELL TO FAMILY MEMBERS

Irrevocable Grantor Trust

CR *What is an irrevocable grantor trust?*

A very effective technique for selling a rapidly growing business is to sell it to a special kind of trust, called an irrevocable grantor trust (IGT), of which the business owner is the trustmaker-grantor. A business owner would usually use this arrangement to sell to family members, not nonfamily.

By creating an IGT and then selling your company to the trust, taking back a note, you will not recognize any capital gain on the transaction. This is because for income tax purposes the trust assets are considered your assets. You receive annual or more frequent loan payments and charge interest at a rate the government considers a market rate. Because this is a sale for fair market value, there is no gift and thus no gift taxes, yet a highly appreciating asset has been removed from your estate for estate and gift tax purposes.

We also discuss the IGT in Chapter 5, Wealth Transfer Techniques. This is a sophisticated transaction that requires significant coordination with the rest of your estate and succession planning, but under some circumstances this technique can be very effective.

Self-Canceling Installment Note

C**Q** *What is a self-canceling installment note, and how can I use it to transfer my business?*

A *self-canceling installment note (SCIN)* is an installment note with a contingency, that being the death of the seller. At the seller's death, the SCIN is canceled, even if it has not been paid in full. Cancellation of the SCIN prevents the inclusion of the unpaid balance of the SCIN in your estate, unlike an ordinary installment note. To compensate you, as the seller, for the risk of early cancellation, the buyer must pay a "risk premium," which can take the form of a higher principal amount or a higher interest rate. The term of the note must be for a period shorter than your life expectancy.

Otherwise, the SCIN also has most of the same advantages and disadvantages of the ordinary installment sale, but you would usually use the SCIN only for a sale to family members.

As an estate planning tool, the self-canceling installment note has significant potential for reducing estate tax (but not income tax) if you die before the note is paid.

C**Q** *What is the term of the SCIN?*

As a general rule, the term of the note should not exceed the seller's actuarial life expectancy. The premium the buyer pays for the self-canceling feature is determined by the term of the note and the seller's age—the longer the term, the higher the premium. Thus, the buyer may want to repay the note as quickly as possible. Also, both parties typically want the note paid off as soon as is practical.

CR *Which is the better way to structure the SCIN risk premium, as a higher rate of interest or as a higher purchase price?*

That depends on your goals. Interest on an installment note for the purchase of a business is generally deductible. Consequently, if the risk premium is reflected in the interest rate, the buyer will get a higher current deduction. However, if a higher sales price is utilized for the risk premium, this will increase the tax basis in the business for the buyer. This can allow the buyer greater depreciation over the life of the assets of the business in an asset sale or can reduce the gain recognized by the buyer on a subsequent sale of the business.

CR *What are the tax consequences of a SCIN?*

The capital gain consequences of a SCIN are the same as those of an ordinary installment sale. However, the risk premium on the SCIN increases the amount of income you, as the seller, will recognize over the term of the note. If you die before the buyers repay the note, the deferred gain is accelerated and your estate must pay capital gain tax on the unrecognized gain, even though the note payments have ceased. If the note carried a proper risk premium, there is no gift.

The primary benefit of a SCIN is that if it is properly structured, neither the value of the business you sold nor the promissory note itself is subject to estate tax when you die. Remember that with an ordinary installment sale, the unpaid amount of the note is included in the seller's estate. With a SCIN, the note is canceled and so has no value at death.

Private Annuity

CR *How can I use a private annuity to sell my business to my children?*

With a private annuity, you sell the business to a buyer (or buyers), who is usually a member of your family, in return for the buyer's promise to pay a fixed amount to you for the rest of your life. The annuity is "private" because the buyer of the property is not in the business of writing annuity contracts. The property you sell in exchange for the annuity is not included in your estate for federal estate tax purposes.

℺ How is the annuity payment calculated?

The present value of the annuity is the fair market value of the company. There are specific formulas for calculating a payment schedule that will create a net present value equal to the purchase price on the basis of your statistical life expectancy. The payment obligation terminates on your death. If you die before your statistical life expectancy, your children will pay less than the business is worth at the time of sale. However, if you live longer than the statistical life expectancy of someone of your age, your children have to continue the fixed payments over your lifetime and will pay too much for the company.

Thus, private annuities are sometimes recommended when the actual life expectancy of the seller is less than the average life expectancy of the seller's statistical age group. The seller must live more than 1 year after the transaction, however, or the Internal Revenue Service (IRS) may ignore the actuarial tables and treat the transfer as a gift.

℺ What if I want to provide an income stream not only for my own life but also for my husband's life?

A private annuity will allow you to do that. You can require that the annuity payment be made for your life and for the life of your husband. The result is that the buyers will make smaller payments but over a longer period of time.

℺ When should I consider an annuity as an appropriate means for selling the business to my children?

You should consider an annuity if you are in any of the following situations:

- Your estate will be subject to estate tax at your death.
- You want to exchange the burden of ownership for a fixed payment payable over your life.

- Your family history suggests that it is unlikely that you will live to your actuarial life expectancy.

- The business is likely to appreciate in value.

- The business produces an annual cash flow equal to or greater than the required annuity payment, or the buyer has sufficient other resources to make the annuity payment.

○ℛ *What rules do I have to follow so that the private annuity isn't considered a gift?*

If you abide by certain rules, chances are strong that you can avoid making a taxable gift in setting up a private annuity. The rules are:

- Do not tie the payments in any way to the amount of income earned by the business after the sale.

- Do not retain any interest whatsoever in the property you exchange for the private annuity, not even a security interest. You cannot have any right to control or manage the property, to vote stock or a partnership interest, to sell the property, to mortgage the property, or to exchange the property for another asset. This limitation is absolutely critical.

- Make sure that the children are personally liable for the payments, regardless of how well the business does, and that the payments are *not* secured by the business or any other assets—you must rely only on the children's promise to make the lifetime annuity payments.

- Use the IRS annuity tables to calculate the amount of the annuity payment.

- Death cannot be imminent when you arrange the private annuity.

- Don't set up a private annuity with your children if they have no way of making the payments without your making gifts to them. Be sure the business provides enough cash flow to make the payments, and avoid setting up a private annuity with children who are not involved in the business.

○ℛ *How are my husband and I taxed on the payments we receive from this transaction?*

The IRS views each payment that you receive as two parts: the capital part and the annuity part. The capital part is considered a return of your basis (the amount you paid for the business) plus any capital gain you earned. The annuity part is taxed as ordinary income, and the capital gain is subject to capital gain tax.

℞ *What are the estate tax results of a private annuity?*

Generally, neither the annuity nor the business is included in your or your husband's estate at death. However, if you do not follow the rules in establishing the annuity, it could be seen as a gift in which you retain a lifetime interest, and thus it would be at least partially includable in your estate.

℞ *What are the advantages of using a private annuity to sell the business to our children?*

There are a number of advantages to your selling the business through a private annuity:

- You retain income for life.
- The value of the annuity is not includable in your taxable estate.
- Provided that the annuity payments equal the fair market value of the property sold, you have not made a gift.
- The future appreciation of any assets you sell via the private annuity is kept outside your estate.
- Because the private annuity calls for payments to be made over your lifetime, you can spread any gains from the sale over your life expectancy (or over your and your husband's joint life expectancy).

℞ *What are some of the disadvantages of a private annuity?*

Some of the disadvantages are:

- The sale and the private annuity contract must be irrevocable.
- You run the risk that you may outlive your scheduled life expectancy. Consequently, your children may pay more than the original value of the business.
- Your children are not allowed a tax deduction for the annuity payment or the interest on the payment; the payment is treated as a business capital expenditure.
- You risk nonpayment, since the children's promise is unsecured.

If the business fails or your children have other financial difficulties, the money for paying the annuity may not be there. If you are depending on the annuity payments for financial support, the private annuity may not be the best approach.

SELL TO ALL EMPLOYEES

℞ *Is there a way to sell the business to all of my employees when I have no key employees or family members to sell the company to?*

Yes. If your company is a C or an S corporation, consider using an *employee stock ownership plan (ESOP)*. An ESOP not only enables owners to accomplish a number of business succession planning objectives but can provide an excellent qualified retirement benefit for all long-term employees. Some of the benefits of an ESOP are:

■ Creates a market for the privately held stock

■ Creates a tax-deductible method of financing the buyout

■ Enables a key-employee group to borrow the money for a buyout through leverage opportunities available in a specially designed variation of the ESOP

■ Receives tax-favored treatment if at least 30 percent of the stock is sold by a C corporation business owner

■ Allows the owner to sell part, or eventually all, of the business without recognizing any immediate gain for tax purposes

℞ *How does an ESOP work?*

First, the company establishes an ESOP as a qualified retirement plan for its employees. The shareholders sell their stock to the ESOP trust at an appraised value. The ESOP either borrows funds to purchase the stock all at once or buys the stock over time with the funds contributed each year by the company (a tax-deductible contribution). Each year the ESOP allocates the stock among the participants in a manner similar to the way a profit-sharing plan does. When employees leave the company, they receive their vested ESOP shares, which the company or ESOP may buy back. One major benefit of the ESOP is that it allows the company to repurchase shares with pretax dollars; this generally saves thousands of dollars. Employees who sell their shares back to the ESOP also win, as they can defer capital gain taxes by reinvesting their gains in stocks of other companies.

❧ *What factors should I consider in determining whether my company should implement an ESOP?*

Some of the factors you want to consider are:

- Do you have middle managers who are progressing in their ability to run the company without you?
- Is your company growing and in a trade or industry that will continue to grow during the next decade?
- Can you or should you convert your company to a C or an S corporation to establish an ESOP?
- Is your payroll at least $500,000 per year?
- Is your company a U.S. domestic company?

❧ *Which companies should not implement an ESOP?*

A company should select another alternative if it has a poor record of earnings and is not likely to improve its earnings in the future. A company is not a candidate if it does not have sufficient payroll to service an ESOP loan and to generate tax savings.

❧ *How does an ESOP get the money to buy company stock?*

There are two basic types of ESOPs, a regular ESOP and a leveraged ESOP. In a *regular ESOP*, the company makes cash contributions to the ESOP (as with any retirement plan), and the trust then buys the stock from a shareholder. If the plan is new and does not have the cash to purchase all the shares immediately, the ESOP can purchase the stock over time or can buy all the stock in exchange for a promissory note, in either way using the company's annual contributions to pay.

In a *leveraged ESOP*, the trust formed to administer the ESOP borrows money from a lender to buy the shares, and in most instances the shareholders guarantee the loan or the company cosigns or guarantees repayment of the loan. Alternatively, the company borrows the money and makes a loan to the ESOP trust.

CR *How does the company reduce its income taxes by implementing an ESOP?*

If the company contributes to the ESOP to purchase the shares, the contributions are fully deductible (within limits). Contributions of newly issued stock are tax-deductible. If the ESOP borrows money to buy the stock, the loan will be repaid from contributions to the ESOP, making both interest and principal payments deductible.

CR *How does the selling shareholder avoid capital gain on the sale of shares to an ESOP?*

Under the Internal Revenue Code (IRC), if a selling shareholder of a C corporation sells at least 30 percent of the company stock to the ESOP, the shareholder will not recognize a capital gain on the sale if he or she invests the proceeds in "qualified replacement property" within 12 months. The selling shareholder must own the stock for at least 3 years before the sale to qualify. (This "rollover" technique is not available for S corporation shareholders.)

Qualified replacement property is defined as securities of domestic corporations not controlled by foreign companies. The corporation must use more than 50 percent of its assets in the active conduct of a trade or business to qualify, and it must not have passive income (rents, royalties, dividends, interest, etc.) that exceeds 25 percent of its gross receipts. Mutual funds, real estate investment trusts, and governmental bonds do not qualify.

CR *What are the rules for an ESOP?*

The primary requirements for a qualified ESOP are that the plan must:

- Be in writing and provide all the information necessary for qualification.
- Be established by the employer and intended to be permanent.
- Be communicated to employees in the form of a summary plan description.
- State who can make contributions—the employer, the employee, or both.
- Be for the exclusive benefit of the participants and their beneficiaries, with the primary benefits for the participants.

- Meet the Employee Retirement Income Security Act's (ERISA's) minimum vesting, participation, and coverage standards.
- Not discriminate in favor of highly compensated employees.
- Meet the minimum funding rules of a defined-benefit plan and comply with the maximum contribution and benefits under the IRC.
- Include a clearly definable statement of the benefits.

GIVE THE BUSINESS TO FAMILY MEMBERS

Considerations

℞ *I've decided to give the business to my children and grandchildren. What should I be thinking about before I do that?*

For parents, gift giving is the simplest, most frequently used, and often the most powerful method for transferring the business to children and other family members. There are several techniques for giving the business to members of the next generation, so it is important that you consider all the issues and define your goals in order to select the appropriate technique for your situation. Your advisors can help you establish your goals, recommend the best technique, and prepare the required documents to implement it as part of your overall exit strategy and succession plan. In giving the business to family members, business owners usually want to achieve goals in the following categories:

- *Family succession planning:* The business represents the family heritage, and the owners want it to continue for future generations, protected from the loss of its current leadership, as well as from creditors and ex-spouses. They want to begin the formal transition process while they are still present to give the younger generation the benefit of their skills, experience, and knowledge. They want to ensure that the business is owned by the family members they choose, not by family members who do not want to run the business or lack the ability to do so. Owners want to facilitate the family culture represented by the business and to promote family values with regard to wealth and its creation.

- *Estate tax planning:* One reason people make gifts is to remove the value of the assets from their estates and thus to reduce the amount of estate taxes when the donor dies. Giving assets away also transfers to the recipient all postgift appreciation in the value of those assets. Even if the estate tax is repealed in 2010, a giving program, which can include the business, may still make sense for estate and income tax reasons until then and perhaps after then as well.

- *Income tax planning:* If business owners want to shift excess income to other family members, giving income-producing business interests to family members may be wise.

- *Asset protection:* Business owners want to ensure that the business interests they are giving to children and other family members are not subject to the claims of the recipients' creditors or entangled in divorce proceedings.

- *Valuation adjustments:* Lifetime gifts of partial ownership interests often produce lower valuations than will be the case if the total asset is valued for death tax purposes; such gifts result in lower estate and gift taxes for the business owner. For example, three gifts of a one-third interest in a business will have a total value, for gift tax purposes, of less than 100 percent of the business held by one owner at death.

ଔ *What other issues should I consider?*

In establishing your goals and choosing the best method for giving the business to your children, consider the following factors:

- *Type of entity:* Your current ownership structure will determine how you transfer the business or whether you must change the entity in order to make the transfer.

- *Control:* The type of entity and your desires for giving up or maintaining control of the business go hand in hand. For example, if your company has only one class of ownership, such as a general partnership, adding a new owner would generally mean giving up significant control.

- *Income needs:* When you give away an asset, the assumption is that you are willing and financially able to give up all rights to that asset. You must consider the cash-flow consequences of giving business interests to family members. If you need the income generated by the company, consider all the aspects of the transfer before making your gift. Giving a gift with "strings," such as the continued right to receive income from the business you give away, is ineffective in removing the value of the business from your estate.

■ *Other assets:* If your business is the greater part of your estate and you plan to give it to just some of your children, you need to consider what you will give or leave to the other children to "equalize" your estate, as well as how you will care for your spouse after you are gone.

■ *Estate and gift taxes:* Each of the techniques for giving the business to your children produces different results for purposes of estate and gift taxes. It is important that you understand the basic concepts of the unified gift and estate tax system, as it exists today and as it will change in the near future, in order to make the appropriate choices.

Despite the impact that taxes can have on your decision of whether to make a lifetime or a testamentary gift of the business to your children and family members, taxes may not always be the most important consideration. Some parents place more weight on the nontax reasons for choosing one technique over another.

℣ *I have two children. Julie runs my company and does a very good job. Harry is a schoolteacher and wants nothing to do with the company. The problem is that 90 percent of my net worth is tied up in this company. What should I do?*

You should consider diversifying your assets over time. Develop a financial plan that allows you to balance and to build your nonbusiness assets while maintaining your viable business. In this way, you can leave the nonbusiness assets to your son, Harry, and leave the business to Julie who runs the company. You can also use some of the revenue from the company to purchase a life insurance policy through an irrevocable life insurance trust for Harry. Thus, Julie can inherit the business, and Harry can inherit the life insurance.

ℭℛ *What are the techniques for giving business interests to my family?*

The most common techniques for giving businesses to family members are:

- outright gifts of business interests to family members, and
- the irrevocable grantor retained annuity trust.

Each technique achieves different goals, as we will discuss in the balance of this chapter.

Outright Gifts of Business Interests

ℭℛ *What is the simplest way of giving my business to my children?*

The least complicated method of giving the business to family members is simply to give ownership interests outright by assigning the interests directly to them or by issuing stock in their names. Your attorney can help you with the documentation.

ℭℛ *Are there any drawbacks to giving the business outright to my children?*

The most common drawbacks are that you may not want to give up control or may want to retain the income rights to the ownership interests. Beyond that, there may be important business continuity reasons that would discourage outright gifts of ownership interests. For example, an equity interest owned outright by a child may be subject to attachment by the child's creditors or an ex-spouse. As long as the interest is not S corporation stock, using a grantor retained annuity trust (GRAT) or an irrevocable grantor trust to give ownership interests to children would protect against these problems.

Grantor Retained Annuity Trust

ℭℛ *Can I use a grantor retained annuity trust to transfer my business to my children?*

Yes. You create the GRAT and give the business to it. The GRAT receives the income from the business and uses it to pay you an annuity for a specified term of years. After the specified term expires, the remaining trust property is distributed or held in trust for the remainder beneficiaries—children or other family members. Because this is a gift of a future interest, the gift does not qualify for the annual gift tax exclusion. Instead, you must use all or part of your gift tax applicable exclusion.

✿ How do I determine the amount of income I will receive from the GRAT?

As its name implies, the GRAT pays an annuity. The trust pays a fixed rate of return (e.g., 8 percent) on the value of the business as established when you transfer it to the trust, regardless of the actual income realized by the business once it is in the trust. The returns generated by the business in excess of the amount needed to pay the annuity are added to the trust principal for eventual distribution to the children.

✿ What are the income tax implications of a GRAT?

There is no income tax gain or loss recognized at the time you transfer your business to a GRAT, and you do not report the annuity payments as income. However, all income earned by the trust, whether or not distributed to you, is attributable to you, and you will be responsible for the payment of income tax on those amounts. Consequently, your children will receive your tax basis in the business (carryover basis) when they receive the business from the trust.

✿ Is the value of the gift to the trust the value of the business?

No. Because the children are required to wait for a term of years before receiving any benefit from your gift, the value of the business is reduced by their opportunity cost of having to wait for the benefits. The IRS publishes monthly the applicable federal rate (AFR), an interest rate for determining the present value of the remainder interest for the value of the gift.

For example, let's assume that you give your business valued at $1 million to a grantor retained annuity trust that is going to pay you an annuity equal to 7.5 percent of the trust property for a period of 12 years. Assuming the AFR for valuing the remainder interest is

3.2 percent, the value of the gift for gift tax purposes is $290,222. If you have enough of your $1 million gift tax applicable exclusion available to offset the gift, you owe no gift tax.

Not only have you removed the $1 million business from your estate, but you have also removed all future appreciation of the business from your estate. If the business grows at the rate of 10 percent annually, at the end of 12 years, your children will receive property having a value of more than $1.5 million with no additional estate or gift tax on the appreciation. If the value of the property in the trust is increasing faster than the rate the IRS uses to calculate the value of the gift, you will transfer significant property to your children at greatly reduced gift tax costs.

⊙ℛ *What are the advantages of using a GRAT to give my business to my children?*

A grantor retained annuity trust is a popular device in business succession planning when you want to achieve the following:

- Create an ongoing income stream.
- Remove the value of the business from your taxable estate.
- Remove appreciation on the business from your taxable estate.
- Maintain management control of the business until the expiration of the term, and then distribute it to the beneficiaries of the trust.
- Realize significant valuation discounts on the value of the gifts.
- Protect the business from family members' creditors and ex-spouses.
- Give S corporation stock to family members.

⊙ℛ *Are there any disadvantages of using a GRAT for succession planning?*

Yes. If you die before the trust term ends, a portion of the value of all assets transferred to the trust becomes includable in your estate.

In addition, if the business does not generate sufficient income to make the required payments, property of the trust must be distributed "in kind" to meet the payment obligation. As a result, the business would have to be valued annually to determine the in-kind distributions and equity interests being transferred back to you.

Is there any way to mitigate the damages that can occur if I die before the end of the trust term?

A GRAT is especially useful when the business owner has a long life expectancy, no significant health problems, and a family history of longevity. However, if you want to protect your plan against a premature death, you can purchase a life insurance policy to cover the amount of taxes that will have to be paid if the property is included in your estate. To ensure that the life insurance proceeds are kept out of the estate, you will purchase the policy through an irrevocable life insurance trust.

VALUATIONS FOR BUSINESS PLANNING

What does a business valuation do?

A business valuation establishes the value of a business as a whole or the value of a partial interest in a business through quantitative and qualitative analysis. A value is placed on the business assets, both tangible (building, land, and equipment) and intangible (goodwill, trademarks, customer lists).

Why do we need to have the business valued for succession planning?

As part of the business succession planning process, business owners need to predetermine the value of the business for the following reasons:

- If they are entering into a buy-sell agreement, they must know the price of redeeming another owner's interest on his or her death, disability, retirement, or other triggering event. In this case, the business appraiser recommends a valuation formula that is representative, in the years to come, of the present and future values of the business. That formula is incorporated into the buy-sell agreement.

- If they are going to sell the business, the appraiser will usually establish a range of values so that the business owner can set an asking price.

- For estate planning purposes—that is, for purposes of transferring business interests to family members during life or at death—tax value is not always fair market value. The business appraiser must apply the special rules imposed by the IRC and case law that govern the valuation of the various types of privately owned business enterprises for transfer tax purposes. Without a properly prepared report by a qualified appraiser, the business owner may find himself or herself assessed with undervaluation penalties if the IRS audits the estate or gift tax returns.

℣ *Will appraisers apply discounts in valuing the business for any of the purposes you mentioned?*

In valuing a privately owned business enterprise, the appraiser may adjust the value based on the following discounts:

- *Lack-of-marketability discount:* This discount reflects the inherent difficulty in marketing a business that is not registered for sale to the general public and is not freely traded on any stock exchange.
- *Lack-of-control, or minority-interest, discount:* This discount is a reduction in value applicable to the valuation of an equity interest that represents less than 50 percent of the ownership of the company. A valuation discount for noncontrolling equity interests in a business recognizes that an investor will probably pay more for control and will pay less in the absence of control.
- *Key-person discount:* The death or permanent disability of a key employee can be ruinous to a company. The key-person discount recognizes the potential reduction in income, and corresponding impairment of equity value, if business performance truly depends on the continued participation of the few key employees.

The appraiser may also apply premiums to the value, such as a control premium, which is the converse of the lack-of-control discount. If an owner has more than a 50 percent share of the business and the right to control it, a buyer will usually pay more for control.

℣ *I heard that if I own a farm or a small business, I might be able to avoid some estate taxes. Is that true?*

The IRC contains a *special-use valuation* provision by which the land on which a farm or a small business is operated can be valued for estate tax purposes at an amount well below its fair market value.

Generally, land is valued at its highest-and-best-use value, meaning that if the property would be worth more if you had been using it in a different way, then the property is valued at a higher value as though you had been using it in that different and more valuable way. For instance, assume that you owned a building in the middle of downtown in which you rented apartments. If valued as an apartment building, that building may be worth $500,000, but if you had been renting out office space in that building, rather than apartments, the building would be worth $600,000. The building is valued for estate tax purposes at its highest-and-best-use value—$600,000—even though you were not using it for its highest and best use.

Farmers and owners of small businesses are typically hardest hit by this highest-and-best-use rule. There can be a huge difference between the value of land used for farming and the value of the same land if it were subdivided and developed into a new neighborhood. Also, land often is the primary asset of farmers and small-business owners. So, in order to meet the high estate taxes attributable to the land, farmers and small-business owners might have to sell the land, usually at distress prices.

Recognizing that this result is often inequitable, Congress amended the IRC to permit farmers and small-business owners to value their land at its special-use value rather than at its highest-and-best-use value. The total decrease in value, from the highest-and-best-use value to the special-use value, cannot exceed $840,000 (2003 figure, indexed for inflation).

CR *How do I know if my estate will be eligible for the special-use valuation?*

Numerous detailed requirements must be met to be eligible for special-use valuation. These requirements can be summarized as follows:

- The land must be located in the United States.

- The decedent or a member of the decedent's family must have owned the land for 5 out of the 8 years immediately preceding the decedent's death.

- The decedent or a member of the decedent's family must have used the land as a farm or in another business for 5 out of the 8 years immediately preceding the decedent's death.

■ The decedent or a member of the decedent's family must have actively participated in the farming or other business for 5 out of the 8 years immediately preceding the decedent's death.

■ Fifty percent or more of the adjusted value of the decedent's estate (valued at its highest-and-best-use value) must consist of the adjusted value of the land and personal property that was used for the farm or business. The *adjusted value* is the value of the land or personal property reduced by any debt that is secured by the land or personal property.

■ Twenty-five percent or more of the adjusted value of the decedent's estate must consist of the adjusted value of the land that was used for the farm or business.

■ The land must pass from the decedent's estate to members of the decedent's family, and the members of the decedent's family who receive the land must agree to continue to operate the farm or business on the property for at least 10 years after the decedent's death.

PAYMENT OF FEDERAL
ESTATE TAXES

CR *Is there any way to arrange installment payments of federal estate taxes if the estate consists mostly of a family business?*

Yes. If a substantial portion of your wealth consists of an interest in a farm or a closely held business, your estate may not have enough liquid funds to pay the estate taxes attributable to that farm or closely held business. Unless your estate can postpone the payment of some of the estate taxes, your estate might be forced to sell the farm or business interest at a distressed price in order to pay the estate taxes within 9 months after your death.

The IRC contains an exception to the 9-month rule for estates that consist largely of a farm or business interest. If certain requirements are met, your estate can elect to defer the payment of the estate tax for 14 years. For the first 4 years, your estate will have to pay only interest on the deferred taxes.

Not all of your estate taxes can be paid in installments. Only that portion of your estate taxes which is attributable to your farm or business interest can be paid in installments.

To be eligible for installment payments, the following requirements must be met:

- The decedent must have been a U.S. citizen.
- The value of the farm or business interest must be more than 35 percent of the decedent's adjusted gross estate.
- The person who files the decedent's estate tax return must make an election on the return to pay the taxes in installments.

ACTION STEPS

We respectfully present the following action steps to summarize the concepts that we discussed in chapter 10 and to suggest steps that you can take to prepare for meetings with your estate planning team of professionals.

❑ *Identify advisors who can help with your business succession plan.* In our experience, the benefit of having objective, resourceful professionals look at your business and the prospects for its continued success are tremendous. Most small-business owners are too busy running their businesses day to day to focus on the best way to get out of the business when the time comes.

❑ *Understand your objectives.* Business owners should have realistic expectations and specific goals when making succession plans. Simply wanting the business to continue is not enough. With the help of your advisors, your must first identify when you want to leave the business and under what terms. Ask yourself the following questions:

   ■ Who can manage the business if I can't?

   ■ Who wants to own the business and has a reasonable chance of succeeding?

   ■ Am I willing to stay on and help with the business after I sell it?

   ■ Is my goal to sell the business to outsiders or to keep the business in the family?

❑ *If your goal is to keep the business in the family, start early with your planning.* Many business owners want to found businesses that will stay in their families for generations. If that's your goal, you must start planning *now* to make that a reality. You face the following issues:

   ■ Can you afford to give away your business, or do you need to sell it to your children to afford retirement?

- What about children who don't work in the business—What will they inherit?

- How will other employees react when your children take over the business?

❑ *Work closely with a business attorney and valuation expert.* Business succession documents are complex legal documents that require drafting by a skilled attorney. Make sure you are working with an attorney skilled in business planning. But before you get to the implementation stage, you must know what your business is worth. A business appraiser is essential to developing a successful business succession plan.

chapter 11

Asset Protection Planning

THE PURPOSE OF ASSET PROTECTION ESTATE PLANNING

Ⅸ What is asset protection?

Asset protection is positioning your property in such a way that it is not subject to the claims of plaintiffs in lawsuits. Corporations, limited partnerships, and trusts are asset protection devices. They were invented in part to protect assets from the claims of creditors.

A good asset protection plan allows an individual to keep control over assets that might otherwise be subject to court control because of the claims of plaintiffs. Without such a plan, a defendant can virtually be held hostage to the extortionate demands of plaintiffs and their attorneys. An asset protection plan, if properly set up, will avoid these threats and put the potential defendant on a level playing field with the plaintiffs.

Ⅸ Why do I need asset protection estate planning?

Just because someone is competent and careful doesn't mean that he

411

or she will not be sued. We live in a litigious society where a person's competence is no longer as important as who can be blamed for someone's misfortune. Typically, juries like to blame the professional or businessperson because he or she has wealth, income-producing capacity, and insurance.

We spend a lot of time building and learning how to build our fortunes; unfortunately, we spend very little time—and very little is ever taught—on the subject of protecting our fortunes from creditors. Asset protection planning has as its objective the protection of a family's property and income from the attacks of gold-digging plaintiffs or creditors.

○R *Are any assets exempt from creditors?*

By statute, most states and the federal government have defined certain assets as "exempt" from execution by creditors, including the Internal Revenue Service (IRS). *Exempt assets* are those assets that a person is entitled to keep even if the person files bankruptcy or if judgment creditors attempt to seize a person's assets to satisfy a judgment. The amount and type of assets that qualify as exempt vary from state to state. However, state law does not define which assets are protected from execution by the IRS; these assets are specifically defined by federal law.

FRAUDULENT CONVEYANCES

○R *Why is asset protection planning in advance so important?*

You might compare planning for asset protection to buying insurance on your boat. You cannot legally insure the boat after it has sunk. In fact, you cannot buy insurance after the engines have quit and you are taking on water. To carry the analogy even further, you cannot even buy the insurance when the boat is fine if you are out on the ocean in the midst of a raging storm. You need to insure your boat while it is shipshape, the seas are calm, and there is no storm on the horizon.

Fraudulent conveyance laws vary from state to state, but they always have the same general goal: to prevent people from making transfers with the intention of hindering, delaying, or defrauding present or subsequent creditors. Present creditors are easily ascertained.

Questions usually arise about which "subsequent," or future, creditors are protected by fraudulent conveyance laws. Did the individual doing the estate planning make the transfers with the intent to hinder, delay, or defraud specific future creditors?

Fraudulent conveyance laws are not designed to protect everyone who could someday be a person's creditor. They pertain only to those creditors against whom a person harbored an actual fraudulent intent on the date of the transfer, or creditors who were harmed by a person who acted with reckless disregard after conveying assets.

It clearly is *not* a fraudulent conveyance when a transfer is made by a person who has no pending or even threatened claims or has no reason to believe that legal problems will develop in the future, but simply wants to plan for his or her family's future well-being. It clearly *is* a fraudulent conveyance when an individual makes a transfer just before filing for bankruptcy or divorce or immediately after being sued for malpractice. In between these two extremes lies a large gray area of legal interpretation.

If a transfer or conveyance is found to be fraudulent, the remedy serves to "unwind" the transfer so that the asset is again available to the judgment creditor.

⌘ *What if I'm already involved in a lawsuit?*

Under the fraudulent conveyance rules, if you are currently involved in a lawsuit, you will not be able to set up an asset protection trust. This is the general rule unless the maximum potential of the claim is less than your entire net worth. In this situation, it may be possible to transfer some of your assets while still leaving enough to honor the existing claim.

But in such situations, you should always seek proper legal advice.

TOOLS FOR ASSET PROTECTION

Irrevocable Gifts

⌘ *Is giving my assets away an effective asset protection planning technique?*

Giving your assets away is one of the quickest and easiest ways of protecting them from your creditors. However, the transfers should occur before any creditor claim or possible claim arises, or you risk having the transfers considered fraudulent. If they are deemed fraudulent conveyances, the recipients can be forced to give the gifts to your creditors. Thus, at the time that you have no liability or malpractice claims or alleged claims against you is the best time to make gifts.

There are, however, several problems associated with giving property away through a direct gift:

- You lose total control and enjoyment of the assets you give away.
- If the value of the gift in any year to any one person exceeds the annual gift tax exclusion, you must file a federal gift tax return and use a portion of your gift tax applicable exclusion. Once your applicable exclusion is exhausted, you will have to pay federal gift tax and possibly state gift tax as well.
- There is a risk that the recipient of your gift might lose the asset to his or her creditors or to his or her spouse in a divorce action.
- If the recipient of your gift is a minor, he or she cannot own or control property.

Tenancy by the Entirety

ℭ� *I understand that in my state, real estate that is held by my spouse and me in tenancy by the entirety is not subject to the claims of our creditors, and we thereby have some protection for our home or other real estate. Is this true?*

In most states a home or other property held by spouses as tenants by the entirety is protected from the claims of each spouse's separate creditors but is *not* protected from the claims of both spouses' joint creditors. Therefore, if you alone are the debtor or if your spouse alone is the debtor, your tenancy-by-the-entirety property is protected. But if both you and your spouse are liable for the same debt (e.g., a mortgage on the home), your property is not protected.

This protection is available only to property held by a husband and wife as tenants by the entirety. If you hold property jointly with a person other than your spouse, this protection is not available. Also, in some states, you must clearly show that you and your spouse intend to own property in tenancy by the entirety. If the title to the property merely states that you and your spouse own the property as joint tenants with right of survivorship, the protection given to tenancy-by-the-entirety ownership may not apply.

Revocable Trusts

ℭℛ *Can my revocable living trust protect my assets?*

No, but if your trust has "spendthrift" provisions in it, your trust may be able to protect your beneficiaries' inheritance from their creditors. A *spendthrift trust* is a trust which, by its terms, imposes a restraint upon the voluntary or involuntary transfer of the interest held in the trust for the benefit of a beneficiary.

The purpose of a spendthrift trust is to protect a particular beneficiary's inheritance from his or her own improvidence. The beneficiary cannot force the trustee to make distributions upon demand. Similarly, creditors of the beneficiary cannot attach the assets held in the spendthrift trust for the beneficiary or force their early distribution to pay the beneficiary's debts. Creditors can, however, attach assets once they have been distributed to a beneficiary, even if the assets were distributed from a spendthrift trust.

Irrevocable Trusts

ℭℛ *Is there a trust that I can create for my benefit that protects me from my creditors?*

The laws in every state do *not* allow a person to set up a trust, name himself or herself as a trustee and beneficiary, and avoid creditors. The wisdom of this rule is obvious because otherwise trustmakers facing significant liability could simply transfer all their assets into trusts for their own benefit.

In the past few years, the States of Alaska, Delaware, Nevada, and Rhode Island have passed legislation that significantly increases the asset protection of *self-settled trusts* (a trust in which you are the maker and the beneficiary). Under this legislation, you can transfer assets to an irrevocable trust set up in one of these states, and your creditors will be unable to make claims against those assets (even though you are the beneficiary).

The requirements vary from state to state, but there are certain common requirements for creating this type of trust:

- The assets must be located in the state, such as in a bank, bro-kerage, or trust company in the state.
- At least one trustee must be located in the state.
- You, as the trustmaker, may not have the power to revoke the trust.
- The trustee must have sole discretion to make or withhold dis-tributions to you.

Even with the restrictions imposed on these trusts, they are one of the few ways to protect your assets without giving them away entirely.

℞ Can you summarize the features of a self-settled asset protection trust?

The trustmaker establishes an irrevocable trust for his or her family in one of the states that offers this type of trust. The trustmaker is also a beneficiary eligible to receive distributions of income and principal at the discretion of the trustee. The trustmaker then funds the trust with whatever amount of assets he or she is willing to give up control of in exchange for the benefit of creditor protection. Generally, at least some of the assets must reside in the state or with a financial institution in the state in order to be protected. In some states the creditor protection features do not "switch on" for 2 or 3 years; this delay should keep the transfer from being declared a fraudulent transfer by a court.

The transfer to this type of irrevocable trust may be a completed gift for gift tax purposes, which would use up the maker's gift tax applicable exclusion and possibly trigger gift tax. But if the trust-maker retains a special power of appointment or a power to veto pay-ments, the gift is incomplete for federal tax purposes, meaning that no gift occurs unless the trustee makes a distribution to a family member.

℞ Are these trusts an ironclad asset protection plan?

Unfortunately, they are not. The statutes prohibit levying (enforcing judgment) against trust assets for judgments against the maker-beneficiary but do not remove the trustee from the personal jurisdic-tion of any federal court, anywhere in the country. Also, certain types of debts cannot be avoided through these trusts, namely ali-mony, child support, and taxes.

A federal court could still order the trustee to hold up distribution of assets and even to transfer assets to the custody of the court. Refusal to comply could subject the trustee to contempt proceedings by the court. Remember, the true purpose of asset protection is not to cheat creditors to whom the maker owes legitimate debts but to create a level playing field against the predatory tactics of unscrupulous plaintiffs and their lawyers.

Limited Partnerships

ℭ *What asset protection does a limited partnership offer?*

A *charging order* is, in most states, the exclusive remedy available to a creditor who has a judgment against a limited partner. The charging order is served upon the general partner, instructing the general partner to forward any distributions to the creditor instead of the limited partner. The general partner has complete control over distributions; if the general partner makes no distributions, which is the right of the general partner, the creditor has no recourse.

ℭ *What protection do general partners have?*

A limited partnership offers no liability protection for the general partners. Each general partner is responsible for the liabilities and contractual debts and obligations of the partnership.

As a general partner, the way to avoid personal liability is to have another entity with limited liability features as the general partner. It is possible, and even preferable in most cases, for the general partner to create a separate entity to be the general partner to avoid exposure to personal liability.

The entity chosen to be the general partner should insulate its owners from personal liability for its debts and activities. This is usually best accomplished by forming a corporation or limited liability company to be the general partner. For example, you can own a corporation that becomes the general partner of the partnership. As long as you exercise control and management of the partnership through the corporation, your personal liabilities of the limited partnership are limited to your investment in the corporation.

Each type of business that you can use as a general partner has advantages and disadvantages that you must review to determine which type would produce the greatest overall benefit.

ᛃ *As a professional, I'm concerned that the assets I've accumulated could be subject to seizure in a lawsuit. How can I prevent that from happening?*

You can create a limited partnership to hold your assets. The general partner will have to be someone other than you to protect the assets from collection by the judgment creditor. If you are a limited partner, the best that a creditor can do is step into your shoes through a charging order. In that case, the general partner would not authorize distributions, so that the creditor would receive phantom income from the partnership and would be required to pay income tax on it without having the cash flow that created the tax.

The general partner should be a corporation or limited liability company. This should insulate the assets from any attempt by a creditor to collect after a lawsuit.

Limited Liability Companies

ᛃ *What is a limited liability company?*

The *limited liability company (LLC)* is a new business form that is becoming very popular because of its simplicity and flexibility. An LLC offers the following asset protection benefits:

- Like a corporation, all members (owners) of an LLC enjoy limited liability.
- There is no requirement that any member have unlimited liability, as is the case with the limited partnership.
- The management function can be completely severed from ownership so members of an LLC can be actively involved in management without losing their limited liability, which is not the case with the limited partnership.

ᛃ *What protection does an LLC offer its members from the liabilities of the company?*

An LLC offers great protection for its managers and members from the liabilities of the LLC. For example, if the limited liability company fails to repay a bank loan and a lawsuit arises, the limited liability company can be held liable for the bank loan, but the managers, officers, and members generally cannot be held liable. Exceptions exist as to this general rule for situations where the limited liability company is used to perpetrate a fraud or the members fail to follow the rules for holding meetings and documenting decisions made on the LLC's behalf.

ભ *What protection does the LLC have from my personal creditors?*

Property owned by an LLC is generally not available to someone who has a claim against you personally. Thus, someone who has obtained a judgment against you cannot seize a motor vehicle that is titled in the name of the LLC.

However, your ownership interest in the LLC is subject to the claims of your personal creditors. For example, in Wyoming the exclusive remedy for a creditor of an LLC member is to obtain a charging order, just like with a partnership.

A TECHNIQUE THAT
DOESN'T WORK

ભ *I attended an estate planning seminar recently where the speaker discussed the use of a pure-equity trust to protect all one's assets from creditors. Does this trust work, and if it does, why isn't everyone using it?*

The easiest answer to this question is the old proviso, "If it sounds too good to be true, it probably is." Some people claim that the "pure-equity trust" (also called a "constitutional trust," "business trust," and similar names) is perfectly legal, and they can even cite court cases to claim support for their claims. But, in fact, the law offers no support for the legality of these trusts or the benefits they allegedly convey. The IRS has made clear that it considers these trusts "abusive" and contrary to established law.

ACTION STEPS

We respectfully present the following action steps to summarize the concepts that we discussed in chapter 11 and to suggest steps that you can take to prepare for meetings with your estate planning team of professionals.

❑ *Assess your need for asset protection.* Whether you need asset protection planning is a function of your potential exposure to lawsuits. Consider the following as you decide your asset protection needs:

- Are you employed in a profession or activity that makes you a potential defendant?

- Have you been sued before?

- Are there any gaps in your liability insurance? Do you need to raise the policy limits?

❑ *Implement your asset protection plan before trouble starts.* The best time to engage in asset protection planning is when things are going smoothly. Once you have been sued, it's too late to shield your assets from the plaintiff. Even if litigation is only threatened, it may be too late.

❑ *Work with an asset protection attorney.* Asset protection is a complex legal field; only an attorney skilled in asset protection planning can adequately assist you. Ask your current attorney if he or she has expertise in this field. If the answer is no, ask him or her to refer you to an attorney who regularly does this type of planning for clients.

chapter 12

Planning for Seniors

ELDER LAW

CR *What is elder law?*

Elder law, by definition, is helping the elderly. *Elder law* is a special area of legal practice that focuses on issues of particular relevance to senior citizens. Elder law attorneys typically advise their clients on Social Security, Medicare, Medicaid, and other governmental assistance programs for the elderly. They also provide guidance on planning for incapacity, long-term-care insurance, and all aspects of retirement benefits. Elder law attorneys provide Medicaid planning to protect assets from being consumed by nursing home costs.

CR *Can my financial advisor help me with some of these things?*

Although financial advisors cannot practice law, many financial advisors today specialize in planning for the elderly, especially as these issues relate to their clients' financial plans. They are also the most qualified to evaluate long-term-care insurance products. As we've mentioned throughout this book, your financial advisor and attorney should work together to provide you with the best plan and the best solutions to specific problems.

421

CR *I'm worried that as I get older, I may need someone to handle my
finances for me. What is the best way to prepare for this situation?*

The safest way for you to handle the possibility that you may
become unable to act on your own behalf is to use the protections
afforded with a revocable living trust.

You can designate one or more cotrustees whom you can authorize to act for you in the event that you become unable to handle
your affairs. They can be individuals or institutions, or a combination
of both.

You can give them a broad range of authority to cover foresee-
able problems that may arise, including authority to make decisions
concerning your living arrangements, finances, and legal matters.
You also want to be sure to have all the other documents we discussed in Chapter 8, Planning for Disability.

CR *Should I seek out an attorney who specializes in elder law?*

Yes. Elder law is a distinct specialty that requires enormous knowledge with regard to the nuances of federal and state statutes and
compliance regulations. As with any other area of law, there are
many intricacies and frequent changes, and someone who concen-
trates in elder law will be able to provide you with the most accurate
and up-to-date information.

LONG-TERM CARE

CR *What is the greatest financial risk in my retirement years?*

As you plan for retirement, remember that your doctor and hospital
bills are not your largest financial risk. The high cost of long-term
convalescent health care presents the greatest financial risk for retirees.
Unfortunately, most people do not recognize this problem. According to a survey conducted by AARP, 79 percent of those expecting to
need nursing home care believed incorrectly that Medicare would
pay the bill.

CR *What is long-term care?*

For purposes of governmental programs and insurance, *long-term care* is care or assistance provided to individuals who are functionally impaired. *Functional impairment* means that a person needs care because of cognitive or other impairment and/or is unable to perform at least two of the six *activities of daily living* without assistance. These activities are bathing, dressing, toileting, eating, medicating, and transferring in and out of bed or a wheelchair. Long-term care is further defined as a stay of more than 30 consecutive days in an establishment where food and shelter are furnished to four or more persons unrelated to the owner or operator and where some treatments or services are provided that meet some need beyond the basic provision of food and shelter.

Such care may be provided by adult-care homes, hospitals, psychiatric facilities, licensed nonmedical residential-care facilities, and other facilities that meet the provisions in the definition of long-term care.

◌ঽ *Are there different levels of long-term care?*

There are four levels of long-term care defined and provided by nursing-care providers:

1. *Skilled care:* Skilled care is care that demands the greatest expertise and requires that care be provided on a 24-hour basis by personnel such as registered nurses; licensed practical nurses; respiratory, occupational, physical, or speech therapists; and related professionals. Typically, skilled care is a half step away from full hospitalization.

2. *Intermediate care:* Intermediate care is care with some skilled services and is not required on a 24-hour basis.

3. *Custodial care:* Custodial care is the most basic level of care provided and the care category within which most benefit recipients fall. It is care in which the patient receives assistance in the six activities of daily living. Typically, providers in the custodial-care area are not necessarily licensed professionals.

4. *Home care:* When medical care or therapy is required, home care is provided at the patient's home. Home care can include such personal services as preparing meals, cleaning the house, and helping the patient bathe and dress. Other home-care services include transportation, assistance with nutritional meals and the securing of goods and services, and certain psychological support systems to raise patients' spirits.

Depending on the severity of an individual's functional impairment, the first three levels of care can be made available and be appropriate at home or in an assisted-living or skilled-care facility.

◌ঽ *Why should I plan for my long-term care or disability?*

Let's start with some statistics to evaluate the likelihood that you may need assistance with long-term care. Today, the average life expectancy for a person who reaches the age of 65 is 18 more years—or age 83. A national study done in 2001 concluded that 6.4 million people age 65 and older need long-term care; people age 65 and older face a 40 percent lifetime chance of entering a nursing home.

Home health care has become a burgeoning industry primarily because it tends to run about one-half the cost of nursing home care. The effect this cost differential will have in coming years is hard to estimate, although it is likely that the number of people entering nursing homes will decrease as more and more people seek assistance in their own homes.

If you are destitute and qualify for public assistance through Medicaid, your alternatives are limited to making sure that appropriate exemptions have been provided and planned for. If you are among those who would not immediately qualify for benefits, you have the choice of divesting yourself of your assets in order to qualify or doing whatever you can to provide for your own care through financial planning and the acquisition of long-term-care insurance.

◌ঽ *I'm concerned about how the cost of care during a long-term illness or nursing home stay will affect my assets. Is this a legitimate concern? What is the cost of long-term care?*

It is a legitimate and important concern. The cost of long-term care varies from city to city, but the national average cost for in-home care runs $37 an hour for a licensed practical nurse; and the average annual cost for custodial care in a skilled- or intermediate-care nursing home is $57,700.

The two most common sources of payment, however, remain payment from individuals' own assets and payment by the Medicaid system. Medicaid has become known as the "payer of last resort." In recent years, assisting clients with qualification for Medicaid benefits has been a growth industry. In stark contrast to earlier views, both Congress and the state governments have begun to develop incentives encouraging the use of privately purchased long-term-care insurance.

⚬⃰ *Isn't elder planning just for people who don't have money?*

There are people who have substantial assets whose estates are dramatically affected when one or both spouses require long-term care. It may be emotionally devastating for your spouse or your children to have to liquidate your assets to pay the exorbitant costs of nursing home care, even when you have sufficient assets to liquidate. It is also difficult for family members to deal with the administrative and financial hassles of the Medicaid application process.

If it is possible for you to consider long-term-care insurance, you should. Many people feel peace of mind in knowing that they will be taken care of properly when the time comes. Also, many plans offer the option to cover in-home care. This may enable your family members to take care of you in a way that they may not have otherwise been able to do. You can view your long-term-care insurance policy as a gift to your family members, protecting their inheritance.

⚬⃰ *What is a prudent way to plan for our senior years?*

The first line of defense is to purchase long-term-care insurance while you are in your forties or fifties, when the cost is manageable. In your fifties or sixties, you should consider putting your name on the waiting list at one or more continuing-care retirement communities. These are facilities that offer a range of care and housing options depending on your needs. Many residents start out living in apartments or townhouses while they are self-sufficient but eventually move to adjoining facilities that offer more care as the resident requires more assistance with daily living activities.

The biggest mistake people make is not putting their names on lists just as if they were applying to one or more colleges. Applying is not a commitment to move to the facility. Often it simply involves paying a nonrefundable processing fee and leaving a refundable deposit.

⚬⃰ *Why should I worry about long-term-care planning when my children have promised to take care of me when I grow old?*

While our children may want to return the loving care we gave them when they were too little to care for themselves, they may not be able to care for us when that need arises. They may live too far away to provide daily care. They may have families of their own to care for. There may not be adequate room for you to live with them in their home. In spite of these limitations, your need for daily care will remain. The best way for you to maintain as much control as possible over your own destiny is to plan and pay now for the care you will inevitably require in the future.

 CR *Won't there always be a governmental program to pay for my care?*

There have been several legislative attempts to limit and cut back senior citizen programs. Given the emphasis on attempting to balance the federal budget, it is not unreasonable to expect that fewer, rather than more, resources will be made available to these programs in the new millennium.

SOCIAL SECURITY

CR *What is Social Security?*

Social Security is a federal program that provides retirement, disability, and survivor benefits to wage earners and their spouses, former spouses, widows and widowers, and children. A wage earner's eligibility for retirement benefits is based upon his or her work history— the years during which the wage earner paid taxes into the Social Security trust fund. The amount of monthly retirement benefits Social Security pays is a function of a variety of factors, including the number of years of past work and the amount of earnings.

CR *How do I find out what my Social Security benefits will be?*

Your income from Social Security will depend on your work history. If you are not already receiving this statement automatically, Social Security makes it easy for you to find out what work history has been reported in your name. You can obtain a Request for Earnings and Benefit Estimate Statement (SSA-7004) from your local Social Security office. After you have completed the form, mail it to Social Security Administration, P.O. Box 3600, Wilkes-Barre, PA 18767-3600. You will receive a copy of your work history and an estimate of your benefits when you retire. You can also request the information online from the Social Security Administration at www.ssa.gov.

CR *How does early retirement affect my ability to receive Social Security benefits?*

Difficult social and economic issues face many older workers when they are forced to take early retirement by companies that are either downsizing or going out of business. Many of these workers believe that early retirement includes the right to begin receiving Social Security retirement benefits, but full benefits are not available until people reach the age of 65. A person may elect to begin receiving benefits at 62, but the amount of the benefits is reduced.

Individuals and couples planning for retirement should understand that there is pending legislation that proposes to increase the minimum age at which Social Security benefits will be paid. This potential change in the Social Security system may have a substantial financial impact on many retirees and should be considered as part of an overall retirement plan.

MEDICARE

What Medicare Is

CR *What is Medicare?*

Medicare is a federal "health insurance program." Within the Medicare program, there is a Part A and a Part B.

Medicare Part A is the Medicare hospitalization insurance program and is similar to private health insurance, containing many of the same concepts and notions of hospitalization insurance. It provides benefits for hospital care and post-hospitalization skilled care. Part A involves deductibles, co-insurance payments, and benefit limits.

Part B is the Medicare medical (nonhospital care) insurance program that provides broader coverage, primarily for outpatient services, and is also similar to private health insurance, imposing deductibles and co-insurance payment requirements. Part B is optional and requires a monthly premium.

Eligibility

♋ *Who is eligible for Medicare?*

The following are automatically eligible for Medicare Part A benefits without the payment of any premiums for such coverage:

- Individuals who are 65 years of age or older and who are also eligible to receive Social Security payments or Railroad Retirement benefits
- Persons of any age who meet certain disability requirements
- Individuals who suffer from permanent kidney failure
- Certain spouses, divorced spouses, and widows and widowers of certain wage earners
- Disabled children of certain wage earners
- Individuals born before 1909, even if they are not eligible for Social Security retirement benefits.

Everyone who is eligible for Medicare Part A is also eligible to participate in Medicare Part B and is automatically enrolled in Part B. For individuals who do not opt out of the Medicare Part B coverage, they pay a monthly premium that is automatically deducted from their Social Security checks.

♋ *What if I'm not eligible to receive Social Security or Railroad Retirement benefits. Can I still apply for Medicare?*

Medicare is available to all qualified individuals regardless of their income or economic status. Even if you are not eligible for Social Security payments or Railroad Retirement benefits, you are eligible to receive Medicare benefits as of age 65. You must voluntarily enroll in the Medicare program and must enroll in both Part A and Part B and must pay a premium for both.

♋ *How do I apply for Medicare benefits?*

You are eligible for Medicare the first day of the month that you turn age 65. So if you are 65 on March 30, you are eligible for Medicare benefits on March 1 of that same year. How you apply depends on your situation:

- If you are not yet 65 years of age and not yet receiving Social Security benefits, you apply for Medicare by filling out a Medicare application at your local Social Security office. When you apply, you elect to receive Part A benefits and may opt out of receiving Part B coverage. You can go to your local Social Security office and apply in person before you turn 65, and your benefits will then automatically begin when you turn 65.

- If you are not yet 65 but are already receiving Social Security benefits, you will automatically be enrolled in Medicare Part A and Part B when you turn 65; however, you will have to opt out of the Part B coverage if you do not wish to pay for it.

- If you are 65 years of age or over and are just submitting an application for Social Security benefits, then you will also automatically be enrolled in Medicare.

What Medicare Covers

ca *What does Medicare Part A cover?*

Medicare Part A primarily covers care that is associated with hospitalization. It covers the following:

- Inpatient hospital care and short-term acute medical emergencies, such as doctors' bills and hospital expenses for surgery to a broken bone or treatment for a bout of pneumonia

- If the recipient has no Part B coverage, Medicare Part A will cover some home care stemming from an illness or injury from which the patient is expected to recover.

- Hospice care

ca *Does it cover any other expenses?*

On a limited basis, Medicare Part A also covers:

- a limited number of days' stay in a nursing home or other Medicare-approved convalescent facility, and
- skilled care for rehabilitation needs after an acute condition strikes.

For the limited services covered, there may be a deductible, and in many instances Medicare requires a copayment.

❦ *What skilled care will Medicare pay for?*

For skilled care to be covered by Medicare Part A, these four requirements must be met:

1. The patient's residence in the Medicare-approved facility must follow a hospital stay of at least 3 days.

2. The patient must enter the facility within 30 days of the hospitalization stay.

3. The patient must require the skilled services on a 24-hour basis under a doctor's care.

4. The patient must have the potential for improvement.

❦ *What are the limits of Medicare Part A payments for skilled care?*

Even if a person satisfies all of the four requirements for Medicare Part A payment of skilled care, it will only pay a "limited" benefit for these skilled services in a nursing home or other convalescent facility.

For example, if you were hospitalized for a period of 3 days and your doctor prescribed medical care that must take place each day, Medicare will pay for skilled care for a period of up to 100 days following the hospitalization. If you are on Medicare, the first 20 days are fully paid; and provided the beneficiary can demonstrate improvement over those first 20 days from the skilled care, the next 80 days are paid by Medicare on a co-insurance basis (you pay part of the cost). After this additional 80 days, all Medicare Part A payments to the nursing home for the skilled care stop. The 100-day coverage is the lifetime maximum number of days that Medicare will cover. Within the 100-day limitation, you can qualify for further care, but only with a new illness and a new hospital stay.

To make matters worse, there are often disagreements as to the definition of skilled care, and they frequently result in disputes over whether the patient qualifies for Medicare during the initial 20- and 80-day periods.

It cannot be overemphasized that, as a general rule, Medicare is *not* an available resource for paying the costs associated with long-term skilled care in a nursing home.

If I need to have nursing care, but don't want to go into a nursing home, will Medicare pay for my in-home medical care?

Medicare will cover skilled in-home health care stemming from an illness or injury from which the patient is expected to recover. In order to qualify for home health care, the patient must meet Medicare's definition of homebound. The care must be provided by a Medicare-certified home health agency. It will cover only intermittent visits, and the number of visits is limited and varied based on the patient's condition.

What does Medicare Part B cover?

Optional Medicare Part B primarily covers bills associated with outpatient care. This includes visits to doctors, durable medical equipment, laboratory tests, X-rays, ambulance services, therapy, dressings, splints, and related services. Medicare Part B also covers home health care stemming from an illness or injury from which the patient is expected to recover.

These services are *not* paid 100 percent by Medicare. Rather, after satisfying an annual deductible payment, Medicare Part B will pay 80 percent of the allowed amount. The Medicare Part B recipient will be required to pay the remaining 20 percent.

What Medicare Doesn't Cover

What doesn't Medicare Part A cover?

Medicare Part A does not cover physician and surgery expenses, ambulance services, outpatient hospital services, diagnostic care, or custodial care. Once you have recovered as much as you can from an acute medical condition, you may still need assistance with the six activities of daily living. The level of care you would need then is not of a skilled nature, but of a custodial level. Medicare will not pay for such custodial care. You will have to provide for and pay for such care yourself.

Supplemental Medicare Insurance

What is Medicare Part C or Medicare+Choice?

You may also have the option of receiving Medicare Part C, also known as Medicare+Choice. Medicare+Choice is a more recent option for Medicare recipients. It is an alternative to Medicare Part A and Part B and may be available from your state in different versions. Most Medicare+Choice plans are HMO-style plans that tend to cover more than Medicare Parts A and B but may require a higher premium than Part B.

> ଔ *I received a brochure in the mail about medigap insurance. What is it?*

It is important to remember that Medicare coverage is only partial, and in many circumstances, there is a significant copayment. Therefore, anyone eligible to receive Medicare should seriously consider purchasing some kind of supplemental insurance.

For example, optional Medicare Part B primarily covers bills associated with outpatient care but are not paid 100 percent by Medicare. Rather, after satisfying an annual deductible payment, Medicare Part B will pay 80 percent of the allowed amount, and the patient will be required to pay the remaining 20 percent. This difference of 20 percent that is required to be paid by the Medicare patient is often referred to as a Medicare "gap." Medicare Part B recipients have the option of privately purchasing "supplemental" or "medigap" or "mediplus" health insurance to cover this gap and other costs not paid for by Medicare Part A or Part B. The costs that the Medicare supplement will cover are:

- Part A and Part B deductibles
- Part A copayments
- Part B co-insurance
- Hospital expenses after the lifetime reserve days have been exhausted
- Certain treatments or services not covered by Medicare
- Part B excess charges

Medicare supplemental insurance does *not* reimburse for care that Medicare does not cover, such as long-term care in a nursing home.

> ଔ *I have been told that Medicare supplemental insurance policies are not a good buy. Should I consider such a policy?*

Medicare supplemental policies have drawn a lot of attention from consumer groups and legislators because, in the past, many policies did not cover what they promised, and some did no more than duplicate coverage already provided by Medicare. The products were sometimes "oversold." There are examples of elderly people having bought ten or more policies, all in force at the same time, paying a large percentage of their income on premiums. It is important for you to discuss the purchase of this insurance with your financial advisor, your accountant, or a qualified insurance professional.

MEDICAID

What Medicaid Is

❧ *What is Medicaid?*

Medicaid is a joint federal and state medical assistance program for the aged, blind, and disabled with limited or no means of paying for medical care. The federal government provides funding assistance for each state's Medicaid program, but each state makes its own eligibility rules. There are very strict eligibility requirements for this program, because it was created to serve people in severe financial need. It will pay for almost all long-term-care costs, some home- and community-based services, as well as many of the Medicare costs for which the insured is responsible. A Medicaid recipient does not actually receive direct cash benefits but, rather, receives benefits by way of payments made directly to his or her health care providers, such as doctors, hospitals, nursing homes, medical testing facilities, pharmacies, and dentists.

❧ *How is the Medicaid program administered?*

Although Medicaid is a federal program, Medicaid is administered by each state's welfare agency, such as the Department of Human Services. Approved care and services under Medicaid are funded almost equally by the federal government and each state. While Congress has created federal guidelines for the administration of many programs that may assist the elderly, each state, and even local communities, can alter the general rules and regulations. Specific services and payment rates are established by each welfare agency, which reviews and periodically adjusts them. It is essential that you check with competent professional advisors to determine how the laws in your state and community affect a particular program's benefits as they would apply to your situation.

Eligibility

⚕ *Who qualifies for Medicaid?*

A person qualifies for Medicaid if he or she is determined to be categorically or medically needy. Persons who are *categorically needy* are eligible only because they meet requirements relating to old age, blindness, or disability and are below certain asset and income levels such as those who are receiving state public assistance or who receive Supplemental Security Income. *Medically needy* persons qualify for eligibility only because they fall within certain categories (e.g., the blind) and their income and other resources fall below set levels set by each state. Not everyone who is poor and in need of medical care qualifies for Medicaid.

⚕ *Who would qualify for the long-term-care benefits from Medicaid?*

Although each state may impose slightly different conditions for a patient to be eligible for Medicaid benefits, in general Medicaid covers long-term care in a skilled-care facility provided the patient can satisfy two conditions:

1. Personal income and asset holdings are under strict limits.
2. Medical criteria are satisfied by being unable to perform at least two of the six activities of daily living.

⚕ *I don't own much. Will I be eligible for Medicaid long-term care?*

It is important to remember that Medicaid is a program intended for people requiring public assistance; therefore, the amount that a single person can have, and still be considered eligible for Medicaid, is extremely low. This means that almost any single person who owns a retirement plan, life insurance, or an investment account will need to do some type of planning before becoming eligible for Medicaid long-term care.

Medicaid eligibility requirements are different for couples when one spouse is living outside of a nursing home facility (the *community spouse*). The Medicaid long-term-care program takes into consideration that the community spouse will continue to require means to support himself or herself. Therefore, the community spouse is able to retain significantly more assets and income than the spouse who is living in the nursing home.

Asset Limits

C⅋ *What is the asset limit you mentioned?*

The asset limit for Medicaid qualification involves the determination of what assets are "countable" towards this limit. If a person has nonexempt assets that exceed the limit, then the applicant will not qualify for Medicaid.

Assets are divided into three classes:

1. Countable assets (also called "nonexempt" or "available" in some states)
2. Exempt assets (also referred to as "noncountable" assets in some states)
3. Inaccessible assets

C⅋ *What are countable assets?*

Countable assets are any personal financial resources owned or controlled by the applicant and are specifically used by the applicant for his or her care. They generally include:

- Cash
- Stocks and bonds
- All general investments
- All tax-qualified pension plans if the applicant is retired
- Deferred annuities if not annuitized
- All life insurance policies with cash surrender value if the death benefit exceeds $1,500
- Vacation property
- Inherited property

❧ What are exempt assets?

Exempt assets are acknowledged by Medicaid but are not used in determining eligibility. They generally include:

- A small sum of money, usually under $3,000
- Primary residence
- Prepaid funeral (some states limit its cost)
- Term life insurance
- Business assets, if applicant derives a livelihood from them
- A car for personal use (some states cap its value)
- Personal items

❧ What are inaccessible assets?

Inaccessible assets are assets that have been transferred by the applicant to other people or to trusts prior to application.

❧ How much in value can a person have and still qualify for Medicaid?

In order to be eligible for Medicaid benefits, a nursing home resident may usually have no more than $3,000 in countable assets. The community spouse is limited to one-half of the couple's joint countable assets, which can range from approximately $18,000 to $90,000, depending on the state in which you live.

❧ I have a policy for long-term care. How will payments from this affect my eligibility for Medicaid?

Insurance coverage is available to help pay the cost of long-term care. Generally, most of the policies allow for payments to be made either to the individual or to the nursing facility. The benefits are counted as income and either cover the monthly cost of long-term care or are applied toward it with Medicaid paying the difference. Thus, the long-term-care insurance is treated as a third-party resource, which does not adversely affect eligibility for Medicaid.

❧ I heard that I will have to give up my home in order to qualify for Medicaid. Is that true?

If you state on the application for Medicaid that you intend to return home, the agency responsible for administering the Medicaid program will not take your home. However, they will attach a lifetime lien to your home. If your home is sold during your lifetime, the state will then be reimbursed for any medical expenses that Medicaid has paid on your behalf. Depending on your state, the governmental agency may also attach a postmortem lien to your house to ensure reimbursement after your death. If you do not intend to return home, your house becomes a countable asset, which may disqualify you from Medicaid eligibility by putting you over the asset limit.

There are a few exceptions to these general rules. Your house will *not* be considered a countable asset and a postmortem lien will not be attached if any of the following people continue to live in your home: your spouse, a minor or disabled child, or your adult child who has been providing in-home care as an alternative to nursing home care.

Income Limits

CR *How much income may I keep and still qualify for Medicaid?*

It depends on the eligibility group into which you fall. Each state sets an income limit for each Medicaid eligibility group and determines what income counts toward that limit.

CR *How do I apply for Medicaid?*

The basic Medicaid rule for nursing home residents is that they must pay all of their income, minus certain deductions, to the nursing home. The deductions include a small amount for personal needs; a deduction for any noncovered medical expenses; and in the case of a married applicant, an allowance for the community spouse who continues to live at home and needs income for his or her support. The income of the community spouse is not counted in determining the Medicaid applicant's eligibility.

Estate Recovery

CR *Can a state agency recover payments made to a Medicaid recipient for nursing home costs?*

Federal law requires each state to seek recovery of amounts paid by the state for certain Medicaid beneficiaries. The state must, at a minimum, seek recovery for services provided to a person of any age in a nursing facility, intermediate-care facility for the mentally retarded, or other medical institution. The state may, at its option, recover amounts up to the total amount spent on the individual's behalf for medical assistance for other services under the state's plan. For individuals aged 55 or older, states are required to seek recovery of payments from the individual's estate for nursing facility services, home- and community-based services, and related hospital and prescription drug services. States have the option of recovering payments for all other Medicaid services provided to these individuals.

What Medicaid Covers

CR If I need to be in a nursing facility, will Medicaid pay the cost?

Residential (custodial) long-term care is covered. *Residential care* is defined as supervised, nonmedical care in a residence that has been assessed, licensed, or registered by the appropriate state agency.

The facility is to provide care that matches the individual's needs, limitations, and abilities. Care includes assistance with making and keeping appointments for regular or emergency medical care; meeting nutritional needs; taking medications; contacting and maintaining relationships with family and friends; and gaining access to recreational, social, religious, and other community activities. Laundry services and necessary transportation are also included. Each of these services is in addition to assistance with the necessary activities of daily living.

CR Does it cover any medical needs outside of a long-term-care facility?

Although each individual state may include its own benefits, every state is required to cover the following long-term-care-related services under Medicaid:

- Inpatient hospital services (except in institutions treating mental disease or tuberculosis)
- Outpatient hospital services and rural health clinic services
- Other laboratory services and X-ray services

- Physicians' services provided to the patient in the doctors' offices, the patient's home, the hospital, a skilled-care facility, or elsewhere
- Skilled-care-facility services
- Limited home health care services
- Transportation to medical facilities

Medicaid does not pay for any home care nor does it provide for any community-based facilities.

MEDICAID PLANNING

C**R** *What is Medicaid planning, and how does it relate to my estate plan?*

Medicaid planning involves the structuring of an individual's income and assets to attempt to ensure eligibility for benefits available under Medicaid.

Each state, as well as the federal government, sets limits on the assets and income one can own and still remain eligible for Medicaid. When one's assets exceed Medicaid's limits, they must either be properly disposed of or be used to pay for expenses Medicaid would otherwise cover.

When countable assets render individuals ineligible for Medicaid assistance, these people must "spend down" their assets until they have few enough remaining to meet the eligibility requirements. Medicaid planning invokes a variety of strategies to reduce a person's assets—often years before illness or death—to achieve Medicaid eligibility.

C**R** *Why should I include Medicaid planning as part of the estate planning process?*

Medicaid's eligibility requirements—and the related implementing rules imposed by each state—are complex, far-reaching, and very limiting. More important, they are often inconsistent with estate planning strategies that might be employed in the absence of a goal of establishing Medicaid eligibility. Medicaid planning contemplates, in large part, reducing your estate long before you might need long-term health care. Estate planning contemplates, generally, control of most of your assets during your lifetime and the dispersal of your assets on your death.

People with substantial wealth will be able to afford whatever long-term-care expenses they incur. For such people, there is no reason to structure their affairs so that they will qualify for Medicaid benefits. Some are reluctant, on ethical grounds, to accept Medicaid benefits to pay for services that they could afford without Medicaid eligibility planning. For others, however, ensuring access to Medicaid is an important planning goal.

Whether Medicaid planning is appropriate for you depends on a consideration of many factors, including your age when planning is considered; your health; the assets you anticipate being able to apply to any long-term care you may eventually need; the range of possible long-term-care costs; the cost of appropriate long-term-care insurance, if available; other insurance and benefit plans such as employee benefit plans, which might provide you with financial support if you should require long-term care; and the eligibility criteria of the state in which you reside.

Keep in mind that there is continuing political pressure to reduce governmental benefits in general. Medicaid eligibility rules change frequently, and there can be no guarantee that Medicaid benefits will continue to be available indefinitely in their present form.

☙ Should I plan to avoid Medicaid?

Many people do. Here are some reasons why long-term-care planning for many people is planning for Medicaid avoidance, not Medicaid eligibility:

- *Medical necessity requirement:* In addition to establishing financial eligibility, a Medicaid applicant must prove a medical necessity for nursing home care. If you are lucky and healthy, you may never be able to meet that requirement.

- *Better care:* If you can afford to live in one of the better facilities, you may well prefer to do so rather than try to preserve assets for other family members—especially if there is no community spouse or if available resources are likely to be sufficient to privately pay for your life expectancy.

- *Lack of facilities:* Because "Medicaid beds" pay less than "private pay" beds, many facilities have only a limited number of Medicaid beds.

- *Your values:* Many people see Medicaid as a stigmatizing form of welfare and are resistant to applying for it, even if it is clear that they will probably be eligible eventually.

You should begin by analyzing your income and income-producing assets to determine whether you have sufficient income to provide for your own needs in the event that you do need assistance. You should also determine your cash shortfall on a monthly basis in case you, your spouse, or both of you need assistance. Then you should consider ways to enhance income.

Your planning options include long-term-care insurance; life insurance with long-term-care, loan, or cash-value provisions; annuities; and turning non-income-producing assets into income-producing assets.

ᑐ *My grandmother is going into a nursing home. Her caseworker said that the nursing home would fill out her Medicaid application for free. Should we have the nursing home fill out the application, or do we need to hire an attorney to do it?*

It is worthwhile at the outset to consult an attorney, because the attorney may find ways that the nursing home might never consider for her to preserve some of her assets for her heirs. Furthermore, once her Medicaid application has been submitted, she may have no further opportunity to transfer any assets to her heirs. An attorney might find ways of saving assets from being absorbed by Medicaid, whereas the nursing home may lack both the expertise and the incentive to do so. It is important to note that this must be done before the application is submitted.

What Not to Do before Seeking Professional Assistance

ᑐ *Are there common mistakes that people make when considering Medicaid?*

The top mistakes people make with Medicaid:

- Thinking it's too late to plan
- Giving away assets too early
- Ignoring important safe-harbor rules
- Failing to take advantage of protections for the spouse of a nursing home resident
- Applying for Medicaid too early
- Applying for Medicaid too late
- Not getting expert help

Planning Options

CR *What are some commonly used strategies in Medicaid planning?*

Making asset transfers earlier than the 36-month look-back period before an application for Medicaid is the most common planning technique relied upon by practitioners. In some states divorce is used as a strategy to maximize the assets that the healthy—divorced— spouse may use and enjoy. Life estates, income trusts, and, with careful planning, outright gifts, can also be effective planning tools.

Outright Gifts

CR *I was told by a friend of mine that if my mother gave all of her assets away to her children and grandchildren, she would then be eligible for Medicaid and not have to pay for her long-term-care coverage in any facility. Is this true?*

There are strict rules against transferring assets just to qualify for Medicaid benefits. In the past, some people gave substantial assets to family members and then applied for Medicaid. In general, if a person now transfers assets for less than fair market value within 36 months (the look-back period) of applying for Medicaid, they will lose eligibility for a certain number of months, based on a formula set by each state. Your parents should check with competent professionals before doing anything, including applying for Medicaid.

CR *How does the look-back-period rule work?*

A common misconception is that if you give anything away within 36 months of entering a nursing home you are permanently ineligible for Medicaid assistance. In reality, a gift only imposes a period of ineligibility. As an illustration, if you give away $100,000 and the average monthly cost of a nursing home is $5,000 in your area, you divide the amount of the gift by the monthly nursing home cost, which gives an ineligibility period of 20 months. If your gift was over 20 months ago, you are now eligible for Medicaid assistance if you meet the income and asset tests.

  ◌ᴙ *This is the second marriage for both my wife and me. We made a prenuptial agreement before our marriage. Are my assets exempt from being consumed to pay for my wife's needs if she requires nursing home care?*

No. The Medicaid agency in your state will look at both your and your wife's assets to determine her eligibility for Medicaid. They will ignore your prenuptial agreement and will allow you as the community spouse to keep only a certain amount of countable assets as determined by your state before your wife will qualify for Medicaid.

Life Estate

  ◌ᴙ *If I go into a nursing home, I don't want the state to take my home. How can I protect it?*

In some states, you can create a life estate and, upon your death, your heirs can inherit your house without being subject to Medicaid reimbursement. However, federal regulations allow states to recover Medicaid expenditures based on the value of the life estate interest. If your state has adopted this portion of the federal guidelines, then your state Medicaid agency can recover up to the value of your life estate interest from your estate, so a life estate would protect only a portion of your house from recovery. These laws change constantly, so it is important to remain in touch with your attorney.

  Any gift, including your house, will disqualify you from receiving Medicaid benefits for a period of time. There are also tax consequences to making gifts. It is important to consult with your attorney regarding capital gain, income, and estate tax considerations.

  ◌ᴙ *What is a life estate?*

A *life estate* is a particular type of home ownership arrangement with two different ownership interests: a life estate interest and a remainder interest. Often, for Medicaid purposes, elders keep the life estate interest in their home and give the remainder interest to their heirs. The life estate interest allows you to essentially retain control of your home while you are alive. You can live in your home as long as you like and cannot be removed against your will. You can make any improvements or additions to the property that you want. You continue to pay taxes associated with the home and can rent the property to tenants if you choose.

The remainder interest is a partial ownership interest in your home, which remains after your death. Upon your death, the remaindermen (the heirs to whom you gifted your home) receive the property without a probate proceeding.

There are a few things to consider when you create a life estate. First, when you create a life estate, you are making a gift of the remainder interest. This gift will render you ineligible for Medicaid for up to 3 years from the date of the gift. The period of ineligibility will depend on the value of the remainder interest and the monthly cost of nursing home services in your area.

Second, you will need the consent of your remaindermen if you want to sell or refinance your home during your life. To sell your home, you must first gain approval from everyone who has an interest in the property. In addition, the remaindermen are entitled to their share of the proceeds. If your home is sold while you are in a nursing home, the proceeds of the sale to which you are entitled will have to be spent on nursing home care.

Irrevocable Income Trust

℞ *What is an income trust?*

An *income trust* is applicable only to individuals who require nursing home care and whose monthly income exceeds the amount necessary to qualify for Medicaid. It must be an irrevocable trust.

℞ *How does an income trust work?*

You establish the trust and transfer your property to it. The purpose of an income trust is to reduce an individual's income below that required to qualify for Medicaid. The sole beneficiary of the income trust is the individual, during his or her life. All income received by the trust must be made available to pay for the individual's cost of care each month, with the exception of a small amount for trust-related expenses and a personal-needs allowance.

The state welfare agency and the estate recovery unit are the beneficiaries after the death of the individual, and the trust must provide that the state's estate recovery unit will be compensated for the amount of medical assistance paid on the individual's behalf from any amount remaining in the trust at the time of the individual's death.

LONG-TERM-CARE INSURANCE

℞ What is long-term-care insurance?

Long-term-care insurance has become increasingly popular as the cost of nursing home care and other extended-care alternatives has steadily increased. It covers part or all of the insured's cost of home care, nursing home care, or similar extended care should it become necessary. It is designed to help pay for expenses you will incur if you lose the ability to take care of your own activities of daily living due to chronic medical conditions or cognitive disabilities. It is important to understand that long-term-care insurance is not provided by Medicare, Medicaid, Social Security, or Medicare supplemental insurance.

Some states are permitting holders of long-term-care insurance policies to treat their policy proceeds as exempt from consideration for Medicaid eligibility purposes. These programs create additional incentive for obtaining such coverage.

Long-term-care insurance is one of the few alternatives to self-paying the costs of long-term care. This type of insurance generally provides an amount of money per day for a fixed period of time or for the remainder of the insured's life. Premiums are generally level, meaning a fixed amount per year. Most policies do not provide guarantees that the premiums will not be increased but do provide that your premium can be increased only if rates are raised for everyone in your state carrying the same policy.

The major advantages of funding your potential long-term costs through insurance are simplicity and control. Having your own dollars to spend the way you want gives you power over your circumstances.

You can let your loved ones know and can direct in your estate planning documents how you want your affairs conducted if a major disability strikes. With long-term-care insurance you will not be subject to the whims of government. You can go to the facility of your choosing and get the level of care that you want and desire.

Because the Medicaid system does not reimburse nursing homes at the same rate that a private patient pays, there is always a risk that the quality of care you receive will not be the same if you rely on the Medicaid system to pay your way. By "paying the freight" yourself, you'll have better peace of mind that you'll get the care you expect and desire.

Is there a way to combine the purchase of long-term-care insurance with other planning strategies?

One of the most common and effective strategies being used under the current Medicaid rules is to have an estate plan prepared that utilizes a revocable living trust and a special durable power of attorney and to purchase long-term-care insurance for a benefit period long enough to cover the Medicaid 36-month look-back period.

In this way, a person can pay for a period of time from his or her assets and have all the benefits of control, including selection of facility. If the need for assistance turns out to be long term, the person has positioned his or her trustees and agents to make the transfers necessary to preserve assets without having to spend down personal funds beyond the cost of the premiums for the long-term-care policy.

A drawback of this strategy is that the person will eventually be dependent upon the whims of government, but it seems to be a popular "middle ground" because of the difference in the premiums for policies providing 3 or 4 years of benefits and for those providing lifetime benefits.

One caution with this type of planning is that the federal government may, at any time, increase the look-back period to longer than 36 months. If this happens, there may be a shortfall in coverage. You should discuss this potential problem in detail with your advisors before you use this approach.

Are long-term-care insurance and nursing home insurance the same thing?

Long-term-care insurance was introduced in the early 1980s as nursing home insurance, but with our population aging and people maintaining more active lives, long-term-care insurance has changed dramatically and now covers much more than nursing home care. This insurance can provide the assistance to keep you out of the nursing home. A good long-term-care policy will pay for services delivered in your home or in an assisted-living facility.

◌⅋ *How are the costs of long-term-care insurance determined?*

Long-term-care policies have many features that can afford you the protection you want. The cost of the insurance is dependent on which of these features you desire:

- The amount of coverage
- The duration of benefits (with 5 years covering more than 95 percent of the cases, or guaranteed renewable policy for life)
- The waiting period before benefits begin (e.g., 6 months, 1 year, etc.)
- The "benefit trigger"
- The level of benefits such as home health care (if required), skilled, intermediate, custodial
- An escalation or inflation provision
- A waiver of premium if you become ill
- A discounted premium if both husband and wife secure coverage under the policy
- Coverage for Alzheimer's disease
- No requirement for prior hospitalization

With the rise of managed care, more and more long-term-care insurers are providing case management to reduce costs.

◌⅋ *How are the benefits paid under a long-term-care policy?*

- *Expense-incurred method:* The insurance company must decide if and when you are eligible for benefits and services. It will pay you or your provider for the cost of the services rendered up to the limits of your policy.
- *Indemnity method:* This policy specifies a maximum dollar coverage, and when this amount is spent, the coverage ends. With this

type of policy, the insurance company decides if you are eligible for benefits, based upon the definitions stated in the policy. The insurance company will pay benefits directly to you, up to the limits of the policy, regardless of the actual expenses incurred. This has become a more popular type of policy.

☞ *How does the insurance company determine when a person is eligible to receive benefits under a long-term-care insurance policy?*

"Benefit triggers" is the term an insurance company uses to describe the way it decides when to begin paying benefits under a policy. This is one of the most important parts of a long-term-care insurance policy. Older policies required at least a 3-day hospital stay to trigger benefits, which is harder to achieve in this day and age (because health insurance companies often don't allow their insureds to remain in the hospital more than overnight even after major surgery) and rather impossible to achieve if Alzheimer's is the triggering event. Modern policies speak in terms of inability to perform one or more of the six activities of daily living, which are eating, toileting, bathing, dressing, medicating, and transferring from a bed to a chair.

Policy benefit triggers differ from company to company. Some policies use more than one way to decide when to pay the benefits. Some states require certain benefit triggers. You should check with your state insurance department to find out what your state requires.

☞ *What is the escalation provision?*

The escalation feature is usually an "inflation rider" to the policy, which is advisable to include. Coverage of $90 per day will only be worth half that amount in 14 years if nursing home costs increase at the rate of 5 percent per year. An inflation rider can provide for a fixed percentage increase each year or an increase that is tied to the consumer price index. You can purchase a policy with an inflation rider calculated using simple or compound interest, with or without a cap.

☞ *How do I know how much coverage is the right amount for me?*

This can be a very confusing decision because of the great number of companies selling long-term-care insurance and the great variety of options. The decision is part emotional and part financial. Generally speaking, the greater your liquid financial assets, the less coverage you need. For example, someone with $1 million of liquid assets will be able to finance a higher percentage of their nursing home costs than someone with $200,000.

The next consideration is how long you can wait before the long-term-care policy begins payments. Policies typically have a waiting period ranging from 30 to 360 days before the benefits commence. The longer the waiting period, the more you will need to finance yourself, but the lower the premium cost.

Once you have decided on the length of the waiting period, you need to decide how much of the daily cost of care you will pay and how much you want the insurance policy to pay. Remember that you do not need insurance to pay for everything because you will still be receiving Social Security, pensions, and investment income while you are in the nursing home.

○ʔ *How long a benefit period should I purchase?*

You can choose benefit periods from 1 to 10 years, or for lifetime. Your choice will depend on your personal goals. If you want to ensure care for the rest of your life, you should consider a lifetime policy. This may be important if you have a family history of a condition such as Alzheimer's that may require you to stay a number of years in a nursing home.

You may only want coverage for a long enough period of time to carry out a gifting strategy that will leave you eligible to qualify for Medicaid immediately after a 3- to 5-year waiting period from the date of your last gift.

○ʔ *What if I do not want to stay in a nursing home?*

In recent years, long-term-care insurance providers have developed policies that allow choices to use your insurance benefits to provide care for yourself outside of a nursing home. You can arrange for care at your home, in an adult day-care facility, in an assisted-living arrangement, or in adult foster care. Some more liberal policies will even pay benefits to family members who give care in the home—for a higher premium, of course. Thus, you can appropriately call such coverage "nursing home avoidance" insurance.

❧ *A friend of mine says that long-term-care policy premiums are tax-deductible. Is this true?*

If you have a qualified long-term-care policy and you itemize your deductions, you can deduct the annual premium you pay for the policy. The premium is considered a deductible medical expense that you can deduct if the premium and your other unreimbursed medical expenses exceed 7½ percent of your adjusted gross income for the year. There is a maximum amount you can deduct each year, which is adjusted annually for inflation. The amount you can deduct increases with your age.

❧ *If I elect to receive benefits to help pay for or to reimburse me for my home health care needs, will I pay income tax on those benefits?*

Under current law, benefits from a long-term-care policy up to $220 a day (2003 figure, adjusted annually for inflation) are not subject to federal income taxes.

❧ *What are the main concerns people have about long-term-care policies?*

The two biggest concerns are field underwriting and policy gatekeepers.

1. *Field underwriting* is a business practice in which the agent takes health information directly from the proposed insured, and the company issues a contract with little or no review of the client's actual medical records. When the policyholder applies for benefits under the policy, the company then conducts an in-depth review of his or her health situation. In such cases, the company is sometimes able to claim that the original information provided on the application was incomplete or even misleading. In these situations, it is not uncommon for the company to deny a claim.

2. *Policy gatekeepers* are provisions included in a policy to make it difficult for the policyholder to ever receive benefits. For example, a gatekeeper provision might specify qualification by level of care. Early long-term-care policies provide that a policyholder must receive skilled care, typically in a hospital, before applying for custodial-care benefits under the policy. Skilled care is care aimed at rehabilitating a client. Direct entry into a nursing home, therefore, would almost never be covered. Another more

direct example is a provision that requires transfer from a hospital to the nursing home. Again, direct entry to the home would not be covered.

Every state has some sort of counseling system from which you can benefit. Call your state's department of insurance to find out how the program works in your state. The state counselors can assist in determining your needs and can generically describe the background of the type of agent you're looking for. Your other professional advisors can also assist you in locating a skilled professional long-term-care agent.

A very helpful brochure is *A Shopper's Guide to Long-Term Care Insurance.* You can get it from your insurance professional or by contacting the National Association of Insurance Commissioners, 120 West 12th Street, Suite 1100, Kansas City, MO 64105-1925.

ACTION STEPS

We respectfully present the following action steps to summarize the concepts that we discussed in chapter 12 and to suggest steps that you can take to prepare for meetings with your estate planning team of professionals.

❑ *Determine how you are going to pay for medical care during your later years.* The greatest financial risk to seniors is long-term convalescent health care. There are only three places the money is going to come from to pay these costs: Your savings, long-term-care insurance, or Medicaid. In addition to ensuring that you are covered for routine medical care and prescriptions, you need to decide how you will pay for long-term care.

❑ *Estimate your Social Security payments.* You should regularly verify your employment history with the Social Security Administration to make sure you are properly credited for your work. Working with your financial advisor, estimate what your monthly Social Security income will be at the time you retire.

❑ *Evaluate your Medicare options carefully.* For most people, Medicare Part B is essential. But even with full Medicare Part A and Part B coverage, you may still have uninsured medical needs. Consider one of the Medicare HMO options that offer enhanced coverage or supplemental insurance to cover the gaps in Medicare coverage.

❑ *Shop carefully for long-term-care insurance.* Work with an insurance professional whom you trust and who can offer first-rate policies. The quality of long-term-care policies varies widely, so you must learn all that you can about these policies, determine how much coverage you need and can afford, and then rely on your insurance professional to find the best policy that suits your needs.

❑ *Begin Medicaid planning early.* If qualifying for Medicaid is an important objective for you, you should begin planning early. The time to start Medicaid planning is *not* just before you have to enter a nursing home, but years before that.

❑ *Work with a Medicaid planning specialist.* Medicaid eligibility rules are largely determined by each state, and, in our experience, the interpretation of those rules can even vary from county to county within each state. You must work with an attorney who knows these rules and is experienced in working with local Medicaid officials.

chapter 13

Finding and Working with Professional Advisors

DO-IT-YOURSELF
AND ONE-SIZE-FITS-ALL
PLANNING

❧ I purchased a software program that will prepare a trust for me. Why shouldn't I do my own?

Software programs typically provide only very general or generic tax advice; they are not likely to address relevant personal and local law issues. This is inadequate for people with taxable estates. Innocent mistakes or oversights in tax planning can disqualify major exemptions, deductions, and credits. The real issue here is not whether the trust is right for you, but whether you are receiving the counseling that you need to make the right decisions. Forms, whether they are preprinted or programmed software, are no substitute for experience, judgment, and legal training. In the end, a computer program is only as smart as the operator; if you're not already an expert in estate planning, a software program isn't going to make you a competent estate planner.

455

These "canned programs" use a one-size-fits-all approach to estate planning. If you are a one-size-fits-all kind of person, then it may be perfect for you, but we know of very few people, if any, who actually fit these trusts. Does the program give you the ability to customize different areas of the trust to fit your individual circumstances and state law requirements? Probably not.

There are some projects that are naturally "do-it-yourself" projects, and there are some that require a skilled person to lead you through the process. Estate planning is definitely one project that should not be attempted alone.

ᘓ *What about estate planning packages sold by companies?*

Estate planning documents prepared by nonattorneys create major problems for you and your loved ones, including any or all of the following:

- They may not work in your state because they may have been prepared under another state's laws.
- They are pure boilerplate and not likely to meet the specifics of your planning situation.
- They may cause unnecessary taxes and expenses.
- Even if drafted properly, they most likely will not work unless they have been funded properly as well.
- The many mistakes or deficiencies in the documents will not come to light until after your death.

People should seek out the advice of qualified attorneys with regard to living trusts and other estate planning tools.

ᘓ *There's an ad in the newspaper for an attorney who will do my estate plan for $400. Won't that be sufficient?*

Some attorneys and nonattorneys who say they "do estate planning" use fill-in-the-blank forms for their clients. They are able to quote low fees for estate planning before they even meet with clients because they do the same documents for every client; thus "one size fits all." Attorneys who provide these types of documents to their clients are really doing the clients a great disservice.

Proper estate planning requires detailed analysis of each client's assets and personal financial situation, as well as his or her individual hopes, plans, dreams, and ambitions. A true estate planning professional will make certain that the documents are individually tailored to satisfy the immensely personal concerns and goals of each client.

℆ *Why should I work with a financial advisor when I can buy investments over the Internet?*

There are lots of web sites now where, in addition to purchasing dinette sets and alpacas, you can also purchase investments, insurance, and estate plans. Are you willing to trust a strange company on the Internet with your money?

To make informed investment decisions, an investor needs to know about the various types of investments available and which ones are suited to his or her goals. For example, let's say you need life insurance. How much and what type of life insurance should you buy? A life insurance professional can learn what your goals and requirements are and present the best policy or policies to meet your planning needs. Over time, the insurance specialist can continue to work with your attorney and financial advisor to modify your insurance policies by fine-tuning, updating, and making small changes that will keep your policies in line with your goals.

PROPER PLANNING

℆ *My attorney suggested that I involve my accountant, insurance agent, and financial planner in planning my estate. Why should all these individuals be involved?*

Proper estate planning combines financial, tax, business, retirement, and insurance planning—in fact, all the areas covered by the contributors in *Love, Money, Control*. These diverse subjects must be addressed in an integrated fashion to create the best estate plan for you.

We have discovered that a client's interests are best served by a multidisciplinary approach that combines the skills of estate planning attorneys, financial advisors, and accountants; with assistance as needed from other professionals such as insurance experts, business consultants, bank trust officers, and others, depending on each client's specific needs.

ℂℛ *How do attorneys view working with other professionals?*

A qualified attorney will welcome input from other advisors and, if circumstances warrant it, will initiate putting together a team of advisors on your behalf. For example, you may need a charitable trust or an irrevocable life insurance arrangement, and implementing these more sophisticated techniques requires the combined services of individuals who are experienced in those areas. The resulting synergy of professionals tends to prove the adage, "The whole is greater than the sum of its parts."

THE TEAM

ℂℛ *What should I look for in a professional who is qualified to help me with my estate and financial planning?*

Following are some of the characteristics that qualified professionals will undoubtedly possess:

- An attitude that puts your well-being ahead of everything else
- A good reputation for the highest levels of honesty, integrity, and ethical propriety
- Discipline and diligence in staying current in their respective disciplines through constant study, research, reading, and interaction with other members of their particular profession
- Organizational methods and technological systems, which allow them to provide superior services and/or documents in a timely manner
- The ability to freely acknowledge when a matter is beyond their experience or expertise
- Relationships that enable them to enlist the aid of skilled colleagues in situations that call for that expertise

ℂℛ *What should happen after my first meeting with an advisor?*

First, you should evaluate the meeting. Was the advisor prompt, courteous, organized, and knowledgeable? Did he or she speak in plain and understandable language and fully answer your questions? Did he or she seem genuinely interested in you and your family?

Second, you should trust your instincts. If you feel good about the experience, you should proceed. If something just does not feel right, you should look for another advisor because you will probably never form the necessary relationship with that professional to trust his or her advice.

The Accountant

CR *What role does my accountant play in estate planning?*

That depends on what your current relationship is with your accountant. Many people use their accountants as advisors for almost all personal and financial decisions. If that's your situation, then the accountant's participation in the process is essential. If you simply see your accountant once a year for tax return preparation, he or she can still be helpful because of his or her knowledge of your financial holdings and tax situation.

In addition to their advisory role, accountants need to prepare tax returns for most irrevocable trusts. Accountants might serve as successor cotrustees with family members to help them with financial matters, and often serve as trustees of irrevocable life insurance trusts to ensure their proper administration while the insured is living.

The Attorney

CR *My stockbroker says I need a revocable trust. She has recommended three estate planning attorneys. I was in an automobile accident 2 years ago, and my attorney for that case was very nice; can we use him for our trusts?*

Estate planning laws are highly technical and complicated, and unless the practitioner possesses a high degree of professional training in them, he may innocently do a great deal of harm. Like doctors, most attorneys now limit their practices to specialized fields. Even the best trial lawyer is highly unlikely to possess the skills needed to adequately prepare your estate plan. Attorneys who concentrate either solely or predominantly on estate planning can appropriately spot and solve potential problems and provide sophisticated techniques that will save your beneficiaries probate expenses and taxes.

The peace of mind that you seek for yourself and your family is best achieved by working with an attorney who focuses his or her practice on estate planning.

↷ *How do I find a qualified estate planning attorney?*

There are a number of resources for meaningful referrals:

- *Friends, relatives, and business associates who have had their estate planning done:* There is nothing like a satisfied client. A recommendation from one of these people to his or her attorney is definitely worth pursuing.

- *Non-estate planning attorneys:* Attorneys you know who do not emphasize estate planning in their own practices will usually be able to refer you to an attorney who does practice estate planning.

- *Accountants, financial planners, insurance professionals, and stockbrokers:* These professionals frequently work with estate planning attorneys. When they refer their clients to attorneys, they make it their business to know how well the attorneys perform. Most advisors can thoughtfully refer you to estate planning attorneys whom they respect personally and professionally.

- *Bank trust departments and private trust companies:* These institutions are in the trust business and undoubtedly know the most competent professionals in their communities. If asked, they will be pleased to give you a number of names.

- *Your local estate planning council:* Estate planning councils include lawyers, accountants, life insurance agents, financial planners, and bank trust officers who meet regularly to discuss estate planning trends and new ideas. These councils are in most major metropolitan areas, and they are listed in local telephone directories. They will be pleased to provide you with a list of their members.

- *Professional organizations:* There are several national organizations whose members practice predominantly in the estate planning field. For information on how to contact these organizations, see Appendix B, Professional Resources; Table B-1, Referral Organizations.

The attorneys who are contributors to *Love, Money, Control* focus their practices on estate planning.

CR *I've seen advertisements in the newspaper for estate planning seminars. Should I go to one of these seminars before making an appointment with an attorney?*

Attending one or more seminars can only heighten your knowledge. The more information you can acquire on the estate planning process, the better position you will be in to talk knowingly to the attorney you ultimately select.

If you attend an educational seminar, be attuned to whether the seminar turns into a sales pitch for a particular product or service. First and foremost, a seminar should be dedicated to providing information. The host of the seminar should provide an overview of the subject and not attempt to give specific legal advice from the dais. If you are invited to participate with the host or one of his or her associates one-on-one after the seminar, be sure that doing so is on a no-cost, no-obligation basis.

CR *When I meet with an attorney for the first time, what questions should I ask?*

Consider asking the following types of questions:

- How long has the attorney been preparing estate plans?
- What kind of clientele does the attorney have?
- What is the size of his or her average client's estate?
- Does the attorney belong to estate planning–oriented organizations or have any specialized degrees or training in estate planning?
- How long will it take to complete the process? (If an attorney is not willing to commit to a reasonable schedule for completing your plan, you might try another attorney.)
- Is the attorney a member of a large firm? If so, who in the firm will supervise and be responsible for his or her work?

CR *How long does the planning process take?*

There are essentially three blocks of time that will be required of you during the estate planning process:

1. The first block constitutes the time in which the estate planning attorney will gather detailed information from you about your

family and your assets and will talk to you about your goals and planning expectations.

2. The second block of time will be when you meet with the attorney to design the specifics of your plan and to ultimately review and sign the estate planning documentation that he or she prepares on your behalf.

3. The third block of time involves transferring the ownership of your assets into your various trust and planning vehicles.

The amount of time needed for the first and last blocks is largely dependent on the number of assets you own and the degree of organization that exists before the planning process. In addition, some attorneys hold postsigning educational workshops for trustees and beneficiaries so that they will understand their roles.

○R *What factors will an attorney take into account in establishing his or her fee for my estate plan?*

Some or all of the following factors usually determine fees:

- *Cost of doing business:* The amount of overhead and other expenses involved in running the practice are usually considered.

- *Credentials:* The attorney's level of expertise, experience, training, and reputation will be important criteria.

- *"Turnaround" requirements:* Emergencies and unusually quick timelines almost always require higher fees.

- *Responsibility and liability:* The degree of responsibility and liability that the attorney must assume plays a huge role in determining the fee. Because malpractice insurance rates are raging upward, this is a sensitive issue with most attorneys.

- *Value of the estate:* The complexity, nature, and value of the assets that make up the estate are most always taken into consideration.

- *Results and benefits:* The economic value resulting from the avoidance of probate and ancillary administration and the dollar value of saving estate, gift, income, capital gain, and excise taxes are always taken into consideration in determining the appropriate billing.

- *Complexity:* The involvement of extraordinary legal, financial, or business issues is important in the billing decision.

- *Novelty:* The novelty of the issues presented and the question, "Are the issues routine or uniquely difficult?" play a large part in the billing decision.

- *Service:* The speed and the overall level of service provided throughout the relationship are important to many attorneys. If the attorney determines that a particular client demands "right-now service," the billing will usually be higher.

- *Time:* How much time did the attorney spend on the matter that could not be spent on other equally or more profitable matters?

ℭℛ *How can I determine if I am getting a high-quality living trust plan?*

There are several factors that distinguish a comprehensive, high-quality estate plan from a run-of-the-mill or inadequate plan. A quality living trust–centered estate plan is:

- *Prepared by an attorney who emphasizes estate planning in his or her practice:* Usually, attorneys who devote substantially all of their practices to estate planning attend extensive continuing legal education courses devoted to estate planning and are best-suited to draft plans that most accurately capture their clients' needs.

- *Prepared in a "user-friendly" manner:* Many attorneys feel that it is necessary to draft trusts in legalese to make their clients feel that they are getting their money's worth. Actually, the main goals of an estate planning attorney are to draft documents that meet the client's objectives and that the client can understand. The mark of a caring attorney is his or her zeal to incorporate easy-to-read instructions into a living trust plan that explain for the family and the trustmaker's fiduciaries—trustees and personal representatives—how the plan works on the death or incapacity of its maker. Some attorneys offer educational workshops for their clients in which they thoroughly explain how revocable living trusts function.

- *Funded with the appropriate assets after the documents are made operational:* All too often we see plans for which the attorneys did not take the appropriate steps to ensure that the clients' assets were transferred into the trusts. Vehicles without fuel do not operate, nor do trusts without assets.

- *Prepared by an attorney who has a desire to maintain a continuing relationship with the family:* After the preparation of an estate plan, it is essential that the clients have access to the attorney and his or her staff, at the very least, for interpreting matters concerning the plan. Some attorneys offer updating programs, which are formal arrangements where the attorneys automatically review clients' documents and funding at regular intervals.

ᘓ *My wife and I have a very large estate. Though we are very impressed with your experience and qualifications, we were wondering if it wouldn't be advisable to have more than one attorney planning our estate. Is this possible?*

No one attorney can have all the answers, and you are entitled to the very best representation you can afford. For large estates, it is common for several attorneys to work on different components of the overall estate plan. For instance, if your estate plan contains complex asset protection aspects, it may be advisable to bring in an attorney who focuses on domestic and offshore asset protection planning.

The Financial Advisor

ᘓ *What does a financial advisor do?*

Most financial professionals usually fit into one of two categories: financial planners or investment managers. Both types are needed for estate and financial planning. Ideally, you will find one person capable of acting as both a planner and an investment manager. But if not, it would be better to have both financial professionals on your team.

■ *Financial planners* look at all aspects of your financial life—including making and spending money, debt, taxes, investments, estate planning, and insurance needs. They are primarily involved in what might be called the "big picture"—analysis and planning. A financial planner will review your current situation and future goals and then propose ways of getting "from here to there." This typically includes analyzing your investment mix, current insurance coverage, tax situation, and estate planning considerations, and then making recommendations regarding what you should do in order to achieve a designed plan. Frequently, a formal, written financial plan document is part of this analysis.

- *Investment managers* tend to be more concerned with managing investments on a day-to-day basis; they generally do not do the initial big-picture planning. Investment managers are usually specialists in stock, investment counseling, or money management and are very familiar with the investment markets.

A competent financial advisor can provide you with a wide variety of professional and educational services. Depending upon the advisor's level of expertise, qualifications, and certification, he or she may perform comprehensive financial planning analysis; assist in the creation, development, and implementation of short- and long-range financial planning goals; act as the registered broker-dealer for purposes of purchasing investments; recommend estate planning concepts; and act as a sounding board regarding the performance of investments.

☙ *In what ways can I benefit from consulting a financial planner?*

Meeting with a financial planner offers significant benefits:

- *Integrating all aspects of financial planning.* He or she will help you compile a complete financial statement and analyze your current and future financial pictures. Often, individuals simply implement investments, tax strategies, or insurance without regard to the complete picture. You hear people ask, "What's the hottest investment for this year? Shouldn't I put my money there?" A financial planner cannot answer that question without first knowing your tax bracket, your income needs, your current portfolio situation, your estate tax situation, your risk tolerance level, and your insurance needs.
- *Pinpointing weaknesses and recommending improvements.* You do not meet with a financial planner just to hear "Everything looks great." You want to find out if there are weaknesses and potential problems with your plan and to learn ways to solve those problems.
- *Coordinating the implementation of your plan.* The financial planner will focus not just on planning, but also on keeping you accountable in implementing your plan.
- *Monitoring your progress.* Because it is important to monitor your progress, you and your financial planner will review your portfolio and your progress toward meeting your goals at least annually or, for larger portfolios, quarterly.

■ *Ensuring continuity of management.* A financial planner can provide continuity of management if you are ill, disabled, or die and your spouse, children, or others must step in to handle your financial and legal affairs.

⚭ What role does the financial advisor play on my team?

As you have seen throughout this book, there are probably many things that you have not considered about all of the aspects of estate planning. The role of the financial advisor is to identify these major challenges and opportunities as they apply to you and then coordinate the implementation with the other experts on your team.

A good financial advisor will spend considerable time learning about you, your family, your goals, and your financial situation. After taking a thorough inventory, he or she will illustrate the feasibility of achieving your financial and estate planning goals and will make recommendations to help you achieve them.

⚭ What is the best way to find a financial planner?

There are a number of ways to find a financial planner. Talking with friends about who handles their money and asking your attorney, accountant, and other professionals for recommendations are just two ways that you can find out about competent financial planners.

Perhaps the easiest way to get the names of several planners in your area is to contact one of the associations of financial planning professionals. Well-known professional associations that provide referral services for consumers are listed in Appendix B, Professional Resources, Table B-1. The financial planners who are contributors to *Love, Money, Control* would also be available to help you.

⚭ What credentials should I look for when choosing a financial advisor?

In the increasingly complex world of finance, it is more important than ever that consumers be knowledgeable about a financial professional's training, licenses, and history. Therefore, you should be aware of their licensing and registration requirements:

■ Professionals who sell investment securities (stocks, bonds, mutual funds, variable life insurance, etc.) for a commission in the U.S. must be licensed by and registered with the Securities and Exchange Commission (SEC) and the securities divisions of the state(s) in which they practice. These professionals are known as *registered representatives of broker-dealers.* The SEC has delegated their regulation and supervision to broker-dealers through the National Association of Securities Dealers (NASD). The NASD requires that the managers and representatives of broker-dealers pass certain tests to ensure that they understand SEC and NASD rules and are competent to perform their duties.

■ Professionals who manage $25 million or more worth of clients' investments in the U.S. must be registered with the SEC as *registered investment advisors.* If they manage less than $25 million, they must be registered with the state(s) in which they practice as *registered investment advisors, investment advisor representatives,* or such other designation as the state requires.

Many individuals and companies are both registered representatives and registered investment advisors. This allows them to provide investment advice, to manage investments, and to sell securities. Being a registered representative *or* a registered investment advisor does not guarantee competency other than the minimal regulatory requirements.

⊂ℛ *Is there a way I can check to see if my financial advisor is licensed with these regulatory agencies?*

Table B-2 in Appendix B, Professional Resources, lists the telephone numbers, street addresses, and web-site addresses of the regulatory agencies. You can check with these agencies to determine the "standing" of your financial advisor.

⊂ℛ *What are all the acronyms that I see after my financial advisor's name?*

Many training organizations and schools within the financial services industry offer educational programs for financial advisors to improve their competency. Other organizations are formed by financial planning practitioners to promote advanced study. These organizations limit their membership to professionals who have a certain number of years' experience, have earned specific designations, and follow specific standards of conduct.

All of these organizations allow their graduates or members to use their particular professional designations as long as they achieve and maintain required standards. In Appendix B, Professional Resources, Table B-3 lists most of the designations available and the requirements for attaining them; Table B-4 is a comprehensive list of the organizations that award the designations. Some of the most respected designations are:

- Certified Financial Planner (CFP) practitioner
- chartered financial consultant (ChFC)
- registered financial consultant (RFC)
- chartered life underwriter (CLU)
- certified financial analyst (CFA)

ৎ *How do I choose an investment manager?*

If you want an investment manager to assist you, the following questions will help you select one:

- How many years has the financial advisor been assisting clients in investing?
- How many dollars of assets does the advisor have under management?
- How many accounts does he or she manage?
- Who owns the broker-dealer or company for which he or she works?
- How many investment professionals are in the company?
- What is the minimum account size for the company?
- Who are some representative clients?
- How long have the key personnel been there, and what qualifications do they have?
- What is the process they use to choose the investments?
- What areas do they specialize in (e.g., estate planning, retirement planning, insurance)?
- How will the advisor analyze your particular situation?
- How does he or she go about preparing a plan? How detailed is it?
- Does the advisor research all products he or she recommends, or does the advisor rely on someone else's research? How does the manager pay for that research?

- How often will the advisor meet with you to review your goals and investments? (This should be at least once a year.)
- Does the advisor charge fees, commissions, or both? (Ask how he or she sets fees.)

ℭ *What standards should an investment professional be held to?*

The Uniform Code of Fiduciary Conduct stipulates that investment professionals should:

- Prepare written investment policies, and document the process used to derive investment decisions.
- Diversify portfolio assets with regard to the specific risk-return objectives of the client.
- Use professional money managers (prudent experts) to make investment decisions.
- Control and account for all investment expenses.
- Monitor the activities of all money managers and service providers.
- Avoid conflicts of interest.

ℭ *Once I identify several advisors, how do I choose the one I want to work with?*

Meeting with several financial advisors will give you a good idea of which one makes you feel most comfortable. Although all of the financial planners you meet with may be excellent, one personality may fit best with yours and have more in common with you. Another advisor may be more specialized in a field that is more important to your financial success, and another might be surrounded by other professionals who will help you not only now but in the future.

Similar to selecting the best estate planning attorney for you, the best financial advisor for you is the one who makes you feel most comfortable and wants to form a lasting relationship with you. Your financial advisor will be someone who is interested in helping you establish your goals, designing the plan for achieving those goals, and finding the solutions that will best fit your plan today and in the future. The relationship and the security that your financial advisor will provide do not come on day 1. What comes on day 1 is a feeling of comfort and a feeling that a relationship can form that will enhance your financial plan.

Life Insurance Professional

Our estate plan requires life insurance. What should we know about working with a life insurance agent?

Trust and objectivity are two prerequisites for working with life insurance professionals. Since you already know that you need more insurance, you may want to have your financial advisor secure a number of quotations on your behalf. A qualified life insurance agent will be able to give you comparative information on several companies' policies, as well as a variety of possible solutions to your insurance needs. You should confirm several things at the beginning of the process, namely, that the life insurance agent is:

- licensed to sell variable insurance products if they are appropriate,
- experienced in working with the estate planning tools you are putting in place, and
- willing to spend time to confirm that the recommended insurance is consistent with your overall goals.

ACTION STEPS

We respectfully present the following action steps to summarize the concepts that we discussed in chapter 13 and to suggest steps that you can take to prepare for meetings with your estate planning team of professionals.

❑ *Select a team of the best advisors you can find.* Find one professional with whom you feel comfortable and who can spearhead your planning. For most people, this will be an attorney or a financial advisor. From there, build your team of advisors.

❑ *Ask friends and relatives for referrals.* This is perhaps the most satisfactory way of finding an estate planning attorney or financial advisor.

❑ *Ask the attorney or financial advisor for referrals.* These professionals routinely work with other professionals to whom they can refer you, or they can help you choose your team from referrals you received from your friends and relatives.

appendix A

Estate Planning Resources

TABLE A-1 Governmental Resources

Organization	Services
Centers for Medicare & Medicaid Services (CMS) 7500 Security Blvd. Baltimore, MD 21244-1850 877-267-2323 www.cms.hhs.gov	The Health Care Financing Administration (HCFA) is now CMS. Its purpose is to educate seniors & other Medicare beneficiaries about their options, allowing them to make better decisions.
The Federal Web Locator www.infoctr.edu/fwl/	This site is provided by the Center for Information, Law & Policy, as "one-stop shopping" for federal governmental information on the Internet. It contains a comprehensive listing of federal governmental web sites.
Internal Revenue Service 1111 Constitution Ave., NW Washington, DC 20224 800-829-1040 www.irs.gov	Web site includes information & publications for individuals & small businesses regarding income, estate, & gift taxes; & retirement plan contributions & distributions.

TABLE A-1   Governmental Resources, *continued*

Organization	Services
Medicare www.medicare.gov	Features include directories of contacts for each state & downloadable publications on Medicare, nursing home selection, & advanced medical directives.
National Association of Insurance Commissioners 120 W. 12th St., Ste. 1100 Kansas City, MO 64105-1925	Distributes a very helpful booklet for consumers titled *A Shopper's Guide to Long-term Care Insurance.*
Small Business Administration (SBA) 409 Third St., SW Washington, DC 20416 800-U-ASK-SBA www.sba.gov	Provides programs, services, training, counseling, & information on a wide range of topics. Web site includes small-business start-up kit, free software, & extensive guidance for small-business owners.
Social Security Administration (SSA) P.O. Box 3600 Wilkes-Barre, PA 18767-3600 www.ssa.gov	Provides comprehensive information regarding the SSA & its programs & services. Some online services are also available on this web site including ordering a replacement Medicare card, changing your address or phone number, & applying for Social Security retirement benefits.
Social Security Handbook www.ssa.gov/OP_Home/handbook/ handbook.html	Provides an online *Social Security Handbook*; your basic guide to the Social Security programs.

TABLE A-2   Private Resources

Organization	Services
AARP 601 E St., NW Washington, DC 20049 1-800-424-3410 www.aarp.org	AARP is a nonprofit, nonpartisan membership organization dedicated to enhancing the quality of life for people aged 50 & over. AARP provides a wide range of unique benefits & special products & services for its members.
Advance Choice DocuBank 603 Revere Rd. Merion Station, PA 19066-1007 610-667-3524	Maintains file copies of living wills & other health care documents for its members, allowing access 365 days a year, 24 hours a day. Upon notification, it will fax copies of the documents to whatever hospital or medical facility needs them.
American College of Trust and Estate Counsel (ACTEC) 3415 S. Sepulveda Blvd., Ste. 330 Los Angeles, CA 90034 310-398-1888 www.actec.org	A professional association of attorneys. Web site includes public information & frequently asked questions on estate planning & administration.
BBB Wise Giving Alliance 4200 Wilson Blvd., Ste. 800 Arlington, VA 22203 703-276-0100 www.give.org	Provides information on charities, including their stated purpose, kinds of programs sponsored, management & fundraising methods, tax status, financial status, & administrative & fundraising expenses as they relate to program expenditures & total assets. Provides the charity's IRS Form 990.

Center on Nonprofits and
  Philanthropy
2100 M St., NW
Washington, DC 20037
202-833-7200
www.urban.org/content/
  PolicyCenters/
  NonprofitsandPhilanthropy/
  overview.htm
	Provides statistics on charities, including their IRS Form 990, which states who runs them, where & how they spend money, major expense categories, management/operation, & fundraising.

TABLE A-2   Private Resources, *continued*

Organization	Services
Ethical Wills Bookstore (Internet only) www.ethicalwill also at: amazon.com & local bookstores by order	Some of the books that help families write ethical wills & legacy statements are *Ethical Wills: Putting Your Values on Paper* & *The Ethical Will Writing Guide Workbook*, Barry K. Baines; *Choice at the End of Life: Finding Out What Your Parents Want Before It's Too Late*, Linda Norlander & Kerstin McSteen. The Ethical Wills Bookstore lists many other titles on these topics.
Financial Planning Association (FPA) 3801 E. Florida Ave., Ste. 708 Denver, CO 80210 800-322-4237 www.fpanet.org	Provides free information to consumers about financial planning.
FirstGov for Seniors www.seniors.gov	One of many projects created at the direction of the National Partnership for Reinventing Government. Provides secure & easy access to governmental services & benefits for seniors.
Life & Health Insurance Foundation for Education (LIFE) 2175 K St., NW Washington, DC 20037 202-464-5000 www.life-line.org	Provides information & education on life, health, & disability insurance.
The Motley Fool® personal finance newsletter To subscribe: www.Fool.com	Free Internet e-mail newsletter on basic personal financial issues, including budgeting, saving, credit, etc. (Note: The newsletter does include advertising but there is no "spam" e-mail connected with this publication & you may unsubscribe at any time.)
National Association of Financial & Estate Planning (NAFEP) 525 E. 4500 South, Ste. F-100 Salt Lake City, UT 84107 801-266-9900 www.nafep.com	Primarily for estate planning professionals but their web site contains a substantial amount of basic information for the public on estate planning topics.

TABLE A-2 Private Resources, *continued*

Organization	Services
National Committee on Planned Giving (NCPG) 233 McCrea St., Ste. 400 Indianapolis, IN 46225 317-269-6274 www.ncpg.org	The NCPG is the professional association for people whose work includes developing, marketing, & administering charitable planned gifts. Those people include fundraisers for non-profit institutions, & consultants & donor advisors working in a variety of for-profit settings.
The Philanthropic Initiative, Inc. 77 Franklin St. Boston, MA 02110 617-338-2590 www.tpi.org	Founded in 1989, this organization helps donors develop strategies for increasing the impact of their donations.
Quantum Press LLC 621 17th St., Ste. 2250 Denver, CO 80293 303-893-2663 www.quantumpress.net	The exclusive publisher of the Esperti Peterson Contributory Book Series written for the public by America's leading planning professionals on a wide range of estate, business, tax, charitable, & retirement planning subjects. Books can be purchased on amazon.com.

appendix B

Professional Resources

TABLE B-1   Referral Organizations

Organization	Services
American Academy of Estate Planning Attorneys 9360 Towne Centre Dr., Ste. 300 San Diego, CA 92121 800-846-1555 www.estateplanforyou.com	Makes referrals of its members.
American College of Trust and Estate Counsel (ACTEC) 3415 S. Sepulveda Blvd., Ste. 330 Los Angeles, CA 90034 310-398-1888 www.actec.org	Makes referrals of its attorney members. The web site allows ability to search for an ACTEC fellow by state, city, area code, zip code, or name.
American Institute of Certified Public Accountants (AICPA) 1211 Avenue of the Americas New York, NY 10036-8775 888-862-4272 www.aicpa.org	Makes referrals of licensed CPAs by specialty, e.g., personal financial specialists (PFS) & those accredited in business valuation (ABV).

TABLE B-1   Referral Organizations, *continued*

Organization	Services
Appraisal Institute 550 W. Van Buren St., Ste. 1000 Chicago, IL 60607 312-335-4100 www.appraisalinstitute.org	Makes referrals of its certified real estate appraisers (MAI, SRA, & SRPA).
Certified Financial Planner Board of Standards (CFP Board) 1700 Broadway, Ste. 2100 Denver, CO 80290-2101 303-830-7500 www.cfp-board.org	Makes referrals of Certified Financial Planner® (CFP) practitioners.
Esperti Peterson Institute (EPI) 1605 Main St., Ste. 700 Sarasota, FL 34236 941-365-4819 www.epinstitute.org	Makes referrals of its registry of masters & fellows in estate & wealth strategies planning.
Financial Planning Association (FPA) 3801 E. Florida Ave., Ste. 708 Denver, CO 80210 800-322-4237 www.fpanet.org	Makes referrals of its financial advisor members. Provides information about how to choose a financial planner.
Institute of Business and Finance (IBF) 7911 Herschel Ave., Ste. 201 La Jolla, CA 92037-4413 800-848-2029 www.icfs.com	Makes referrals of certified fund specialists (CFS).
International Association of Registered Financial Consultants (IARFC) P.O. Box 42506 Middletown, OH 45042 800-532-9060 www.iarfc.org	Makes referrals of registered financial consultants (RFC).
National Academy of Elder Law Attorneys (NAELA) 1604 N. Country Club Rd. Tucson, AZ 85716 520-881-4005 www.naela.org	Makes referrals of its members & provides help on its web site for how to choose an elder law attorney.

TABLE B-1 Referral Organizations, *continued*

Organization	Services
National Association of Estate Planners and Councils (NAEPC) 270 S. Bryn Mawr Ave. P.O. Box 46 Bryn Mawr, PA 19010-2196 610-526-1389 www.naepc.org	Makes referrals of its members. The web site allows the ability to search for a member by state & specialty.
National Association of Family Wealth Counselors (NAFWC) P.O. Box 308 Franklin, IN 46131 888-597-6575 www.nafwc.org	Makes referrals of its members. The web site allows the ability to search for a member by name, state, & status.
National Association of Financial and Estate Planning (NAFEP) 525 E. 4500 South, Ste. F-100 Salt Lake City, UT 84107 801-266-9900 www.nafep.com	Makes referrals of its members. The web site allows the ability to search for a member by specialty.
National Network of Estate Planning Attorneys (NNEPA) One Valmont Plaza, Fourth Floor Omaha, NE 68154 888-337-4090 www.nnepa.com	Makes referrals of its members. The web site allows the ability to search for a member by state or name & provides member profiles.
Society of Certified Senior Advisors 1777 S. Bellaire St., Ste. 230 Denver, CO 80222 1-800-653-1785 www.society-csa.com	Makes referrals of its members. The web site allows the ability to search for a member by state.
WealthCounsel, LLC P.O. Box 68449 Portland, OR 97268-0449 999-659-4069 www.wealthcounsel.com	Makes referrals of its members. The web site allows the ability to search for a member by state or name & provides member profiles.

TABLE B-2   Licensing and Regulatory Agencies

Agency	Functions
National Association of Securities Dealers (NASD) Regulators 1735 K St., NW Washington, DC 20006 800-289-9999 www.nasd.com www.nasdr.com	Self-regulates the securities industry & the NASDAQ stock market through registration, education, & examination of broker-dealers & their employees; creation & enforcement of rules designed for the protection of investors; surveillance of markets operated by NASDAQ; & cooperative programs with governmental agencies & industry organizations.
Securities Investor Protection Corporation (SIPC) 605 15th St., NW, Ste. 800 Washington, DC 20005-2215 202-371-8300 www.sipc.org	Protects customers of SEC-registered broker- dealers against losses caused by the financial failure of a broker-dealer (but not against a change in the market value of securities); funded by its member securities broker-dealers.
State Bar Association American Bar Association (ABA) Center for Professional Responsibility www.abanet.org/cpr/ regulation/ scpd/disciplinary.html	Each state's bar association administers the bar examination, licenses attorneys, & regulates the practice of law in that state. Contact your state bar association for the standing of any attorney who practices in your state. The ABA provides a complete list of all state bar associations.
State Board of Accountancy National Association of State Boards of Accountancy (NASBA) 150 Fourth Ave., North, Ste. 700 Nashville, TN 37219 615-880-4200 www.nasba.org	Each state's board of accountancy administers the Uniform CPA examination, licenses CPAs, & regulates the practice of public accounting in its state. The NASBA provides a complete list of all state boards.

TABLE B-2 Licensing and Regulatory Agencies, *continued*

Agency	Functions
State Department of Insurance National Association of Insurance Commissioners (NAIC) 2301 McGee St., Ste. 800 Kansas City, MO 64108-2604 816-842-3600 www.naic.org/state_contacts/ sid_websites.htm	Each state administers & enforces its own laws & regulations regarding insurance & its sale. Contact your state insurance commissioner for the standing of any insurance sales professional in your state. The NAIC provides a complete list of all state insurance commissioners.
U.S. Securities and Exchange Commission (SEC) 450 Fifth St. Washington, DC 20549 800-732-0330 www.sec.gov	An independent, quasijudicial regulatory agency that helps establish & administer federal securities laws; regulates firms engaged in the purchase or sale of securities, people who provide investment advice, & investment companies.

TABLE B-3   Professional Licenses and Designations

Designation	Accrediting institution and requirements
ABV: accreditation in business valuation (available to CPAs)	AICPA: meet experience requirements, pass exam, be licensed CPA & member of AICPA; maintain substantial involvement in business valuation & take classes to maintain certification.
AEP: accredited estate planner (available to estate planning practitioners who have completed certain estate planning graduate courses)	NAEPC & American College: pass exam in trust banking, insurance, accounting, law; meet NAEPC's continuing education requirements.
AIFA: Accredited Investment Fiduciary Auditor™ (for investment advisors, investment committee members, and money managers)	Center for Fiduciary Studies: Complete a 3-day program covering components of comprehensive investment process & related fiduciary standards of care. Designees are certified to conduct investment fiduciary audits and reviews.
Broker-dealer (One who is licensed to buy & sell investment products for or to clients. "Brokers" buy & sell securities on behalf of investors; "dealers" sell securities they own.)	SEC
CEA: certified estate advisor	NAFEP: candidates are either attorneys, CPAs, or financial planners with securities licenses. Estate planning curriculum is developed by the NAFEP & recipient must pass the CEA exam & attend continuing education courses.
CFP: Certified Financial Planner® practitioner (available to those with a bachelor's degree who have completed a financial planning curriculum at a U.S.-accredited college or university & have 3 years of financial planning experience or 5 years without a degree)	CFP Board of Standards & American College: pass exam, adhere to CFP Board code of ethics, periodically disclose investigations or legal proceedings related to professional or business conduct, take 30 hours of continuing education every 2 years, complete biennial licensing requirement with CFP Board, submit to regulatory authority of the CFP Board.

TABLE B-3 Professional Licenses and Designations, *continued*

Designation	Accrediting institution and requirements
ChFC: chartered financial consultant (for CPAs, attorneys, bankers, insurance agents, brokers, & securities representatives with 3 years of business experience)	American College: complete 10-course curriculum, pass exams, adhere to code of ethics, take 60 hours of continuing education every 2 years.
CLU: chartered life underwriter (for insurance & financial services professionals with 3 years of business experience)	American College: pass 10 college-level courses, abide by the college's code of ethics.
CPA: certified public accountant	Licensed by state: pass Uniform CPA exam, satisfy work experience & statutory & licensing requirements of the state(s) in which one practices.
CSA: certified senior advisor	Society of CSAs: attend 3-day program or complete correspondence course & testing in all aspects of issues specific to seniors. Take home-study exams to maintain certification.
CSPG: certified specialist in planned giving	American Institute for Philanthropic Studies & California State University, Long Beach Foundation: course work on financial investment planning, tax planning, elder care, charitable giving, estate & gift planning, & administration & operations of planned giving programs.
CTFA: certified trust and financial advisor	ICB: Must meet experience, education, & competency requirements in the areas of fiduciary responsibilities & trust activities; personal finance, insurance, & estate planning; tax law; & investment management. Take self-study course & pass exam.
CVA: certified valuation analyst	NACVA: have a CPA license, be a member of NACVA, take classes, submit references, complete exam.

TABLE B-3   Professional Licenses and Designations,
continued

Designation	Accrediting institution and requirements
fellow of the Esperti Peterson Institute (EPI) (for attorneys, financial advisors, & CPAs who have technical knowledge of financial, estate, insurance, & investment tools)	Complete program, attend classes annually, participate in monthly conference calls, prepare a case design book for a hypothetical client.
J.D.: juris doctor, or doctor of jurisprudence (basic law degree; replaced the LL.B. in the late 1960s)	Accredited law schools: complete required studies, pass exam.
LL.M.: master of laws (advanced law degree)	Accredited colleges & universities: complete required studies; pass exams, usually in a specialized area of law (e.g., taxation). Prerequisite: juris doctor.
M.B.A.: master of business administration	Certain colleges & universities: complete required studies, pass exam.
MS: Master of Science (in taxation) (graduate-level study in financial planning, wealth management, tax planning, retirement planning, & estate planning)	College for Financial Planning: complete 12 courses with 3.0 (B) grade-point average.
MSFS: master of science in financial services	American College: complete 36 course credits, including 2 residency sessions.
M.S.T.: master of science in taxation	Accredited colleges & universities: complete required studies, pass exam.
PFS: personal financial specialist (available to CPAs)	AICPA: meet experience requirements, pass exam, be a member of AICPA; experience & course work required to maintain accreditation.
registered investment advisor (one who recommends stocks, bonds, mutual funds, partnerships, or other SEC-registered investments for clients)	SEC/NASD and/or state securities agencies: pass required NASD exams for series licenses, & annually file an ADV (Advisor) form detailing educational & professional experience & a U-4 form disclosing any disciplinary action.

TABLE B-3   Professional Licenses and Designations,
continued

Designation	Accrediting institution and requirements
registered representative (also called stockbroker) (one who is affiliated with a stock exchange member broker-dealer firm, recommends to clients which securities to buy & sell, & earns a commisson on all trades)	NASD &/or state securities agencies: pass NASD & any exams required by the securities agency of the state(s) in which one practices.
RFC: registered financial consultant (for those with a securities/insurance license or one of the following: CPA, CFA, CFP, CLU, ChFC, J.D., EA, or RHU)	IARFC: meet education, examination, experience, & licensing requirements, take 40 hours per year of continuing education, abide by IARFC code of ethics.
RFP: registered financial planner	RFPI: complete study course, have experience in field.
RHU: registered health underwriter (available to those involved in the sale & service of disability income & health insurance)	American College: complete 3-course curriculum; meet experience, ethics, & continuing education requirements.

TABLE B-4   Professional Associations and Accrediting Institutions

Organization	Functions
American Academy of Estate Planning Attorneys (AAEPA) 9360 Towne Centre Dr., Ste. 300 San Diego, CA 92121 800-846-1555 www.estateplanforyou.com	Membership organization of attorneys who focus their practices on estate planning. Provides members with technical & practice management tools & education.
American Bar Association (ABA) 750 N. Lake Shore Dr. Chicago, IL 60611 312-988-5522 www.abanet.org	Professional association of attorneys. Ensures continuation of programs promoting quality legal services, equal access to justice, better understanding of the law, & improvements in our justice system; provides members with information & tools; sponsors workshops, seminars, continuing legal education sessions, & publications.
American College Bryn Mawr, PA www.amercoll.edu	Nonprofit, accredited educational institution for the purpose of raising the level of professionalism of the financial services industry. Provides educational curriculum for the CFP®, ChFC, CLU, RHU designations, among others; & awards the MSFS degree.
American College of Trust and Estate Counsel (ACTEC) 3415 S. Sepulveda Blvd., Ste. 330 Los Angeles, CA 90034 310-398-1888 www.actec.org	Professional association of attorneys whose practices include preparation of wills & trusts; estate planning; probate; & administration of trusts & estates of decedents, minors, & incompetents.
American Institute for Philanthropic Studies www.plannedgivingedu.com	Accrediting institution for CSPG. Provides professionals & others involved in the planned giving process with the knowledge & skills required to implement & to maintain a successful gift planning program.

TABLE B-4   Professional Associations and Accrediting Institutions, *continued*

Organization	Functions
American Institute of Certified Public Accountants (AICPA) 1211 Avenue of the Americas New York, NY 10036-8775 888-862-4272 www.aicpa.org	Professional association of CPAs. Provides resources, information, & leadership focusing on advocacy, certification & licensing, communications, recruiting & education, & standards & performance.
Association for Advanced Life Underwriting (AALU) 2901 Telestar Ct. Falls Church, VA 22042-1205 703-641-9400 www.aalu.org	Professional association of advanced life insurance professionals. Proposes & monitors legislation & regulation regarding advanced life underwriting; provides education & leadership in improving the business environment for its members.
Certified Financial Planner Board of Standards (CFP Board) 1700 Broadway, Ste. 2100 Denver, CO 80290-2101 303-830-7500 www.cfp-board.org	Sets the initial & ongoing education & ethical standards for the CFP® practitioner designation.
Esperti Peterson Institute (EPI) 1605 Main St., Ste. 700 Sarasota, FL 34236 941-365-4819 www.epinstitute.org	Provides initial & ongoing education in wealth strategies planning through its 2-year Advanced Studies & 3-year Masters Programs. Awards fellow of the Institute status to graduates of Masters Program.
Estate planning councils	Professional associations organized at local level by & for those who specialize in tax, estate, & business planning. Provides opportunity to interact, exchange ideas, & pool knowledge.
Financial Planning Association (FPA) 3801 E. Florida Ave., Ste. 708 Denver, CO 80210 800-322-4237 www.fpanet.org	Professional association (formed by the merger of the International Association of Financial Planners & the Institute of CFPs). Embraces the highest principles of financial planning. Open to everyone affiliated with the financial planning profession.

TABLE B-4 Professional Associations and Accrediting Institutions, *continued*

Organization	Functions
Institute of Certified Bankers (ICB) 1120 Connecticut Ave. NW, Ste. 600 Washington, DC 20036 202-663-5092 www.aba.com/icbcertifications	Nonprofit organization of certified professionals in the financial services industry & sponsored by American Bankers Association. Accrediting organization for CTFA.
International Association of Registered Financial Consultants (IARFC) P.O. Box 42506 Middletown, OH 45042 800-532-9060 www.iarfc.org	Professional association & accrediting organization for RFC designation. Fosters professional development through education; provides a clearinghouse of industry information; distributes information on legislation affecting financial planning, including taxes.
Million Dollar Round Table (MDRT) 325 W. Touhy Ave. Park Ridge, IL 60068-4265 847-692-6378 www.mdrt.org	Professional association of top 6% of life insurance producers worldwide. Provides members with resources for improving technical knowledge, sales skills, & client service while adopting high ethical standards.
National Academy of Elder Law Attorneys (NAELA) 1604 N. Country Club Rd. Tucson, AZ 85716 520-881-4005 www.naela.org	Professional association of attorneys & others who work with older or disabled clients & their families. Provides information, education, & networking. Members' practice in the areas of public benefits, probate & estate planning, guardianship/ conservatorship, & health & long-term-care planning, among others.
National Association of Certified Valuation Analysts (NACVA) 1111 Brickyard Rd., Ste. 200 Salt Lake City, UT 84106 www.nacva.com	Professional association of CPAs with certification as valuation specialists. Provides training, certification (CVA), & continuing education in business valuation, litigation consulting, & fraud prevention; offers tools & technical support.

TABLE B-4 Professional Associations and Accrediting Institutions, *continued*

Organization	Functions
National Association of Enrolled Agents (NAEA) 200 Orchard Ridge Dr., Ste. 302 Gaithersburg, MD 20878 301-212-9608 www.naea.org	Professional association that promotes professionalism & interests of its members. Acts as advocate of taxpayer rights.
National Association of Estate Planners and Councils (NAEPC) P.O. Box 46 Bryn Mawr, PA 19010-2196 610-526-1389 www.naepc.org	Professional association of estate planning professionals. Provides education to its members.
National Association of Family Wealth Counselors (NAFWC) P.O. Box 308 Franklin, IN 46131 317-736-8750 www.nafwc.org	Membership organization of attorneys & financial advisors who practice estate planning. Provides opportunities for education & networking.
National Association of Financial and Estate Planning (NAFEP) 525 E. 4500 South, Ste. F-100 Salt Lake City, UT 84107 801-266-9900 www.nafep.com	Professional association of attorneys, CPAs, & registered investment advisors. Accrediting institution for CEA designation.
National Association of Insurance and Financial Advisors (NAIFA) 2901 Telestar Ct. Falls Church, VA 22042-1205 877-866-2432 www.naifa.org	Professional association. Serves as advocate for insurance agents & consumers; encourages legislation to protect policyholders, develops policy, advances its position with lawmakers & regulators; enhances professional skills of members, promotes ethical conduct, & offers education; organized at state & local levels.
National Association of Personal Financial Advisors (NAPFA) 355 W. Dundee Rd., Ste. 200 Buffalo Grove, IL 60089 888-FEE-ONLY www.napfa.org	Professional association of fee-only financial professionals to enhance skills, market services, & gain a voice with government & consumers. Publishes monthly *NAPFA Advisor* & offers educational opportunities to members.

TABLE B-4   Professional Associations and Accrediting Institutions, *continued*

Organization	Functions
National Network of Estate Planning Attorneys (NNEPA) One Valmont Plaza, Fourth Floor Omaha, NE 68154 888-337-4090 www.nnepa.com	Membership organization of attorneys who focus their practices on all aspects of living trust–centered estate planning & after-death administration. Provides members with technical & practice management tools & education.
Registered Financial Planner Institute (RFPI) 2001 Cooper Foster Park Rd. Amherst, OH 44001-1251 440-282-7176 www.rfpi.com	Professional association of financial planners & accrediting organization for RFP designation.
Societies of CPAs	Professional associations of CPAs to promote the accounting profession within government & to the public. Provide members with education, information, & opportunities to interact with colleagues & to participate in community service projects. Organized at local level.
Society of Certified Senior Advisors 1777 S. Bellaire St., Ste. 230 Denver, CO 80222 1-800-653-1785 www.society-csa.com	Organization of professionals & accrediting organization for CSAs who are involved in working with & helping seniors. Includes attorneys, CPAs, financial advisors, home health professionals, physicians, long-term-care consultants, clergy, realtors, etc.
Society of Financial Service Professionals (SFSP) 270 S. Bryn Mawr Ave. Bryn Mawr, PA 19010-1295 888-243-2258 www.financialpro.org	Sets & promotes standards of excellence for professionals in financial services; supports members' commitment to advanced education & high ethical standards. (Formerly, Society of CLU & ChFC.)
WealthCounsel, LLC P.O. Box 68449 Portland, OR 97268-0449 999-659-4069 www.wealthcounsel.com/	Professional organization of advisors who practice estate planning. Provides tools & educational workshops.

appendix C

The Contributory Book Series and Protocol for *Love, Money, Control*

Eileen Sacco, Publisher

History of the Contributory Book Series

With the publication of the first edition of *Wealth Enhancement and Preservation* in 1995, the Esperti Peterson Institute (EPI) formally established its Contributory Book Series, in which 52 highly regarded professionals from across the United States participated to create a comprehensive book on financial planning. Since 1995, EPI established research projects that culminated in the following texts:

- A second edition of *Wealth Enhancement and Preservation* (1996), with research from 10 additional contributing authors.
- *Legacy: Plan, Protect, and Preserve Your Estate* (1996), with a select contributor group of 87 members from the National Network of Estate Planning Attorneys, which focused on the most commonly asked questions about estate, business, and tax planning.
- *Generations: Planning Your Legacy* (1999), a reconceptualization

493

of *Legacy*, with 49 new contributors who added up-to-date information after passage of the 1997 and 1998 tax laws.

- *Ways and Means: Maximize the Value of Your Retirement Savings* (1999), EPI's first multidiscipline text, merged the expertise and experience of both the legal and financial planning professionals to assist individuals in how to plan properly for retirement and how to coordinate the results of that effort with their estate planning.

- *21st Century Wealth: Essential Financial Planning Principles* (2000), which incorporated research from 51 expert financial planning professionals, presents to the planning public the most up-to-date and simple and sophisticated financial planning strategies made available by the Taxpayer Relief Act of 1997, the IRS Restructuring Act of 1998, rulings issued during that period by the Department of the Treasury and the Internal Revenue Service, and the excitement surrounding the new millennium. This book also launched EPI's relationship with its new publisher, Quantum Press LLC.

- *Strictly Business: Planning Strategies for Privately Owned Businesses* (2002) was developed to help business owners understand and plan for their unique situations. Ninety-one professional authorities contributed their experience, knowledge, and skills to this text. The Economic Growth and Tax Relief Reconciliation Act of 2001 was passed just as *Strictly Business* went to press, which required a massive rewrite and reconciliation of the text with the act. As a result, it was the first book published for business owners that includes details of the new law.

- *Giving: Philanthropy for Everyone* (2003) is an essential reference on charitable giving for people at all economic levels. Eighty of the country's expert estate, tax, and charitable planning attorneys, accountants, and financial advisors explained how families can successfully incorporate charitable giving concepts and strategies into their financial and estate plans.

- And Quantum Press now presents *Love, Money, Control: Reinventing Estate Planning*, which is an up-to-date foundation text on estate planning—post-2001 tax act. Since publication of *Generations* in 1999, the emphasis in estate planning has switched from tax planning, because of the public's understanding of the 2001 tax act, to planning for loved ones after our death and how to control our own finances and well-being if we become incapacitated.

Contributors to *Love, Money, Control* are 69 of the top estate planning attorneys and financial advisors in the country.

The objectives of each book in the series are to:

- be the most professional research project of its kind;

- ascertain the critical planning questions that clients are asking their professional advisors nationwide and the answers of those advisors;

- ensure readers that they can get immediate assistance from professionals on the basis of the planning concepts and strategies they learned from reading the book;

- heighten the public's understanding of the knowledge and contributions that highly experienced financial advisors, attorneys, and accountants make to the lives of their clients;

- improve the quality of financial and estate planning services offered by professionals to clients by sharing the ideas and techniques of a number of authorities in a highly condensed, user-friendly form; and

- be recognized as a major contribution to financial and estate planning literature.

EPI staff invested many hundreds of hours in establishing protocols for the first *Wealth Enhancement and Preservation* research project. EPI and, now, Quantum Press (QP), its publisher, have added elements to the protocols and have diligently adhered to these protocols in all subsequent contributory book series projects.

Protocol

Definition of "Authority" or "Expert"

EPI and QP define an "authority" or "expert" as an outstanding professional who is technically competent, is an effective communicator, and has a proven record of a minimum of 5 years meeting his or her clients' needs.

Research Protocol

As with all previous contributory books, the first step in following the protocol was to create the "Research Questionnaire" for *Love,*

Money, Control, which was an outline of potential topics for the book, organized in a cohesive chapter format. However, every contributing author was encouraged to provide his or her own input outside the parameters of the "Research Questionnaire." Time, demanding schedules, and the difficulty for the contributors to explain very complex technical laws and regulations in clear and concise English led EPI and QP to establish a protocol of a minimum of 25 questions and answers from each contributing author.

Qualifying Professionals: The Application Process

When originally developing the protocol for the first research project, EPI submitted its definition of *expert* and the objectives of the research project to trusted financial planning colleagues and asked them to design the criteria that would help EPI not only identify potential contributors but also judge the level of their expertise and credentials. On the basis of the input of these colleagues, EPI established criteria for an authority and an expert and developed an extensive "Application and Profile" for the financial planning professionals and the criteria for evaluating each applicant, which are weighted according to the input received from our colleagues and established by Robert A. Esperti, Renno L. Peterson, and EPI staff prior to the first research project. Before contacting prospective contributors for every book project, QP staff asks several of the fellows of the Esperti Peterson Institute in Wealth Strategies Planning to review and update the criteria, application, and requirements for attorneys, financial advisors, and accountants.

Applicants must provide a completed "Application and Profile," along with "ADV Part II" if they are registered investment advisors with the Securities and Exchange Commission and U-4 forms if they are registered with the National Association of Securities Dealers (NASD). QP staff carefully reviewed and graded each professional under the established evaluation procedures. Depending on the discipline in which each applicant is licensed, QP checked the NASD web site, state securities division, state insurance commission, state board of accountancy, or state bar association for disclosures (arbitrations, claims, lawsuits, etc.). Before QP finally accepted an applicant for *Love, Money, Control,* editors Robert A. Esperti and Renno L. Peterson reviewed the "Application and Profile" and conducted telephone interviews of every applicant whom they did not know personally.

The telephone interviews allowed the editors to determine the level of each applicant's knowledge of estate, tax, financial, retirement, charitable, and business planning and to satisfy themselves that the applicant was committed to the project and understood all its parameters. The interviews also allowed the applicants to ask any additional questions about the individuals who would be editing their research.

QP then mailed to each applicant a letter of either nonacceptance or acceptance. With an acceptance letter, QP also mailed a "Contributing Expert and Authority Agreement," a "Research Questionnaire," and specifications for submitting a photograph, a personalized introduction, and biographical information.

The applicants who were ultimately accepted into the *Love, Money, Control* project submitted a total of 1,700 questions and answers, amounting to more than 500 manuscript pages.

Research Editing Protocol

The QP staff combined and organized the research from all the contributing authors by "Research Questionnaire" category. The managing editor reorganized and outlined the research, based on its content, into a standard book structure and delivered the manuscript to the senior legal editor, who eliminated those questions and answers that were *not* common to a majority of the contributors. The remaining research *and* the eliminated questions and answers were delivered to Bob and Renno. They read the research questions (and confirmed that the eliminated research was not applicable), combined similar material, and edited the remaining questions and answers into the cohesive and understandable questions and answers that appear in this text.

The managing editor and senior legal editor reviewed the resulting working manuscript for clarity and technical accuracy. QP provided a working manuscript to each contributing author for review. In this way, the contributors increased the level of their participation in the research project by validating that the questions were the most common that they received and by confirming the technical accuracy of the answers. A number of contributing authors supplied revisions and additions to the working manuscript.

The logistics of a Contributory Book Series project is daunting, to say the least. The process of initiating the project; creating the materials for the invitees, applicants, and contributing authors;

following up on all of the invitations; checking the applications and credentials; collecting all the necessary information and paperwork, including the questions and answers; updating the manuscript to be current with new laws and regulations; and turning the material into a book calls for extraordinary organization and commitment from the contributors, editors, and Quantum Press and its staff. In fact, this brief overview of the process does not do justice to 24 months of work simply because the volume of information and protocol developed for these projects consists of hundreds of pages of material and thousands of hours of effort. The Esperti Peterson Institute and Quantum Press are proud of the degree of professionalism displayed by all participants in the creation and completion of *Love, Money, Control.*

appendix D

Contributing Authors

Daniel S. Ahmad, CFP, EA, ATA, CSA
Advance Wealth Strategies
2520 Douglas Boulevard, Suite 110
Roseville, CA 95661
916-773-6078 fax 916-773-6453
dahmad@surewest.net

Mitchell C. Barnes, ChFC
Family Wealth Counseling Inc.
800 Stone Creek Parkway, Suite 3
Louisville, KY 40223
502-394-9294 fax 502-394-0628
mitchfwc@aol.com

Suzann L. Beckett, J.D.
Estate Planning Law Center LLC
543 Prospect Avenue
Hartford, CT 06105
860-236-1111 fax 860-236-0050
suzannb@beckett-law.com

William R. Black, J.D.
William R. Black, P.A.
2691 E. Oakland Park Boulevard,
  Suite 402
Fort Lauderdale, FL 33306
954-561-2233 fax 954-561-6633
blackesq@bellsouth.net

William R. Black, *continued*
Second Office:
Covert & Black, LLC
311 Park Place Boulevard, Suite 360
Clearwater, FL 33759
727-449-8200 fax 727-450-2190

James T. Blazek, J.D.
Blazek & Associates, P.C., L.L.O.
11580 West Dodge Road
Omaha, NE 68154
402-496-3432 fax 402-496-4519
jim@blazeklaw.com

Steven W. Brown, J.D.
Brown & Vogel, Chartered
2035 East Iron Avenue, Suite 101
Salina, KS 67401
785-826-2525 fax 785-826-2588
steve@brownvogellaw.com

David K. Cahoone, J.D., LL.M.
Esperti Peterson & Cahoone
1605 Main Street, Suite 700
Sarasota, FL 34236
941-365-4819 fax 941-366-5347
dkcahoone@aol.com

Michael W. Conway, CFP, ChFC
Summit Financial Resources, Inc.
4 Campus Drive
Parsippany, NJ 07054-0413
973-285-3640 fax 973-285-3644
mconway@sfr1.com

Robert P. Copeland, J.D.
Robert P. Copeland, P.C.
1827 Powers Ferry Road
Building 11, Suite 200
Atlanta, GA 30339
770-937-9444 fax 770-937-9229
bob@copelandlaw.com

William P. Corry
The Corry Group, Inc.
2 North Tamiami Trail, Suite 508
Sarasota, FL 34236
800-833-0989 fax 941-955-6044
corrygroup@aol.com

Neil R. Covert, J.D.
Covert & Black, LLC
311 Park Place Boulevard, Suite 360
Clearwater, FL 33759
727-449-8200 fax 727-450-2190
ncovert@covertlaw.com

Keith L. Davis, J.D., LL.M. (tax), CPA
Davis & Associates, P.C.
523 Park Point Drive, Suite 100
Golden, CO 80401
303-670-9855 fax 303-670-5381
kldavis@davisassocpc.com

Austin J. Doyle, J.D., CPA
Doyle Law Firm
3201 New Mexico Avenue, NW,
  Suite 350
Washington, DC 20016
202-785-8900 fax 202-274-1986
austind@verizon.net

Robert A. Esperti, J.D.
Esperti Peterson & Cahoone
3561 East Sunrise Drive, Suite 135
Tucson, AZ 85718
520-529-9060 fax 520-529-9360
bobesperti@aol.com

Anthony R. Fantini, J.D.
The Fantini Law Firm, P.C.
7 Foster Plaza, Suite 220
661 Andersen Drive
Pittsburgh, PA 15220
412-928-9200 fax 412-928-9207
anthony@fantinilaw.com

Richard L. Ferris, CLU, ChFC, J.D., LL.M. (tax)
Ferris & Associates Attorneys at Law
460 McLaws Circle, Suite 200
Williamsburg, VA 23185
757-220-8114 fax 757-220-8029

Martin J. Fogarty, J.D., CFP
The Heartland Planning Group
2222 Chestnut, 2nd Floor
Glenview, IL 60025
847-729-3300 fax 847-486-9970
mfogarty@heartlandplanning.com

David M. Frisse, J.D.
Frisse Law Offices, LLC
307 West Wood Street
Paris, IL 61944
217-465-1234 fax 217-463-4005
dave@frisselaw.com
Second Office:
4531 South Seventh Street
Terre Haute, IN 47802
812-234-2777 fax 812-232-1209

Robert A. Goldman, J.D., CPA
Goldman & Associates
100 Larkspur Landing Circle,
  Suite 112
Larkspur, CA 94939
415-461-1490 fax 415-461-1497
rgoldman@goldmanattorneys.com

Carol H. Gonnella, J.D.
Gonnella Geittmann, PC
575 South Willow Street
Jackson, WY 83001
307-733-5890 fax 307-734-0544
carol@jhestatelaw.com

Suzanne M. Graves, J.D.
Law Offices of Suzanne M. Graves
1317 West Foothill Boulevard,
  Suite 245
Upland, CA 91786
909-981-6177 fax 909-981-8859
graveplan@aol.com

Theron M Hall Jr., J.D.
Morris, Hall & Kinghorn, P.L.L.C.
3300 N. Central Avenue, Suite 920
Phoenix, AZ 85012
602-249-1328 fax 602-248-2887
tim@morristrust.com

Gregory C. Hamilton, J.D.
Mall, Hamilton & Associates, P.C.
31000 Northwestern Highway,
  Suite 220
Farmington Hills, MI 48334
248-538-1800 fax 248-538-1801
ghamiltonesq@aol.com

Daniel O. Hands, J.D.
Daniel O. Hands, P.C.
1301 West 22nd Street, Suite 603
Oak Brook, IL 60523
630-574-0123 fax 630-574-0319
dhands@danhands.com

Dean R. Hedeker, J.D., CPA, CFP
Dean R. Hedeker, Ltd.
510 Lake Cook Road, Suite 105
Deerfield, IL 60015
847-236-9900 fax 847-236-9901
dhedeker@taxdean.com

Benjamin J. Hill, CFP, CLU, CSPG
Wealth Enhancement &
  Preservation, Inc.
2835 Townsgate Road, Suite 204
Westlake Village, CA 91361
805-449-1132 fax 805-449-1158
benjamin@wealth-inc.com

Edward F. Hooper, J.D., CLU, ChFC
Hooper Law Office
4650 West Spencer Street
Appleton, WI 54914
920-993-0990 fax 920-968-4650
hooperef@execpc.com

**Reid S. Johnson, MSFS, MSM, CFP,
  ChFC**
The Planning Group
8800 N. Gainey Center Drive,
  Suite 279
Scottsdale, AZ 85258
480-596-1580 fax 480-596-2165
reid@theplanninggroup.com

Scott Keffer
Wealth Transfer Solutions, Inc.
2535 Washington Road, Suite 1120
Pittsburgh, PA 15241
412-854-7860 fax 412-854-7864
skeffer@preserve-wealth.com

Kevin F. Kinghorn, J.D.
Morris, Hall & Kinghorn, P.L.L.C.
1050 East River Road, Suite 100
Tucson, AZ 85718
520-320-5100 fax 520-320-5200
kevin@morristrust.com

W. Vito Lanuti, J.D.
323 Main Street
Seal Beach, CA 90740
562-596-7550 fax 562-596-3661
habaeous@aol.com

Jerry W. Lawson, CLU, ChFC
Lawson & Watson, LLC
823 North Elm Street, Suite 100
Greensboro, NC 27401
336-379-8207 x143
  fax 336-379-8349
jlawson@lawson-watson.com

**Jeffrey M. Levine, J.D., LL.M. (tax),
  CFP**
Jeffrey M. Levine Financial Planning
  Consultant
4 Executive Park Drive
Albany, NY 12203
518-489-8538 fax 518-489-8677
jmlevine@lnc.com

Stephen J. Livens, J.D., CPA
The Livens Law Firm
2516 Harwood Road
Bedford (Dallas/Fort Worth),
TX 76021
817-545-3425 fax 817-545-9847
slivens@livenslaw.com

Christopher J. Lubbers, CFP, CFS
Heartland Financial Group of
Kansas, Inc.
1603 Crawford Avenue
Parsons, KS 67357
800-421-6227 fax 620-421-4389
heart@par1.net

Constance O. Luttrell, RFC
CC & Associates
604 Cotswold Park Court
Franklin, TN 37069
615-591-3260 fax 615-591-3280
luttrell@mindspring.com

Chris J. Mares, J.D.
The Law Firm of Chris J. Mares, S.C.
420 East Longview Drive
Appleton, WI 54911
920-734-7000 fax 920-735-5500
cmares@execpc.com

Amy Kaufman McLellan, J.D.
The Law Office of Amy Kaufman
McLellan
23 Main Street, 2nd Floor
Andover, MA 01810
978-475-2400 fax 978-475-1267
amym@lifetimetrusts.com

Stephen A. Mendel, J.D.
The Mendel Law Firm, L.P.
1155 Dairy Ashford, Suite 104
Houston, TX 77079
281-759-3213 fax 281-759-3214
steve@mendellawfirm.com

**Donna M. Miller, CPA, CFP, CVA,
CPMA**
Miller Musmar, P.C.
1861 Wiehle Avenue, Suite 125
Reston, VA 20190
703-437-8877 fax 703-437-8937
info@millermusmar.com

Dan R. Morris, J.D.
Morris, Hall & Kinghorn, P.L.L.C.
3300 North Central Avenue,
Suite 920
Phoenix, AZ 85015
602-249-1328 fax 602-248-2887
dan@morristrust.com

W. Aubrey Morrow, CFP
Financial Designs, Ltd.
5075 Shoreham Place, Suite 230
San Diego, CA 92122
858-597-1980 fax 858-546-1106
aubrey@financialdesignsltd.com

Debbie J. Papay, J.D.
Bayer, Papay, & Steiner Co., LPA
1925 Indian Wood Circle
Maumee, OH 43537
419-891-8884 fax 419-891-8889
papay@plansthatwork.net

Renno L. Peterson, J.D.
Esperti Peterson & Cahoone
1605 Main Street, Suite 700
Sarasota, FL 34236
941-365-4819 fax 941-366-5347
rennopeterson@worldnet.att.net

John S. Pfarr, J.D.
Pfarr & Wallin, LLP
37 Sunset Terrace
Essex, CT 06426
860-767-6555 fax 860-767-3068
pfarrlaw@aol.com

Dagmar M. Pollex, J.D.
Law Offices of Dagmar M. Pollex
424 Adams Street, Suite 200
Milton, MA 02186
617-698-2100
dagmar@pollexestateplanning.com

Lawrence K.Y. Pon, CPA/PFS, CFP
Pon & Associates
240F Twin Dolphin Drive
Redwood City, CA 94065
650-508-1268 fax 650-508-1233
lkypon@aol.com

Chester M. Przybylo, J.D.
Law Offices of Przybylo,
  Kubiatowski and Associates
5339 North Milwaukee Avenue
Chicago, IL 60630
773-631-2525 fax 773-631-7101
trustnow@sbcglobal.net

W. Dennis Renter, CFP, CEPA
Associated Planner's Investment
  Advisory, Inc.
245 Fischer Avenue, Suite A4
Costa Mesa, CA 92626
714-546-2100 fax 714-546-0840
drenter@afgweb.com

Bernard M. Rethore, J.D.
Graves & Rethore, P.C.
2400 East Arizona Biltmore Circle
Building 1, Suite 1135
Phoenix, AZ 85016
602-381-6253 fax 602-381-6260
www.gravesandrethore.com

Kevin P. Rex
Summit Financial Resources, LLC
4 Campus Drive
Parsippany, NJ 07054
973-285-3661 fax 973-285-3666
krex@sfr1.com

David Reyes Jr., CEP, CSA
Quantum Advisors
5075 Shoreham Place, Suite 200
San Diego, CA 92122
858-509-0505 fax 858-597-8884

Mark J. Rogers, J.D.
Angermeier & Rogers, LLP
312 East Wisconsin Avenue, Suite 210
Milwaukee, WI 53202
414-289-9200 fax 414-289-0664
mrogers@execpc.com

Mark S. Rothstein, E.A., CFP
Tri Star Income Tax & Financial
  Services
1426 Aviation Boulevard, Suite 204
Redondo Beach, CA 90278
800-734-7408 fax 310-374-2223
tristaretg@aol.com

Richard A. Sarner, J.D.
Law Offices of Richard A. Sarner
184 Atlantic Street
Stamford, CT 06901
203-967-8899 fax 203-967-8886
rsarner@sarnerlaw.com
Second Office:
465 Park Avenue, Suite 10C
New York, NY 10022
800-392-8550

Scott C. Schultz, J.D.
Schultz & Associates Law Center, P.C.
969 Willagillespie Road
Eugene, OR 97401
541-485-5515 fax 541-485-5518
scott@schultz-law.com
Second Office:
445 Union Street NE, Suite 203
Salem, OR 97301
503-362-4645

Peter B. Scott, J.D., LL.M., AEP
Peter B. Scott, P.C.
777 South Wadsworth Boulevard,
  Suite 2-103
Lakewood, CO 80226
303-914-1111 fax 303-914-1112
pbscottpc@aol.com

Simon Singer, CFP
The Advisor Consulting Group
4266 Valley Meadow Road
Encino, CA 91436
800-350-0909 fax 818-728-5965
simon@advcg.com

Cecil D. Smith, J.D.
Smith Bray & Associates, PC
6799 Great Oaks Road, Suite 110
Memphis, TN 38139
901-754-7540 fax 901-754-3010
cecil@smithbraylaw.com
Second Office:
2900 Vanderbilt Place, Suite 102
Nashville, TN 37212
615-320-5313 fax 615-320-5745

Steven B. Spewak, J.D., LL.M.
Estate Plan Strategies, LLC
1067 North Mason Road, Suite 3
St. Louis, MO 63141
steves@spewakatlaw.com

Chris E. Steiner, J.D.
Bayer, Papay, & Steiner Co., LPA
1925 Indian Wood Circle
Maumee, OH 43537
419-891-8884 fax 419-891-8889
steiner@plansthatwork.net

David A. Straus, J.D., LL.M., CPA
Law Offices of David A. Straus
900 Rancho Lane
Las Vegas, NV 89106
702-474-4500 fax 702-474-4510
david@strauslaw.com

David N. Sutton, J.D.
Law Offices of Sutton and Conover
Center for Lifelong Planning
  Concepts
1805 South Bellaire, Suite 222
Denver, CO 80222
720-524-2111 fax 720-524-2112
dave@suttonlaw.net

**Jerry G. Sutton, J.D., CFP, CIMC,
  AIFA**
SuttonAdvisors, PLC
2201 East Grand River Avenue
Lansing, MI 48912
517-487-5555 fax 517-487-5770
email@suttonadvisors.com

**John C. Watson III, CLU, ChFC,
  AEP, RFC**
Lawson & Watson, LLC
823 North Elm Street, Suite 100
Greensboro, NC 27401
336-379-8207 x130 fax
  336-379-8349
jcw3@lawson-watson.com

Danniel J. Wexler, J.D.
Quinlivan & Kaniewski LLP
6 Hutton Centre, Suite 1150
South Coast Metro, CA 92707
714-241-1919 fax 714-241-1199
d.wexler@quikanlaw.com

Charles D. Wilder, J.D., LL.M. (tax)
Estate Planning and Legacy Law
  Center
1131 Symonds Avenue
Winter Park, FL 32789
407-644-2216 fax 407-644-2194
cwilder@wilder-law.com

William N. Yakobovich
Yakobovich & Company
P.O. Box 1745
Carmel, CA 93921
831-620-1130 fax 831-620-1165
yakobovich@aol.com

Jeffrey M. Zabner, J.D.
Jeffrey M. Zabner, a Law Corporation
4165 East Thousand Oaks
  Boulevard, Suite 301
Westlake Village, CA 91362
805-374-2777 fax 805-381-0787
jmz@zabnerlaw.com

appendix E

Geographic Listing of Contributing Authors

Arizona
Robert A. Esperti
Theron M Hall
Reid S. Johnson
Kevin F. Kinghorn
Dan R. Morris
Bernard M. Rethore

California
Daniel S. Ahmad
Robert A. Goldman
Suzanne M. Graves
Benjamin J. Hill
W. Vito Lanuti
W. Aubrey Morrow
Lawrence K.Y. Pon
W. Dennis Renter
David Reyes Jr.
Mark S. Rothstein
Simon Singer
Danniel J. Wexler
William N. Yakobovich
Jeffrey M. Zabner

Colorado
Keith L. Davis
Peter B. Scott
David N. Sutton

Connecticut
Suzann L. Beckett
John S. Pfarr
Richard A. Sarner

District of Columbia
Austin J. Doyle

Florida
William R. Black
David K. Cahoone
William P. Corry
Neil R. Covert
Renno L. Peterson
Charles D. Wilder

Georgia
Robert P. Copeland

Illinois
Martin J. Fogarty
David M. Frisse
Daniel O. Hands
Dean R. Hedeker
Chester M. Przybylo

Indiana
David M. Frisse

Kansas
Steven W. Brown
Christopher J. Lubbers

Kentucky
Mitchell C. Barnes

Massachusetts
Amy Kaufman McLellan
Dagmar M. Pollex

Michigan
Gregory C. Hamilton
Jerry G. Sutton

Missouri
Steven B. Spewak

Nebraska
James T. Blazek

Nevada
David A. Straus

New Jersey
Michael W. Conway
Kevin P. Rex

New York
Jeffrey M. Levine
Richard A. Sarner

North Carolina
Jerry W. Lawson
John C. Watson

Ohio
Debbie J. Papay
Chris E. Steiner

Oregon
Scott C. Schultz

Pennsylvania
Anthony R. Fantini
Scott Keffer

Tennessee
Constance O. Luttrell
Cecil D. Smith

Texas
Stephen J. Livens
Stephen A. Mendel

Virginia
Richard L. Ferris
Donna M. Miller

Wisconsin
Edward F. Hooper
Chris J. Mares
Mark J. Rogers

Wyoming
Carol H. Gonnella

glossary

activities of daily living. Bathing, dressing, toileting, eating, medicating, and transferring in and out of bed or a wheelchair.

affidavit of trust. An affidavit setting out the essential elements of a trust without disclosing the private information contained in the actual trust document. An affidavit of trust can usually be given to banks and other third parties in lieu of giving them a copy of the full trust document.

AFR. An abbreviation for *applicable federal rate*. An estimated investment return that the government determines and publishes monthly. Used for calculating the value of gifts made to split-interest irrevocable trusts, such as charitable remainder trusts and grantor retained interest trusts, and the amount of the annuity payments in private annuities.

amendment. Written changes to a trust document. If the changes are complex or extensive, the original trust may be *restated* as a new trust document incorporating all the changes but maintaining the name and date of the original trust to avoid having to "re-fund" assets to a new trust.

ancillary administration. The probate and administration of a decedent's estate performed in a state other than the one where the decedent lived at the time of death. Occurs if decedent owned property in more than one state at death.

annual exclusion. See **gift tax annual exclusion.**

annuity. A fixed amount of money which is paid to the annuitant (person establishing the annuity) for his or her life or for a fixed period of time.

applicable credit. See **estate tax unified credit; gift tax unified credit.**

ascertainable standards. A limitation on distributions from a trust for the "health, education, maintenance, and support" of a beneficiary.

asset protection. Positioning property in such a way that it is not subject to the claims of a plaintiff in a lawsuit. In estate and business planning, corporations, limited partnerships, and certain trusts are used as asset protection devices.

bargain sale. A sale in which the property owner sells the property to a qualified charity for less than the fair market value. The difference between the fair market value and the sales price to the charity is the "bargain" part of the arrangement and is considered a gift to the charity.

basis. Generally the cost of property. Basis can be increased by such items as capital improvements or decreased by items such as depreciation. Basis is used to compute taxable gain on the sale, exchange, or other disposition of property.

beneficiary. One who receives property pursuant to a trust, a will, an insurance policy, an individual retirement account, or other third-party beneficiary contract.

business succession plan. The succession plan details the steps for implementing the business owner's chosen exit strategy allowing the smooth transfer of control and ownership of the business in the event of the death, disability, or retirement of the owner.

buy-sell agreement. A succession plan for business co-owners in the event of death, disability, disagreement, or retirement (often known as *triggering events*) to protect both the departing owner and the integrity of an ownership group. There are three types of buy-sell agreements: (1) cross-purchase agreement, (2) entity-purchase agreement, and (3) hybrid of the first two.

bypass trust. See **family trust.**

capital gain (loss). The difference between the amount received in a sale or exchange of a capital asset and its basis.

carryover basis. Generally for gifts of property made after 1976, the donee takes the basis of the donor, with some increase in the basis if the donor paid gift tax on the transfer.

charitable planning. Structuring donations into a unified plan so that donors maximize for themselves, their families, and their worthy causes the tax and nontax benefits of their gifts while they are alive and after their death.

CLAT. An abbreviation for *charitable lead annuity trust*. Pronounced "klat." A charitable lead trust in which a fixed dollar amount or a percentage of the initial value of the trust assets is paid annually to a charitable beneficiary for a period of time, after which the trust principal is transferred to the noncharitable beneficiaries designated in the trust. See also **CLT**.

CLT. An abbreviation for *charitable lead trust*. An irrevocable trust in which a charity has the right to receive distributions from the trust for a period of time, after which the balance of the trust principal is paid to noncharitable beneficiaries. The charitable interest "leads" the noncharitable beneficiaries' interests in a CLT. Depending on how the distributions to the charitable beneficiary are calculated, the CLT may be a *CLAT* or a *CLUT*. A CLT can be created and operational during the maker's life (*inter vivos*) or created at death (*testamentary*) through a will or a living trust and funded with all or part of the decedent's property. See also **CLAT; CLUT**.

CLUT. An abbreviation for *charitable lead unitrust*. Pronounced "klut." A charitable lead trust in which a fixed percentage of the value of the trust assets, revalued annually, is paid annually to a charitable beneficiary for a period of time, after which the trust principal is transferred to the noncharitable beneficiaries designated in the trust. See also **CLT**.

common trust. Often incorporated by parents into their wills or living trusts to hold assets in one common or "pot" trust for the benefit of all their children until some event occurs—which the trust-maker designates in the document—such as the youngest child reaching a certain age. Ensures that all of the parents' assets are available to care for all of the children in all circumstances until all of the children are old enough to care for themselves.

community property. Form of ownership in which all property—real and personal, wherever located—acquired by a married person during the marriage while domiciled in a community property state is deemed to be owned equally by both spouses. The community property states are Alaska, Arizona, California, Idaho, Louisiana, Nevada, New Mexico, Texas, Washington, and Wisconsin. Each community property state has a slightly different set of rules about how and when couples acquire the community property.

compound interest. Interest that accrues on principal and unpaid interest.

contractual ownership. A form of ownership generally referring to a person's right to direct the disposition of an asset at death as part of the agreement that creates the asset itself; such as a life insurance policy.

contribution base. For purposes of calculating a taxpayer's charitable income tax deduction, a taxpayer's adjusted gross income not including any net operating loss carry-back deduction.

convenience trust. A type of trust set up under a will or a trust that permits the beneficiary of the trust to withdraw assets at any time and for any reason, without restriction.

CRAT. An abbreviation for *charitable remainder annuity trust*. Pronounced "krat." A charitable remainder trust in which a fixed dollar amount or a percentage of the initial value of the trust assets is paid annually to noncharitable beneficiaries for period of time, after which the trust principal is transferred to the charitable remainder beneficiaries designated in the trust. See also **CRT**.

credit shelter trust. See **family trust**.

cross-purchase agreement. A type of buy-sell agreement in which the remaining co-owners agree to purchase the interest of a deceased or departing owner.

CRT. An abbreviation for *charitable remainder trust*. An irrevocable trust in which the trustmaker and/or other designated noncharitable beneficiaries (usually the trustmaker's spouse) have the right to receive payments annually for a period of time, after which the balance of the trust principal is paid to the charitable beneficiaries designated in the trust. Depending on how the distributions to the noncharitable beneficiaries are calculated, the CRT may be an annuity trust or a unitrust. A CRT can be created and operational during the maker's life (*inter vivos*) or created at death (*testamentary*) through a will or a living trust and funded with all or part of the decedent's property. See also **CRAT; CRUT; NIMCRUT**.

Crummey power. See **demand right**.

CRUT. An abbreviation for *charitable remainder unitrust*. Pronounced "krut." A CRT in which a fixed percentage of the value of the trust assets, revalued annually, is paid annually to noncharitable beneficiaries for period of time, after which the trust principal is transferred to the charitable beneficiaries designated in the trust. See also **CRT**.

death probate. The court proceeding that establishes the validity of a will; appoints personal representatives and guardians of minor children; and provides legal oversight to ensure accuracy in accounting for a decedent's assets, fairness in the treatment of heirs, and protection for the rights of the decedent's creditors.

death tax. A phrase commonly used to refer to the federal estate tax and state inheritance and estate taxes.

defined-benefit plan. An employer-sponsored qualified retirement plan in which the benefit that the retired employee will receive is defined as a specific dollar amount or a percentage of the employee's compensation before retirement.

defined-contribution plan. An employer-sponsored qualified retirement plan in which the contribution, not the benefit, is defined. Employers contribute to the plan on employee-participants' behalf, and each employee has a separate account within the plan. Retiring or departing employees receive the balance of their accounts (subject to vesting rules), either in a lump sum or in some form of periodic distribution. The amount employees receive is largely a factor of investment performance. The most common defined-contribution plans are profit sharing, 401(k), SIMPLE IRA, and SEP plans.

demand right. The right of a beneficiary to withdraw property transferred to an irrevocable trust. Used to convert a future-interest gift to a present-interest gift so that the gift qualifies for the gift tax annual exclusion.

disability. For legal, insurance, and government purposes, to be physically or mentally disabled, or both, for an extended period of time.

disability insurance. Insurance that provides income to an individual if he or she becomes disabled. The disability income paid is based on the premium the insured pays and the insured's age, occupation, and health status.

disclaimer. An irrevocable refusal by a beneficiary or other recipient to accept a gift or bequest.

discounts. In estate planning, discounts reduce the value of a gift for estate and gift tax purposes. Discounts also apply in business planning in valuing a business for sale. Types of discounts include lack of marketability, lack of control or minority interest, and key person.

donee. The person receiving a gift.

donor. The person making a gift.

durable power of attorney. Generally a power of attorney expires at the death or disability of the principal. If it specifically states that it is to continue upon the incapacity of the principal, the power is *durable* and is used in disability planning to allow the agent to act on the principal's behalf during periods of disability. Durable powers of attorney can be (1) *general*, granting the agent powers to deal with all of the principal's assets and to take any action on his or her behalf; and (2) *limited* or *special*, allowing the agent to perform only certain acts or to control specific property.

durable special power of attorney for financial affairs. A power of attorney that limits the agent's power to transferring property only to the principal's living trust in the event of the principal's legal incapacity. May be titled differently by practitioners.

durable special power of attorney for health care. A power of attorney that limits the agent's power to making health care decisions for the principal if the principal cannot make health care decisions for himself or herself because of incapacity.

dynasty planning. Also referred to as *generation-skipping transfer tax* or *multigenerational planning.* Extending the benefits of an estate plan beyond children to grandchildren and even future generations. It is a family wealth management plan that also sustains the parents' or grandparents' values and traditions after their deaths.

early distribution. A distribution from an employer-sponsored plan or individual retirement account taken before the participant-owner reaches 59½ years of age.

elder law. A special area of legal practice that focuses on issues of particular relevance to senior citizens, such as Social Security, Medicare, Medicaid, and other governmental assistance programs for the elderly; guidance on planning for incapacity; long-term-care insurance; and all aspects of retirement benefits. Some elder law attorneys provide Medicaid planning to protect assets from being consumed by nursing home costs.

elective-share statutes. Statutory provisions that give a surviving spouse a share of the assets of a deceased spouse. Can override the terms of a trust or will.

entity-purchase agreement. Also known as a *redemption agreement.* A type of buy-sell agreement in which the business agrees to purchase (redeem) the interest of a deceased or departing owner.

ESOP. An abbreviation for *employee stock ownership plan.* Pronounced "ee-sop." A type of qualified retirement plan for corporations and a business succession plan because the owner(s) can use an ESOP to sell the company to all employees.

estate administration. The legal process by which assets and obligations of the decedent are ascertained, so that the decedent's obligations can be paid, and the remaining assets distributed to beneficiaries without fear of further claims against the estate. Will planning utilizes the probate process, and trust planning uses the trust administration process.

estate planning. The process of individuals and families planning for the management and disposition of their assets and resources when they are deceased or no longer able to manage their own affairs. It incorporates family legacy, charitable, business succession, tax, disability, asset protection, retirement, gift, and elder law planning. While estate planning is about assets and minimizing income and estate taxes, it is also about people accomplishing goals during life and beyond.

estate tax. A federal tax assessed on the net value of all property transferred at a person's death. *Net value* is the gross value of the decedent's assets—including home, business interests, bank accounts, investments, personal property, individual retirement accounts, retirement plans, and death benefits from life insurance that he or she owned—less debts and administration expenses. There are also state estate taxes, but they are more often referred to as inheritance or sponge taxes depending on the type of tax the states impose. See also **inheritance tax; sponge tax.**

estate tax applicable exclusion. The amount that the unified credit equates to in terms of how much an individual can transfer free of estate taxes. Put another way, the applicable exclusion is the dollar value of a person's estate that is sheltered from estate taxes by the estate tax unified credit.

estate tax unified credit. Also called *estate tax applicable credit.* A tax credit that reduces or eliminates a decedent's estate taxes. Once the value of a decedent's estate is determined and all of the appropriate deductions are taken, the remaining net value is the *taxable estate.* A tentative tax on that amount is calculated, and then the credit is applied. This credit reduces the amount of the final tax due. It is a "unified" credit because transfers during life subject to gift tax reduce the amount of the estate tax unified credit available to offset transfers at death (estate tax). The estate tax unified credit equates to the estate tax applicable exclusion amount.

ethical wills. Personal legacy or family mission statements that pass on in written form the decedents' life stories and core values; the hopes, dreams, and aspirations that they had for themselves and for their families and heirs; and messages of love and gratitude to families and friends. Might contain instructions, guidance, and even prohibitions intended to influence what heirs do with their inheritances.

executor (or executrix). See **personal representative.**

exit strategy. A long-range plan for how a business owner wants to divest himself or herself of the ownership of the business when any of certain events occur. Usually these events are retirement, disability, and death.

fair market value. The value at which property would change hands between a willing buyer and a willing seller, both having full knowledge of all relevant facts and neither being under any compulsion to buy or to sell.

family trust. Also called *credit shelter, B,* or *bypass trust.* In the most basic plan, on the first spouse's death, an amount of cash and property equal to the then applicable exclusion amount passes to a family trust so there is no estate tax on that amount. The family trust will often provide for income and discretionary distributions of principal to the surviving spouse; drafted so that when the surviving spouse dies, none of the trust assets are included in the surviving spouse's estate. Can be set up in either a will or a living trust.

fiduciary. A person who is entrusted with the assets of another and who is obligated to carry out the direction set forth by the person entrusting those assets. Personal representatives and trustees are examples of fiduciaries.

financial planning. The process of individuals and families understanding their money and their total financial pictures; and planning in advance so they can financially achieve their family legacy, charitable, business, tax, disability, and retirement planning goals. Financial planning bridges tax law, elder law, estate planning, investing, accounting, actuarial science, and life insurance.

529 Plans. Savings plans for higher education. Although they are federally legislated, they are created, regulated, and administered by each state. The child can use the money to pay for his or her tuition, fees, books, and some living expenses. Each state has slightly different rules for its specific plan, so parents and grandparents need to read the details of their particular state's 529 Plan, although they can use almost any state's 529 Plan since most do not have residency requirements. Some states allow tax-deductible contributions, and most states do not tax the earnings within the plan; and the 2001 tax act made earnings in the 529 Plan federal income tax–free until they are distributed.

flip unitrust. An abbreviation for *charitable remainder unitrust with flip provisions.* A charitable remainder trust that starts out as a charitable remainder unitrust with net income makeup provisions but "flips" to a standard charitable remainder unitrust upon the occurrence of a certain predetermined event. See also **CRT; CRUT; NIMCRUT.**

FLP. An abbreviation for *family limited partnership*. A limited partnership established under state law in which all the partners are family members or entities that are owned by family members. Typically used by the senior generation to facilitate the transfer of assets to younger family members, often at a discount (i.e., the value of the partnership interests are discounted from the value of the assets held by the partnership and represented by those partnership interests).

401(k) plan. An employer-sponsored qualified retirement plan that allows employee-participants to contribute a portion of their pay to their own retirement accounts free of withholding for income taxes.

fraudulent conveyance. A transfer of property that occurs shortly before or during legal proceedings against the person making the transfer. Fraudulent conveyance laws vary from state to state, but they always have the same general goal: to prevent people from making transfers with the intention of hindering, delaying, or defrauding present or subsequent creditors.

funding. The act of retitling (changing ownership of) your assets from your name individually to the trustee of a trust or naming the trustee as the beneficiary of assets such as life insurance and qualified retirement plans.

future interest. A gift the benefits of which the donee won't actually enjoy or control until some future date.

gift tax. A tax on the value of property that an individual gives away during life.

gift tax annual exclusion. An annual federal tax exclusion of $11,000 per donee (2004 figure; indexed annually for inflation) for gifts of a present interest, without limit as to the number of recipients. These gifts are often referred to as *annual-exclusion gifts*. For married couples who consent to "split" gifts, the exclusion is double the gift tax annual exclusion allowed for the year of the gift.

gift tax applicable exclusion. The amount of cash or property an individual can transfer gratuitously without paying gift taxes. The gift tax applicable exclusion is $1 million under the current law. If a person uses this gift tax exclusion by making taxable gifts, then it reduces, dollar for dollar, the amount of that person's estate tax applicable exclusion. See also **gift tax unified credit.**

gift tax unified credit. Also called *gift tax applicable credit.* A credit available to offset the tax on lifetime taxable gifts. The gift tax unified credit equates to the gift tax applicable exclusion amount of $1 million in total. It is a "unified" credit because transfers during life that are subject to gift tax reduce the amount of the estate tax unified credit available to offset transfers at death (estate tax).

grantor retained interest trust. An irrevocable trust that allows the trustmaker (the grantor) to make gifts of property while retaining the property's use and enjoyment or retaining an income interest in the property for a term of years, after which the balance of the trust assets pass to the remainder beneficiaries designated in the trust. See also **GRAT; GRUT; QPRT.**

grantor trust. Under the Internal Revenue Code, a trust for which all income, deductions, and credits of the trust are attributable directly to the grantor-trustmaker. In essence, the trust is ignored for federal income tax purposes.

GRAT. An abbreviation for *grantor retained annuity trust.* Pronounced "grat." A type of grantor retained interest trust into which the trustmaker transfers appreciating or income-producing property in exchange for the right to receive a fixed amount paid at least annually for a term of years. When the term of the trust ends, any remaining balance in the GRAT is transferred to the remainder beneficiaries named in the trust.

GRUT. An abbreviation for *grantor retained unitrust.* Pronounced "grut." A type of grantor retained interest trust into which the trustmaker transfers appreciating or income-producing property in exchange for the right to receive a fixed percentage of the trust, as valued annually, paid at least annually for a term of years. When the term of the trust ends, any remaining balance in the GRUT is transferred to the remainder beneficiaries named in the trust.

GST tax. An abbreviation for *generation-skipping transfer tax.* A federal tax assessed on property transferred to a donee who is more than one generation removed from the donor of the transferred property (e.g., a gift of property from a grandparent to a grandchild). This tax is in addition to gift or estate tax imposed on the transfer.

GST tax exemption. An exemption ($1.5 million in 2004) for the benefit of each transferor with respect to federal generation-skipping transfer tax.

honorary trusts. Trusts that some states allow individuals to create for their pets. The pet owner may leave a sum of money to someone, with the condition that he or she agrees to take the pet in and to properly care for the animal.

hybrid agreement. Also called a *two-tier buy-sell agreement.* A type of buy-sell agreement in which the individual equity owners *and* the business itself has rights, duties, and/or obligations within the same agreement to acquire the interest of a deceased, disabled, or retiring owner.

IGT. An abbreviation for *irrevocable grantor trust.* Sometimes referred to as an *intentional grantor trust* or an *intentionally defective grantor trust.* An irrevocable trust that is drafted so that the trustmaker is treated as the owner of the trust for income tax purposes, but not to such an extent that the trust assets are included in the estate of the trustmaker at death. In addition, the assets in the trust appreciate outside of the maker's estate during the term of the trust.

ILIT. An abbreviation for *irrevocable life insurance trust.* Sometimes referred to as a *wealth replacement trust.* Pronounced "eye-lit." A trust which holds life insurance as a principal asset, the death proceeds of which are neither estate-taxed in the estate of the insured nor income-taxed to the beneficiaries of the trust.

incidents of ownership. Any rights or privileges that the insured has in a life insurance policy, such as the right to change the beneficiary of the policy or to access its cash value in any way.

income trust. An irrevocable trust used by individuals who require nursing home care and whose monthly income exceeds the amount necessary to qualify for Medicaid.

independent trustee. A person named in a charitable trust to perform certain duties, especially if the trust owns an annuity policy or a hard-to-value asset such as real estate. An independent trustee is someone who is not related to the trustmaker, the trustmaker's spouse, or to any other income beneficiary, and is not subordinate to or controlled by the trustmaker or these other individuals, such as an employee.

inheritance tax. A state tax levied by state governments on the privilege of inheriting wealth. The recipient of the property pays the tax based on the value of property and the recipient's relationship to the decedent.

installment sale. Sale of an asset in exchange for an interest-bearing promissory note payable over 2 or more tax years.

inter vivos **trust.** See **living trust**.

intestate. Dying without a will or living trust. The decedent's property is distributed to his or her heirs under what is known as the *law of intestacy* of the state where the decedent resided. The law of intestacy is a statutory inheritance framework that favors spouses and family bloodlines.

IRA. An abbreviation for *individual retirement account.* A traditional form of retirement account authorized under the Internal Revenue

Code. Contributions are usually tax-deductible when made (within limits); and both contributions and earnings accumulate on a tax-deferred basis until the owner of the account withdraws them, at which time the owner will pay the tax at his or her then-current tax rate. Owner must begin taking withdrawals soon after reaching age 70½.

IRD. An abbreviation for *income in respect of a decedent*. Income that has been earned by an individual but not yet realized prior to his or her death. Heirs are responsible for paying the taxes on this income. The most common IRD assets are qualified retirement accounts and traditional individual retirement accounts.

irrevocable trust. A trust that the maker cannot change or amend after he or she signs it. Irrevocable trusts with demand-right provisions are often used to qualify gifts for the gift tax annual exclusion. Also, if the trustmaker retains no rights in the trust and is not a beneficiary of the trust, the assets of the trust are excluded from the trustmaker's gross estate for estate tax purposes, thus allowing the trustmaker to lower and, at times, eliminate federal estate taxes.

joint tenancy with right of survivorship. A form of ownership where two (or more) people each own an equal, undivided interest in an asset and upon the death of one owner, the surviving owner(s) is vested with ownership through operation of law.

last will and testament. See **will**.

life estate. A particular type of ownership arrangement with two different ownership interests: a life estate interest and a remainder interest.

lifetime trust. A type of trust that is set up under a will or a trust that keeps the inheritance in trust for the lifetime of the beneficiary.

living probate. Technically known as *guardianship*. A legal proceeding to appoint a guardian or a conservator for a minor or other person who cannot manage his or her own affairs (ward). Provides legal oversight to ensure accuracy in accounting for a ward's assets and protection for the rights of the ward.

living trust. Sometimes referred to as an *inter vivos trust*. A trust created by and operational during the maker's lifetime and surviving the maker's incapacity and death. A living trust can be either revocable or irrevocable.

living trust–centered estate plan. A plan that uses the revocable living trust as the foundation document in lieu of a will.

living will. Depending on the state, this may be called a *medical directive* or a *physician's directive*. Not actually a will, but a set of instructions or an expression of wishes and desires regarding the use or nonuse of medical treatments or "extraordinary" means or procedures that would artificially prolong life should the maker be in a terminal condition or a permanently unconscious state.

LLC. An abbreviation for *limited liability company*. A fairly recent hybrid business form that combines characteristics of a corporation and a partnership. The LLC can elect to be taxed as a partnership or a corporation. Owners are "members" and their ownership interests are percentage interests in the LLC. All members of an LLC enjoy limited liability.

long-term care. For Medicaid purposes, assistance provided to individuals who are functionally impaired. *Functional impairment* means that a person is unable to perform at least two of the six activities of daily living without assistance and/or needs care because of cognitive or other impairment. Further defined as a stay of more than 30 consecutive days in Medicaid-approved adult care homes, hospitals, psychiatric facilities, and licensed nonmedical residential care facilities.

long-term-care insurance. Covers part or all of the insured's cost of home care, nursing home care, or similar extended care should it become necessary. Designed to help pay for expenses that insureds may incur if they lose the ability to take care of their own activities of daily living due to chronic medical conditions or cognitive disabilities. Not provided by Medicare, Medicaid, Social Security, or Medicare supplemental insurance.

marital deduction. Unlimited deduction against estate and gift taxes on the value of property that spouses transfer to each other.

Medicaid. A joint federal and state medical assistance program for the aged, blind, and disabled with limited or no means. The federal government provides funding assistance for each state's Medicaid program, but each state makes its own eligibility rules. There are very strict eligibility requirements for this program because it was created to serve people in severe financial need. Not everyone who is poor and in need of medical care qualifies for Medicaid. It will pay for almost all long-term-care costs, some home- and community-based services, as well as many of the Medicare costs for which the insured is responsible.

Medicare. A federal health insurance program. Within the Medicare program, there are Part A, the Medicare hospitalization insurance program with deductibles, copayments, and benefit limits; and Part B, the medical (nonhospital care) insurance program that provides broader coverage, primarily for outpatient services, and also imposes deductibles and copayments. Part B is optional, and it requires a monthly premium.

memorandum of personal property. Prepared as part of an estate plan, this document gives specific items of tangible personal property, such as the rocking chair or the doll collection, to specific people. The benefit of this memorandum is that it can be changed any time without assistance from an attorney. Is not valid in all states.

modified carryover basis system. In 2010, replaces the step-up-in-basis system for property acquired from a decedent. This means that, with some important exceptions and adjustments, the basis for property acquired from a decedent will be equal to the decedent's basis before death or the fair market value of the property at death, whichever is less.

multigenerational planning. See **dynasty planning.**

NIMCRUT. An abbreviation for *charitable remainder unitrust with net income makeup provisions.* Pronounced "nim-krut." A charitable remainder unitrust which provides for annual distribution to the noncharitable beneficiary of the lesser of the unitrust amount or the trust's income. If and when the trust earns sufficient income, the trust can distribute additional amounts to make up for prior years when the full unitrust amount was not distributed. Allows for some flexibility in income planning; often used in retirement planning. See also **CRT; CRUT.**

nonqualified plans. Retirement plans that are employer-sponsored but not controlled by the Employee Retirement Income Security Act of 1974 (ERISA) or subject to Internal Revenue Code limits imposed on qualified plans. Employers can tailor these plans to meet the goals and objectives of individual participants; but in return for this flexibility, the employers and participants forgo many of the tax benefits associated with qualified plans.

personal representative. The modern term for *executor* and *executrix* (female executor) but is without gender. This is the person named in a will and subsequently approved by the probate court to administer and to distribute the property of a person who has died with a will.

POD designation. An abbreviation for *payable-on-death.* Also called *TOD,* an abbreviation for *transfer-on-death.* In the states that allow this designation, it is used primarily for bank checking, savings, and money market accounts; and brokerage accounts. Similar to a beneficiary designation in that it gives ownership of an asset to a named beneficiary or living trust at the owner's death.

pour-over will. A document that acts as a safety net to transfer any assets that you own at your death outside of a revocable living trust to the trust; appoints a guardian for minor children; and revokes any previous wills and codicils so that they cannot interfere with the new estate plan.

power of appointment. A power granted to a person allowing him or her to designate the recipient of the property controlled by the power.

power of attorney. A document by which a *principal*—the person giving the power—appoints an *attorney-in-fact* or *agent* to perform specific acts on the principal's behalf. The two basic types are (1) *general*, granting the agent broad powers to deal with all of the principal's assets and to take any action on his or her behalf; and (2) *limited* or *special*, which allows the agent to perform only certain acts or to control specific property. A power of attorney automatically terminates when the principal dies, and, unless it is a *durable power of attorney*, terminates when the principal becomes disabled.

present interest. The recipient of a gift can control, use, and enjoy the gift immediately. This is a requirement for gifts to qualify for the gift tax annual exclusion.

private annuity. An agreement under which an owner transfers an asset to a buyer in exchange for the buyer's unsecured promise to make fixed periodic payments to the seller—the annuitant—for the rest of his or her life. When the seller dies, the buyer's obligation to make payments ends. The buyer's obligation to make the annuity payments is personal and is not tied to or secured by the property transferred or its income.

private foundation. A tax-exempt charitable entity typically established by a single contributor or a single family for carrying out charitable purposes. Does not qualify as a public charity and does not seek support from the general public. In some instances a foundation is created at death through a will or a living trust and funded with all or part of the decedent's property.

probate. See **death probate; living probate.**

public charity. The best known and most common type of qualified charity (churches, educational institutions, hospitals, medical research institutions, etc.). To qualify as a public charity, the organization must receive broad-based public support through contributions.

Donations to public charities are subject to more generous deductibility limits than donations to most other qualified charities.

QDOT trust. An abbreviation for *qualified domestic trust*. Pronounced "q-dot." For noncitizen spouses, functions like a QTIP trust, but there are some important differences regarding who can be the trustee and how principal distributions are made from the trust.

QPRT. An abbreviation for *qualified personal residence trust*. Pronounced "q-pert." A type of grantor retained interest trust into which the trustmaker transfers his or her personal residence while retaining the right to live in the residence for a term of years. At the end of the term, the property passes to beneficiaries designated in the trust. Removes the future value of the house from the trustmaker's estate.

QTIP trust. An abbreviation for *qualified terminable interest property trust*. Pronounced "q-tip." A form of marital trust in which the surviving spouse has an income interest for life. Property left for the benefit of a surviving spouse in a QTIP trust qualifies for the estate tax marital deduction. Can also be created while the trustmaker is living (*inter vivos* QTIP trust) to benefit the donee spouse for his or her lifetime.

qualified charity. The Internal Revenue Code defines qualified charity in a series of complex regulations, and taxpayers only receive deductions for gifts to qualified charities. There are three basic types of qualified charity: public charities, supporting organizations, and private foundations.

qualified plan. An employer-sponsored retirement plan governed by the Employee Retirement Income Security Act of 1974 (ERISA) and the Internal Revenue Code. Most common types of qualified plans are *defined benefit, profit-sharing, 401(k), SIMPLE IRA*, and *SEP* plans.

reciprocal trust doctrine. A common-law doctrine which states that if two trustmakers create identical trusts for each other, the trusts are disregarded and the property is included in the trustmaker's estate.

retirement planning. Formulating a plan for the time when a person will no longer be earning an income. It is individuals deciding how they want to live out their dreams for themselves and their families after retirement and planning so that those dreams come true. Retirement planning will include setting goals, analyzing income, estimating retirement income needs, budgeting, saving, investment and income tax planning, and planning for the proper distribution of retirement plan proceeds after death.

revocable trust. A trust that the trustmaker can change or revoke after he or she signs it. See also **living trust.**

RMD. An abbreviation for *required minimum distribution.* The minimum amount that you *must* begin to withdraw each year from your traditional individual retirement account or qualified retirement plan beginning the year after you reach age 70½ (*required beginning date*). The Internal Revenue Service proscribes the rules for calculating how much the RMD must be.

Roth IRA. An abbreviation for *Roth individual retirement account.* A variation of the traditional individual retirement account. Contributions are *not* tax-deductible, but contributions and earnings grow inside the Roth IRA tax-free. No requirements for taking withdrawals (required minimum distributions) at age 70½, so funds can continue to grow. Distributions after retirement are generally tax-free.

rule against perpetuities. This rule can be enormously complicated, but the upshot is that, in most states, a trust can exist for only 90 or so years before it must end. Some states have abolished the rule against perpetuities altogether. In those states, a trust can go on indefinitely and never terminate.

salary continuation plan. An employer-sponsored nonqualified retirement plan under which the corporation promises to pay a stated benefit to the employee at retirement.

salary reduction plan. An employer-sponsored nonqualified retirement plan under which the employee defers a portion of current compensation, and the company invests these funds to accrue benefits for the ultimate purpose of providing an income payout at the employee's retirement.

SCIN. An abbreviation for *self-canceling installment note.* Pronounced "skin." A promissory note given by a buyer to a seller that calls for installment payments of principal and interest over a set period of time. It also provides that if the seller dies before the note is fully repaid, the remaining payments are automatically canceled and the buyer owes nothing further.

second-to-die life insurance. Also called *joint-life, survivorship,* or *last-to-die* life insurance. A policy that insures two lives and only pays when both insureds are deceased. Second-to-die life insurance is far less costly than life insurance on the life of any one spouse or policies purchased separately on each spouse's life since the insurance company's risk is minimized by insuring two lives under one policy.

self-settled trust. An irrevocable trust of which the maker can also be the beneficiary. In the past few years, a few states (Alaska, Delaware, Nevada, and Rhode Island) have passed legislation that allows a trustmaker to transfer assets to an irrevocable self-settled trust established in one of these states, and creditors are unable to make claims against those assets (even though the maker is the beneficiary), which significantly increases the asset protection of these trusts.

SEP plan. An abbreviation for *simplified employee pension plan*. A low-cost, IRS-approved, employer-sponsored IRA (individual retirement account) for employees. Under a SEP plan, the employer, and in some cases, the employee, contributes funds to the IRA, which the employee owns and controls.

SIMPLE IRA. An abbreviation for *savings incentive match plan individual retirement account*. A low-cost, IRS-approved, employer-sponsored retirement plan for employees. Allows employee and employer contributions to an IRA or individual retirement annuity, which the employee owns and controls.

situs. The "location" of the trust—the state under whose laws the trust is established or administered.

SO. An abbreviation for *supporting organization*. A type of charity created under the Internal Revenue Code and that operates to support the activities of one or more other public charities. As long as the SO is organized and operated exclusively to support one or more public charities, it is considered a public charity whether its funds come from the general public or from only one donor.

Social Security. A federal program that provides retirement, disability, and survivor benefits to wage earners and their spouses; former spouses, widows, and widowers; and children. A wage earner's eligibility for retirement benefits is based upon his or her work history—the years during which the wage earner paid taxes into the Social Security trust fund.

special-needs trust. See **supplemental-needs trust**.

special-use valuation. For estate tax calculations, valuing land used for farm or business purposes based on its current use instead of fair market value, resulting in reduced estate taxes.

spendthrift provisions. Provisions in a trust that may be able to protect the beneficiary's interest in the trust from his or her creditors.

sponge tax. Also called *pickup estate tax*. A state-imposed estate tax that is tied to the federal estate tax: a state estate tax equal to the amount the federal government allows as a credit for state tax against the federal estate tax. The federal credit will be repealed in 2005, and many states have begun to "decouple" their estate tax from the federal tax. By decoupling the state death tax from the federal tax, a state can charge whatever amount of estate tax it chooses.

spousal IRA. An individual retirement account for a spouse who doesn't work or who doesn't earn enough compensation income to make the maximum annual contribution to an IRA as allowed by law.

staggered distributions. Pattern of distributions from a trust to a beneficiary over a period of years (e.g., distributions at age 30, 35, 40, etc.)

step-up-in-basis system. When heirs inherit property, their basis in the property becomes the fair market value of the property on the decedent's date of death.

supplemental-needs trust. Also called *special-needs trust*. A trust that provides items and services that are not provided by any public or private agency for the comfort and happiness of a person with disabilities. A supplemental-needs trust can enable a person with disabilities to inherit property without jeopardizing eligibility for governmental benefits.

T-CLT. An abbreviation for *testamentary charitable lead trust*. A charitable lead trust created at death through a will or a living trust and funded with all or part of the decedent's property. See also **CLT**.

T-CRT. An abbreviation for *testamentary charitable remainder trust*. A charitable remainder trust created at death through a will or a living trust and funded with all or part of the decedent's property. See also **CRT**.

tenancy by the entirety. A form of joint ownership in some states when the two joint owners are husband and wife. Like joint tenancy with right of survivorship, each spouse owns an equal, undivided interest in the property and upon the death of one spouse, the surviving spouse is vested with sole ownership through operation of law.

tenancy in common. A form of ownership between two or more individuals who each own an undivided interest in the property. Their interests may or may not be equal. Each co-owner can control who receives his or her interest in the property at death; the surviving tenant does not automatically become the sole owner.

testamentary trust. A trust that is created under a will or a trust and does not come into existence until after the maker's death. Since a testamentary trust is not in force during the maker's lifetime, no assets can be placed in the trust until death. If it is a trust created under a will, the testamentary trust may be subject to court supervision until all assets have been distributed and all trust purposes have been completed.

total control trust. A type of marital trust established under a will or trust for the benefit of a surviving spouse and over which the surviving spouse has total control.

total return trust. A fairly new type of marital trust established under a will or trust for the benefit of a surviving spouse that pays the spouse the greater of the trust's income or a fixed percentage of the trust's value, determined annually.

trust. A contract between its maker and a trustee. In the contract, the trustmaker gives instructions to the trustee concerning the holding and administering of trust assets for the benefit of the trust's beneficiaries.

trust ownership. A form of ownership in which legal title to assets is held by the trustee of the trust for the beneficial enjoyment or use by the beneficiary or beneficiaries of the trust.

trust protector. A person or corporation that, depending on the terms of the trust, has authority to oversee the trustees; to change provisions of the trust; to veto acts of the trustees; and, in general, to ensure that the trust is properly administered.

trustee. A person or a licensed corporation appointed by a trustmaker to oversee the trust. The person or corporation owes a fiduciary duty to the beneficiaries of a trust. When the trustmaker appoints several persons to serve as trustees together, they are known as *cotrustees*. A *successor trustee* is a trustee who the trustmaker usually appoints in the trust agreement and who takes over for a previous trustee when that trustee is no longer able to perform the trustee duties, for whatever reason.

UBTI. An abbreviation for *unrelated business taxable income*. Income derived by a charity or charitable trust from any unrelated trade or business that it carries on and that is not specifically excluded by statute. Typically, investment income or capital gains are not UBTI (unless the asset is debt-financed). Revenue from an active trade or business, however, is generally UBTI.

unified credit. See **estate tax unified credit; gift tax unified credit.**

UTMA. An abbreviation for *Uniform Transfers to Minors Act*. Also called *UGMA*, an abbreviation for *Uniform Gifts to Minors Act*. Accounts to transfer gifts to minors. With an UTMA or UGMA account, a custodian manages the gifts and makes distributions to the child as the custodian deems necessary. The account terminates and the child receives all the account's property upon reaching the age of majority.

vests. The point at which participants in a qualified employer-sponsored retirement plan will not forfeit the funds set aside for them if they leave their employers, no matter the reason. In some plans, the funds must vest immediately; in other plans, employers are allowed to establish vesting schedules, such as 10 percent of the funds vest if the participants are still with the company in the second year of employment.

wait-and-see life insurance. For spouses, an alternative to irrevocable life insurance trusts. A husband's living trust purchases and owns a policy insuring the wife's life, and a wife's living trust purchases and owns a policy insuring the husband's life.

will. A legal document containing the instructions for the disposition of one's assets after death, revoking all previous wills and codicils, and naming guardians of minor children.

index